BEHIND THE MYTH

BUSINESS, MONEY AND POWER IN SOUTHEAST ASIA

James Clad

Grafton Books

A Division of HarperCollins*Publishers*

GraftonBooks
A Division of HarperCollins*Publishers*
77–85 Fulham Palace Road,
Hammersmith, London W6 8JB

First published in Great Britain
by Unwin Hyman Limited 1989
This edition published by GraftonBooks 1991

10 9 8 7 6 5 4 3 2 1

Copyright © James Clad 1989

The Author asserts the moral right to
be identified as the author of this work

A catalogue record for this book
is available from the British Library

ISBN 0-246-13908-0

Printed in Great Britain by
HarperCollinsManufacturing Glasgow

CONTENTS

To the memory of my mother

FOREWORD

In the 1980s, the world became aware of the extraordinarily economic success of East Asia – Japan, South Korea and Taiwan. Few realise, though, that economic growth in Southeast Asia has been almost as successful. Over the past two decades countries such as Indonesia, the Philippines, Thailand, Malaysia, and Brunei have grown at an unprecedented rate. From 1980 to 1987 their economies increased by 4.8 per cent per annum, a very respectable rate by any standard. So why should one not trumpet the story of Southeast Asian success as well as that of East Asia?

Few are better qualified to do this than James Clad. He has served in the Asian branch of the New Zealand foreign service and understands the diplomatic issues. As a former lawyer specialising in company law, he has a keen sense of the businessman's point of view, and after a year each at Harvard and Oxford on fellowships he has a wide academic knowledge of the area. In his years in Southeast Asia he has developed friendships that give his writing a sense of intimacy. But above all, he writes as a journalist who has covered Southeast Asia for the *Far Eastern Economic Review*, the leading journal of the region. He is fascinated by the throb of each country and writes tersely, as if trying to cram in every detail a page will hold.

Clad searches persistently for the inside story and, alas, the story he finds is often not an entirely happy one. Behind the glossy exterior and the myth of success lie a host of problems. East Asian countries have undoubtedly achieved extraordinary success in providing high levels of education and standards of living for all their people, and in spawning businesses and an economic bureaucracy which enable their nations to be masters of their own fate. In Southeast Asia, however, the base of success is weak, tattered and fragile; large numbers of people still receive only a low level of education and live in poverty. Businessmen and political leaders, meanwhile, have siphoned off enormous fortunes without playing any constructive role in promoting their countries, and the fortunes are not reinvested. Too many local businessmen have been content to sell off their nations' resources – their oil, rubber and tin. Perhaps worst of all, they have profiteered while vast tropical forests have been felled, and are now dangerously close to depletion with no plans for their replacement.

The success of Southeast Asia depends on outside finance, outside technology and outside management. Some local leaders have shared in the fruits of the success, but not enough have learned the secrets of that success and how to capture it for their own country, or how to develop their own initiative. Even Singapore, the best educated country in Southeast Asia, with the finest bureaucracy, is very dependent on outside companies for its economic health. The infrastructure projects instigated by foreign loans and technical assistance are often poorly maintained.

Hovering in the background of Clad's account of Southeast Asia is the re-emergence of Japan as the dominant power in the region. In recent years, direct Japanese investment there has been more than three times that of the

United States. The closest thing to a regional financial institution is the Asian Development Bank, dominated by the Japanese. So far every president of this bank has been nominated by the Japanese and, not surprisingly, a substantial amount of the goods procured by bank loans come from Japanese companies. And yet, for all its managerial skills and information, this bank does not emerge in Clad's account as a very happy or successful one. The Japanese have shown only a limited interest in building up strong local economies and in making direct investment – they prefer self-owned subsidiaries. Since local governments and business do not have the ability to provide a counterweight, one can imagine future conflicts as Japanese power, galloping along at great speed, encounters the forces of local nationalism.

One wonders why the people of Southeast Asia have not been as ambitious as those in East Asia in making their countries strong. Why have so many Southeast Asian leaders been content merely to siphon off the fruits of their earnings while countless East Asian businessmen and bureaucrats have been willing to live modestly and plough the fruits of their earnings into productive assets? Why have so many Chinese in Taiwan built up their own manufacturing plants while Chinese in Southeast Asia (many of whom were originally from the same province of Fujian as those in Taiwan) are apparently happy to stick with commerce, finance and profits? Why would leaders with tens of millions of dollars not be content with their wealth and not be willing to reinvest additional earnings in their country? Clad is not so pretentious as to give systematic answers to these questions, but a careful reader who ponders the meaning of his stories will be able to reach some very informed conclusions.

EZRA F. VOGEL
Clarence Dillon Professor of International Affairs,
Harvard University

PREFACE

This book describes the links between business and politics in Southeast Asia, an unseen system of business favouritism that lies behind the myth of free market enterprise. At a broader level, my central point is this: despite the glitter, Southeast Asia's prosperity rests on shaky foundations and depends on external forces well beyond its control. The region's growth, in its essence, results primarily from outsiders' capital, outsiders' technology, outsiders' management and outsiders' markets.

Although this premiss may appear controversial, I hope this book will prove to be stimulating both to people in Southeast Asia and to those who have business, investment, banking, journalism, trade, travel or other interests in the region. I hope readers will welcome the following pages as a caveat, and a corrective, to the undifferentiated praise of Asia's 'economic miracle' now much in vogue.

Throughout the book, I deal rather sceptically with claims that countries belonging to the Association of Southeast Asian Nations, known as 'Asean', are fast developing sophisticated, self-propelled economies. To be sure, much of the region's impressive economic growth over the last two decades is self-generated, self-sustained and achieved without patronage or insider advantage. But much more is not.

In separate chapters on Thailand, Malaysia, Indonesia and the Philippines I try to probe behind the myth of indigenous success. In a chapter on Singapore, I discuss the vulnerability of that island's phenomenal economic accomplishment. Although I concentrate throughout on the commercial crises of the 1980s, I devote special attention to the financial power of Chinese minorities, to volatile commodity prices, to multinational companies and to the region's casino-like share markets. Separate chapters also analyse both the failure to build economic regionalism through Asean and the slipping reputation of the Asian Development Bank, the world's richest regional financial institution.

All these, I stress, are different issues from the indisputable fact of Southeast Asia's quickly won and highly visible wealth. After a severe recession in the mid-1980s, the region once again has recorded high, if uneven, rates of growth. Yet it is probable that these improved terms of trade are but a temporary respite in a longer-term, downward trend; meanwhile, profoundly anti-market attitudes and habits still retard the region's potential.

My business friends in Southeast Asia usually find these arguments irrelevant. 'Who cares?' they ask. 'Money is money, what does it matter how it is earned?' To underline this point, some of the world's wealthiest tycoons have made their fortunes in Southeast Asia. This rarified circle includes the two richest men on earth, one a Malay sultan, the other a well-connected Chinese. Both are beneficiaries of the system described in this book.

Business practices naturally vary among the Asean's five island states (Brunei, Indonesia, Malaysia, the Philippines and Singapore) and one mainland nation (Thailand). Throughout the region, wealthy manipulators of the nexus between business and politics have different names. In the Philippines they are known as 'cronies'. In Malaysia and Indonesia, the words *towkay* and *cukong* carry a similar meaning. Yet beneath the diversity lies a secretive but similar business culture, one in which public and private interests mix as effortlessly as the shuffled halves of a deck of cards.

The book comes after twelve years either in the region itself or studying it from afar, during sabbaticals in Cambridge, Massachusetts, and at Oxford. I do not attempt to be comprehensive or particularly analytical about the economies, social structures or political élites discussed in these pages. Specialist and general surveys of the region abound, and I refer to some of these in the text itself and, at the end of the book, in a list of recommended further reading. Much of my material rests heavily on my experience in the foreign service or, later, on interviews and research done as a staff writer for the *Far Eastern Economic Review*; to that extent the book is episodic and personal.

It should not be necessary to add that I have an extremely high regard for most Southeast Asians, whether powerful or peripheral, whom I have met during the last twelve years. To some extent they are all inheritors of the culture of business patrimonialism, which is basically a frame of mind consolidated over hundreds of years of native and colonial rule.

In writing this preface and the words that follow I am acutely aware that people, wherever they live, must deal with the world as they find it. The sphere of political and business power has its own rules, in Asia and elsewhere. Staying in power or keeping the family business afloat, from street peddling to multinational corporate finance, requires Southeast Asia's business families to play the game by the locally prevailing rules.

In this part of Asia, these rules are invariably antithetical to liberal market capitalism. That is the essential point. It will take a long time to tease out these habits but, until this happens, Southeast Asia will continue to be a reactive player in the world economy, not a proactive one. There is still a slim chance that the region may yet lead, rather than follow, the trends now shifting the world's centre of gravity to Asia and the Pacific. But that chance is quickly slipping away.

New Delhi, India
31 August 1989

JAMES CLOVIS CLAD

ACKNOWLEDGEMENTS

Many friends and colleagues, some no longer living, have helped to sharpen my perceptions of Southeast Asia. Many kindly offered advice while I was writing this book. I have learned much from all of them and wish to express my appreciation to the following people in particular:

the late Senator Benigno Aquino, Jr, Joker Arroyo, Susumu Awanohara, Robert Barnes, James Bartholomew, John Berthelson, Rodolfo Biazon, Ian Buruma, Peter Carey, Paul Chan, Jenny Clad, Sir Ralf Dahrendorf, Lester Dally, K. Das, Derek Davies, Eduardo del Fonso, C. S. Eu, Carlos Fernandez, Jonathan Friedland, José Galang, Tony Gatmaitan, Tenku Ghafar, Philip Gibson, Goenawan Mohamad, Kim Gordon-Bates, Nigel Holloway, Dorojatun Koentjoro Jakti, David Jenkins, Jomo K. S., Clayton Jones, Kamal Hassan, David Kersey, V. G. Kulkarnee, Paul Leong, Victor Limlingan, John McBeth, Hamish McDonald, Jeffrey McNeeley, Rosnah Majid, Nono Makarim, Robert Manning, Matt Miller, Musa Hitam, the late Neil Naliboff, Adnan Buying Nasution, Richard Nations, Roger Peren, Raphael Pura, Ron Richardson, Anthony Rowley, Nelly Sandayan, Margaret Scott, the late Robert Shaplin, Greg Smith, Juwono Soedarsono, Anthony Spaeth, Paisal Sricharatchanya, Rodney Tasker, Nic Thorne, Marites Vitug, Ezra Vogel, Paul Wachtel, Wahjudiono, Roger Ward and Wu An.

There are a dozen other friends whom I would wish to thank but, given the prevailing climate in their respective countries, it would be doing them scant service to mention them by name. They will know I am in their debt.

Especial thanks are due to Philip Bowring, Editor of the *Far Eastern Economic Review*, for allowing me to rewrite much material which appeared originally in that magazine's pages; to Mary Butler at Unwin Hyman and to David Cox, my long-suffering but ever patient editor.

Finally I shall always be grateful for the understanding I have received during the preparation and writing of this book from my two daughters, Katherine and Rachel, who have only rarely shown impatience at Daddy's long absences. And I owe more to my wife and friend, Carmen Jones-Clad, than I can say.

The author and publishers are grateful to the following for permission to reproduce copyright material:

Asian Development Bank for Table 4 (Chapter 8); *Far Eastern Economic Review* for Table 1 (Chapter 4); International Monetary Fund for Tables 7 and 8 (Chapters 8 and 11); PA Consulting Group, Australia for Tables 5 and 6 (Chapter 8); UNESCO for Table 2 (Chapter 5); Vita Development

Corporation, Manila for Table 3 (Chapter 7) from V. Limlingan *The Overseas Chinese in ASEAN: Business Strategies and Management Practices* (1987); and the World Bank and International Monetary Fund for Table 9 (Chapter 12). Especial thanks are also due to James Bartholomew for quoting from his book *The World's Richest Man*, published in 1989 by Viking Press.

1

THE END OF AN ERA

A Reluctant Farewell

On 25 February 1986 President Ferdinand Marcos of the Philippines took a long hard look outside his palace gates. Judging the moment both opportune and pressing, he dashed off to a comfortable though bemoaned exile, helicoptering over chanting crowds. Neighbouring Southeast Asian politicians watched his twenty-year presidency collapse with fear and relief.

Fond of his fading photographs as a Manila muscleman, the 67-year-old Marcos left behind a country so thoroughly ravaged that the incoming regime, led by a woman he called 'a mere housewife', needed months just to count the missing money. To the disquiet of Manila's hungry new politicians, it soon became clear that hair-raising amounts of cash had left the country long before the dictator did. He was indulged right to the last minute, the Americans allowing him to stack hundreds of millions of his country's sadly eroded pesos on board his farewell plane. For Marcos it must have been force of habit; he would not be able to spend them in Hawaii, his place of exile.

Relief at the dictator's departure cascaded elsewhere in Asia, although for different reasons from those animating the jubilant crowds in Manila. Marcos had long since become a colossal embarrassment to the Southeast Asians living around him, a region home to 300 million people in six different countries, from tiny Brunei's 250,000 subjects to giant Indonesia, whose 170 million people make this 13,000 island archipelago the world's fifth most populous nation. For years, Marcos's extravagances and mutterings had attracted barely muted ridicule and censure from his fellow Asians. By its indiscipline, his blundering military had added thousands of recruits to the New People's Army, communist insurgents gaining an ever stronger hold in the countryside. Southeast Asia shed few tears while watching him go.

But the region watched in fear also, an unvoiced anxiety. These ageing leaders, also of Marcos's generation, could empathise with the wily old politician from Ilocos Norte, the northernmost of the Philippines' seventy-three provinces. 'Crony capitalism', the habit of giving business favours to one's friends, may have reached state-of-the-art perfection during the Marcos years, but the expression described equally well the type of commercial wheeling and dealing prevalent in many of Asia's other market economies. While the muscleman's local friends added a breathtaking dimension to the word 'favouritism', they had followed a path of patronage very familiar in this part of Asia. Business and political power form two sides of the same coin in many more places than the Philippines.

Tycoons elsewhere in Southeast Asia differ in some respects from their Philippine peers. They generally take more care to avoid the glare of international publicity. But for every one of Marcos's most notorious business associates, such as 'Kokoy' Romualdez and 'Bobby' Benedicto, a George Tan, a Lorrain Osman or a Liem Sioe Liong also figures in Malaysia, Hong Kong or Indonesia. The inner workings show many similarities, with anchor lines of influence leading to the governing élite. In the same year the Marcoses left for their Hawaiian exile, the Malaysian tycoon politician Tan Koon Swan went to gaol after a string of financial scams pummelled Singapore's stock market. In the same year too, another Chinese banker, Khoo Teck Puat, was involved in a flaming row with the world's richest man, the Sultan of Brunei, over missing money.

In nearby Kuala Lumpur meanwhile, government reports admitted that Hong Kong real estate swindles and kick-back commissions had drained at least US$1 *billion* (that is, one thousand million US dollars) from the country's biggest bank, Bank Bumiputra. In Thailand, business vendettas during 1986 had led to the burning of businesses at Phuket and Bangkok. In Indonesia, Suharto family relations held an enervating grip on various import monopolies, stifling the business climate, reinforcing feudal commercial habits and, not least, earning withering private criticism from the World Bank. In short, while American media attention put the spotlight on Philippine cronies, the extravagance and intrigues of other tropical tycoons lay mostly hidden from view. And unlike Marcos, who faced possible imprisonment in 1989 if various fraud charges go to trial in the US, they will almost certainly avoid any legal accountability.

And that is exactly how these business kingpins, and their political protectors, want matters to remain. They know only too well that the region's breakneck rush to wealth has generated fortunes that almost defy description. A real estate boom has put soaring glass towers amid Kuala Lumpur's rapidly retreating rainforest. In just ten years of growth, Singapore's shophouse skyline had become a soaring silhouette closely resembling Manhattan's towers. The world's second longest suspension bridge now connects Penang to Malaysia's west coast, its towers visible to the steady queue of ships passing through the adjacent Strait of Malacca, the world's most strategic naval bottleneck. In short, the tourist image of sleepy, coconut-lined seashores now yields to another vista – huge furnaces, car factories, off-shore drilling rigs and refineries as large as those in Rotterdam; open-cast mines and hydroelectric dams that are drowning river valleys and their ancient Dayak longhouses.

Rightly so, proclaim the region's modernising missionaries. Asian businesses, led by Asians, have worked these wonders. Yet behind these marvels lie many tales of princely patronage and influence-trading; a well-connected Malaysian company, capitalised at a tiny amount, hires foreign expertise to build the US$1.4 billion highway connecting Penang's bridge to mainland Malaysia and Singapore. The inducement? This firm, a mere conduit for government loans and possessing next to no skills of its own, also has a monopoly on levying a toll charge. Nor is this an isolated exception; behind Indonesia's cement plants, some of Asia's largest, stand Chinese middlemen far richer than Marcos's much vilified 'cronies'.

His plundering rule in the Philippines spanned the same two decades during which his more discreet neighbours also amassed colossal riches. Well-connected families in Indonesia, Malaysia, Brunei and Thailand have harvested a business bonanza, sometimes as more or less genuine 'entrepreneurs' but more often as free-riders (riding 'free' on the back of immigrant Chinese or foreign investors). Government-backed monopolies have become a favoured, fast-track route to wealth; ostensibly created to avoid Chinese or colonial era 'middlemen', these businesses in reality may interpose the open palms of presidential or prime ministerial offspring. The grip of free-riders has fastened especially firmly on the food import business, on the many Japanese franchises, on plantation investments still tied to Western capital, or on the companies conducting 'delicate' commercial dealings (such as trading with China, an especially sensitive activity in countries with big Chinese minorities).

A laughh-it-off business culture surrounds the rampant free-riding. A favourite story in Manila boardrooms concerned the fate of two ambitious men, schoolboys together in the US before returning to their native Philippines and Indonesia. Years passed. Then one day an invitation arrived for the Filipino to come and see his old friend in Jakarta. When he arrived in the Indonesian capital he received impeccable, five-star treatment. His friend's house had every modern convenience.

Impressed, the Filipino asked his friend for the secret of his success. 'Look out of that window there,' the Indonesian replied. The Filipino did as he was asked. 'Do you see that power station there?' the Indonesian said. The Filipino looked again. He nodded. There it was. 'So, what about it?' asked the man from Manila. The Indonesian then gestured to all the glittering possessions around him. Knowingly he tapped his chest. 'Ten per cent,' he giggled and touched his wallet.

When the Filipino went home he pondered this explanation deeply. More years passed, taking him – and the Philippines – to the height of the Marcos era. And, yes, one day a reciprocal invitation reached the Indonesian who, when he came to Manila, was met by a limousine so long that it took five minutes to go around a corner. The guest house where he stayed was marbled, with gold taps in the toilets.

Yet the guest house also paled in magnificence to the Filipino's grand home, in every way a superlative for extravagance and poor taste. Awed and overwhelmed, the Indonesian could only marvel at the success of his Filipino friend. 'How have you done this?' he gasped. 'Look out of the window at the power station out there,' came the reply. The Indonesian went to the window and scanned the horizon. But try as he might, he could see nothing at all. Baffled, he turned back to his friend. 'What power station? There's no power station out there.' The Filipino's smile broadened hugely. 'One hundred per cent,' he winked. A fast learner, said the boardroom jokers.

Apart from a business culture with a lot in common, Southeast Asia's market economies spawned many common commercial habits. They gave *carte blanche* to foreign forest concessionaires and mining companies in league with privileged business cronies. Debt financing became a regional vogue as foreign banks, flush with petro-dollars, branched out from Singapore offices to adjacent capitals. Politicians used tax holidays and customs duty waivers to lure electronics assembly plants, especially the incipient semiconductor business, into 'export processing zones' – fenced-off tax havens for onward assembly. And the companies came, their capital plant quickly written off as depreciation against taxes in their country of domicile, their factories filled each day with bused-in workers whose docility became the boast of itinerant Southeast Asian finance ministers.

But most of all, the Philippines and its neighbours rode high on a dizzy, twenty-year swell of prices buoying up the tropical commodities upon which they still rely heavily. Rubber, palm oil, coconut oil, copra, timber, spices, sugar, rice and petroleum flowed out of Southeast Asia. Money – great golden rivers of it – flowed back in, enriching many with its touch. Thai and Javanese generals, Malay princes and bureaucrats, Singaporean counting houses, Filipino speculators, secretive Brunei sultans, Hong Kong and Taiwanese financiers and their ethnic Chinese compatriots – all of them grew very rich.

Behind them grew the middle classes, steadily becoming more commercially competent. Especially explosive was the growth of the financial, transport, real estate and communications industries. This constituted a real growth of mass capitalism although, to be sure, the patronage instinct permeated even the smallest business corners. Yet by the 1980s reports in regional newspapers began, circumspectly, to describe the business strangleholds of families and friends of those in power. The list of those targeted by the foreign press and by domestic rumour mills included particularly the scions of Indonesian president Suharto and Malaysian prime minister Mahathir Mohamad's village kin ('kampong cronies'), notably his finance minister Daim Zainuddin. Thai generals are also reported to have done very well. This type of investigative reportage by foreigners received only paper-thin tolerance. By the end of the decade even that margin of forgiveness had narrowed to the merest sliver.

In vigilant Singapore, the government – not the press – ensured an extraordinarily impressive standard of public service. Yet, even here, the government faced erupting scandals in the mid-1980s. Prime minister Lee Kuan Yew's long-ruling government discovered city-state bureaucrats fingering funds from foreign arms dealers. His housing minister, Teh Cheang Wan, committed suicide over corrupt contract payments. Months earlier Singapore's share market had crashed in a wreckage of phoney 'forward contracts', recycling never-never money. The paper mountain was shored up again for a while – only to take a disproportionate drubbing in the world-wide share market crash of 19 October 1987. Stock markets throughout Asia shed a cumulative 33 per cent off share values in one day, far more than Western bourses had lost.

Southeast Asia's rush to wealth spread down to other levels of society. In the fast-growing suburbs of the capital cities, swollen armies of middle-tier bureaucrats erected air conditioned stucco mansions sporting Corinthian pillars and barbecue pits. Some of their peers in the military did the same, especially in Thailand and Indonesia – where retirement from the armed forces almost never results in retirement from business. To meet their new demands, the full array of Western-style, mass retailing businesses emerged, adding unfortunately to import swindles, portside corruption and smuggling. But drenching though this leakage of wealth was, enough money still washed through to splash society's lower, larger layers.

Although milked furiously by various well-connected officials, public works projects extended and patched up roads neglected since colonial times. An ever growing number of motor cycles and utility vans, stamped out by Japanese-licensed factories, travelled on them. They brought news of construction jobs in expanding cities, stirring new aspirations among millions of farmers and rural people. The proliferating television sets and radios also beamed out the same gilt-edged promise. Health and agricultural schemes did make some difference, often not much, but still a difference all the same. Compared with the socialist ruin in Indochina, where Vietnam after 1975 joined the world's fifteen poorest countries, the prosperity seemed to prove that 'trickle-down' spreading of wealth worked after all. (Trickle-down is shorthand for development policies that prefer growth rather than equity in expectation that benefits will 'trickle down' to the less advantaged.)

The two-decade boom brought huge changes to the business landscape. The comfortable, colonial era picture of cash-cropping farms watched over by trading houses and privileged importers yielded to a much more vibrant tableau. Commodity houses in Singapore went public and branched out. Government-run oil firms – Philippine National Oil Company (PNOC) in Manila, the Thai Petroleum Corporation (TPC) in Bangkok, Pertamina (Perusahaan Umum Tanah Minyak) in Jakarta and Petronas (Petroleum Nasional Berhad) in Kuala Lumpur – became major centres of contracting and patronage.

The region's financial industry grew at almost incredible rates, a straight reflection of the huge wash of money pouring into Southeast Asia: for example, from US$240 million in assets in 1965, Malaysia's banking system alone had grown to thirty-four commercial banks having a US$25 billion book value by 1988. Total bank assets in the region reached US$165 billion in the same year, according to one financial reporting service in New York.

Apart from the financial industry, Southeast Asia's first multinational corporations stretched their wings. Malaysia's plantation and rubber manufacturing giant Sime Darby expanded into nearby countries. Malay businessmen bought into Britain's venerable old Dunlop PLC, the tyre maker. Indonesian Chinese presided over the blossoming of the PT Astra Group, a diversified conglomerate active in plantations and car franchising. Liem Sioe Liong, the Indonesian Chinese kingpin mentioned earlier, began shifting assets to his offshore flagship, First Pacific Holdings of Hong Kong.

Meanwhile, transport networks have also expanded exponentially. From colonial-owned 'mosquito' services, the region's airlines branched out at breakneck speed. Malaysian Airline System, Philippine Airlines, Thai Airways, Garuda Indonesian Airways and Singapore Airlines girdled the globe. Passenger miles travelled went up logarithmically, reflecting an urge to travel for shopping weekends or to send children abroad for education, often as a 'finishing school' status symbol. Foreign education for the millions of young Southeast Asians abroad at any one time during the 1980s amounted to the biggest single 'invisible' drain on the region's balance of payments; in Malaysia alone the remittances abroad for educational purposes (including the luxury of having mum and dad visit during end of term holidays) amounted to US$500 million annually.

Naturally the airlines benefited from this, and from the huge increase in Asia Pacific tourism, although elsewhere in the transport sector the old shipping cartels of Europe and America held their place. Plans for starting a regional shipping line failed miserably in the face of foreign monopoly muscle of older and more experienced vintage than that of local shippers. Thai, Indonesian and especially Filipino seamen by the hundreds of thousands remained the most poorly paid, non-unionised baseline crews for the world's shippers, especially for the tramp liners or the charterers braving the fusilades of the Iran–Iraq war in the Gulf. Only rust bucket lines, such as the Philippines' Sulpicio Lines and several Chinese owned Indonesian lines, stayed afloat.

In financial as well as business affairs the Southeast Asian engine room (invariably manned by Chinese stokers) operated at full-speed-ahead for two delirious decades. And despite all the pilfering and leakage from these hurrying business vessels, archipelagic Asians had good cause to be self-satisfied by the late 1980s. Gross domestic product (GDP) grew at heart-stopping rates. Even populous, poor Indonesia clocked up 5 to 6 per cent annual growth rates; at the other end of the scale the Singaporeans, followed closely by the Thais, hovered at around 10 per cent per annum rates in most years. It was not only growth in trade that ushered in those twenty golden years. Money came in debt-finance dollars from hundreds of foreign banks eager to lend. It also poured in from the world's biggest and richest multilateral lending bank, the Asian Development Bank, or ADB, whose loans went into hydroelectric projects, roads and ports with a lot of cash going to Japanese contractors. Nor was the ADB alone in the race to lend. The World Bank and big foreign aid donors – the US, Japan and West Germany – also followed suit. By the 1980s just one of these aid consortia, IGGI (the Intergovernmental Group on Indonesia), was lending about US$2.4 billion every year. As one Indonesian finance ministry official put it in his dead-pan way: 'It wasn't hard to get a loan in those days.'

All in all therefore, the region comprising the Association of Southeast Asian Nations, known as Asean, had good cause to feel smug alongside the economic fiasco and social misery of neighbouring communist Indochina. A comfortable political environment contributed strongly to the boom times. Within the Asean archipelagic arc, hitherto squabbling leaders were becoming better acquainted with each other. This usually happened on golf courses but the region's leaders also, squirming in neckties, attended get-together dinners during the 1970s and 1980s at Singapore Prime Minister Lee Kuan Yew's home to meet Henry Kissinger, John Kenneth Galbraith and other guests.

The Asean Way

Using informal methods like this, which the local press quickly dubbed 'the Asean way', Indonesia and Malaysia patched up a bitter quarrel over the 1963 incorporation of Sarawak and Sabah into the Malaysian federation. Informality also eased the conclusion of many useful bilateral agreements for patrolling borders, provision of services (water, telecommunications and the like), delineation of boundaries and, if the problem seemed intractable, then at least an amicable deferral of awkward issues.

Backroom diplomacy has certainly scored successes. Indeed, informal contacts among and between Southeast Asia's military and business élites bind much more strongly than a plethora of sonorously titled bureaucratic committees. Asean conferences have created scores of these, ostensibly aimed at integrating the region's economies which, alas, remain stubbornly competitive, not complementary.

The longer one works in Southeast Asia, the more obvious it becomes that the name 'Asean' really serves as a type of convenient shorthand, a way to describe a still narrow area of convergent opinion among the still narrow circles of people holding power. Many cynics believe that Asean, when seen from a historical perspective, will come to denote little more than a temporary moment of relaxation among six conflict-prone countries within an even more obviously conflict-ridden region.

When Bad News Is Good News

As passive beneficiaries of dynamic commodity markets in Europe, the US and Japan, the Southeast Asians passively received another gain during the 1970s, though not in the strictly economic sense. The communist victories in Indochina after 1975 finally forced the Asean Five (Brunei became the sixth member in 1984) into more common purpose. Four years later a Vietnamese invasion of Cambodia not only evicted a deranged tyranny from that country but also drew a conveniently sharp line between friend and foe.

Asean diplomats perked up: they had a new job to do, bolstering a cardboard government-in-exile that carried the name 'Democratic Kampuchea', the Khmer Rouge terror state. The exiled 'government' was a ramshackle coalition hatched with Asean mothering in 1982 and grouping the Khmer Rouge with two non-communist but perennially squabbling factions.

Year after year, the Asean missions at the United Nations won empty victories in the General Assembly denying a seat to Hanoi's puppet government in Phnom Penh. Year after year, the Vietnamese forces won battlefield victories on the ground, consolidating the latest Marxist imposition on a once peaceful country.

The end of Vietnamese occupation, announced in 1989, resulted more from increasingly cordial Sino-Soviet relations than from the impotent flurries of Asean diplomacy. (Vietnam drained US$3 billion a year from the Russians during 1979–89.) Yet even the fleeting diplomatic unity which Cambodia bestowed on Asean, another 'gift' from outsiders, needed careful qualification. Indonesia insisted on keeping a door open to Vietnam throughout the dispute, mindful of Vietnam's usefulness as a buffer between China and Southeast Asia.

Asean's anti-Vietnamese policy strengthened business confidence in the region because the Cambodia dispute kept the big powers interested in the region. Soviet support for Hanoi became a cheap and easy way to keep the Americans interested in Southeast Asia. The Asean countries, especially Singapore and Thailand, sounded the tocsin happily. Hanoi's 1978 friendship treaty with the Soviet Union provided Washington with a good reason for retaining its naval and air bases in the Philippines. Despite non-aligned noises from Indonesia and Malaysia, the region's leaders wanted them to stay.

Watch What We Say, Not What We Do

Yet the anti-Vietnamese rhetoric did not run very deep, for all the bluster. Always conscious of its commercial priorities, Singapore continued to trade with Hanoi. Estimates put the annual two-way trade flow at US$210 million by the later 1980s, not a particularly large sum but a gain all the same. Other countries did the same, albeit more circumspectly. Malaysia approved plantation expertise going to Hanoi on commercial terms, for example, and the Indonesians by 1989 had approved banking and commodity trading joint ventures with the Vietnamese.

None of this prevented Singapore roundly criticising countries which opted, for humanitarian or commercial reasons, to breach Asean's nominal boycott of Vietnam. Lee Kuan Yew disparaged foreign donors, such as Sweden or Australia, which sent aid to alleviate the harsh internal consequences inflicted by Vietnam's rulers on their own countrymen.

On another occasion, Asean countries hounded Japan for trading with Hanoi. Only the US effectively hobbled its businesspeople from dealing with Hanoi, a policy later to cripple American petroleum companies which watched in irritation as European firms snapped up production agreements after 1988.

Meanwhile, in the Cambodian dispute, its direct victims continued to suffer from the tender mercies of contending socialisms. Although the Indonesians fretted that Southeast Asia had become an unwitting tool of China, the Thais felt better after China taught Vietnam a three-week 'lesson' in January 1979. The teaching of it cost the lives of 55,000 Chinese youths, more than all of America's battlefield deaths in its own, long war in Indochina.

No Shortage of Shooting

Seen in this unflattering way, the Asean success formula boils down to a simple equation: outsiders' markets plus outsiders' quarrels equals peace and prosperity.' The publicists of Southeast Asia's economic performance invariably overlook the persistence of conflict in the region, a factor even within the region's market economies.

Active or residual rebellions still troubled the four major Asean members by the beginning of 1989. These included a communist insurgency entrenched in sixty of the Philippines' seventy-three provinces; guerrilla warfare in Indonesia's East Timor and West Irian provinces; growing signs of renewed religious trouble in Thailand's southern, Muslim-influenced provinces, and residual guerrilla movements in West Malaysia coupled with a slower, more worrying emergence of ethnic unrest in Malaysian Borneo.

That picture of unrest is just within the Asean grouping. Within the broader Southeast Asian region there was more trouble than just the Cambodian war. In 1988, heavy fighting between Lao and Thai troops erupted over disputed borders. In the same year, the Burmese military brutally suppressed a popular revolt in Rangoon. Complex insurgencies continued in Burma's tribal and mountainous provinces. Chinese troops remained stationed threateningly near Vietnam. Is this a region destined, in the words of a Malaysian diplomatic plan, to become a 'zone of peace, freedom and neutrality'?

It is a measure of the reduction of intra-regional conflict that Asian specialist writers now enthuse over the 'Asean Six'. The grouping began in 1967 as a by-product of the interplay of convivial politicians, buoyed up by the ending of Indonesian hostility to Malaysia and by the consolidation of Malay chauvinism within a Malaysia from which the troublesome Chinese island of Singapore had just been ejected.

As it began so it continues; twenty years later, Asean still rests on a thicket of informal understandings. But this period of easy conviviality may be passing; leadership changes have already begun, or are expected to occur, during the next few years in Indonesia, Malaysia and Singapore. The Philippine transition from Marcos has become, as Chapter 2 shows, a restoration of old-money families devoid of even the most feeble political will to effect change. In Thailand the unspoken question is, what happens when the current, widely respected monarch passes from the scene? Can the military continue to be eased out of their half-century of political and economic importance?

An end to the dispute over Cambodia may presage a time of preoccupation with pre-existing problems. These include many, long-dormant quarrels among the Asean members themselves. All in all, regional *bonhomie* may begin to show signs of strain. The mixed achievement of Asean receives treatment in detail in Chapter 11.

Commodity Windfalls

Until very recently observations like these seemed churlish conjecture. The mid-1980s showed how regional prosperity rested on shaky foundations but the long period of growth after the 1960s still lulled economists and businessmen. World trading trends, two meteoric oil prices, the marketing gains from multilateral trade diplomacy, the opening of the US market to Asia, the massive Japanese direct investment, the bringing of new commodities (such as cocoa and nickel) to world markets and, in the background, Indochina's continuing security troubles – all these trends or events conspired to consolidate and enrich the market economies of Southeast Asia.

During the region's early boom years, the paths of earnings from each commodity rose ever higher, one after the other, like separate rockets finding loftier trajectories. The timing of each windfall was perfect; as each preceding moneyspinner fizzled out, another commodity boomlet occurred. Timber, then rubber. Palm oil, then copra. Cocoa, then minerals – copper, nickel, coal and even tin – which held their own until prices crashed decisively in 1985. And up they mostly inched again after that, only to slump sharply down after October 1987, one of many consequences of that month's share market collapse, a flattening of sentiment that shook confidence badly around the region. Then prices rose again in 1988 while levelling off in early 1989.

Behind these oscillations loomed Southeast Asia's petroleum resources, the mostly known reserves of Indonesia and Brunei plus Malaysia's expanding offshore fields. All in all, three to four million barrels came out each day at the height of the 1970s boom. Of the three major Asean producers, only Indonesia belongs to the OPEC cartel.

Hopes also rose in Thailand and the Philippines as they joined the search for natural gas and oil. Even Burma, once it emerges from the disaster of its self-imposed 'Burmese Way of Socialism', has large reserves. The Thais, ever lucky, found enough oil to pipe out of the Gulf of Siam; the Filipinos, ever unlucky, had recurrent disappointments.

Singapore's eager refineries stood ready to take the flow although steadily growing capacity, in the region and in the Arab Gulf states, undercut Singapore's competitiveness. New discoveries in western China and offshore Vietnamese fields also promised to shift investment away from archipelagic Asia. Yet even with oil wealth – and this is a key point – economic autonomy remained elusive. Outside events and outsiders' markets provide the 'dynamism' so many observers mistook for a home-grown phenomenon in Southeast Asia.

Chinese Financiers and Footloose Factories

As a repository for overseas Chinese money, Singapore clocked up truly extraordinary rates of growth, reaching over 10 per cent a year. Oil riches fuelled a rush to wealth in Brunei, Malaysia and Indonesia, while debt-financed investment took a giddy hold of a Philippines adjusting to Marcos's grandly titled plan for a 'New Society'. Thailand capitalised on its strong agricultural base – and on its equally strong Chinese minority.

Twelve per cent of the Thai population are of Chinese descent: their integration into the pork-eating, liquor-loving and wholly Buddhist mainstream Thai society has proceeded much more easily than anywhere else in the region. In Malaysia or Indonesia, Chinese minorities receive much less tolerant treatment, partly because of finely drawn communal balances (in Malaysia), partly because of Islamic dietary and recreational prohibitions and partly also because of an unhappy history, as in Java, in which the Chinese acted as colonial middlemen and tax farmers.

Thailand's two t's helped push its growth especially. Tapioca was grown for Europe's cows while beach and bar-girl tourism drew sex-tour enthusiasts from Tokyo to Stockholm. By the approach of the 1990s these twin wellsprings of wealth looked vulnerable: fears of an Asian AIDS epidemic were voiced in an international conference in Bangkok in 1989. While boosting orders for Malaysian-made condoms, the prospect cast a chill over the sex industry just as the approach of a unified market in the European Community after 1992 spelled possible trouble for tapioca's continuing access as cattle feed.

Still, more and more footloose industries set up temporary shop in Thailand, using give-away tax exemptions and docile labour. Japanese direct investment doubled each successive year after 1985 as Tokyo's major consumer goods manufacturers sought to shift production offshore in response to a rapidly appreciating yen. Meanwhile, the diminutive oil-producing Brunei, a Malay sultanate resembling an autocratic Gulf potentate, just pumped and pumped. A Gurkha battalion secured the royal household, and the royal household secured the oil: wags in Bandar Seri Begawan, the country's tiny capital, said the 250,000 Bruneians lived in a 'Shell-fare state' giving them a per capita GDP of US$23,000 a year.

Second Time Around: Japan's Regained Ascendancy

Over these varying success stories flowed another sweet tide. In just three years, from 1985 to 1988, Japan's direct investment flow to Asia totalled US$8.63 billion, compared with US$2.67 billion over the same period from American investors. During the two decades after 1967, Japanese investment came to predominate foreign capital flow. By the late 1960s, two-thirds of Japanese private investment and three-quarters of its foreign aid flow to Asia went to Southeast Asia.

By the mid-1980s Tokyo had become the top foreign private investor in Asean, a trend that accelerated with the 60 per cent appreciation of the yen from 1985 to

1987. Apart from the US market, Southeast Asia had become the most important area for Japanese investors. Indeed, if Tokyo's ministry of finance statistics had included (which they did not) the reinvested profits of Japanese subsidiaries in Southeast Asia, the scale of Japanese penetration would have been even more vividly portrayed.

Indonesia alone took almost half of all Japanese direct foreign investment to Asia during the 1970s, and all regional countries have gained from a shift away from resource-based industry investment and towards technology-intensive manufacturing. In Thailand, Japanese direct investment 'more than doubled over the two decades', as a World Bank report of September 1988 explained. The leading types of manufacturing investment in Southeast Asia were electrical consumer goods, textiles and chemicals.

To this must be added Tokyo's official, concessionary loans from its Overseas Economic Cooperation Fund (OECF). By the end of the decade they came close to the equivalent (in 1988 terms) of US$12 billion. To this must be added various Japanese funds, notably insurance companies and pension schemes, which have increasingly sought to invest some of their enormous liquidity in quality listings on the region's growing equity markets, still tiny by comparison with Tokyo's stock exchange, after 1987 the world's largest with a capitalisation of US$3 trillion.

Yet the results did not please everyone in the region. As political analyst Donald McCloud notes in his book *System and Process in Southeast Asia* (1986),

> Growing economic imbalances between Japan and Southeast Asia have had important political consequences . . . Japanese investment policies and practices have done little to establish a positive image. Japanese businessmen in Southeast Asia have sought the best local business expertise but this [comes] invariably from the Chinese community . . . [their] corporate policies for introducing local management remain very limited [and] their rigid demeanour and strict business practices alienate the more ebullient Southeast Asians, thereby leaving an image, rightly or wrongly, of exploitation.

By the mid-1980s all the Japanese aid money and much of its private investment was going to Asean's 'Four Farms', so called because Indonesia, Malaysia, the Philippines and Thailand still rely predominantly on commodities. Singapore, one of Asia's 'Four Dragons' because of its industrial strength, benefited in other ways however. Despite a steadily rising GDP per capita that finally pushed Singapore beyond Tokyo's means-tested scale for concessionary loans, the appreciating yen after 1985 kept Singapore's inward capital flow from Japan in healthy surplus. (Hong Kong, South Korea and Taiwan are known as the other three 'Dragons'.)

This turnaround followed a period of depression when the lustre had begun to fade from the golden gamble. After 1983 the petro-dollars, rubber-yen, palm oil-pounds and timber-marks no longer made the impression they once had done on the ledgers. Not only did *every* regional commodity price nose-dive in 1985, but outside investors were becoming nervous.

There were several reasons for this. First, the overvalued US dollar at the start of the decade kept US corporate funds at home chasing interest rates. Yet once the dollar's depreciating slide started in earnest after September 1985, the currency movements also closed off American investment – which in any event remained far too concentrated in the oil industry.

These trends accelerated in the late 1980s. Though large, Japanese offshore production line investment was sporadic and choosy, bypassing the chronically unstable Philippines and the rule-bound, racial mix of Malaysia for greener pastures in Thailand and Singapore. In December 1987, Tokyo moved to put more into the region. The equivalent of a US$2 billion investment fund, the Asean-Japan Development Fund, emerged from the third Asean heads of government summit held in Manila that month.

Thus the underlying trends pointed, not to regional self-reliance or intra-regional commerce, but to increasingly ascendant Japanese tutelage in both industry and finance. Beneath the surface appearance suggesting little change in the pattern of Japanese investment lay shifting ground; much of the cheap labour production moved out of Japan into Asean, centred on consumer goods directed back into the Japanese market. Twin systems of quality control, the better standards pegged to Japanese sales, emerged in many recipient countries.

Although a soaring yen did mean extra investment, this came as scant consolation for the stranglehold of Japanese licensing arrangements that forced ever heftier local currency conversions to pay for imported Japanese components. To make matters worse, all governments in the region, except for frugal, high-saving Singapore and oil slippery Brunei, borrowed heavily in yen-denominated instruments. Their squeals of protest reached a shrill pitch by the later 1980s; Japan, to no one's surprise, found talk of rescheduling payments distasteful and chose instead to offer plentiful credit albeit on easier terms.

Industrial Images, Industrial Mirages

Despite a recovery after 1988, the signs still pointed to an end of the type of headlong growth experienced during the region's sunny two decades after the mid-1960s. True, during 1973–85 the region's economies had achieved twelfth place, or better, among all developing countries striving for more manufactured output. (Indonesia reached twelfth place, the bottom Asean rung. Singapore, on the other hand, was number two.)

But where was this industrial dynamism and capital coming from? The World Bank's 1988 *World Development Report* said that for most developing economies, and 'especially [for] those in Southeast Asia, . . . the attraction [for multinational corporations to invest] has been the availability of semi-skilled industrial labour at low cost.'

More than any other factor, the presence of docile, disciplined and cheap labour explains why foreign companies account for such a large proportion of total manufactured exports from Southeast Asia. In the Four Farms foreigners make more than 50 per cent of all manufactured exports; in Singapore it exceeds 90 per cent. But the region's cheap labour cannot forever be taken for granted.

On the labour side, the region's educational systems, with the notable exception of Singapore, have failed to direct young people into the sort of hands-on, applied technology that foreign-owned industries need most. Ironically, Singapore's decision in the early 1980s to price up labour costs (to encourage efficiencies and more technological upgrading) badly hampered the island republic's ability to attract new foreign investment, especially during the deep recession of 1984–86. Singapore's switch back to cheap labour policies came in time to ride on the back of the strengthening yen after 1985, which did more than any other factor to turn around the tiny country's economy.

Another element in the industrial equation promised longer-term problems for sustained regional recovery. Permanent changes in industrial production have begun to rewrite factory textbooks. Robotics, computer-assisted engineering and inventory cutting systems are forcing siting of foreign plants closer to consumers. To take just one example, the textile industry, often seen as a loser in the West's competitive war with Asian productivity, regained its competitive bounce in the late 1980s.

'Surprisingly,' a World Bank *World Development Report* (1987) said, 'the textile industry has consistently registered higher-than-average labour productivity gains in the industrial market economies in recent decades.' The Bank noted 'dramatically higher speeds in spinning, weaving and knitting . . . and the introduction of radical, new techniques.' Even in the clothing industries, microelectronics now made it possible to regain productivity – which meant regained competitiveness against much of the bulk textiles from Asia. 'Recent innovations promise substantial savings in material and labour costs,' the Bank said, 'as well as other advantages in the pre-assembly phase of production.'

Although their effect is likely to be slow, the new technologies are rearming the advanced Western economies and reviving some smokestack industries, even in Japan. The competitiveness of US and British steel makers is a case in point; despite higher labour costs, retrenchments and retooling have achieved their purpose.

Sub-contracting or Substitution?

Beyond that, regional industries have not escaped the even more important design grip of foreign companies. Alert to consumer demand in Western and Japanese markets, foreign investors impose product design specifications and changes on their subsidiaries, a system the World Bank describes as 'akin to the putting-out system in textiles adopted in pre-industrial England.'

Equally profound changes have also occurred in the nature of demand for traditional, out-of-the-ground commodities. This adds up, ultimately, to shrinking markets – for vegetable oil, for example, a major plantation crop in Indonesia and Malaysia. Tired of sky-high prices, major buyers such as India and Pakistan made domestic investments in their own oil crops. Competitors from South America to Papua New Guinea, Asean's near neighbour, have planted oil palm.

To explain this trend a little more, basic consumer preferences are also changing even *within* the spectrum of increasingly static demand for Asean's edible oils. Ferocious public relations wars erupted in 1987 over American soyabean growers' claims that coconut and palm oils have, literally, heart-stoppingly high cholesterol levels.

The US campaign used brochures depicting a flamboyant tropical fat cat, replete with cigar and wide-brimmed hat. This 'grease-ball', as the character was called, was shown selling coconuts with lighted fuses. 'What you don't know about Tropical Fats can kill you,' the advertisements said luridly. Whatever American, European, or Japanese consumers might think, the region still needed Tropical Fats.

This 'viscous infighting', as one wag put it, presaged other attacks by increasingly mobilised lobbies against tropical products. Sugar is one example; sugarbeet farmers in the US and Europe have exerted increasing influence. Another area is animal feeds, a threat to oil mill by-products, tapioca and even fishmeal. Synthetic rubber marks yet another threat to regional commodities, riding high or low depending on petroleum pricing.

All in all, most commodity analysts at the end of the 1980s saw two trends slowly converging. First, the region's market share of all commodities will slowly drop. Secondly, so will the unit prices commanded by these products. Substitutes, conservation and alternative sources of supply will add up to 'reducing uptake', as the commodity trading jargon goes, of the region's raw materials. Changing technologies, some of them rather esoteric (dehydrated preservation techniques displacing the need for tinplate, for example) are also adding to the trend.

Cutting Down a Resource

The supply side of commodities also portends uncertainty in the years ahead. Petroleum is an example already cited; so are other mineral deposits. The end of one particular resource is already at hand.

By the end of the 1970s, Europe's and Japan's voracious appetite for tropical woods had already led to unprecedented havoc in Southeast Asian timber lands, some of the world's oldest tropical rainforest. By the approach of the 1990s, the devastation is nearly complete. In 1970 the Philippines had 15 million hectares of tropical hardwood trees. By 1987, this had slipped to 1 million. Indonesia's Borneo and Sumatra forests tell a similar tale of devastation. Thailand's, Burma's and Malaysia's forests have the same, grim future. Southeast Asia, including Burma, now supplies 70 per cent of global tropical woods but in a few decades the forests will completely disappear.

When pressed, however, to prevent extinction of the resource by banning new logging, Malaysia's Mahathir and other regional politicians usually ridicule the conservation lobby – which, admittedly, often uses sentimental and imported 'love-of-nature' arguments alien to the region. Mahathir and his peers refuse to allow constraint of the resource in Malaysia, any more than demand and supply allow. Trees, they reason, should stop appearing on the market only when they get used up. Full stop.

The problem is that very little replanting or reafforestation work is proceeding. Some signs promise a glimmer of hope; in January 1989, Thailand's government took the unprecedented decision of ordering an immediate halt in logging, a decision shocking the Chinese timber barons and their many military patrons. Whether Thailand's often compromised local administration can muster the will to enforce the ban remains an open question.

The end of Southeast Asia's timber business, a hugely profitable industry in the 1970s, has thus become a grotesque race. Which will ruin the timber market faster? Slowing end-user demand for wood, for everything from furniture panels to use-once, throwaway chopsticks? Or the dwindling number of trees themselves? The odds favour the supply-siders.

Other commodities and crops face tenacious viruses that are cutting back productivity. Pepper, cloves and other smallholder crops have suffered production declines. The Philippines bought sugar in 1987 although it is the region's biggest supplier. Indonesia's need for cloves, with which the country's smokers love to lace their tobacco, resulted in profitable imports from

Zanzibar. Indonesian agronomists insist the country can grow as many cloves as it needs.

The effect of deforestation is increasingly felt: siltation and erosion are increasing, leading to results like the Thai flooding. At the onset of the 1990s, even the continued presence of the land itself can no longer be taken for granted: each year the equivalent of 100,000 hectares of topsoil, half a metre thick, washes into the sea from the eroded Philippine slopes. Watersheds and fisheries are suffering acute damage. Monoculture cash crop plantations also exhaust the land, especially in upland terrain where soils are thinner and leach quickly without tree cover.

Commodity Con Games

By the end of the 1980s therefore, the gilded promises sustaining the growth of these stellar Asean economies seem to be losing much of their gloss. Although the commodity river still flows bountifully, the fluctuating rapids of the 1980s reveal a rockier bottom beneath. Revised estimates in the mid-1980s showed a 30 per cent drop or more on projections of demand for major commodities by the year 2000, compared with studies made just five years earlier.

K. N. Kohli, chief economist for the Asian Development Bank, forecast (1987) permanently reduced demand, describing the two golden decades as an 'aberration'. Most commodity analysts tend to agree. 'The optimism and confidence encountered in the "fastest growing region of the world" has given way to pessimism and gloom over the prospects for further growth,' wrote Dr Hans Christoph Rieger, an authority on regional economics in 1986.

The moderate recovery since 1987 has revived the hosannas for the region's market-minded dynamism. Apart from trade performance or foreign investment flows however, the conventionally benign view of Southeast Asian economies has to contend with various business scandals. During the 1980s these afflicted Indonesian, Malaysian and Philippine banks, harming foreign confidence.

Accounts of monopoly mania among prominent families have also become commonplace. For example, in Malaysia sugar 'czar' Robert Kuok still has a tight hold on the business. Family firms like the Kuoks have bought sugar from countries far more distant than the neighbouring Philippines, burdened during most of the decade by unsold mountains of sugar. Importing can be tricky in Indonesia. Many of that country's imported commodities – wheat, meat or cloves – are priced dearly by import monopolies.

The market mechanism is distorted in many other ways throughout the region. In Malaysia a government-enforced New Economic Policy (NEP) resulted in a twenty-year programme starting in 1970 to transfer corporate wealth to indigenous Malays. The programme has given head starts to well-connected Malays. The burgeoning banking, plantation, transport and communications companies have been fought over.

The same monopoly habits resurfaced in the Philippines after Marcos. President Corazon Aquino's immediate and extended family members have moved into waterside and other transport businesses – port-clearing, cargo agencies and river transport. Her family, the Cojuangcos, has consolidated through its various wings an early family grip on various banking and sugar businesses. Even a new government agency, given the task of recovering the former president's stolen millions, moved to create new networks of patronage. The agency's name, the

Commission on Good Government, has acquired an ironic ring. (An account of the Philippines' business culture is found in Chapter 2.)

The direct and indirect economic costs from these habits is now better understood. 'Economists are now taking a closer look at unproductive activity,' the World Bank said in 1988. The term most often used for the taking of unearned benefits is 'rent-seeking'. Another expression is 'Directly Unproductive Profit-seeking', or DUP for short.

To apply the idea to Southeast Asia, the region's 'duppies' capture what economists call the 'scarcity premiums' that accrue to government-enforced advantages like monopolies, quotas or licences. DUP means easy profit but little or no authentic production. It means 'economic activities that produce zero output while using up real resources', in the words of one World Bank report. DUP theory applies well to the many, poorly managed infant industries in the region with their restricting effect on the economy.

It was not as if the gloomy mid-1980s suddenly burst the region's bubble, stopping revellers in their tracks. A type of anticipatory shudder of these tremulous times had shot through Asean once before, at the end of its *first* dizzy decade.

A financial crisis in Indonesia's state oil monopoly Pertamina badly shook confidence in Jakarta in the mid-1970s, imperilling the nation's credit-worthiness. Scandals in Malaysia also piled up one on another in the 1970s. Afterwards controversies erupted over Bank Rakyat, the country's biggest cooperative bank. A litany of Philippine financial failures also became unnerving in the 1970s with the flight from Manila of banker Dewey Dee, a close Marcos associate.

The argument, however, is that the New Economic Policy and similar policies in Southeast Asia distort market rigour so drastically that the dead weight of government sits too heavily on the 'hidden hand', pinching off its circulation. Just as much as Chinese or Indians, the Malays chafe under their government's paternalism. Javanese generals have also heightened the asymmetry of wealth in Indonesia, retaining private business pacts with predominantly Chinese financiers while championing the rights of small *pribumis*, the 'indigenous' (non-Chinese) businessmen and women. The 1950s era, 'Filipino First' campaigns in Manila also had the same, distorting effect and achieved the opposite from that intended: forcing the Chinese out of agricultural businesses propelled them into industry, then and now the most vibrant part of the economy.

Malaysia's NEP has attracted enormous attention during its nearly two-decade run. Describing the programme as an Asian brand of positive discrimination, Malay politicians compare it benignly to American affirmative action programmes to enhance the opportunities of blacks, women and other groups under-represented in the economy.

But others, quite apart from resentful Malaysian Chinese, have different views. Canadian economist Ozay Mehmet (1986), who has studied the NEP more than any other foreign economist, says 'making millionaires by patronage is not only inconsistent with the rules of fair play, it is also contrary to the rules of economic efficiency.' He says government programmes transferring corporate shares to Malay trustee corporations have become 'a zero-sum economic game . . . the trustees have gained at the expense of the losers, the large number of poor families who have remained poor.' Indonesia's public enterprises, ostensibly displacing the Chinese on behalf of *pribumis*, also enrich only small fractions of the 'native' élite.

Projectitis

Yet at this time, when foreign debt burden was still small, Malaysia, Indonesia, the Philippines and Thailand each caught and then passed on an enervating virus called 'projectitis'. Even the region's affluent small-fry such as Brunei and Singapore, caught the bug; Brunei's royal palace, with 257 bathrooms, provided one example while Singapore's most expensive project (a telling contrast) was an underground mass transit system.

Malaysia's vanity provides a good example. Huge natural gas, methanol, liquid natural gas, cement, steel, shipyard and refinery projects emerged along the coconut-fringed seashores. Mahathir's ambition for a showpiece, 'made-in-Malaysia' motorcar resulted in a comically look-alike version of a Mitsubishi saloon car punched out by an imported but already obsolete stamping plant.

To make the plant work (Mitsubishi trading and manufacturing corporations capitalised 30 per cent of the venture and the Malaysian government the rest), the country built up its tariff structure on imported cars. The cumulative effect gave so many direct and indirect preferences to the new company, named Proton, that most existing assembly plants had to shut down. When sales fell victim to the 1984–86 recession, Mahathir embraced plans to sell Proton's car, to the US and Britain, even if the agents chosen to do the job had a doubtful sales track record.

Before the recession of the 1980s hit hard, projectitis had reached the epidemic stage. Mimicking their central government, some of Malaysia's thirteen state governments puffed up like toads. One of them, the happy-go-spending, timber-felling state of Sabah, had encumbered its 1.2 million citizens with a US$2.2 billion foreign and domestic debt by 1985, an US$18,300 per capita burden for the state's fishermen, subsistence rice growers and forest dwelling tribes.

Indonesian, Thai and Philippine experience also mirrored Malaysia's disappointed dreams although there are exceptions. Sector by sector, big projects usually became grandiloquent failures. A prime example is the region's patchwork-quilt motor industry, now almost totally in thrall to the Japanese multinationals. Despite ten years of official Asean talks to devise a complementary motor industry throughout the region, the ultimate result was an agreement, now honoured in the breach, to make three interchangeable parts.

In another example, a vast US$3 billion aluminium plant and hydroelectric scheme in northern Sumatra roared into red ink from its first day of operation. And there it mostly has stayed, although a sustained recovery in the market finally began in 1988. The same fate seemed to grasp an Indonesian joint venture with Spain that assembles aircraft touted as Indonesia's own. This factory, sited in West Java, remains technology minister Mohamad Habibie's pet project. He enjoys a *Wunderkind* reputation with his boss, President Suharto, but his enemies call him *sok tau*, 'know-it-all'. His planes find few buyers outside the country's captive air force.

Overlooking Maintenance

There is no question but that impressive achievements were won during Southeast Asia's two decades of boom. Schools, hospitals, roads, dams, and power facilities were built in record numbers. Yet, sadly, these have not been well maintained. The International Monetary Fund's fiscal affairs director, Vito Tanzi, said cautiously in a 1987 Asian Development Bank publication that 'these countries have been more successful at building infrastructure than at its adequate maintenance or use.'

In the Philippines, he continued, 'operation and maintenance expenditures [in 1985 real terms] were only 60% of their 1977 levels' while 'in Indonesia much of the infrastructure built over the past two decades is reported to be deteriorating . . . only 40% of national and provincial roads are considered in a stable condition and [the same is true] for irrigation canals.' Tanzi is an international Civil Servant and perforce must use diplomatic language; other reports, including direct observation from the field, confirm the lamentable state of many roads, bridges, irrigation systems and hydroelectric facilities throughout the region.

A Primitive Business Culture

At the core of this mixed record, in which spend-happy 'duppying' so often clouds success, lies a predatory business culture that, despite local variations, runs through the region. Doing business in the Asean archipelago usually depends, first, on personalities and, second, on patrimonial largesse. Corporate label comes a poor third; expertise a dismal fourth.

In its 'rainy day' mentality, the drive behind making and hiding wealth in Southeast Asia has a distinctly cultural overtone. Southeast Asians keep more London flats or San Francisco condominiums than the Arabs. They hold thousands of Zürich bank accounts and remain steady clientele of Bahamian tax havens.

These habits are old. They were already robust by the tenth century, when the first regular sea-traders from China and India passed through the Malacca Strait and bought protection from local rulers. That underlying instinct – slicing off a cut of someone else's wealth rather than creating it yourself – runs very deep. In moments of candour, Westernised Southeast Asians acknowledge the tenacity of these habits.

This need not be the only face of Southeast Asian business. In countries accepting Chinese, Filipino and other migrants from the region, the drive and will to succeed has become blindingly apparent. In Joel Kotkin's and Yoriko Kishimoto's book *The Third Century: America's Resurgence in the Asian Era*, published in 1989, 'Amer-Asians' are described as comprising the bulk of recent immigration into the US.

Although just 2 per cent of total US population, by 1988 Amer-Asians formed 25 per cent of the student body at the University of California's Berkeley campus and 14 per cent of Harvard's undergraduates. Nearly 50 per cent of all Amer-Asian adults hold university degrees. They form a disproportionate number of technicians at work in California's Silicon Valley or in Massachusetts. Apart from those of Korean and Japanese ancestry, the rest are overseas Chinese from the Asean region. Some are Filipinos.

Back 'home', business habits often remain rooted in feudal obligations. Southeast Asia's rulers traditionally exploited the entrepreneurial energies of Chinese and other immigrants, just as they were 'used' in return. As McCloud (1986) notes,

> The class of wealthy merchants was so powerful in the economic world
> of traditional Southeast Asia that it often controlled the political system.
> Merchants were not part of the royal élite . . . and for the most part were not

even indigenous peoples but, instead, consisted of Arabs, Chinese, Indians and, later, Europeans . . .

The Chinese Connection

Tightly secretive clan groups began moving out of the southern provinces of China to the *Nanyang*, 'South Seas', in successive waves starting four hundred years ago. Some Chinese have lived in the region even longer, although the greatest numbers migrated in the forty years after 1870. Many of the richest descendants are happy to close the time-honoured feudal circle, paying their new rulers for protection. This picture of a corrupt circle of favours is not universal, nor is it complete; but enough truth still resides in it to define one of the region's most enduring characteristics.

As recession bites harder and with greater regularity into Southeast Asian business, the reality of extensive Chinese control becomes harder to disguise. Manila's 'Binondo Central Bank' – meaning Chinese money-lenders in the city's old Binondo commercial core – still has enormous influence on the peso exchange rates. The same fact of business life hangs over Jakarta's Jalan Gajah Mada in the city's old Chinese quarter, or among Kuala Lumpur's backlane counting houses.

In the unreported 'black' economies the links are many and manifold: for example in each regional country the retailers of smuggled goods, also overwhelmingly Chinese, keep up their cordial links with the customs service. The same applies to the Philippines, whether Ferdinand Marcos or Corazon Aquino (herself from a Chinese *mestizo* (mixed blood) family) sits in the presidential palace. Via Hokkien, Fukien, or Hakka clan networks, or out of Taiwan or Hong Kong, virtually every piece of Southeast Asian business has a slice of Chinatown.

The Chinese remain the region's most effective risk financiers; next to their powerful, adroit marshalling of money, the state-led financial institutions pale into insignificance. Government lending criteria, as for example in the crisis-plagued Indonesian Development Bank or in Malaysia's Bank Bumiputra, place patronage and favouritism ahead of regular business. At least with the Chinese, the figures usually add up.

A redoubled anxiety surfaced in the late 1980s among the overseas Chinese. More funds went into tax and real estate havens in Europe, Australia or the US. A senior Australian diplomat told me in 1986 that Chinese businessmen in Singapore and Malaysia alone had remitted a net positive capital inflow to Australia of US$1 billion during just the twelve months ending September 1985.

As political uncertainties mounted in Indonesia and Malaysia so did fears of changing times ahead. A determination to get a US 'green card', the American permanent residence permit, or to migrate to Australia or Canada gripped Chinese families. This happened even in prosperous Singapore, a troubling fact for Lee Kuan Yew's government. The crucial if inconvenient role still played by the Chinese in Southeast Asian business is more fully explored in Chapter 7.

The Shadow of Debt

The anxieties at play among the Chinese simply reflected their commercial horse sense, reacting to the steadily accumulating economic problems. By 1989 the foreign debt of Indonesia, Malaysia, Thailand and the Philippines had soared to just under US$110 billion. Ten years earlier, it had stood at less than US$17 billion; without the Pertamina oil company corruption in Indonesia the figure would have been less than US$7 billion.

The debt was one side of a more complicated problem. In each major regional country the so-called 'invisible payments' such as insurance, travel or remittances abroad, are now routinely pulling their balance-of-payments account well into the red. Only Malaysia's better export performance differentiates it from the Philippines experience; otherwise anxiety over Kuala Lumpur's US$22 billion foreign debt (three-and-a-half times higher on a per capita basis than in the Philippines) would have been more visible.

The true debt position is difficult to determine. In Southeast Asia, money goes in and out of the region, with no questions asked. Most capital flow monitoring systems are timid, deliberately or conveniently so. Every day, millions of dollars move about in quick despatch, mostly within the banking sector but often, especially among the Chinese, in closed, clan accounting systems in which a debit for a million dollars in an Amsterdam noodle shop becomes a credit for the same amount in a Bangkok jewellers after a direct dial telephone call and a hurried burst of Cantonese.

The movement of capital, free of exchange controls, reigns supreme in the region. Jaffar Hussein, governor of the Malaysian central bank, might well have been speaking for all of free market Southeast Asia when he told a New York audience that '[Malaysia] has been well ahead in maintaining a free system of exchange control. Indeed, we hardly have exchange controls in practice.' On payments abroad, 'both residents and non-residents are allowed to do whatever they like with their own money.'

What buttresses the system more than anything else is the certainty that ruinous capital flight would follow any imposition of controls. Whenever the Chinese feel nervous they buy dollars or Deutschmarks so fast that Jaffar's colleagues will decimate reserves in an effort to protect their currencies. This happened in Indonesia several times during the late 1980s; the Chinese unloaded trillions of rupiah over three, one-week periods in 1987.

The free exchange principle reaches highest enshrinement in the region's Chinese-dominated casinos. At Genting Highlands overlooking Kuala Lumpur, at Jakarta's Horison Hotel or Manila's Playboy Pagcor dens, the haemorrhaging of local currencies went on during the boom. Takings were exchanged for dollars on the black market, stuffed into steel boxes and, for one Malaysian casino, put each morning on a light plane to Singapore.

This is gambling in the literal sense. Metaphorically however, small businesses have also wagered recklessly. In an atmosphere of seemingly endless expansion, debt finance fuelled too many small traders, convinced that rapid expansion was the only way to position themselves for even bigger profits. The risks to which these businessmen exposed themselves became evident in fears of banking collapse.

The Blunt Side of the East Asian Edge

The fixation with Asia has grown in tandem with the manufacturing export successes of Northeast Asia, coupled with increasing direct foreign investment by Japan. Southeast Asia, home to a very different temperament, became the passive beneficiary of a gathering mythology about Asia. Western media uncritically lumped the Southeast Asians in the same category as the self-sustaining, high-saving, technologically innovative Northeast Asians. A more fundamental error would be hard to imagine.

Within Southeast Asia an abiding preference for opulence over excellence has not changed. Why should it? Productive investment is usually done by outsiders – first the Indian merchants, then the colonial powers and, lastly by the immigrant Chinese. If these remarks seem harsh, just look at the nest eggs maintained by the privileged themselves. To the simple question, 'where do you put your money?', far too often comes the answer, 'anywhere but here.'

The smallest but wealthiest regional countries, Brunei and Singapore, have generally refused to invest their US$50–75 billion reserves in the economies of their adjoining neighbours. They were not foolish: they wanted reliable, low-risk securities. Singapore's hard-nosed approach to the region became legendary. When prime minister Lee Kuan Yew came to Manila in July 1986 he presented a gift of nearly US$2.5 million to the Philippines treasury. Diplomats were stunned: none could remember Singapore having given anything to anyone *free*.

Lee's successful enclave receives more attention in Chapter 6. The diminutive republic revealed, by invidious comparison with its neighbours, the veneer of Southeast Asia's modernity.

An Indigenous Technological Culture?

A key purpose of these pages is to question the market myths of the Southeast Asian economies, not to dispute their achievement. Not all the wealth has gone to waste. More children have learned to read, more highways have been cut through tropical forests, more engineers, technicians and innovators emerged from steadily expanding universities.

Yet despite the great advances, a self-generating technological culture in the Asean region remains a highly elusive quarry. There are few technical innovators, and even fewer men or women of influence who urge their nurture. Spending for research and development shows little truly autonomous achievement anywhere in Southeast Asia.

Singapore provides an exception in this regard. Its Science Park and other attempts to inculcate technical expertise, show signs of success; so also to some extent does Malaysia's effort to create a self-reliant software programming capability, via the creation – at the prime minister's behest – of a government-financed unit. In Thailand and in Indonesia, 'technology' is fashionable. But homegrown results remain meagre.

The regional figures tell a great deal. The R & D amounts lag far behind expenditure in advanced countries. Even within those budgets, much of the spending is 'captive', linked to retailing gimmicks (e.g., changing the shape of a toothpaste tube). Fewer than 12 per cent of Thai university students enter engineering or applied science courses; in Japan over 40 per cent do.

Where tertiary education reaches many more, as in the Philippines, the brightest students still seek rewards elsewhere, searching for a green card at the end of the rainbow but, if that proves too hard, then applying their skills to austere jobs such as mechanics in the Middle East. Apart from the Singaporeans, the best applied researchers remain Malaysians and Thais, mostly in foreign-owned or -managed mining and plantation companies.

One way to measure the inventiveness of the region's people is to consult foreign managers, especially other Asians. In the mid-1980s the prestigious Kyoto University surveyed Japanese managers' opinions of Asean staff.

In Malaysia, not one of several thousand managers surveyed gave local staff a 'good' rating on the question of ability 'to adapt to changing situations.' Three-quarters of the respondents called local employees 'not very adaptable.' Especially among non-Chinese employees, the notion of guaranteed employment is strong. Accounts from other countries told the same, if slightly varying, story. Singapore and Thailand scored best. Indonesia and the Philippines scored lowest after Malaysia.

Another study, from Singapore's Institute of Southeast Asian Studies in 1987, said that most middle-sized entrepreneurs in the region suffer from 'a total lack of, or only limited·knowledge of book-keeping, costing, financing, procurement and . . . quality control.'

Boasts that basic, 'market-minded' changes have occurred in the region seem particularly shallow in the area of intellectual property and manpower. Although the Philippines remains a special case, hundreds of thousands of Indonesians, Malaysians and Thais also work abroad, even in the biggest boom times, unable at the lower end of the labour market to find well-paid work or, at the top end, to find satisfying or challenging goals. Singapore, meanwhile, preaches the free market so long as this does not involve free movement of labour. And each country made little effort to protect copyright, trademarks or patents until the Reagan administration forced them to confront the issue. Pirated books, cassettes, videos and fashions filled the marketplaces.

The much-vaunted growth in the region's financial industry has some drawbacks. Capital markets have not developed much beyond casinos. Even Southeast Asia's biggest, the Hong Kong exchange with its US$35 billion capitalisation in mid-1986, amounted to less than 3 per cent of Tokyo's share market. Hong Kong's share market woke up one morning in December in 1987 to find the stock exchange director in gaol, arrested on corruption charges.

'What stands out', says Asian stockmarket analyst Anthony Rowley, 'is the relative insignificance of other markets in Asia . . . Asian markets are often tiny in relation to the size of the economies they operate within.' More to the point, Rowley claims in his 1987 book *Asian Stockmarkets: the Inside Story* that 'insider trading is accepted as part of the culture of making money. Small investors do not mind too much whether company directors are making money from dealing on the inside – provided those on the outside can make something too.'

Hong Kong's reaction to the 1987 crash was to try to hold it back, closing down for three days. Bourses in Singapore, Kuala Lumpur, Bangkok and Manila went for a straight free fall, slicing as much as half the paper value off speculative high-fliers registering impressive gains just two weeks before. Once again the point needs little labouring. As in industry, as in commodities, so also in the capital markets. Led, but not leading. Passive and not proactive.

The mythology of the Southeast Asian marketplace has a political as well as business rationale. For two decades after the end of the Second World War, this region of archipelagic Asia remained preoccupied by the post-colonial reckoning.

Just forty-five years ago, it was not at all clear that what we now call 'Indonesia', 'Malaysia', 'Singapore', or 'Brunei', would emerge as independent countries. Nor was it clear what racial and geographic shape they would take. Together with

Thailand, Burma and the Philippines, these names conjured a vista of swaying coconut trees in the tropical Indies, and not much more. Nothing pointed towards the future bonanza.

Today, Europe and America hear spellbinding tales about a calm, politically stable and free-marketeering Southeast Asia. US politicians pay homage to the achievement. The six 'dialogue partners' of Asean – the US, Japan, Canada, Australia, New Zealand and the European Community – pour on the praise at annual meetings.

In regional economics as in regional politics however, the impression of cohesion is as brittle as glass. Very little needs to happen before these fragilities are exposed: a renewal of border squabbling could cause enormous strains. So could tense political succession in Indonesia, racial uproar in Malaysia or a geopolitical shift by Thailand, ever sensitive to the broader currents of world affairs.

A major communist insurgency is consuming one Asean country, the Philippines. Minor Red crusades still trouble Thailand and Malaysia. Two Muslim separatist movements, in Thailand and in the Philippines, could boil up again into major problems. Sabah, on northern Borneo's tip, is claimed by Malaysia and the Philippines. Fundamentalist Islam creates headaches in Malaysia and Indonesia. Timor and West Irian, both the scene of past rebellions against Jakarta's authority, still spawn bloody trouble.

The old golf course chumminess is already passing. The leaders do not feel so comfortable with each other any more: Thailand's long-serving Prem Tinsulonond reportedly found Malaysia's Mahathir an irritating person. Indonesia's Suharto and Singapore's Lee shook their heads over Aquino's naïveté, and over her government's initial instability. The Brunei sultan has little reputation for intellectual depth. The pendulum may be shifting back to mutual suspicion, especially if a gap between the generations reinforces differing policies among the various national leaderships.

As they enter the 1990s, Malaysian, Indonesia, Thai and Filipino economists are now asking themselves 'what might have been done differently?' For a start, they acknowledge that Southeast Asia's wellspring of wealth basically has never moved past a reliance on commodities, a feature discussed in more detail in Chapter 8.

'Value-added', the economist's favoured phrase, never became a favoured mode. As in the Middle East, oil became the region's great corruptor. Its influence – direct in Brunei's royal ostentation and only slightly more muted in Indonesian or Malaysian extravagance – became corrosive. Even Singapore, more than its leaders ever admitted, grew a little lazy with its oil wealth.

Home Movies

Many foreign advisers stressed these points to Southeast Asian leaders. Just how pervasive this advice was became apparent when I viewed a mystery videotape which arrived at my front doorstep in Kuala Lumpur one morning without warning or ceremony. When I put it into the recorder the tape cassette revealed a curious scene.

The camera panned along a line of faces – the Malaysian cabinet in session. Head after head was nodding in agreement as an Americanised Japanese voice droned on about commodity marketing. Astonishingly, Mahathir had brought his personal adviser, Kenichi Ohmae, to his cabinet and had filmed the result. Mahathir repeated the exercise for senior Civil Servants.

Ohmae and others criticised the Southeast Asians' infatuation with raw resources. Still mesmerised by the 1970s oil price hikes, many in the region dreamed that Asean might one day become an 'EEC without pain', as one Thai economist put it, escaping the hard work of economic integration by erecting one tropical commodity cartel after another. Commodity Price Agreements (CPAs) became the vogue. Demand would be insatiable, production steady. Get a grip on the supply, and the money would flood in forever, or so the reasoning (and panicky Western reportage) went. These fantasies had gripped Asia's collective imagination for a decade. After all, the multilateral trade diplomacy, preferential tariffs, the oil cartel and (for a while) the tin, rubber and lesser CPAs worked magic.

To be sure, Southeast Asia's new industries have added more local content. But the footloose factories settling in Jakarta, Singapore, Penang, Bataan or Bangkok still rely on little more than local labour; with the exception of Singapore, most value-added still comes from docile hands doing the things that new generations of robots will do as dexterously in coming decades. Singapore economist Chia Siow Yue notes that Southeast Asia's 'non-resource based product groups . . . the electrical machinery, clothing, telecommunications equipment and switchgear' are all labour-intensive. 'Much of the technology is imported.'

The Japanese have the fewest illusions about the region. Perhaps this is because their own, pre-industrial past lies so close to their own surface, or perhaps it is because they had a much more recent experience at the tail end of Southeast Asian manufacturing themselves, making the cheap consumer goods produced during Japan's first industrial phase.

Whatever the reason, Tokyo's business and financial conglomerates have a good grasp of the region. An almost admirable brutality stiffens Japanese thinking – clear, no illusions, successfully self-interested. Even the Asian Development Bank, one of Japan's vehicles for a sanitised reappearance in Southeast Asia after the Second World War, now carries forward the struggle for Japanese contracts and advances Tokyo's interest, a phenomenon receiving more attention in Chapter 10.

The End of an Era

As their second fast-earning decade ended, Southeast Asian leaders feared a portent in the swinging palace doors left behind by Marcos. His authoritarian neighbours stared, aghast, as the foreign press invaded Manila's presidential palace, nibbling the deposed leader's sandwiches and prodding bedsprings in flagrant lèse-majesté.

Much maligned among its Asean neighbours, the post-Marcos Philippines is now reverting to familiar ways as politics comes full circle under the haphazard authority of Corazon Aquino. Marcos's departure was the first of many other leadership changes in this region, all as inevitable as death and the passing of time.

Free market Southeast Asia enters the closing years of this century largely bereft of new ideas, saddled with growing populations and watching in resentful fascination as market dynamism fashioned elsewhere widens the gap between the region's unchanged role as a receiver of technology and the West's (and Northeast

Asia's) authentic, technological competence. And the backlog of problems can no longer be met by evasion.

The World Bank forecasts Indonesia's population reaching 363 millions by AD 2010 – just two decades distant. In the Philippines, where Aquino remains at peace with papal dogma on fertility control; human numbers will reach 100 millions in the same year. Thailand, which has a serious fertility control programme, will attain the same numbers that year while Malaysia, the only country with open space, wants more than the Bank's estimate of 33 millions. (Mahathir in the mid-1980s urged a '70 million policy'.) Singapore would inch up to 3 millions. All this means more than a doubling of the region's numbers in under twenty years. It signals again the old, if unfashionable question: at what point do human numbers become a vice? It is hard to see how these economies will cope.

'It is difficult to foresee the repetition' of the 'exceptional and perhaps unprecedented' post-war Southeast Asian prosperity, wrote the noted development economist Harry Oshima in a 1986 issue of an Asian Development Bank journal. The root cause of the abnormal bonanza, in his view, lay in 'the demand side due to the opening of the large US domestic market to the world.' Given the chronic US balance of payments problem, few analysts believe that another headlong sales drive into the American market can happen again.

Nor do businessmen or economists imagine for one moment that Japan will readily become a surrogate Uncle Sam for directionless exports. Exports to Tokyo will rise – they have risen on the back of the dear yen since the late 1980s - but the internal Japanese market will not work the same wonders.

If all this were not enough, two decades of high living have whittled away at Southeast Asian competitiveness. The trends point to a real chance that the region's infant, protected industries may be crushed by the emerging industrial power of India and China. It has already been happening in textiles and some cheap, retail electronic lines. The writing seems to be on the wall.

Richer but not a great deal wiser, debt-burdened yet borrowing still, profligate in habit yet believing that outside markets and muscle will always come to the rescue, the region's authoritarian leaders now ponder their own passing from the stage. In the next few years, all of them – Lee (the prudent exception), Suharto, Mahathir and perhaps even the antiquated Brunei monarchy – will be gone. The Thai monarchy and the Aquino government could face serious transitional problems. So will many of their financial backers. And waiting just a few years ahead lies the passing of Hong Kong back into Mother China in 1997, an end also of another era, and a drying up perhaps of a vital regional lubricant – overseas Chinese finance – if Peking redirects it into the mother-land.

Ironically, Marcos led the way down the development road that other Southeast Asian economies have since travelled. He carried his country into ruinous debt to finance vanished dreams. His Asian neighbours followed suit, with better but still varying success. Ironically also, the old dictator began his economic career, not as creator of cronies, but as role model for 'development'.

Both the 'model' itself and the man who fostered it are now discredited; the notion of Marcos as innovator seems strange today. But it is, after all, no stranger than the notion that the muscleman's ignominious exit might herald yet another era, this time a slowing down of the economic miracle in the rest of Southeast Asia.

References

Kohli, K. N. (1987) 'An assessment of the impact of falling commodity prices', Manila: Asian Development Bank. Unpublished

Kotkin, J. and Kishimoto, Y. (1989) *The Third Century: America's Resurgence in the Asian Era*. New York: Random House

Mehmet, O. (1986) *Development in Malaysia: Poverty, Wealth and Trusteeship*. London: Croom Helm

McCloud, D. (1986) *System and Process in Southeast Asia*. Boulder, Colorado: Westview Press

Rieger, H. C. (1986) 'Asian economic performance', *Current History*, vol. 28, No. 2

Rowley, A. (1987) *Asian Stockmarkets: the Inside Story*. Hong Kong: Review Publications

Tanzi, V. (1987) 'The public sector in the market economies of developing Asia', *Asian Development Review*, vol. 5, No. 2

World Bank (1987) *World Development Report*. Washington, DC

World Bank(1988)*World Development Report*. Washington, DC

2

FULL CIRCLE IN THE PHILIPPINES

Portent of Things to Come?

Although the events of February 1986, focused attention on impending changes in Southeast Asia, the region's mood was already in flux well before Marcos's twenty-year tenure came to an ignominious end. The slowing of Southeast Asia's era of easy growth had begun to be apparent by the early 1980s; one sign of the changing times was a tendency for foreign correspondents to run foul of business and political sensitivities.

These prickly feelings show little sign of lessening. Since the mid-1980s, regional governments have gaoled, expelled, prosecuted, prohibited entry to, or revoked working visas from, foreign journalists. Clamps on circulation and deliberate delays in the distribution of foreign publications have become more frequent. Local reporters and their publications are also experiencing rising risks; newspapers have been shut down in Indonesia and Malaysia. Publishing permits, usually issued with a validity of one year, are becoming more difficult to renew.

Behave or Go Home

Singapore's long running skirmish with the foreign media underlines a regional phenomenon. Prime minister Lee Kuan Yew's government has expelled some foreign journalists and denied visas to others during the past decade. In one instance, the Singapore judiciary imposed a fine for contempt of court on an American-owned, regional newspaper.

After 1985 a new approach became apparent in Singapore's dealings with recalcitrant foreign journalists. The authorities have ordered severe cuts in the Singapore circulation of such publications as the *Asian Wall Street Journal*, *Asiaweek*, *Far Eastern Economic Review* and *Time*. In a related move, the government has amended a freshly enacted copyright law (see Chapter 6) to allow a compliant trade union to photocopy, reproduce and distribute the weekly issues of the Hong Kong-based *Far Eastern Economic Review*, minus the advertising pages.

Similar vigilance became the norm after 1983 across the narrow strait separating Singapore from Malaysia. Prime minister Mahathir Mohamed expelled

two American correspondents in September 1986. A year earlier I was arrested
and charged with offences under Malaysia's Official Secrets Act; soon after my
conviction, which resulted in a fine of about US$4,000, the government's parlia-
mentary majority amended the statute to make a two-year term of imprisonment
mandatory upon conviction, even for first-time offenders.

By this time Indonesia had already become less hospitable to the foreign press.
Jakarta-based writers began to receive invitations to come in for 'friendly chats'
with information ministry officials. Some correspondents had their travel plans
vetoed while others had their requests for an extension of working visas denied.
Foreign publications carrying displeasing articles still can enter the country, but
they often arrive with sweeping blotches of black ink across objectionable pages.

Elsewhere in Southeast Asia, the local press remains tame in Brunei, a country that closely monitors the entry of foreign correspondents. Before Marcos's
overthrow, only Thailand could boast a relatively open environment. Yet, even
in Bangkok, the foreign press needs to be alert to various 'no-go' areas, especially
the avoidance of comments deemed *lèse-majesté* to the Thai monarchy.

Southeast Asia's free marketeering countries have accepted that their application
of this sort of discipline does incur some risk. Not only are relations with Western
governments passingly affected, but the occasional fuss about a media 'crackdown'
leads naïve foreign investors to misinterpret the government's moves as a sign of
political instability.

Nothing could be further from the authorities' intention. As it happens, quite
the opposite motivation prompts these highly publicised wrist-slappings. A deputy
premier of one Asean country told me that 'reminding the foreign press that there
are limits to our tolerance helps prevent the creation of false impressions about
stability here.' Those 'false impressions' arise from investigative stories about the
nexus between business and politics, he added.

Such attitudes have made sense to governments at a time when economic
recession is exacerbating internal problems. From an era of oil price booms,
vigorous leadership and rapidly mounting foreign finance, Southeast Asia moved
to a time of high debt, stagnating national income, ageing leaderships and failing
industrial projects. Stricter control over foreign reporting has seemed a good
thing.

Drawing Comparisons

These general anxieties became finely focused after the change of government
in the Philippines. Neighbouring countries watched in dismay as hordes of
'parachute' journalists (freelance writers who arrive in, and report from, a country
about which they know little) dissected intimate connections between Marcos and
his many business 'cronies'.

This type of investigative journalism could, and did, find rich veins to mine
elsewhere in Southeast Asia. After Marcos's departure the foreign press turned
its unwelcome attentions to President Suharto's family. Articles appeared about
business dealings among members of Mahathir's cabinet.

Even Thailand, accustomed to cosy relationships between the military and
Chinese businessmen, stirred a little as articles about corruption surfaced with
less than normal circumspection. Nor was little Brunei spared. In connection
with a political scandal in Washington, the American press embarrassed Sultan

Hassanal Bolkiah by reporting his secret donations to Swiss banks to help finance the Contra rebellion against the Nicaraguan government.

The particular circumstances of Marcos's downfall sent shivers down spines in neighbouring countries. Consider for a moment the reaction of Indonesia's custodians to the February 1986 'People Power' uprising against Marcos.

The aghast Indonesians did not know how to start cataloguing the sins. Virtually every element of social chaos vilified by President Suharto's 'New Order' government in Jakarta materialised on Manila's streets. One of the Philippine sins took a capital 's' – to the secular Indonesian government, Manila archbishop Jaime Cardinal Sin's exhortation of popular revolt exemplified the worst kind of politicised religion. Given Indonesia's 90 per cent Muslim majority, the Suharto government still fears that a fusion of faith and rebellion might occur again. Revolts inspired by Islam threatened national unity during the 1950s, and some groups still nourish dreams of an Islamic state.

The mutinous Philippine military and mass demonstrations were also deeply disturbing to Manila's Asean neighbours. They watched communist-influenced labour rallies with horror. Many regional politicians believe the presence in the Philippines of so many foreign journalists fanned the flames they had come to witness.

Yet the wide-open coverage of Marcos's 'crony' business links and widely publicised dimensions of his well-feathered nest proved most unnerving to the watching region. This reportage has stamped Marcos with a looter's reputation, one that will stay with him for as long as he is remembered. Shorn of obsessive media attention, however, the behaviour of his business friends hardly differs from the business culture flourishing elsewhere in Southeast Asia.

Most of the Marcos cronies are neither larger-than-life figures nor a monstrously deranged species of businessmen making a Mephistophelian pledge. Their powers and privileges are not too distant from the influence wielded by business clans elsewhere in the region. Longtime associates of ruling families or parties have also gained commercial favours using methods which Manila's vilified cronies would easily recognise.

As Yoshihara Kunio notes in his excellent book *The Rise of Ersatz Capitalism in South-East Asia* (1988), 'the term "crony" has its origins in the Philippine setting but . . . it can also be applied to some of the Indonesian capitalists who have close relations with President Suharto.' The same words would apply to virtually every Southeast Asian business élite. Informal business methods also characterise the financial empires spreading out from Taiwan and Hong Kong, territories from which overseas Chinese money flows into Southeast Asia (and to which their profits flow back again).

There was another, unwelcome comparison with the events in Manila. Throughout Southeast Asia, both economic planners and political élites experienced renewed anxiety about impending transitions. No one wants a repeat of the Manila débâcle. In Malaysia's case, worries have surfaced about intra-Malay power struggles weakening the political and commercial foundations on which Malaysia has rested since 1969.

With few exceptions, the existing leaders have made little provision for the inevitable transitions. In an unguarded moment, one of Singapore's deputy prime ministers, S. Rajaratnam, compared Southeast Asia's greying élite (to which he also belongs) with a giant banyan tree. Southeast Asians immediately see the point of such comparisons; the banyan's enormous leafy overhang and tangled root structure deny smaller plants any chance of access to the sun or soil.

No Portent from the Philippines

The experience of the Philippines since February 1986 has calmed fears that Southeast Asia's era of stability was threatened by an upsurge of popular discontent. Faces at the top have changed and, on the surface, an atmosphere of repression has yielded to a noisy, wide-open democracy. Yet the colourful fusion of business and political patronage has continued in the post-Marcos period with scarcely a hiccough.

The business cronyism of the Marcos years has received extensive publicity. The business friends of the former president included both Chinese and non-Chinese Filipinos.

Among the most prominent 'native' cronies were Roberto 'Bobby' Benedicto (a media monopolist); Eduardo 'Danding' Cojuangco (a coconut oil monopolist and President Corazon Aquino's first cousin) and Herminio Disini (a tobacco magnate). Others include Rodolfo Cuenca (head of the Philippines' largest construction company) and Antonio 'Tony' Floirendo, the self-styled 'banana king' of Mindanao, the Philippines' second largest island.

The most important Filipino Chinese associates of Marcos were Ralph Nubla, an old Marcos classmate and president of the Federation of Filipino-Chinese Chambers of Commerce and José Campos, chairman of the Philippines' largest pharmaceuticals firm. Lucio Tan, a banker and (since 1988) a beer magnate, also was reported to have gained from close ties with the palace.

This type of chummy business linkage was supposed to disappear with the coming of 'Cory' Aquino. She issued decrees abolishing coconut and sugar marketing monopolies. The new government claimed Marcos and his wife Imelda stole up to US$10 billion during their long years in power, much of it deposited in Swiss or Hong Kong banks, or used to buy real estate in the United States. Since 1987 the Aquino government has filed lawsuits against some of the most prominent cronies, claiming combined damages of over one trillion (a million million) pesos (nearly US$5 billion).

Yet the much praised ending of some monopolistic privileges did not disguise the perpetuation of many others, albeit under new management. A new cronyism has now emerged, more benign perhaps, but with President Aquino's brothers Pedro ('Don Pedro') Cojuangco, and José ('Peping') Cojuangco standing at the centre of controversy.

The Conjuangco Factor

The younger brother Peping is much more prominent than his reticent, Chinese-speaking brother, Don Pedro. Peping is a horse-racing enthusiast who also breeds fighting cocks. He holds high positions in a loosely organised coalition of patronage-based political parties. Peping's and Don Pedro's careers since 1986 illustrate the tenacity of old habits in the Philippines.

Families dominate business life in the Philippines, as elsewhere in Southeast Asia. Normally a family becomes pre-eminent in a particular province; the

Cojuangco influence in Tarlac, a pivotal central Luzon province, is no different. Tarlac provides the base from which different Cojuangco family factions have extended their influence over the last three-quarters of a century.

This span of time began with the rising fortunes of Corazon Cojuangco Aquino's grandfather, Don Melecio Cojuangco. His land-holdings have guaranteed the family's ascendancy in Luzon's affairs. Don Melecio came from a Chinese *mestizo* (mixed-blood) immigrant who Hispanised his name ('Ko-Huan-Ko'). Don Melecio's descendants still display many Chinese characteristics.

Despite Marcos's hostility to Corazon's husband Benigno Aquino (murdered in August 1983), the keys to Tarlac stayed firmly in Cojuangco hands during the Marcos era, albeit in the hands of someone on the 'wrong' side of Cory's family – Danding Cojuangco. Relations are still tense: President Aquino is said to believe that Danding conspired with Imelda Marcos to order Benigno Aquino's murder.

Nowadays, Tarlac is still Cojuangco country but the mantle has passed back to Cory's side of the family. All the provincial officials and town mayors have found it prudent to join Peping's political party, the Partido Demokratikong Pilipinas (Democratic Philippine Party, or PDP). Danding, living in Californian exile since 1986, also presides over a strong but parallel patronage network in Tarlac; I met rural officials, even churchmen, who claimed to receive a monthly stipend from 'Kano', another of Danding's nicknames which is taken from the word 'Amerikano' (his mother was American).

For President Aquino's side of the family the Tarlac Development Company serves as the holding company for their interests. Her family remains Tarlac's biggest landlord, with Hacienda Luisita their largest single farm. About 5,000 families dwell on the hacienda, working 6,400 hectares of sugar land. Since Cory Aquino became president, the hacienda's guards have been trained by former officers of the British Strategic Air Services, but apart from this the style of life has continued without break.

The air-conditioned stables for Peping's racing horses still stand within sight of the hacienda's eighteen-hole golf course. Migrant workers from Samar or Leyte are brought in to cut cane each harvesting season. Cojuangco family apologists become lyrical in their descriptions of the measured tone and sense of place that permeates Hacienda Luisita, yet it is not much different from the other large land-holdings which feel little threat from the government's self-styled land reform programme enacted in 1988 but riddled with loopholes.

The Cojuangco family owns more than just sugar land. After cutting, Hacienda Luisita's cane travels to another family firm, the Central Azucarera de Tarlac, which crushes up 7,000 tonnes of cane a day, the country's fourth largest sugar mill. The juice from this operation then moves another step, to the Cojuangco family's Tarlac Distillery Company, Luzon's largest alcohol plant.

Mills of another kind began to hum just a few months after Marcos fled in February 1986. The rumour mills working overtime in Manila's coffee shops churned out tales of new business ambitions by Cory's family. Besides her two brothers, attention also focused on her sister Tessie, married to Ricardo 'Baby' Lopa, a banker and gun collector, who became prominent in negotiations to buy several financial institutions after February 1986. The president's maternal uncle, Francisco Sumulong, has gained a reputation for more business prominence since 1986.

So have her in-laws, such as Teresa Aquino Oreta, who, in the May 1987 legislative elections, won a seat representing a constituency in north Manila. In an internal memo, the normally pro-government National Movement for Free

Elections ('Namfrel') described the behaviour of her supporters as the 'worst' election day abuse in the entire country. Other Aquino kin have moved up in the world since 1986, including Peping's wife, Margarita 'Tingting' Cojuangco. A classic beauty ten years Peping's junior, Tingting has figured in recurrent press accounts alleging influence-peddling in Mindanao.

Specific Charges

By mid-1987, rumours began to crystallise into specific charges. Secretly circulating dossiers sketched out the sort of favouritism among business partners and monopoly 'cash-cow milking' that had given Philippine politics under Marcos its special reputation.

Cojuangco interests seem to have targeted opportunities in cargo-handling – the *arrastre* wharf business. Reports suggested that multi-million dollar trading concessions, operating free of customs levy between Mindanao and Malaysia and Singapore, have also come within the family's orbit. So have slices of the large gambling networks. There seems little doubt that men answerable to Peping's subordinates control an enormous but entirely informal gambling network based on the game of *jueteng*, to which most Filipino males are passionately addicted.

The family's influence also extended after 1986 to control over the management of the Philippine Amusement and Games Corporation. Known as Pagcor, the corporation is a government-owned monopoly of hotel-based gambling casinos. Close associates of Peping also moved into government agencies like the National Food Authority, the National Electrification Administration and the Manila International Airport Authority.

Accusations against these new forms of business opportunism were not long in coming. A 31 October 1986 pastoral letter from Cardinal Sin claimed that 'graft and corruption persists in many offices of government.' Two weeks later, armed forces chief of staff General Fidel Ramos sent a confidential 'statement of concern' to Aquino.

Ramos, who became secretary for national defence in January 1988, said that 'graft and corruption on the part of some officials [is rising] while the old regime continues to be castigated for its corrupt ways.' He said that 'some high-ranking officials as well as at the lower levels in the present administration are reported to be involved in graft and corrupt practices of significant magnitude.'

Shortly after this letter, the president sacked two ministers widely believed to be abusing their prerogative – natural resources minister Ernesto Maceda, and public works minister Rogaciano Mercado. They were not driven from the temple however; with Aquino's endorsement each won a place in the new Philippine senate in the May 1987 elections.

Complaints about corruption in government have become more common since then, many of them coming from Aquino's political opponents whose own record, past or present, scarcely inspires respect. More damning, however, have been the occasional leaked contents of government reports taking to task many officials for malfeasance.

Philippine constabulary chief General Renato de Villa wrote to the president about the problem in 1987, less than a year after she had come to power. 'Many local executives have arrogated unto themselves the authority to allow illegal gambling operators to operate in their respective areas,' he said. 'One hundred local executives and other government officials are either maintaining or protecting illegal gambling' in just two of the country's seventy-three provinces, he claimed. And 'it is more or less the same in the other regions.'

Jueteng is a type of numbers game. So are other (illegal) games such as *sakla* and hi-lo. Rather than legalising these games, the authorities find it more profitable to retain the law making these networks illegal, and to connive in their continued operation. De Villa warned Aquino that gambling corruption had begun to 'erode the moral image projected by the present administration.'

In an interview published in the *Far Eastern Economic Review*, Peping Cojuangco told me he had nothing to do with illegal gambling operations that, on his estimate, yield US$45 million every month from just thirty provinces in Luzon. 'In the first few days of the new administration', he told me, 'the president, Ramos and I talked about gambling.' Ramos had urged its legalisation, Peping said, in the hope of reducing corrupt behaviour among his subordinates.

Peping agreed with Ramos but this did not sway Cory, alert to the views of the Roman Catholic Church hierarchy. Yet whatever the country's 103 bishops might think, any real attempt to suppress gambling in the Philippines will only end in failure. 'If you want to see a real revolution in the Philippines', he told me jokingly, 'take away cock-fighting!'

The *Arrastre* Business

Peping admitted however that he 'was able to give business concessions' after his sister won the presidency. 'Assisting someone into business is a better way to put it,' he reflected. What business concessions? Peping noted the *arrastre* business as an example, but said the people he had helped into business had not gone into them 'with empty pockets' – meaning that men of independent wealth had no need to line them.

It is an open secret in Manila that portside monopolies changed hands swiftly after Marcos fled. Imelda Marcos's own Romualdez family in 1980 seized control of *arrastre* in Manila, imposing a monopoly where previously many small companies had shared the business. After Aquino became president her government seized assets belonging to the business 'cronies' of Marcos; one of the sequestered firms was this Romualdez-linked portside monopoloy.

Meanwhile, a newly reconstituted Philippine Port Authority was moving with extraordinary speed. On 18 July 1986 it sent a notice to the old concessionaire. On 19 July, an executive order from President Aquino cancelled the firm's contract. The next day the port authority awarded a new ports servicing contract to a firm incorporated only two months earlier by Peping's business friends. No public tenders were called for. The new monopoly, Metrostar, began to use the equipment, valued at US$5 million, belonging to the firm it had displaced without, it was claimed, paying any rent.

The Aquino government's decision to pass monopoly control from one set of hands to another, rather than liberalise the business, seems uncannily like the spoils-chasing excesses of the Marcos era. The awarding of a monopoly to Cojuangco family friends also augured poorly for promises of a free market, despite import liberalisation decisions demanded from the new government by the World Bank.

A final irony emerged from the reshuffling of the *arrastre* monopolies. The new supervisor of the port authority's contract bidding committee until his appointment had worked for another cargo-handler, Allied Port Services Inc. This company moves consignments from the harbour up the Pasig river, a body of water described by Aquino's environment and natural resources department as 'biologically dead'. Cory's uncle, Francisco Sumulong, is believed to have an important stake in Allied Port Services; he is also one of Tarlac's three congressmen, together with José Yapi, an old Cojuangco ally, and Hermie Aquino, a relative of the president's late husband.

Gambling Dens, Barter Trade and Other Diversions

Apart from *arrastre*, Peping has conceded that 'a lot of people are using my name'. He has said he wants to discourage this; 'if I need something from [someone] I call them myself,' he said to the *Review*. His appointees to Pagcor after 1986 included such colourfully-named men as 'Tarzan' Lazatin, 'Ray' Pineda and 'Ambit' Antonio. Peping told me that they had raised the government's revenues from Pagcor by nearly 400 per cent. Everything seemed fine – until a nightclub slapping incident involving one of these streetwise new managers reached the ears of the president. In a move obviously lamented by Peping, his sister dismissed this management team of rough diamonds. To Peping's dismay, a new set of appointees, led by a woman banker, moved into Pagcor.

Talk about the Cojuangcos' business activities reached a crescendo when, in 1987, a Sydney newspaper quoted an Australian businessman who claimed that 'Tingting' Cojuangco had accepted a present of US$1 million in cash from him in a Manila restaurant in March 1987. The hard-edged Australian reporting of Philippine business ethics had its price, however. *Australian Financial Review* writer Michael Brynes became, in December 1987, the first foreign journalist ever to receive an expulsion order from the Philippines. The order was later rescinded but Brynes later claimed that his articles equating the Cojuangcos' business interests to old-style cronyism had sparked the move. The Cojuango family denied any wrongdoing and sued the Sydney newspaper.

Tingting's connections in Mindanao have caused comment. Presidential advisers told me about Tingting's involvement in selecting appointees for the Southern Philippines Development Authority, the agency responsible for supervising concessions for Muslim Filipinos trading with Malaysia. The duty-free trade, misleadingly known as 'barter trade', was originally conceived in the 1970s as a way of accommodating the traditional, seaborne commerce of the minority Muslim Filipinos (who comprise about 7 per cent of the population). Philippine government import duties had helped to spark a separatist war in the 1970s.

'Barter trade' is thus exempt from customs levies. The gross misuse of the system in the latter Marcos years became an open scandal. Although limited by law to just a few ports of entry, such as Zamboanga or Cotabato, barter trade carriers sometimes arrive in Manila to discharge a duty-free bonanza to its charterers. This 'legalised smuggling', as one senior official describes it, results in make-believe voyages from Mindanao. Ships carry a token cargo to Singapore, filling up perhaps one hold in an otherwise empty ship. On the return voyage, they jam the holds with consumer goods hundreds of times more valuable than the outgoing consignment. Ship tonnages also routinely exceed the legal maximum.

Opposition politicians in Manila in 1987 released a transcript of illegally wire-tapped conversations in which Tingting was allegedly recorded discussing, with the chargé d'affaires of the American embassy, various payments to a Muslim faction. The authenticity of the tapes was never directly denied. When I asked Peping Cojuangco about these and other allegations, he denied any improper motives behind his wife's actions. He insists that her involvement in the southern region results from her postgraduate ethnographic studies in the early 1980s.

Peping acknowledges the need for money to run a political machine but claims his PDP party 'is cheap to run'. However that may be, he has become a key power broker in the new, post-Marcos order. He has cemented alliances for the four elections conducted between February 1986 and January 1988. 'My sister is not a politician,' he told me. 'She does not know about these things.' His advisory role continues. 'Even if I wanted to I cannot get out,' he told me in March 1987. Since then he has moved to bring back into the fold many families once discredited by too close a link to Marcos.

Plus Ça Change . . .

Does this, as one wag suggested, seem good material for a new series of the American soap opera, *All in the Family*? Perhaps a better title might be, 'All in the *Families*'. After all, the time elapsing since Marcos's departure has shown the resilience of the dynastic impulses behind Philippine business patronage.

In the May 1987 elections, for example, three of vice-president Salvador 'Doy' Laurel's family contested, and won, seats in the national legislature. Their seats are in Batangas, a province the Laurels 'own' as much as Tarlac 'belongs' to the Cojuangcos. When Doy left Aquino's government after a series of public rows in 1987, the question of his departure was settled at a conference between the two families. The president and vice-president faced each other across a table, flanked by family members on each side.

Other Luzon families have reasserted their claim to business patronage. The Sumulongs (the family to which President Aquino's mother belonged) are an obvious example. Others in central Luzon include the Nepomuceños and the Mercados. In northern Luzon, the most prominent families remain the Singsons, the Crisologs, the Barberos and the Paredes.

In the Visayas region, halfway down the country, the Osmeña clan still rules Cebu, the country's most populous province, much as it has done since the turn of the century. In Panay, a sugar-growing island, the Roxas family retains much of its power. Even the Dimaporo family, once closely allied to Marcos, have remained influential in the violent Lanao area of Mindanao. Throughout the country, hundreds of other names also denote a patch of turf and a cut of business favours.

Even the vitriol-soaked, anti-government 'dossiers' passed around in Manila have not dared to accuse the president herself of impropriety. She remains utterly uninterested in either accumulating wealth, or in its ostentation. Cory has sold her shares in family businesses, including her nearly 6 per cent holding in the Tarlac Development Company. Peping also dismisses talk that his and Danding's wealth have been secretly joined.

Apologists for the Aquino government are quick to point out a distinction between Marcos cronyism and the type of business influence now exerted by the

Cojuangcos. 'People should not look at us like they looked at the past regime,' Peping told me in 1987. 'We had already accomplished something when my sister became president.'

Alluding to the Cojuangcos' business prowess, close family friends always stress that Cory Aquino's family is 'old money', in sharp contrast to the *parvenus* of the Marcos era. 'People are always saying the Filipinos do not want feudalism,' Peping told me as we sat in his office, lined with photographs of racing horses and trophies. 'Is that right? If you look at Philippine feudalism, it's really just a family.'

Plus C'est La Même Chose

A departing American chargé d'affaires once told me that, when he raised a problem concerning governmental corruption with Aquino, she had looked at him tolerantly and replied, 'What can we do? Boys will be boys.' That attributed remark captures much of the president's fatalism about her country. It also reveals the political and business education she acquired as the observant wife of a man of such adroit talents that Filipinos still say he was the only man who could beat Marcos at his own game.

The Aquino era has made little or no impact on the country's business culture, as the foregoing suggests. 'Rational market capitalism enters a type of time warp here,' a Filipino Harvard Business School graduate told me. 'Or at least that is what we feel every time we come home.' He meant that, no matter how much the surface may change, the underlying reality remains locked in old, exploitive habits. That is just one reason why perhaps two million Filipinos have opted to live in the United States.

This damaging trait now hinders the government's privatisation programme, a showpiece of Aquino's new era. Trumpeted as the way to return corrupt state enterprises to the discipline of market forces, the plan to divest most of the nearly three hundred government-owned or -controlled companies has collided with what one businessman calls the 'cuckoo nesting instinct'. He likens the 'interim' managers appointed to these firms to cuckoos settling into other birds' nests. Once nested, the newcomers prove hard to evict.

In retrospect the outcome now seems a foregone conclusion. Yet for a brief moment there was a chance of radically reshaping the face of Philippine business through divestiture that would widen the share market, create employee shareholders and divorce the government from patronage. Aquino's first finance minister, a businessman named Jaime Ongpin, brought a reforming zeal to his position. He moved quickly to create a twin-track system to clear the clutter from the government's books.

On the one hand, an official Committee on Privatisation met in his department to prepare divestiture plans. Down the road, an Asset Privatisation Trust, chaired by David Sycip, a respected banker, sold off various non-corporate and usually non-performing assets held by the state.

Ongpin's allies and subordinates in the finance ministry, many of whom had degrees from the Wharton and Harvard business schools, planned share flotations and other methods of selling off government-owned companies. Here, at last, was a chance to broaden the narrow, oligopolistic base of Philippine crony capitalism. To this end, share offerings were planned as part of the privatisation of the Philippine

National Oil Corporation. The same aim was set for the sale of the Manila Electric Company, known as 'Meralco'.

As the third anniversary of Marcos's fall approached in February 1989, little of these plans had been achieved. The oil company divestiture was blocked by new management. Only eight firms had been sold. Ongpin had quickly run into problems. The patronage-minded 'officers-in-charge', the Philippine expression for the government corporations' interim managers, resisted the committee's edicts. By the end of 1987 the writing was already plain on the wall: Ongpin, dismissed from cabinet the previous September, committed suicide a few months later. Sycip died of a heart attack, an event that deprived the trust over which he presided of its sense of urgency although it had managed to sell nearly 30 per cent of the assets under its charge. The International Monetary Fund, as part of its approval of new credits in 1989, has won a commitment from Aquino that her government will revive the privatisation programme. Old Manila hands are not holding their breath.

What's in a Name?

The Presidential Commission on Good Government was Cory Aquino's first executive action as president. This commission, modelled on similar agencies in revolutionary Iran and Nicaragua, was the test of the new government's reformist credentials. It set itself a large task: the recovery of 'ill-gotten gains' – billions of dollars looted by the Marcoses and their business friends over twenty years.

The commission began in a blaze of publicity. Jovito Salonga, then 67 years old, became the commission's first chairman. As a former senator and longtime Marcos opponent, Salonga was ready to start. American diplomats told me in 1987 that Salonga had already been talking to the embassy for several weeks preceding Marcos's removal – an assertion hotly denied by Salonga.

When Marcos prepared to leave the country, American embassy staff sorted his belongings into two lots at Clark Airfield, one of two important US military bases in the Philippines. Staff were instructed to put 'genuinely personal items' into one pile and to place documents or boxes of cash into another. Yet it was all for nought: Salonga's commission was denied these important papers when President Reagan's advisers decided to let Marcos take whatever he wanted with him on the aircraft taking him to Hawaii.

Despite losing these crucial documents, the commission moved quickly to seize other records left behind in the scamper to leave Malacanang, the presidential palace. Some sensitive papers were moved in the first hours after his departure to various suburban homes for temporary safekeeping. In one episode, seventeen boxes of miscellaneous papers were taken to a doctor's home in the affluent subu:b of Makati. After a short time they were again moved, this time to vaults in the central bank. That is where they still remain.

A hastily formed group examined the contents of the boxes before the commission and the Central Bank closed off access. I have seen the papers. They include messages from Imelda Marcos to Citicorp Bank instructing million-dollar remittances; cables to Swiss investment houses in Geneva from Imelda's brother Benjamin ('Kokoy') Romualdez (who fretted about the foreign exchange risks in his portfolio) and agreements giving agency rights to sell Philippine sugar (perhaps as collateral?) to Banque Paribas.

Other notes show enormous deposits by the palace in Crédit Suisse, Banque Paribas and the Swiss Banking Corporation. European financial advisers, including Walter Fessler of Kusnacht and William Wirth of Zürich, appear frequently in the messages. So do lists of properties held by other families, such as the Tantocos, who may have served as dummies for palace-financed purchases.

The still-secret palace papers, which have formed much of the evidence of the Commission on Good Government, cover more than just business matters. They include highly sensitive lists of broadcast and print journalists receiving regular stipends from Malacanang. Most of these men and women are still working in journalism.

Early Gains

Under Salonga's stewardship the commission scored some initially impressive gains. In 1987 he told me that he had already passed nearly US$100 million to the president's office. The commission had taken back Marcos-owned real estate in the United States; when sold these would realise another US$100 million, he claimed. Title deeds to over two hundred pieces of land in Manila and 'billions of pesos worth of company shares' had also been sequestered.

For all these accomplishments, the commission has become deeply embroiled in charges and countercharges of corrupt behaviour. 'Other revolutions put people in gaol,' a Manila businessman remarked when considering the mysteries of sequestration. 'Here in the Philippines we put their assets in gaol instead.' By this he meant that the powers of the Commission on Good Government to freeze assets have given that agency enormous powers over property and livelihood, enabling its less ethical members to bargain for personal advantage with the hapless 'cronies'.

Even after discounting the calibre of most information impugning the commission, grave doubts began to centre on the commission's competence, motivation and internal cohesiveness. It took over the management of companies and sometimes farmed out their high-turnover revenues. It sparked labour unrest and threw people out of work. Commission 'task forces' went into sequestered companies, often pilfering the assets they were supposed to protect. Cattle shipments were sold for private profit. A commission takeover of much of the broadcasting industry sparked off a confrontation with Aquino's advisers, who installed their own management team.

Perhaps most damaging of all, the commission seemed to yield very early to the temptation of reaching informal understandings with the exiled cronies. Only later did it bother to document many of its cases against them. A US Justice Department team, visiting the commission two-and-a-half years after Marcos's removal, found rooms full of unopened boxes of documents. 'They are holding on to [the documents] in the same way they use the threat of sequestration,' said one American lawyer. 'As ammunition against uncooperative prey.'

The commission's enterprise rests on shaky grounds. What is a 'crony' anyway? Most cash-rich businesses had links to Marcos; indeed, it was difficult not to have been compromised somewhere along the way given the long tenure of his presidency. These included the Philippine Long Distance Telephone Company, in which another Cojuangco, Ramon, had held control over the voting shares. The United Coconut Planters Bank, an outgrowth of a Cojuangco bank started after the Second World War, also profited mightily through its ties to Danding Cojuangco.

The working definition of a 'crony' became very specific: someone on the other side of the political fence who has the misfortune of not having moved his assets out before February 1986. The most obvious candidates, José Campos or 'Banana King' Floirendo, had to come to terms with Salonga's commission. (When fleeing the Philippines, Campos had the supreme bad luck to leave behind a list showing all his dummy business operations for Marcos.)

Duty-free Duppies

In the fight for the Marcos spoils, the Commission on Good Government was just one among many players. The curious affair of Manila's duty-free shops shows how complicated this struggle could become.

By the end of 1987, duty-free shoppers at Manila's international airport were grumbling about the meagre pickings. 'The shelves are bare,' outgoing passengers remarked to John Peterson, a reporter for the *Far Eastern Economic Review*. 'Sometimes there is some gin or chocolate bars, but not much else.'

Sparsely stocked shelves told only part of the story behind a disruptive takeover by the Commission on Good Government of a small but lucrative monopoly, the Tourist Duty Free Shops Inc. (TDFS). This business began in 1977 when Marcos gave his wife's friends in the Tantoco family the exclusive right to sell cigarettes, liquor and luxury items at airport and hotel outlets free of tax. In a typical year, the franchise generated about US$35 million in clear profit and all in foreign exchange.

Much of this money went to Giliceria Tantoco, TDFS's major shareholder and a close intimate of Imelda Marcos, part of the palace coterie known as the 'Blue Ladies', after their royal blue ballgowns. The Tantocos moved to Rome after February 1986 but provided Marcos with a house in Hawaii into which the dictator moved after being deposed.

The 'crony' connection speaks for itself. TDFS seemed therefore an ideal candidate for sequestration by the commission. But while little doubt hangs over past connections between the Tantocos and the Marcoses, the commission stepped well beyond its legal mandate in handling the lucrative franchise.

A struggle for control began immediately after the April 1986 takeover of TDFS. The top contenders for the company's cash flow, apart from the commission itself, included tourism minister Antonio Gonzales and natural resources minister Ernesto Maceda, dismissed in November 1986. Mary Concepcion Bautista of the commission wrote to Gonzales offering him the 'management and operation of Tourist Duty Free Shops Inc.' and noting his 'expressed willingness to assume responsibility.'

In an interim decision, the Philippine Supreme Court ruled that the commission lacked authority to give TDFS to other interests, but this did not impede a quick switch in patronage. President Aquino simply signed a revolutionary decree (which she could do under her temporary 'Freedom Constitution' of March 1986), cancelling the TDFS franchise. Another presidential decree gave the business to Gonzales' officials in the Tourism Authority.

Gonzales spoke candidly about the exercise. 'We sought to take over the franchise from the beginning. Let's face it, TDFS is a very juicy plum.' The description seemed apt. People familiar with the duty-free business say that over-the-counter sales to foreign tourists, the franchise's ostensibly limited clientele, only amount to a small fraction of the business. Much more cash comes from selling luxury goods illegally on the local black market.

Tantoco's lawyers filed a lawsuit after the switch in cash flow, claiming 'close business and friendly relations' between the president's and Gonzales' family. Those ties certainly exist. President Aquino's only son Benigno Junior ('Nonoy'), has worked at executive level in Mondragon Industries, Gonzales' family firm. During her 1986 presidential campaign, Aquino used the Mondragon building as her headquarters.

Similarly close ties between the Marcoses and the Tantacos led to part of TDFS's revenue being siphoned off to various pet projects of the former First Lady. These included the Manila Seedling Bank Foundation, ostensibly an agency to beautify Manila·but by all accounts a conduit for Imelda's spending money.

Yet when Salonga's commission stopped TDFS payments to the foundation, many were less than pleased. Maceda, to whom the foundation was formally answerable, lobbied via allies in the presidential palace for the funding to continue. To no avail. He lost the plum to Gonzales, who had little interest in the Tantocos' predicament. 'We bent over backwards for them. Had the revolution gone the other way, they wouldn't have done anything for us,' he said.

Broadcasting Blues

Other moves by the asset-chasing commission also reveal an unhappy interplay of commerce and politics, this time in broadcasting, a private sector business in the Philippines. Mercilessly manipulated by Marcos, broadcasters savoured the moment when rebel soldiers cut off the former president's last broadcast before he was deposed.

The new government promised a speedy return to private control for the five television and radio networks located in Manila. Yet that is not what happened. The Commission on Good Government sequestered all the television and most of the major radio stations, claiming a need to head off 'Bobby' Benedicto, owner of three of the five television stations.

Aides close to Aquino balked at the spectre of Salonga's overlordship replacing Benedicto's, however. The commission was seen as a platform for Salonga's Liberal Party; four of the five commissioners were party officers, as were many of their wives. Aquino speech writer and confidant Teodoro ('Teddy Boy') Locsin did not like this situation. He persuaded the president to issue a decree limiting the commission's scope. A new management body was set up, directly responsible to Aquino's office.

The sparring continued for many months. During one election, one of Salonga's commissioners sent agents to take physical possession of various provincial radio stations. One station, in Mindanao, was closed down for failing to take the correct, pro-Liberal Party line. The commission had voluble confrontations with the Nenes Olivares, chairwoman of Teddy Boy's management board and a formidable newspaper columnist in her own right. The commission also helped a once prominent family, the Lopezes, to win back control of television stations they had once owned, 'leasing' broadcasting equipment to the family but not taking care to collect the rental when due, according to reliable reports.

The uproar over broadcasting patronage surprised almost no one in Manila. It added to a lengthening chronicle of stories that mocked the commission's ironic name. By 1988, internal rows accelerated the damage further. Significantly, military dissidents in the most violent revolt against Aquino (on 28 August 1987) claimed corruption 'had doubled, if not trebled' during Aquino's short tenure. Compared with Marcos's rapacity these were extreme words, but the new order in the Philippines has done little to change basic habits.

Salonga, a man with a reputation for probity, was badly served by many of his officers. The trail after the Marcos wealth led the commission to the United States, Australia, Hong Kong, Canada, Japan, Singapore and Switzerland. After freezing the dictator's accounts the Swiss had an attack of banker's conscience. Their courts demanded that Manila must first win a criminal conviction against Marcos before the funds, frozen by the Swiss Banking Commission in March 1987, could be transferred back to Manila.

The likelihood of that happening looked increasingly dim by 1989. Marcos's failing health and the still persistent worries about the destabilising effect of bringing Marcos back to the Philippines seemed to rule out a trial of the old man. Most financial experts to whom I have spoken expect his money may never leave Switzerland despite court decisions in April 1989 relating to US$70 million held by him in a Swiss Banking Corporation account. They say it will remain in escrow accounts, frozen for ever like funds once belonging to Tsar Nicholas II when another, rather more earth-shaking revolution deposed that autocrat seventy-two years ago.

Salonga, who left the commission to become Senate President, faced other obstacles in Manila's business jungle. 'Other leopards outwitted him,' a business-man commented. 'Leopard' is another nickname given to Peping Cojuangco by the business community: it refers to the way he approaches new business prey. In 1986, Salonga's commission watched helplessly as Cojuangco family interests joined Paul Aquino, the president's brother-in-law, to bid successfully for a controlling interest in Manila's Security Bank. One of the bank's former owners was 'Bombong' Marcos, the ex-president's son.

Full Circle in the Philippines?

Will something like the Commission on Good Government become a recurrent feature of Philippine business life at the next turn of the political wheel? If so, what will be its targets next time? Will it be the business interests of Corazon Cojuangco Aquino's extended family? What about vice-president 'Doy' Laurel's stake in an array of petrochemical and banking firms?

Meanwhile, there is no final explanation of what has happened to the com-mission's treasure trove. 'During my chairmanship almost two billion pesos were delivered to the Office of the President,' Salonga told me in 1987. But the president's executive secretary, Joker (his real name) Arroyo, told me that none of this had remained in the president's accounts but had gone into the national treasury. A source in the treasury said only 522 million pesos had reached its coffers by mid-1987. Thus, soon after the dictator's departure an unexpected question began to surface: was crony money recycling in the business of new cronies? No one could be sure.

As an exercise in business politics, the coming to power of the Aquino government has taught Filipinos about the limit of good intentions. Rather than broadening the basis of capitalism (which Filipinos, given the right cultural support, are good at) the new rulers have preoccupied themselves with rearranging the cut. Business remains predatory and 'rent-seeking', a plaything of duppies.

The trouble may be, as James Fallows wrote in an influential November 1987 article in the *Atlantic Monthly*, that the Philippines has a 'damaged culture':

> What has created a society in which people feel fortunate to sift through a garbage dump because the money is so good? It can't be any inherent defect in the people; outside this culture they thrive . . . It seems unlikely that the problem is capitalism itself . . . if capitalism were the cause of Philippine underdevelopment, why would its record be so different elsewhere in the region?

What share benefit schemes were tried in the 'crony' companies during the tutelage of the Commission on Good Government? None. What moves did the commission, or the privatisation programme, make to broaden popular participation in the share market? None. (Less than 0.002 per cent of Filipinos own shares.)

Salonga resented criticism of his commission, much of which was inspired by disinformation from newly dispossessed duppies from the Marcos era. 'Under the law,' he told me, 'the moment it is shown that a former government official has wealth way beyond his usual salary or income, the burden of proof is shifted to him [to show he is not corruptly receiving wealth].' It is a sound test, but a broad one. Under this wide-reaching definition of probity, how many among the Aquino government's officials or favoured families will pass the test?

So great was the government's moral tone, in the first months after Marcos, that simply mentioning the appearance of resurgent crony habits seemed the journalistic equivalent of laughter during High Mass. The government held grimly to its moral mantle in the face of the perpetuation of habits ingrained during 350 years of colonial rule, first by the Spanish and then, for forty of those years, by the Americans.

In the personalised fashion of Manila politics, the president herself resented negative reporting about her family. Some in her entourage attributed the bad news to conspiracies among the military or the still active Marcos-loyalists. Yet the same analysis could apply to virtually any prominent politician. That is their strength, and the Philippines' endemic weakness.

References

Kunio, Yoshihara (1988) *The Rise of Ersatz Capitalism in South-East Asia*. OUP, Singapore

3

MALAISE IN BRUNEI AND MALAYSIA

I

Toll Gates: A Cautionary Tale

On 15 January 1988 the Supreme Court of Malaysia dismissed the last challenge blocking a government contract. In other countries – or even a different Malaysian epoch – the decision would have brought up blushes, and brought down governments.

For this was no ordinary contract. Malaysia's rulers had concluded the largest public works deal in the history of this rich federation, a road-building contract worth M$3.42 billion (US$1.35 billion at the exchange rates then prevailing). The deal seemed destined to give a guaranteed income to powerful friends of the ruling party, the United Malay National Organisation, or UMNO.

Malaysia's steadily more quiescent judiciary had been on the defensive throughout 1987. One of their number had provoked prime minister Mahathir Mohamad's ire by reversing his decision to expel a foreign correspondent. The same judge, then allowed another legal challenge against the premier, by allowing the challenge against the highway contract to proceed. This provoked the UMNO dominated parliament to place new curbs on the residual powers of the judges.

When the highway construction case reached the highest court, the justices seemed more disposed towards the government's plans to 'privatise' another piece of government by allowing a company with links to the political leadership to build a four-lane highway from the Thai-Malaysian border to Singapore, a distance of over 500 kilometres. By a 3–2 majority they refused to acknowledge the legal standing of the litigant bringing the suit, the Leader of the Opposition in Malaysia's parliament.

This man, Lim Kit Siang, was not able to hear the judgement in person. The reason was simple: several months before he had been arrested and imprisoned for two years without judicial recourse. That sort of thing is perfectly legal under Malaysia's draconian Internal Security Act however, which gives the country's home affairs minister power to renew detention orders, month after month, year after year. Lim was finally released in April 1989.

Mahathir also holds the internal affairs portfolio. The prime minister, a trained physician, has clear ideas about when the body politic needs surgery; shortly after the highway case some blood-letting (a now discredited method of therapy) occurred when he sacked Tun Salleh Abbas, the Lord President (the country's senior judge). When five Supreme Court judges had the audacity to hear Salleh's own appeal against dismissal he also sacked them. Malaysia's constitutional king, Johore's Sultan Iskandar Mahmood, willingly complied with the doctor's advice.

The *Asian Wall Street Journal* in 1988 described the recipient of the judicially sanctioned highway contract, a firm called United Engineers Berhad, as a 'financially beleaguered, publicly quoted company with scant experience in construction projects of the magnitude of the highway proposal.'

This did not seem too harsh a comment: at the end of 1985 the awardee of the biggest highway contract in Southeast Asia's history had run up losses of M\$91 million during 1981–85; the firm also owed another M\$75 million to Singapore banks. But what was that against projected highway profits exceeding M\$120 million, just from building the road? Then there would be a guaranteed spell, of many years, during which the company would have a monopoly on charging road tolls.

'The [United Engineering highway] awards have prompted renewed allegations of political favouritism in business transactions by Dr Mahathir's administration,' the *Asian Wall Street Journal* continued. But the deal did more than that. The shuffle of business among friends obscured the hands of other players, Japanese and French contractors, who would give substance to United Engineering's claim of highway building know-how. Tokyo's Mitsui & Co. and the French Dragages et Travaux Publics would provide the real technical support.

These government guaranteed gains confirmed the foresight of managers who had lent money to UE's majority holder, an investment company called Hatibudi, which was set up in 1984. A Malay businessman had then acquired this company, backed by another Malay named Daim Zainuddin. Remember that name: Daim (pronounced 'dime') has been finance minister since 1984. He in turn has another friend, a man dubbed by Kuala Lumpur wags as his closest 'kampong krony'.

Mahathir is Daim's longtime friend and older mentor. Mahathir brought his old village companion into the cabinet after a quarrel within UMNO led to the departure of Daim's predecessor, Tunku Razaleigh Hamzah. Razaleigh is a prince from Kelantan state who enjoys describing Mahathir, his intense enemy after 1987, as 'the doc'. He had held the finance portfolio from 1976.

No one would have known, or cared, anything about Hatibudi had not Malaysia's public works minister incautiously mentioned the existence of the firm in Malaysia's parliament. It was typical of the country that this snippet of information, never confirmed nor denied by Mahathir or Daim, should have come from an ethnic Indian.

Samy Vellu said that Hatibudi, little more than a name on an accountant's doorplate, was nothing other than one of UMNO's leading holding companies. Press investigations showed that Hatibudi's credit-rating should not, on the face of it, have inspired much confidence. Information on a court affidavit showed the company spending M\$13.4 million just to prepare its highways bid. A financial statement for the year ending 31 December 1986 revealed accumulated losses of M\$88.8 million.

Vellu runs the Malaysian Indian Congress (MIC), one of thirteen racially organised and racially run parties comprising the *Barisan Nasional*, or National Front. This coalition pads out a government in which UMNO has called all the important shots. Denied much of a role in policy, many of the National Front's component parties have set up separate business empires, each organised within a holding company. Because of these commercial links, the politics of business in Malaysia reaches its highest corporate expression in all of Southeast Asia.

The tangled business and politics, the willingness to use the government apparatus to reward friends and punish enemies, the compliance of other arms of the state – did these not have a familiar ring? The crony excesses of the Marcos era had received extensive international attention towards the close of the dictator's days in power, but this coverage did not extend beyond the Philippines to the nearby Malaysian peninsula.

Political Troubles

Even the word 'dictator', once an improbable appellation in Malaysia, had surfaced in the storm aroused by the arrest of Lim. The author of that description, no mere journalist, was Tunku Abdul Rahman, Malaysia's first prime minister, a combative 85-year-old whose newspaper column was a constant irritant to Mahathir. The old man's dictatorial dictum soon provoked what seemed to be prime ministerial confirmation – the newspaper was closed down in a series of actions during 1988 that resulted in over 150 people going to prison under the Internal Security Act.

Both these episodes, in their way, marked another advance towards an almost complete identity of government and governing party in Malaysia, a distinction once held somewhat touchingly sacrosanct in that country's legacy of Westminster-style administration. But that was during the early days of Independence for this former British colony, when Tunku Abdul Rahman first stewarded this somewhat unlikely amalgam of thirteen states, a grouping of Malay sultanates, a few Chinese-dominated enclaves along the Strait of Malacca and two, huge Borneo territories. The latter were run until the Second World War either by a benevolent trading company, as in Sabah, or by 'white Rajahs', as in Sarawak, where the Brooke family exercised regal powers for almost a century.

After Malaysia took its current form, in 1963, a hard overlay of Malay nationalism cemented this fractured picture. It is one of many unspoken truisms in Malaysia that its nationalism is of the imposed variety: Malays comprise under 50 per cent of the country; Chinese immigrants make up another 35 per cent and the rest are either Borneo natives, usually Christians or animists, or ethnic Indians descended from plantation labourers. Hindu shrines stand in Kuala Lumpur near Chinese temples and Christian churches while, at a more remote distance, splendid mosques built with government largesse stand gleaming in the tropical sun.

Although now mainly a social club for the well-to-do, UMNO once had a salt-of-the-earth flavour. With a membership of schoolteachers and minor clerks, it spearheaded a successful campaign in the 1940s and 1950s to block a British plan to disengage from Malaya by leaving behind a one-man, one-vote system. The principle itself had much to commend it; the problem was that this type of electoral logic could have dispossessed the Malays in their own country, especially if Singapore, a heavily Chinese island, came into the proposed new state. (Singapore did come in during the 1960s under a different power-sharing system but it left the federation after two unhappy years.)

From this initial composition UMNO has evolved into something less provincial. The schoolteachers and lowly government clerks have receded before a new class of businessmen, lawyers, accountants and government free-riders. And over the years the distribution of business patronage has become steadily more intense, paralleling a period in which economic growth routinely clocked up 7–9 per cent per annum, during the 1970s and early 1980s.

The highway contract perfectly illustrates this 'rent-seeking' impulse in Southeast Asian business, economists' jargon for derived unearned profit, or DUP. It also shows the moral distance UMNO has travelled since its early days. United Engineering now has a monopoly in collecting tolls along the highway, to be completed by 1995. The Malay firm has also gained the loans it needs to pay the Japanese and French to do the work. But in the double-think prevailing in Kuala Lumpur, the government bristles at reports that these arrangements expose the most elementary conflicts of interest. Indeed, the imprisoned Opposition Leaders's lawsuit merely attracted derision as a transparent stratagem, as just another entry on the racial chalkboard pitting 'the Chinese against the Malays'.

The Racial Conundrum

That is how it is in Malaysia: just about every commercial issue becomes ensnarled in the communal thicket. Malays rally round, whatever their man's transgression, apparently happy to play the pawn for politicians all too ready to manipulate a racial gap that seems to define Malaysia more as an *arrangement* than as a logical entity in its own right. The same logic applies to the resentments of smalltown Chinese shopkeepers or Indian plantation workers. Barry Newman of the *Wall Street Journal* put it succinctly in an article now a decade old. Malaysia 'is a lucky country,' he wrote. 'It has a small population, rich crop land, abundant natural resources and capable planners. Through 20 years of independence only one thing had held Malaysia back: the race problem.'

One result of the race problem is that the propriety of deals such as the highway contract tend to get lost in communal calculations. Even Samy Vellu's constituency of Tamil plantation labourers, the poorest of Malaysia's 17 million people, have demanded shares in a holding company that mimics the success of Malays and Chinese corporate vehicles. Vellu obligingly formed a company, Maika Holdings Berhad, which the government promptly rebuffed when it tried to 'bring home' a once Indian-owned bank, United Asian Bank, which had passed into majority Malay ownership.

'When I read the recent histories of Philippine corruption,' one Malaysian diplomat commented to me, 'I sometimes think I am reading about the future of Malaysia.' Some might have thought the present moment offered enough parallels; many charge, both within and outside UMNO, that recent political leadership has cultivated a bevy of protégés, with patronage and perks extending up and down the system.

Mohamed Razali Abdul Rahman and Halim Saad are just two of many men helping Daim to buy various companies during the early 1980s. These firms include Cold Storage (Malaysia) Berhad, a food retailing concern, and the United Malayan Banking Corporation (UMBC), Malaysia's third largest bank. These men were young – Halim was only 34 years old in 1987 – and as custodians of Daim's growing business empire they often took directorships in his companies.

In each acquisition, Kuala Lumpur's bankers readily lent to Daim and other members of the UMNO élite, confident that government contracts would keep up the cash flow in the new acquisitions. None of this is illegal in Malaysia and all of it is endemic. This back-scratching can, and does, transcend narrow racial lines, as the following example shows.

When the public works ministry gave its entirely expected approval to United Engineering's highway bid, it did so unanimously. Samy Vellu's own political party, the Malaysian Indian Congress, wrote to Hatibudi immediately after the contract was awarded, offering thousands of lottery tickets to Hatibudi's management. These were bought, for about M$125,000. What was this if not 'trickle-down' economics in action? A perfect expression had been found of the viewpoint that piling wealth on top cannot be reprehensible, because it seeps down to others; as a device for spreading around Hatibudi's good fortune the lottery tickets seemed as good as any other.

Banking Problems

While staffed by many executives of outstanding ability, Malaysia's banks and finance companies had to work increasingly within this unspoken system. During a scandal overtaking the country's seventh largest commercial bank, Perwira Habib Bank, an ex-director, Raja Khalid Harun, was detained on Mahathir's order. A court, however, then ordered Raja Khalid's release. When he came out of prison he caused an uproar by accusing the country's army commanders of planning to have him shot. After learning how much money (Khalid said M$235 million) had been lost by Perwira Habib, it is not surprising that the generals were angry – the army's pension fund owns the bank's controlling stake. Malaysian police later filed an affidavit alleging that Khalid's consulting firm, Malayan Commercial Services, had taken fees for helping to arrange Perwira Habib's loans. The loans often went unpaid, but Khalid's company made money.

Though admittedly an unusual case, the Perwira Habib scandal followed closely behind a train of other financial disasters. Just months before, the United Asian Bank, which had reported M$1.4 billion assets, had to go to the central bank to get a guarantee for a M$60 million recapitalisation.

This in turn followed another fiasco. In this episode the central bank, by now a harried financial fire brigade on continuous rescue duty, had saved twenty-four financial cooperatives from defaulting to millions of Chinese depositors. The collapse of Malaysia's cooperatives came as a special blow: the funds, many of them allied to the Malaysian Chinese Association (MCA), another National Front party, had served as guarantor for the poorer classes of Malaysian Chinese society. The cooperatives even watched over their members in death, paying burial and funeral expenses.

As Malaysia's economy expanded rapidly during the 1970s, new Chinese cooperatives such as Kojati, Mewah and Komuda appeared, each linked to the political aspirations of Chinese politicians or identified with the various ethnic subcategories of the Malaysian Chinese.

The malfeasance went very high: in 1987 deputy minister Wang Choon Wing, the MCA's national organising secretary, and former deputy minister of trade and industry Kee Young Wee faced criminal breach of trust charges relating to over M$2 million of Komuda's assets. By then, the international accounting firm Coopers & Lybrand reported that Komuda was facing a 'capital deficiency' of nearly M$10 million. Komuda's 41,000 members would get no more than 79 cents for every Malaysian dollar deposited. This news caused near-panic: on one occasion furious depositors prevented Mahathir from leaving a building, an event unreported in Malaysia's government-controlled press.

Another cooperative, Mewah, exuded a prosperous, Hainanese air during much of the 1980s. For all practical purposes it worked in harness with the ambitions of Tan Koo Swan, a peddler's son and ethnic Hainanese, whose great opportunity came when he took over the operations of a gambling complex overlooking Kuala Lumpur.

Tan's sights rose ever higher. In 1985 he won the MCA presidency after a bruising money-in-every-direction fight, only to be sentenced shortly afterwards by a Singapore court to two years in jail at the beginning of 1986. Tan's extravagant share market dealings, linked to the collapse of Pan-Electric Industries, had caught up with him. The implications of this major financial collapse are discussed in Chapter 6.

Tan also played the well-worn game of setting up a family company, Supreme Corporation, whose elaborate acquisitions confused the uninitiated. Reverse takeovers (in which a seemingly smaller company acquires a larger one by juggling share values) mixed up Supreme's ownership still more – on paper at any rate. But no one had any doubt that the ambitious, fast-rising Tan presided over Supreme's subsidiaries in real estate, finance, insurance and plantations. Many of these were publicly quoted but Supreme itself was not. This strategy enabled Tan to maximise stockmarket capitalisation of subsidiary assets while keeping tight, overall control.

The racial dimension to the deposit-taking cooperatives scandal became more evident when the UMNO-dominated government took a hard line, refusing to bail out any of the twenty-four aggressors. This stood in sharp contrast, the Chinese grumbled, to ready transfusions of government capital propping up several grievously mismanaged Malay banks. Although thousands of cooperatives operate in Malaysia, only thirty-four have permission to take deposits. They usually offer interest rates well above those on call in commercial banks.

These were but the most striking cases of reckless financial management, compounded by overexposure to a faltering property market and to rampant business favouritism. By the mid-1980s Malaysia's banking system, which had grown to thirty-eight separate banks with an asset-backing of M$62.5 billion, was experiencing a bruising rash of defaulting borrowers.

At a juncture which called for restraint and prudence, Daim's expansionary policies encouraged bank lending for share acquisitions, with far too many of the loans only secured against the purchased stock. 'Daim has made the revival of the stock market a personal mission,' said *South* magazine at the time, in 1986. In all corporate restructuring exercises mandatory share allocations had to be made to *bumiputras*. These shares usually gave quick profits to banks, nominal shareholders and dummy investors alike because most of the *bumiputra* shares are sold immediately. (In Malaysia dummy investors means ostensibly Malay but really Chinese.)

So long as the share market moved up, the system worked. And the banks were not slow to join in, taking shares as collateral for as much as 80 per cent cover for funds lent. But whenever the market plunges, as it did in 1985, revised share valuations can lop huge slices off initially ascribed values. Downturns like this clobbered Malaysia's banks, which had also fallen into the trap of lending too much too often to influential people, many of them members of the banks' boards of directors.

By the mid-1980s, large non-performing loans cluttered balance books, a direct reflection of the glut of office buildings crowding into downtown Kuala Lumpur. The collapse of Hong Kong's Overseas Trust Bank in 1985 provoked worrying follow-on effects: in June the fourth largest Malaysian bank, Public Bank, nearly succumbed to a run by nervous depositors.

Nervousness in Malaysia only added to Singapore's half-way house reputation – gained from the habit of overseas Chinese 'parking' their money in Singapore banks, even at a negative 2.5 to 3 point interest rate differential *vis-à-vis* neighbouring Indonesia or Malaysia.

These financial sector rumblings in the mid-1980s presaged much bigger troubles for Perwira Habib and the United Asian Bank, which came perilously close to receivership. Yet the greed of Malaysia's banks reflected the spirit of the times – easy, get-rich-quick habits that had spread through the exponentially expanding banking community.

Malaysia's central bank, Bank Negara, constantly bemoaned the lack of experience and judgement among the new breed of bankers. The central bank had hoped to introduce secondary mortgage markets, open-market foreign exchange dealing and secondary markets for government securities. A reliable, sophisticated financial industry was needed for these services. Bank Negara also criticised excessive lending to real estate, share-trading and financial company borrowers. In the event however, it was Bank Negara's integrity that appeared to collide with the finance minister's plans. Critics said that post-Independence habits of financial rectitude began to evaporate as Daim exerted more control over Bank Negara.

The Pan-Electric affair rocked both Malaysia and Singapore, highlighting links between business and political leaders. In investigations by the *Far Eastern Economic Review* it emerged that Tan's Supreme Corporation subsidiaries had given security for several bank loans to a key investment vehicle for Daim's family, a private holding company named Pradez.

Daim already had a strong place in the ledgers of the Development and Commercial Bank, the country's sixth largest, managed by a Chinese, Alexander Lee, who served also as treasurer of a small National Front political party. Daim's accounts included a personal M$200,000 overdraft and M$49.5 million in loans to his property and share-trading companies. Oddly also, the guarantor company owned by Tan had shaky financial credentials. In other circumstances this might have made the Tan company something less than an ideal guarantee risk: in the last financial year before the guarantee deal, current liabilities of M$29 million loomed over its M$5 million current assets.

Tan made sure that other *bumiputra* heavyweights kept an interest in his affairs. One of his Supreme Corporation directors was Mohamed Noah bin Omar, a father-in-law of two former prime ministers. Another director of a Tan company, Tunku Mohamed bin Tunku Besar Burhanuddin, brought Tan closer to the royal family of the West Malaysian state of Negri Sembilan.

Similar patterns of influence have also intruded into Kuala Lumpur's stock market, once a part of Singapore's exchange but after 1973 going its own way. The Malaysian government hoped for a second stock trading board for venture capital listings, and gave itself power to name appointees to the Kuala Lumpur Stock Exchange (KLSE) governing committee. New rules allowed the finance minister to 'direct the [KLSE] committee to admit any Malay whom he considers suitable to be a dealer in securities.' The government started appointing compliant people.

In 1985 Daim froze all new KLSE listings, forcing investors to chase existing stocks. This was another free-ride windfall for those holding shares, as more money chased fixed quantities of stock. The next round of new listings was carefully doled out. At one stage a highly leveraged new property firm named Metroplex made a 50 million share début, promptly grabbing one-third of all KLSE trading. Another new issue, of 4.8 million shares valued at M$0.50 each was 65 *times* oversubscribed. Now Daim no longer needed to worry about Bank Negara working at cross purposes; the central bank's Capital Issues Committee, which formally worked under Bank Negara's governor, broke its moorings and was hauled over to Daim's finance ministry.

Daim's extensive personal share holding understandably resulted in a mixed reaction to his various measures to increase trading. He was nothing if not determined. He lengthened scrip delivery time and gave preferential credit lines to banks lending to share investors. He created a US$406 million concessionary finance fund and loosened foreign investment rules to allow more foreign equity holding. He also encouraged merchant banks to set up their own share brokerage operations. On one occasion he pulled in various local fund managers and pressured them to buy shares at the very height of the 'stale bull overhang', brokers' jargon for an over-bought market. In the mid-1980s, most shares (plantation stocks usually excepted) bore high price-earnings ratios, the normal measuring rod of share fundamentals in which the market price of a share is divided by its annual dividend.

This bout of bearish bad luck on the local market had an unfortunate effect on overseas investor confidence in the share market. A joint Arab-Malaysian Merchant Bank/International Finance Corporation issue, in New York, of a US$60 million Malaysia Fund had the misfortune to appear just before the 1987 crash. The fund offered a spread of Malaysian equities and followed a trend of country funds from Southeast Asia. These are discussed further in Chapter 8.

Daim's money-making made an odd pillion passenger to his ministerial duties, a contrast bemusing locals and confusing outsiders. He gained a bare majority stake in the UMBC bank, and then sold it to a government corporation already holding 32 per cent of UMBC. At a cost of US$124 million the deal was reportedly profitable for Daim although the sale came ostensibly in response to Mahathir's decision that cabinet members, and their families, would no longer be permitted to own shares. The sale also happened at the right market moment, and cost the government corporation US$10 million more than it had budgeted to pay one year earlier, according to reports.

Quite apart from nominee shareholdings and other loopholes that riddled effective enforcement of the ban, Mahathir's 'ban' came very much after the horse had bolted. Just weeks before, Daim had also sold a stake of about 7 per cent in Sime Darby, Southeast Asia's largest multinational and based in Malaysia. He is believed to have gained about US$55 million by equal placings of the shares in London and Hong Kong.

Apart from Daim's stockmarket enthusiasm, businessmen found the finance minister obtrusive in other ways. They found themselves approached by real or putative Daim associates demanding favours. In one extraordinary episode, Daim himself prevailed upon his cabinet colleagues to reverse a decision by Malaysian Airlines System (MAS). The airline had opted not to procure jet engines from Pratt & Whitney for a new line of Boeing jets. This seemed sensible: MAS already operated two other engine types, from General Electric and Rolls-Royce. But Daim and his associates allegedly had other plans. The cabinet decision favouring Pratt & Whitney reversed MAS's own technical preferences, provoking enraged airline staff to claim that commissions had been paid to Daim's friends. The finance minister denied any improper motive.

Daim's control over the government's financial machinery also grew. He appointed Malayan Banking chairman Jaffar Hussein as Bank Negara governor in mid-1985. 'I'm becoming an expert on runs,' Jaffar told me jokingly shortly afterwards. And so he was: barely three days into his job, the country's third largest commercial bank, the Public Bank, experienced a headlong run by its depositors, a reaction to the collapse in Hong Kong of the Overseas Union Bank, one of Southeast Asia's major creditlines for overseas Chinese.

In the following months and years, Jaffar's expertise kept growing. Only in January 1988, almost three years later, did he feel confident enough to say that 'the near collapse' of Malaysia's corroded cooperative system 'is now behind us.' Jaffar had helped find M$590 million to repay the 588,000 Chinese depositors.

Jaffar's brave words followed close on the heels of the central bank's emergency takeover of the largest cooperative financier of them all: the Cooperative Central Bank. By the mid-1980s it already had M$250 million in bad or non-performing loans, nearly half its entire portfolio. Incredibly, Bank Negara had allowed the position to worsen after that. Right after the takeover, Jaffar still hesitated to make speedy judgements, as it was 'too early to tell' whether the latest casualty was in 'good or bad shape.'

Even the cooperatives finally released from Jaffar's care still owed M$100 million to their members. What to do? Central banks as a rule do not usually buy equity in banks or finance companies, but in Malaysia the rules often go out of the window. Rather than simply bail out the cooperatives, Jaffar bent to higher advice. As a result, he – and Daim and Mahathir – advanced the Malay/Chinese poker game one more step.

The plan was this: first the government, via Bank Negara, bought a company named Tai Cheng Finance. Renamed the Kewangan Usahasama Makmur, 'Cooperative Prosperous Finance', Bank Negara poured whatever remained of the ailing cooperatives' assets into the new creature. Overnight, Jaffar created the country's largest financial cooperative, with a backing on the books of over US$160 million in paid-up capital. Soon afterwards, Bank Negara put equity capital into the Cooperative Central Bank, Malaysia's biggest cooperative bank.

Commodity Markets Crumble

Daim's expansionary policies, especially on the share exchange, yielded decisions favouring extending credit for share purchases, even when the recession came home with a vengeance after 1985. Export earnings plummeted; in just one year petroleum receipts – a big (about 20 per cent) share of Malaysia's export receipts – declined by 40 per cent in 1986.

The trends worsened during the next year. Prices dropped by 25 per cent across the board for all commodities. Bank Negara rapidly became the last credit line. The chronic crisis also forced the central bank to buy 49 per cent of one major retail bank, and to take over the daily management of another large finance company.

The government even forced Bank Negara to dig into its reserves to buy a privatised stake in the Malaysian International Shipping Corporation, a government owned entity that became the darling of the stock market when listed in 1986. As the *Far Eastern Economic Review*'s *Asia Year Book* for that year put it, 'questions [are] being asked as to the propriety of using all the central bank's general reserves to invest in two companies' just to raise money for a cash-strapped government.

Scandal of Scandals

For all their drama and near-panic, these bank runs paled by comparison to the theft and incompetence that wrecked the reputation and financial probity of Malaysia's biggest bank, the Bank Bumiputra Malaysia Berhad. In the race conscious, business politics of Malaysia, Bank Bumiputra had become the flagship of the New Economic Policy (NEP), a government programme from 1970 to 1990 to shift wealth away from the Chinese and towards the Malays and other *bumiputra*s.

Nowhere in Malaysia's sadly blotched financial record did more red ink seep than from Bank Bumiputra, whose striking headquarters complex in Kuala Lumpur consists of an office tower thrusting up behind a marble-and-glass pavilion modelled after a Malay kampong house. Bank Bumiputra had moved confidently into the financial world after its creation in 1978, relying exclusively on Malay management. It was, and still is, the country's largest bank, with book assets in 1988 of US$15 billion.

In the early 1980s Bank Bumiputra's profits and prestige collided violently with the 'Carrian Affair', a financial scandal without parallel in Hong Kong or Malaysia. As a house of cards built by a Malaysian Chinese named George Tan, Carrian Investments Ltd had rocketed up to achieve US$1 billion of book assets after just *one* year of business. It bought office towers, a taxi company, an insurance group and Hong Kong's fourth largest shipping fleet.

Ten months later the entire enterprise went bust.

The Carrian fiasco formed just one episode of a wider débâcle. The main cause was the eagerness of foreign banks to help finance Hong Kong's greatest real estate boom. As Philip Bowring and Robert Cottrell write in their book *The Carrian File* (1984), the corporate record of Carrian 'seemed to prove that cash and property could not only be regarded as interchangeable commodities, but that each move into property or back into cash would bring with it a fat tranche of profit.'

All the big foreign banks had their fingers burned. These included Britain's Barclays Bank, Peking's Bank of Communications, the West German Westdeutsche Landesbank, France's Paribas and even the territory's own quasi-central bank, the Hongkong and Shanghai Banking Corporation. Yet their various losses seemed trivial by comparison to the reckless lending to Carrian from Bank Bumiputra's 100 per cent-owned Hong Kong subsidiary, Bumiputra Malaysia Finance Limited, or BMF.

In a relationship in which Tan wrote chummy letters to BMF chairman Lorrain Osman ('Dear Uncle Lorrain'), the money went into a bewildering stable of Carrian's swarming private companies, fast-breeding in an overheated reactor. George Tan had interesting business habits. He remained devoted to *fung shui*, a type of Chinese geomancy, and his fascination for intricate numerological portents and lucky signs never abated. He signed loans only at 'lucky times' and on 'lucky days'.

Carrian' diversification included buying a fifth of the Japanese company Nikatsu, which among other things produced do-it-yourself pornographic films. 'Nikatsu will hire the aspirant cineaste a studio and cameras in which to record his own vision of earthly delight,' Bowring and Cottrell comment. In one deal, a joint venture emerged between Carrian and the premier, government-linked Hong Kong Land Company. 'With hindsight', the two authors continue, this arrangement came 'to look less like a joint venture and more like a suicide pact.' Tan certainly had grand plans. He claimed he was building a conglomerate that would 'last centuries.' Using BMF's money he bought a US$350 million investment in California and a 328 hectare real estate development in Florida.

BMF took the whiplash when Hong Kong confidence, alarmed by difficult Sino–British talks over the colony's future, went into a steep nose-dive. The property boom abruptly went bust. Carrian's stable of buildings stood unsold and under-tenanted. Loan servicing costs mounted. The house of cards buckled.

Inside Carrian, a web of cross-financing and cross guarantees simply amounted in the end to zero equations. The complexity of some phoney asset sales over-whelmed criminal fraud investigators. Some new money might have been found to keep the parent company afloat, but just at the wrong moment a visiting Bank Bumiputra auditor named Jalil Ibrahim was found in a banana grove, strangled with a four-foot belt.

In Malaysia itself, a carefully delimited investigatory panel was formed, but soon even this proceeded in ways displeasing to the authorities. One of Bank Bumiputra's past presidents, Kamarul Arifin, told me the 'highest echelons' of government had approved the monies lent to the apparently endless Carrian highflier. But by the time the parent bank had washed out the bad loans, over *one billion* American dollars had been lost.

There were many other facets to the story. The national oil company Petronas was forced ('frog-marched' as one board member put it) to buy the bad debt and to recapitalise Bank Bumiputra. The panel of inquiry, led by a brave auditor general, came awkwardly close to identifying the compliant members of government who had gained from recycled funds coming back to Malaysia.

Fortunately for the highest levels of government, Malya élite solidarity held. But just barely. Some BMF officials went to gaol, notably Hashim Shamsuddin, who received four-and-a-half years for fraud and bribery. But that was in Hong Kong, not Malaysia. Hashim's Hong Kong lawyer claimed that BMF and its parent bank worked on the basis of an 'incestuous attitude between senior political figures and bank officers'; Hashim simply took orders from Mahathir and other senior politicians, his counsel argued. Hashim's defence counsel also accepted a prosecution claim that former Malaysian finance min-ister Tunku Razaleigh Hamzah had on one occasion received HK$25,100 from HK$13.7 million paid by Tan into a conduit Hong Kong front company, owned by Hashim and his wife. The company's name? Silver Present Limit-ed.

Towards the end of the 1980s, Lorrain Osman remained in a London gaol, fighting an intense legal battle against extradition to Hong Kong. Former alternate BMF director Rais Saniman had disappeared in France. Former BMF general manager Ibrahim Ja'afar bought immunity in exchange for testimony against his former colleagues.

Malaysia's legal process went no further than a few civil suits against the bank's erring ex-employees. Bank Bumiputra had lost M$2.4 billion; the largest court-sanctioned restitution, in a 1987 judgment, ordered Hashim (by then in prison) to pay M$47.5 million for loan losses caused, as Bank Bumiputra's civil action pleaded, 'by [his] own neglect, want of skill or misconduct in management.'

In the Bank Bumiputra scandal, Malay executives perverted the financial marketplace far more than in simple pandering to Malaysia's normal business culture. Differing factions within UMNO had quarrelled over territory in the bank; allegations from Hashim, if they are to be believed, described rival UMNO leaders bargaining for credit lines for their respective protégés. Elsewhere in Asia, large commercial banks also tend to become too closely identified with major personalities, invariably local borrowers. In Malaysia the same feature emerged, but with money of *bumiputra* small depositors squandered by rich Chinese in Hong Kong. The irony could not have been greater.

To its credit, Bank Negara tried to blow the whistle many times on Bank Bumiputra and on other scandals. Outgoing governor Aziz Taha said in a 1985 report that the 'banking system badly needs skilled managers. What it does not need are ineptness in management and executives dedicated to self-enrichment.' Soon afterwards, Daim engineered Taha's departure. By now, Mahathir's friend from their old Kedah kampong had achieved ascendancy over the entire banking system.

Daim's friends moved into new positions in the most important commercial banks. The new chief executive for the country's second largest bank, Malaysian Banking Berhad (Maybank), became an amiable 35-year-old Daim associate with no previous bank operations experience. Maybank's new chairman, a former senior Civil Servant named Hashim Aman, engagingly said he 'would do his best' in his new job even though 'I have been a government servant for so long and I have no experience in banking at all.'

NEP-otism at the Share Market

But Malaysia's market distortion does not begin, or end, in the banking industry. The twenty-year New Economic Policy had begun in 1970 with two ambitious goals. The first was to restructure business to give Malays and other *bumiputras* at least 30 per cent of corporate wealth by 1990. The second aim was to reduce poverty among all races – although this quickly became a vaguer goal.

The NEP has a grounding and rationale in hard, social fact: Malay and Malay interests in 1969 owned only 1.5 per cent of the share capital of limited companies in West Malaysia. Chinese owned 22.8 per cent and Indians less than half of one per cent. The rest remained in foreign, chiefly British hands. Malays controlled the political system; in commerce they could only watch in ignorance.

But the NEP's main instrument became a plethora of market-distorting educational, business and public employment quotas, coercive 're-structurings' of corporate stockholding plus a succession of money-losing government corporations that rapidly became mini-fiefdoms. After the late 1970s a massive government-owned National Equity Corporation emerged, known by its Malay name Permodalan Nasional Berhad (PNB).

This creature bought massive numbers of shares using government loans and then farmed out the proceeds through a unit trust scheme, Amanah Saham. By the mid-1980s the PNB had become the largest single equity holder at the KLSE, with US$2.24 billion invested in 178 companies. Amanah Saham was the second largest. Between the two the 1990 goal of a 30 per cent Malay share would be met, even if a few accounting tricks were necessary.

Whatever the percentage, the *spread* of ownership remains absurdly narrow for a government professing devotion to mass capitalism. Surveys showed the trust agencies had increased their share-buying by 50 per cent each year during the 1970s and early 1980s, and that average Malay household income had also risen at about 6 to 7 per cent a year, a major achievement by any reckoning. Yet the ownership base remained rather thin; former deputy prime minister Musa Hitam in 1986 said three-quarters of all Amanah Saham shareholders owned less than 500 trust shares. More damaging still, he claimed that barely a third of all Malays even belonged to the scheme.

'The NEP strategy of equity restructuring by trusteeship resulted in increased wealth concentration,' according to a Canadian economist who has spent years studying the NEP. Ozay Mehmet's 1986 book *Development in Malaysia: Poverty, Wealth and Trusteeship*, also stresses that

> Agencies dependent upon government subsidies operate as if they are insulated from business cycles. In such agencies, performance and success tend to be determined by non-competitive, bureaucratic criteria . . . [each move into corporate business becomes] more subject to manipulation by the rich and powerful, seeking quasi-rents and other forms of unearned economic rewards.

Mehmet offers a tough indictment. He claims that the NEP has had many market-distorting effects. He says the NEP creates dependency and passivity among Malays; that it generates patron-client networks strangling initiative and genuine entrepreneurial drive. He, and other economists such as Paul Chan of the University of Malaya, claim the NEP is an economic 'free-rider' (that is, its beneficiaries gain advantages at no risk or cost) from such ostensibly non-racial policies as industrialisation, nationalisation, land settlement or agricultural development.

In the 1960s only 2 of 47 public enterprises specifically served *bumiputra* interests; ten years later 59 of the 103 mostly new public corporations existed solely to promote Malay business. The proportion is even higher today. These enterprises fall into four categories.

First, portfolio investors such as the PNB or investment funds held by the Muslim Pilgrims Board or by armed forces personnel. Secondly, trading corporations with significant equity interests in other companies – such as Perbadanan Nasional Berhad, or Pernas (the 'National Corporation'), which owns the biggest stake in UMBC.

The third type of *bumiputra* public enterprise mainly offers concessionary services, finance and business training, a category that embraces the Majlis Amanah Rakyat, the 'Council of Trust for the People', and Bank Bumiputra itself. The fourth type of Malay quango, that delightful acronym for quasi non-governmental organisation, are the state economic development corporations, one for each of the thirteen states. Nearly all of them lose money.

The NEP encapsulates and enshrines the free-riding commercial instincts so prevalent in Southeast Asia. It has generated a generation of Malay equity managers skilled at such productive arts as dawn-raiding on the share markets – as when the British plantation firm Guthries fell to the PNB in three hours of frantic trading in London. In short, many analysts believe the NEP has spawned too many businessmen who have become, in the words of one Malay economist, 'upstarts, rather than start-ups'.

From the initial phase of loss-making state corporations (all but two of which were drowning in red ink by the mid-1980s) to the so-called 'mature phase' of the PNB and share buyouts, the NEP has worked mayhem on the free market, an inversion of its declared aim. It did so often with the willing participation of foreigners happy enough to share a wink and take pleasing buyout prices while staying on as management consultants. As Ja'afar reminded foreign audiences, 'both residents and non-residents are allowed to do whatever they like with their own money.' Remittances of profit remain sacrosanct.

Sultans Galore

Another dimension of Malaysia's business culture comes in regal guise. Among Malaysia's thirteen states, nine are little kingdoms; from among their nine sultans a unique, five-year King is chosen. The owner of the United Asian Bank – that bemoaned loss of the Malaysian Indian community, was Tunku Ariff Bendahara, a Pahang state prince. Ariff's father, Tuanku Ahmad Shan (nicknamed 'Tas'), reigned as Malaysia's king after building up TAS Industries, TAS Holdings and buying a majority stake in the large palm oil refining mill Jomalina.

Just as prominent as the Pahang royalty was that of Negri Sembilan, a small landlocked state south of Kuala Lumpur. Two of that state's princes, Tunku Imran Ibni Tuanku Ja'afar and Tunku Naquiyuddin Ibni Tuanku Ja'afar are both sons of the Negri Sembilan sultan. Imran, known to his friends as 'Pete', loves rugby and horses. He and his brother, nicknamed 'Bill', run Antah Holdings, an early, pure Malay entrant to the stock exchange and a wonderfully successful one at that. Antah's thirty subsidiaries or associated companies have spread the interests of these royal businessmen across insurance, reinsurance, property, consumer products and manufacturing.

Their uncle, Tunku Abdullah Ibni Tuanku Abdul Rahman, served as an exemplar to these brothers. Abdullah became a director of many companies, including Malayan Cement, Pacific Development Corporation, San Holdings, Malaysia Vetsin Manufacturing and the large East Malaysian finance firm, Malaysia Borneo Finance Corporation. Not to be outdone, the royal family of Johore also has a bewildering range of interests in airline chartering, property, construction, sawmilling and timber businesses. The Johore sultan, Mahmood Iskandar, became King in 1984 and left the kingship in 1989.

Iskandar is one of Singapore's biggest private landowners. Once sentenced in the High Court for culpable homicide (he shot a Chinese man whom he took to be a smuggler), the Johore sultan is fond of wind-surfing, fast cars and uniforms. He maintains a 200-man private army, the Johor Military Force.

His reputation dogs him still; disturbing rumours surfaced in 1988 about displays of temper on the golf course. Iskandar is known for his intemperate behaviour.

Other Malaysian royal families have drifted into court. In 1979, Tunku Petri Sultan Ibrahim faced charges of attempting to defraud a Chinese businessman by promising, in exchange for M$20,000, to give him one of the many exalted Malay titles. In the same year, the younger brother of the Pahang sultan was charged in court with using a forged letter purportedly approving his request to log a large block of forest. Two other Pahang royal family members also went to court on fraud charges. Another Pahang royal family member, also called Tunku Abdullah, has become executive chairman of the Apera Holdings group, which began with a M$25,000 loan from Citibank to Abdullah's partner, an arms salesman named Jimmy Yusoff. Apera has sold Italian howitzers to the Malaysian army but now holds a majority stake in Universal Life and General Insurance. However the most profitable company revealing Pahang royal interests may be the share market *Wunderkind* Metroplex, a property developer.

A somewhat blanket reputation for eccentricity still hangs over Malaysia's sultans. Those that can afford them build monumental palaces, not always in the best of taste. For many years the Lotus motorcar became a hot favourite among younger royals, whose propensity for driving commoners off the roads usually evaded tough press treatment. Malaysia's royal businessmen are normally indulged, despite occasional kill-joys such as Chandra Muzaffar, a public interest lobbyist whose 1979 book *Protector?* dealt with 'the alleged utilisation of public funds for private purposes, involvement in businesses . . . and most of all the absence of an image of excellence which can inspire emulation – these are some aspects of the [royal] institution . . .'

Chandra may have been thinking of Trengganu's late Sultan Ismail, Malaysia's rotating king during 1965–70, who never again put on his Royal Malaysian Air Force air marshal's uniform after the air force refused to fly him home on one occasion. Or he may have remembered the time the Sultan of Selangor organised a crow-shooting competition: gunmen bagged over 2,000 of them. A former Perak sultan enjoyed nothing more than playing his saxophone at the Ipoh Club, a tin miners' bastion dating from the colonial era.

It was most likely that Chandra was remembering that the sultans command, and have frequently abused, an important source of revenue – land. Until they were logged out, timber concessions earned large revenues. The Selangor sultan has also benefited from the tremendous rise in property values in his state, which adjoins the Kuala Lumpur federal territory. The interplay between royal wealth, considered 'old money', and the more *parvenu* fortunes of modern Malaysia make an interesting study; the two often intertwine happily in corporate boardrooms. As Nick Seaward of the *Far Eastern Economic Review* wrote in 1989,

the business royals form an interesting counterpoint to the Malay *nouveaux riches*. They compete for *bumiputra* special share issues . . . and they lobby for government contracts reserved for *bumiputras*. The competition has become even more formidable since the banking crackdown of 1986 – the royals had got started on their own capital while the self-made Malay tycoons rode on

the back of the cheap, no-questions-asked credit wave of the late 1970s and
early 1980s.

Move over Mat Salleh?

More than just business favouritism fuels the Malaysian economy, of course.
Its industrious Chinese, hard-working Malay rubber-tappers and wide spread of
resources have made it a rich country. Foreign investors, especially in trading
and plantations, have sought to keep a place in the sun. They have not always
been successful.

The Chinese have a bevy of unprintable epithets for foreigners, of which *kwei
loh*, 'white ghost', is the gentlest. By contrast the more genial Malay tag is 'Mat
Salleh', a word whose etymology still baffles linguists. Some think the word
originates from 'mad sailor', of which there were many during the age of sail.
Some stayed to become merchants and adventurers.

How the great have fallen! For example the once-powerful British trading firm
Inchcape sold a majority stake to a *bumiputra* entity owned by Tunku Shahabuddin
Burhanuddin, a member of the Pahang royal family. Inchcape later made ill-timed
acquisitions in the motor trade; meanwhile political ups and downs among the
Malay élite kept Inchcape from the 'right' *bumiputra* connections. This became
evident when it missed out in a bid for the prized distributorship deal for prime
minister Mahathir's pet project, the 'made-in Malaysia' car.

On the other hand, the old British firm Harrisons & Crosfield not only
bowed to the inevitable restructuring but retained a strong minority voice in
its 'Malaysianised' company, now called Harrisons Malaysian Plantations Berhad
(HMBP). This remained well integrated in Harrisons & Crosfield's global network.
HMBP took Tun Ismail Ali as its chairman, the stern ex-chief of Bank Negara and
related by marriage to the top Malay élite.

Harrisons remained within that select group of efficiently run, steady-yielding
plantation companies that include Consolidated Plantations, Kuala Lumpur
Kepong and Highlands & Lowlands. Forty-one plantation listings now crowd
Kuala Lumpur's stock exchange; the only big exception is Kumpulan Guthrie
Berhad, the descendant of the Guthries group whose stock disappeared into PNB's
hands during that London morning.

Despite their colonial 'feel', plantations still deliver the wellspring of Malaysia's
wealth, a tide of money that, together with petroleum receipts, enables the government to finance its grandiose visions. But years of good commodity prices, backed
up by a bull market, lulled even the most cautious corporate and government
advisers, whose warnings about profligate behaviour never materialised. Thus
the blizzard of loans for high-rise buildings and fancy housing estates while
share market speculation continued unabated. Even plantation companies began
to dabble.

The prudent souls were eventually vindicated as Malaysia's growth by the
mid-1980s stumbled from a heady pace to minuscule figures, dropping to
'negative growth' in 1985 and to just 1.2 per cent GDP growth in 1986.
Since then the growth rates have returned to the buoyant, 'normal' state, but
they are also hostage to fickle demand and hindered by a large overhang of debt
and simmering political uncertainties. The export-based manufacturing sector has
pulled in most of the improved returns; industries uncommonly subject to abrupt

changes in demand and technology, such as the semiconductor business, have led
the recovery. Unemployment meanwhile continues to grow, and is now well over
10 per cent. As the country's balance of payments twisted askew due to falling
commodity prices and resilient imports, new anxiety about its invisible payments
for service account items (such as insurance or travel) became more prominent: by
the mid-1980s the deficit in invisibles rose above M$9.5 billion (US$3.8 billion at
the time).

All this uncertainty has punctured the old boom town mentality. The show-
pieces suddenly look shopworn. The flagship money-waster, the National Car
project, had based its sales on a production capacity of 120,000 Proton cars a
year chasing buoyant demand. By 1987 only 20,000 a year could be offloaded.
'Proton's problem is that it was born in 1983 from a market analysis that
proved hopelessly flawed,' *The Economist* commented. 'It was assumed that an
economy that had grown by almost 8% a year for over ten years would do so
indefinitely.'

Mahathir then sought relief in export sales, originally planned to occur in
the 1990s. In July 1987, he signed a letter of intent with a British distributor
who undertook to market 48,000 Protons in the United Kingdom over five
years. This meant adapting the 1.3 and 1.5 litre models to British standards
– and then attempting to shoehorn it into an already overcrowded market.
'Reality has made a farce of the forecasts,' *The Economist* noted tartly, but
accurately.

The Chinese government's import agencies also sniffed at the car, wondering
how to replace air conditioners with heaters. Four hundred and eighty cars have
gone to Bangladesh, Malta, Sri Lanka and New Zealand but few repeat orders
materialised from these insignificant markets. Mahathir, whose brainchild the
motorcar project was, then pushed hard to export the Proton car to the huge
American market.

A relentless power struggle within UMNO absorbed Mahathir during most
of 1987 and the car received scant attention. Then, in an interview with
an American car magazine, Mahathir announced that he had decided to use
the talents of a Malcolm Bricklin to penetrate the US market. Bricklin, an
American entrepreneur whose winged-design 'Bricklin car' had manifestly failed
to fly in Canada's market after two loss-burdened years, reportedly promised
Mahathir that he would sell 100,000 cars during the first year of marketing in
the US.

The Bricklin decision stunned Mitsubishi, the Japanese partners in the 70 per
cent government-owned factory. It also seemed a particularly desperate move for
the concern, which stopped publicly reporting its losses after 1985. In the year to
31 March 1985, accumulated losses reached M$11.6 million. During the ensuing
twelve months, it was reliably learned that Proton lost another M$42.5 million
– much of this, M$14.8 million, from the effect of import costs following the
relentlessly appreciating yen. By 1988, Proton was selling just 23,000 cars a
year – one-third of the originally installed capacity and *one-sixth* of envisaged
capacity.

Import duties on knocked-down car kits for other car assemblers had been
raised through the ceiling to guarantee that Proton would make a profit, but
the market-distorting measures simply spread the misery. Again, the implicit
assumption of a bull market had led the government into a cul-de-sac. In belated
acknowledgement of the fiasco, Mahathir in 1988 stomached the blow to Malay

pride and accepted Mitsubishi's insistence on turning the car plant over to a Japanese manager.

This willingness to do what's necessary, even if at the last minute, is a factor in Malaysia's favour. It surfaced again when the Malaysian Chinese Association sacked managers installed in the party's investment holding company by its gaoled former president, Tan Koon Swan. Instead it brought in Robert Kuok Hock Nien, a Chinese whose prudence during the 1980s stood out in sharp contrast to many of his millionaire peers. Kuok also became more prominent in another troubled public company, Malayan United Industries, when its reclusive chairman, Khoo Kay Peng, left the group. The Kuok family empire receives more detailed attention in Chapter 7, which deals more extensively with the business power of the overseas Chinese.

Other prestige industries have also run straight into the wall. The government's US$600 million Perwaja Trengganu steel mill had to close a direct-reduction method furnace. It claimed the manufacturer, Nippon Steel Corporation, had supplied equipment that failed to meet performance specifications – and the Japanese came to the rescue by offering US$200 million compensation. In truth it had become vastly cheaper to use ordinary scrap steel as feedstock, rather than to make hot briquetted iron at the plant. Another vast scheme, a three-part telecommunications expansion, also had to be scaled down.

By the close of the decade therefore, the government had to face the music. Daim said sixty 'Non-Financial Public Enterprises' needed to be 'closed down, rehabilitated or privatised.' The government had put in equity or held contingent liabilities to the extent of M$2.1 billion; all this at a time when foreign debt servicing inched up towards the danger signal when repayments consume the equivalent of 20 per cent of export earnings.

Damned Dams

Even the grand plans to build Southeast Asia's biggest dam, in the middle of Sarawak, collided with huge cost estimates (as much as M$18.7 billion by 1995) and an increasingly bothersome environmental lobby. Technical worries also gave pause – how would the dam's estimated 2,400 megawatts be carried across the South China Sea to West Malaysia? The proposed underwater cable would be five times longer than the longest transmission line ever installed. This decision disappointed a bevy of foreign corporations keen to build an aluminium plant to use the surplus power. These included Alcan of Canada, Conzinc Rio Tinto of Australia, Reynolds Metals of the US and Sumitomo of Japan.

Biting the bullet, the government sought change in the area best open to manipulation: rules for foreign investors. Very quickly Daim jettisoned NEP rules limiting foreign equity holdings to 30 per cent in most ventures. He lowered statutory reserve requirements for the banks, from 5 to 4 per cent, and decreed across-the-board cuts to the banks' base lending rate.

At Daim's behest the government also created a M$1 billion investment fund for manufacturing ventures and revised the restrictive Industrial Coordination Act, which had previously legislated the mandatory share surrenders to *bumiputra* agencies and individuals. Some import duties and tariffs, the effect of which (or so one confidential UN report said) was to penalise exporters rather than to encourage them, were also revised. Another fund, this one to conserve revenue from dwindling oil reserves, also emerged.

The move to change foreign equity conditions came first, in July 1985. Soon most new ventures could carry 80 per cent foreign capital; after a while even these guidelines went by the board in certain instances, depending on how desirable the investment might be. Even the NEP now looked in doubt, no matter what statistics the government dished out in its reports. *Bumiputra* investment funds dwindled with declining government revenues.

Apart from the stock market, private investment in other areas was also dropping. And the emerging social stratification *within* Malay society made a hash of the promise of mass entrepreneurship. 'There was little talk of "equality of opportunity" within Malay society itself,' says Bruce Gale, a student of the NEP. 'It was in effect the Malay intellectuals, administrators and petit bourgeoisie in the cities and the sons of the more well-to-do peasants who were being invited to improve themselves.'

A sense of perspective must be retained. The bad business habits described above did not burst suddenly into Malaysia's business and commercial affairs although it marked a newer, more breathtaking scale. In the 1970s the government's UMNO élite belonged to a faction from Johore and Pahang states, including Prime Minister Tun Abdul Razak and his deputy. Tun Razak's family radiated outwards in a patronage system. Similarly, marriage-based groupings from Kelantan and Kedah, plus the cement of royal lineage, all did much business bonding, as we have seen.

Other Bright Ideas

Although critics claim that 'cronyism' has run riot during his tenure, Mahathir did not arrive at the premiership with these aims. Slighted by princely Malays because of his mixed Pakistani-Malay background (the word *mamak* to describe a person of his ancestry is fighting talk in Malaysia), Mahathir came to office vowing greater efficiency and less patronage. He is a complex man, brimful with ideas and anxious to dispel lingering impressions that Malays are lazy, free-riding goodtimers. His book *The Malay Dilemma* caused a storm in the early 1970s; he employed tough language against an apparent lack of competitiveness among Malays.

Mahathir made many innovations. Some seemed inspired, some seemed overdue, and some seemed daft. Among those of which I learned at first hand, my favourite non-starter was a plan to hire a vacant transponder on Indonesia's 'Palapa' communications satellite (unused because Philippine television stations belonging to Marcos crony Roberto Benedicto had not paid their rental charges). The idea (which floated somewhere between the first and third categories of usefulness) was to make an end-run around Singapore's grip on regional, high speed telecommunications and data transmission. The idea went nowhere. As noted, Mahathir also dabbled excessively in the running of the 'Malaysia Car' project. On one occasion he intervened to decide which country, West Germany or Japan, should win a contract to supply steering mechanisms for the Proton car. To Mitsubishi's horror, the Germans won the day. The secret of their success should inspire European competitors discouraged by the Japanese leviathan. The Germans brought a working, full-scale model of their device to Mahathir's office. He climbed into the driver's seat, liked the effect, and ordered that the contract should go to the Germans.

'Looking East'

Another Mahathir initiative pleased, puzzled and enraged his countrymen by turns (and by race). Early in his premiership he embraced a 'Look East' campaign to emulate Japanese and Korean work habits and industrial discipline. Soon however, the reaction to this programme prompted Mahathir to deny that he wanted to make Malaysians into little Japanese or Koreans. 'What I say may not make me popular,' he said once, 'hard work is not popular but it is for our own good.' On another occasion he said 'we want only to emulate the good values of the Japanese, such as their capacity for hard work and integrity, and not their bad habits.'

The older Malaysian Chinese especially, with grim memories of the Japanese Occupation, disliked the campaign. Disgruntled voices, especially from Malaysia's building industry, alleged 'bad habits' which included a pronounced and perhaps permanent usurping by the Japanese of major construction jobs – of which there were many during the spend-happy days of Mahathir's first term.

The most prominent Japanese firms – Takenaka Komuten, Kumagai, Shimizu, Kensetsu, Kazami-gumi and Sumitomo for example – won port expansion, bridge-building and high-rise contracts. Local builders, mostly Malaysian Chinese, felt aggrieved. Even Japanese officials, notably Tokyo's ambassador in Kuala Lumpur, had qualms. Privately they urged Mahathir to tone down his campaign.

Mahathir however claimed immediate benefits from Looking East. He cited the creation of five Malaysian *sogo shoshas*, Japanese-style general trading houses. He accelerated the establishment of Japanese-style, in-house unions to replace craft-based unions of British origin. He praised the 'quality control circles' being formed, at his prodding, in many Malaysian factories. Groups of Malay trainees left for training at major Japanese corporations. Double-taxation and visa-abolition agreements with Tokyo were finalised.

Yet a sense of unease persisted. Mahathir himself came to criticise laggard Japanese investors. He was also unhappy about a trade gap with Japan that widened with each passing year. From M$1.7 billion the deficit climbed to M$3.6 billion in 1985; thereafter the yen's continuing appreciation pushed the figures into further imbalance. The local newspapers, with government approval, began printing stories about resentment against Japanese construction companies by *bumiputras* as well. 'They [the Japanese] are so fond of making all kinds of excuses and demands to deny [Malays] their business,' said one Malay contractor.

After three years, Look East was looking frayed at the edges. *The Sun Also Sets* was the title of one anti-Japanese book circulating in Malaysia. Continuous efforts to imitate the Japanese *sogo shosha* fell flat. Taking their cue from the government, most major commodity firms banded together into what they imagined were Japanese-style trading conglomerates. Yet only one firm of the many prodded into being by Mahathir did tolerably well. Sadly for the prime minister, this one – the Malaysian Overseas Investment Corporation – later fell into disrepute. Its Chinese general manager, a Muslim convert, went to court on fraud charges.

The problem was that most of Malaysia's exports have long ago found their markets. Division-of-market arrangements of the type the Japanese have developed proved unworkable. Performance targets – Mahathir urged each new firm to generate M$1 billion a year in new business – simply heightened a sense of disappointment when results fell far behind these artificial expectations. In brief, shareholders of existing firms had no wish to transfer business to new trading arms.

One statistic expanded, however. Japan had already become the most important foreign investor before the yen soared against the US dollar after September 1985. By the late 1980s the Japanese had far outpaced any other contenders, even in aggregate. New money for manufacturing investment came in, seeking cheap labour and easy re-export back to Japan. Yet Japanese managers retained little faith in Malaysian workers. One Kyoto University survey showed managers giving Malaysians an approval rating of just 19 per cent while in the 'care taken in work' category, they gave Malaysians a 5 per cent approval rating. Not one Japanese manager gave Malaysian workers a good rating in response to a question probing assessment of 'ability to adapt to changing situations'.

II

The World's Richest Man

Malaysia's racial plurality makes for a comparatively open society. Despite amendments each parliamentary session to strengthen repressive legislation governing official secrets, publishing, the right of association and detention, this garrulous, money-hungry society dooms these efforts to failure. Despite itself the Malaysian business and political system throws up everyone's dirty laundry, perhaps because the informed gossip reaches fever pitch in the many clubs and golf courses.

A different set of rules applies in neighbouring Brunei however. A Malay sultanate and independent Asean member since 1984, Brunei Darulsalam, as its formal name goes, is the region's El Dorado. This secretive sultanate has been edging slowly into regional affairs during the 1980s, especially since the long-ruling former Sultan, Sir Muda Omar Ali Saifuddin, died in September 1986. His son, Sir Hassanal Bolkiah, assumed full responsibilities although he had been the nominal Sultan since 1979.

Hassanal is thought to be the world's richest man, and is so described by the *Guiness Book of Records* and by *Fortune* magazine. 'How do you find something to give to the richest man in the world?' asks James Bartholomew (1989), who has researched the Sultan's affairs for a number of years. 'If anyone has everything he wants, surely it must be Sir Hassanal Bolkiah . . . innocents might imagine that, in the circumstances, nobody would attempt to give him anything. But nothing could be further from the truth. The Sultan receives presents all the time.'

Bartholomew's work complements research by V. G. Kulkarni (*Far Eastern Economic Review*), Melinda Liu (*Newsweek*), Jared Mitchell (*Maclean's*), Peter Koenig (*Institutional Investor*) and Louis Kraar (*Fortune*); together they have gone some way to reveal Hassanal's network of free-wheeling friends and erratic business decisions. Needless to say, the Brunei media, such as they are, tread a very narrow path and are either uninformative about this issue, or unreliable.

Among the foreign friends reportedly chosen for their financial advice is Adnan Khashoggi, the well-known arms dealer and, after 1988, co-defendant in a US federal case for fraud filed principally against former Philippine president Ferdinand Marcos. Khashoggi figured as the Sultan's friend during the late 1970s and early 1980s, introducing Hassanal to The Belfry Club and other London nightspots.

Mohammed Al-Fayed figured as another royal friend. He is an Egyptian emigré whose purchase of the House of Fraser (which owns Harrods) still causes controversy in Britain. Another Middle Eastern transplant to London, Bobby Manoukian, also counts himself among Hassanal's friends according to reports. He allegedly serves as royal outfitter and supplier; in 1985 he is believed to have bought London's Dorchester Hotel for the Sultan, for a price said to be £88 million.

The picture of royal friendship is rounded out by two other men. One, Shri Chandra Swamiji Maharaj, in press interviews has described himself as a spiritual mentor to Hassanal. His propensity to talk too much about this friendship however may have propelled him from the Sultan's inner circle in recent years. The other friend, now also on the periphery, is Enrique (nicknamed 'Easy') Zobel, a Filipino businessman who reportedly became one of just two foreigners permitted to establish a bank in Brunei. 'Easy' took 20 per cent; Princess Rashida, Hassanal's oldest daughter took 60 per cent and the remainder went to the Japanese bank Dai-Ichi Kangyo.

Zobel also won the construction contract to build the Istana Nurul Iman, Hassanal's colossal new palace in Bandar Seri Begawan, the country's capital. This monstrosity, designed by one of Marcos's favoured architects, displays thirty-eight different types of Italian marble in its internal fittings. On the outside it wears a coat of Travertine marble. Marble also adorns many of the 257 toilets while 564 chandeliers provide the lighting. According to one report, these require 751,490 light bulbs. Zobel's reportedly hurried construction of the Istana, on Hassanal's orders, is said to have contributed to sub-standard workmanship, displeasing Hassanal.

Not content with this extravagance, Hassanal ordered a second palace built for the Princess Mariam, his second wife, a former air stewardess. His first wife, the Raja Isteri, reigns in the large palace. The second palace, known as Istana Nurulizza, is 'small' only by comparison with the first palace. Although its junior, the lesser edifice still has a throne room, five swimming pools and even an extraordinary office for Hassanal – which he has reportedly fitted out in aluminium and flashing lights. Bartholomew notes that 'another observer' [of the Istana Nurulizza] has described [the office] as *Star Trek*, with the Sultan as Captain Kirk.'

The diminutive enclave of contemporary Brunei represents a contraction of a once large but loose empire. The Brunei Malays once ruled the north Borneo coastline and adjoining islands in the Sulu Sea – then, as now, a haunt for pirates. It is as if its territorial contraction last century brought with it a type of narrowing of time and horizon; the postage-stamp sized potentate is an immensely rich and parochial place where the Sultan's younger brothers hold many cabinet posts, such as foreign affairs and finance, and where the royal family's influence is all pervasive.

How parochial? The Sultan is given to lecturing his bureaucrats on closed circuit television. For many years it was considered desirable to keep Brunei's students at home where, as James Bartholomew writes, 'the Special Branch of the police could keep an eye on them and where they could be inculcated with the notion of "the three Ms – the Malay Muslim Monarchy".'

Bribes, Backhanders and Favours

Yet do not imagine that this insularity has shielded Brunei from worldly temptations. Business and politics in this tiny fiefdom mirror those of Brunei's much larger, if not richer neighbours. Bartholomew's book, *The Richest Man in the World: the Sultan of Brunei* (1989) describes how

> Bribes, backhanders and favours for 'cronies' are commonplace in business and government life in Southeast Asia. The 'cronies' in Brunei are those who are given certain advantages because of their connection with the Sultan or some other member of the royal family. Local companies with a member of the royal family or someone influential at court on the board have a better chance of getting contracts. Foreign companies are almost compelled to sell some shares to local interests and most of them pick a royal or royally connected investor. All this is under the respectable cloak of 'technology transfer' or 'teaching the Malay people business expertise'.

As Bartholomew notes, royal family members win both ways – 'getting shares below market value and perhaps also receiving a salary for being a director of the company.' Such companies as Jasra, a firm owned by Prince Jefri, has taken a stake in a Dallas oil company. It also has received shares in the local subsidiary of Harrisons & Crosfield, the British plantation conglomerate still profitably active, with *bumiputra* hands on board, in neighbouring Malaysia.

QAF Holdings, also with royal connections, has stakes in many offshore drilling firms servicing Shell operations in Brunei. QAF sought, and won, a listing on Singapore's stock exchange in 1984; its filing documents showed its owner to be an incorporated firm named Parkwood Investments, incorporated in Jersey and owned by Princess Zariah, the wife of Prince Mohamed.

Bank Scandals

In financial affairs, Brunei adopts a cavalier, *laisser-faire* attitude to banking and business. Brunei banks can – and do – lend to their own officers and board members. Four finance companies collapsed after 1985, a harbinger of more distress to come. And the country's 250,000 subjects awoke one morning in 1987 to the grandest banking scandal in their diminutive country's history. Four defendants went to trial in October that year following the loss of nearly US$600 million in loans from the National Bank of Brunei (NBB). The Sultan had the bank closed in November 1986 and seized all its deposits, including US$200 million in short-term deposits belonging to thirty-one foreign banks. These included Citibank, the Hongkong and Shanghai Bank, Overseas Union Bank, Standard and Chartered and Maybank.

In the rich village of Bandar Seri Begawan, the country's capital, the case had a special edge because the Sultan felt betrayed. The chairman of the NBB was

Khoo Ban Hock; together with three associates he faced conspiracy and fraud charges. But the grey eminence behind this legal shadow play remained Khoo's father, Khoo Teck Puat, once close enough to Hassanal to figure in his inner league of foreign associates. Khoo is a Chinese patriarch in the old tradition and, though not in the Sultan's special category, also an extremely rich man. His downfall in Brunei is discussed more extensively in Chapter 7.

The Shell-fare State

The Sultan constantly receives suggestions on how he might 'park' some of his country's estimated US$30 billion reserves. These come from between 150,000 and 180,000 barrels per day pumped out by Shell, plus natural gas produced at the rate of about 770 standard cubic feet per day in the late 1980s and exported to Japan in liquid form by a Brunei joint venture with Mitsubishi. No one knows the royalty percentage that Brunei receives from these exports, nor what earnings it gains from the public and private joint ownership of the Shell companies working in Brunei. There is, in addition, a 55 per cent corporate tax payable by these concerns to the Sultan's government. Here more than in most places, it is difficult to distinguish the public from the private purse.

Up to now, Hassanal's financial advisers have played it safe, choosing US and European investments and securities while eschewing the region in which their master lives. But the Sultan wants to be seen as reasonable, especially after his country joined Asean in 1984. In September 1987 therefore, he offered a 25-year interest-free US$100 million loan to Indonesia.

Reportedly also, he offered to inject money into the limping Indo-cement conglomerate owned by Liem Sioe Liong, a longtime business associate of the family of President Suharto. (The muttered Jakarta term for which is *cukong*, pronounced 'choo-cong'.) Building a new hotel in Bali also had some appeal to the Sultan. In the same year the Brunei Investment Agency, which is theoretically distinct from the management of the Sultan's personal holdings, also made a placing of 35 million shares in a newly privatised Malaysian Airline System. This secretive agency also bought into Malaysia's sagging property market.

CONTRA-dictory Generosity

Brunei's generosity even extended to other realms, sometimes embarrassingly so. The American press discovered in late 1986 that the Sultan had given US$10 million to Nicaraguan Contra rebels. The money went into a Swiss bank account operated by Colonel Oliver North of the US National Security Council.

US Secretary of State George Shultz wrote to Hassanal, saying 'we greatly appreciate your support for this endeavour which we believe has great importance for the overall security of the free world.' But Hassanal's money went into the wrong account, depriving the free world, but enriching a lucky Swiss businessman, who promptly withdrew the funds after finding them in his own account.

These scandals and occasionally publicised outside investments amount to side issues, so long as the oil keeps flowing. On present estimates, Brunei's proven reserves will last to AD 2014 if the 1989 extraction rate of 150,000 barrels per day remains constant. Even the disastrous slide in prices after 1986 did little to harm these inhabitants of the'Shell-fare state'. Extraction just went up to compensate for the shortfall in earnings. More resistant to price fluctuations is the sultanate's liquefied natural gas – of which Brunei has become the world's second largest producer. By the end of the 1980s, Brunei accounted for nearly 20 per cent of all liquefied natural gas consumed by Japan, just behind Indonesia and Malaysia.

III

Malay Economics: Getting It Right

The experience of Malaysia and, to a lesser extent, Brunei since the late 1960s mirrors that of its near neighbours in Asean. Commodities generated enormous returns and, in the rush to wealth, each country expanded its financial and banking industry at an almost exponential rate. (The assets of Malaysia's banks grew over 3,100 per cent during 1970–85.) In the face of this on-rush of wealth and economic growth, who would dare sound Canute-like denials?

Malaysia and Brunei have much to celebrate. In Malaysia, in any event, the right formulae have been tried and tested. For example, in seeking to add value to its own raw materials, Malaysian palm oil firms have moved quickly and effectively to process raw palm oil at home.

Similarly, the value-added from converting a raw log into a piece of furniture – which can exceed 3,000 per cent – has spurred Kuala Lumpur's economic planners to try a novel approach: instead of slapping on the usual protective tariff to protect the country's several thousand infant furniture industries, they have *reduced* tariffs sheltering slipshod mum-and-dad firms making dressers and the like for the captive local market. New firms, aiming at economies of scale and incorporating more marketable designs, have quickly responded. Overseas Chinese money flowed in from Hong Kong and Taiwan.

When overall management of the economy comes under scrutiny, Daim has won grudging converts after 1987. He took a long time to do what he needed to do, but at least he did it. For a start, he cut government spending down to 9.7 per cent of GDP in that year – a big switch from a mere six years earlier, when the figure had reached a worrying 22 per cent. Daim has also relaxed restrictive equity participation rules for investors and led a revitalised privatisation drive to shed some large white elephants (such as the Malayan Railways) from the national Treasury. He also cut the maximum corporate tax rates by almost a quarter after 1987.

Daim's measures have certainly helped. From a 'negative growth' (that absurd phrase) of − 1.5 per cent in 1985, Malaysia slowly rebounded on another commodity boomlet and as foreign investment, declining each year after 1982, swung around. Japanese spillover investment from Thailand took the lead. All in all these results contrast sharply with the economic indicators from 1981–85. Despite the poor political climate, growth soared back to an annualised 9 per cent by the beginning of 1989. Is this, then, just a replay of the Good Old Days?

Possibly. To reiterate, Malaysia has a diversified and rich resource base. It has become a pivotal exporter of palm oil, tropical timber, natural rubber and tin. It is the fourth largest producer of cocoa and pepper and, after Indonesia, is Southeast Asia's second largest natural petroleum and natural gas exporter. Resource-based industries have grown, including rubber glove and (in the wake of the AIDS scare) condoms. New petrochemicals and palm oil processing plants are planned.

In addition, Malaysia's government administration, while increasingly bent at the top and now synonymous with Malay ascendancy, remains more efficient and (in most daily dealings) more honest than others in the region. The back-up services for industry – water, roads, telecommunications, electricity and security – make an impressive contrast to countries such as the Philippines or Indonesia.

Despite UMNO infighting, government economic and fiscal policies remain fairly consistent. Bank Negara, though still trembling from its ordeal after 1985, held the show together. The budget deficit and the foreign debt, while still troubling, have become less serious than in the mid-1980s. Some of the foreign debt, which grew steeply during the 1980s, has even been pre-paid. Foreign exchange reserves have built up again. Inflation, at mid-1989 is low. All this looks good to outside investors who realise immediately that, in Malaysia, everyone is, or wants to be, a silver spoon capitalist.

Malay Business Culture: Getting It Wrong

All these traits provide, as it were, the raw material that will continue to make Malaysia a growth economy. But many 'buts' still obtrude, throwing up uncertainties in the coming years. Many of these, in one way or another, turn on the tricky question of Malaysia's (and Brunei's) business culture. Many result also from fundamental changes in world demand and in the technology of industrial production.

The old American rejoinder to a 'know-it-all' used to be, 'if yore so smart, why ain't you rich?' The question is worth directing at Malaysia, but in reverse form: If yore so rich, why ain't you smart? The question arises *because* of, not instead of, the phenomenal growth of this middling sized, resource-rich country. Given the litany of patrimonial business habits above, a conclusion that the extraordinary growth has *not* yielded a corresponding rise in business opportunities seems hard to avoid.

A Merrill Lynch special report on the Malaysian economy in 1988 set out the problem areas. What would happen to the NEP after 1990? it asked. What could be done about 'the government's overextended and inefficient intervention in business'? Given that 'bad debts, losses at cooperatives and even some bank runs in 1986 exposed the fragility of the financial system,' could Bank Negara prevent a repetition of banking mismanagement and greed?

Some constraints are unavoidable, as a *Business International* report on Malaysia's business 'Operating Environment' noted in the mid-1980s. The 'relative cost structure of Malaysia is high,' it said. 'Technical and managerial talent is relatively scarce,' while the 'potential of using Malaysia as an export base [to Asean] seems to be diminishing as each country erects further barriers.' Finally, Malaysia's 'small domestic market does not offer economies of scale.'

Yet the biggest question mark hangs over Malaysia's politics. 'Political uncertainty is the single largest risk to sustained economic recovery,' Merrill Lynch advised, saying that 'prolonged infighting [within UMNO] . . . could dampen the recovery and damage the country's long-term political stability and policy predictability.' Since April 1987, UMNO has been consumed by a bitter power struggle pitting Razaleigh and Musa against Mahathir in an often puzzling *ménage à trois*.

The New York firm said that 'conflict between the administration and judiciary also poses concern as it disrupts the country's legal infrastructure and could even jeopardise normal commercial operations.' Indeed the turnaround might have been stronger 'had a more stable political environment been maintained,' the New York analysts suggest, a conclusion difficult to dispute.

Longer-term Problems

Yet other problems bedevil a really sustained recovery, prompting many forecasters to see in the 1988 recovery little more than a repeat of the 1984 commodity boomlet that falsely lifted hopes before dashing them down again. One must be cautious; Harvard economist Joseph Stern remarked several years ago that 'a study of Malaysia's economic fortunes over the past two decades reveals as much about the prognosticating abilities of economists [and still more about journalists!] as it does about the possibility of encouraging rapid growth through sound policies.' At the onset of the 1970s, few economists had much hope. None expected the 9 to 10 per cent annual growth rates that occurred during the following ten years.

But caution cuts both ways. As Stern himself noted in 1984, 'deepening the industrial structure and creating complementarities and links between industries, and between the manufacturing sector and the rest of the economy, is a long-run process and a major challenge for the decade ahead.' What then has occurred?

Malaysia's leaders often boast about the growing component of export sales made up of manufactured items. This has some validity, but should not blind us from noting how electronic components – which are, after all designed by others – now account for over half this total. Surely this must be a narrow and vulnerable base for future prosperity. This makes Malaysia's position as the world's third largest exporter of semiconductors a somewhat hollow achievement; semiconductors account for 90 per cent of total Malaysian electronic exports. One in every four Malaysian workers depends on this notoriously footloose industry.

Moreover, the turnaround in investment after 1987 comes almost entirely from foreigners. Local sentiment remains doubtful. The deregulation efforts, the higher capital limits and other guidelines benefit foreigners. The government-led, yen-indebted heavy industry programme remains inefficient and now uses obsolete motor car assembly and steel-making equipment bought from Japanese suppliers. Throughout Malaysia there are serious shortages of technician-level workers plus a huge supply of politically volatile but unemployed university graduates – a problem discussed below. Unemployment remains high, by Malaysian standards, at 10 per cent in 1989.

Although much discussed, the plans to add value to indigenous raw materials have come only a little way. 'In spite of all our talk about resource-based industry, progress towards value-added has been minimal in the last decade,' a senior timber official admitted in a 1988 article in *South* magazine. For example, Malaysia buys back its rubber wood, sold in bulk to Korea, as 'Japanese pine' furniture. Only 5 per cent of annual timber production ends up as mouldings, joinery or furniture.

Much of the longer term bad news for the region's commodity producers is discussed in Chapter 8. But Malaysia's particular problems, given that it has been rescued from its own mismanagement yet again by rising commodity prices after 1987, strike an especially troubling note.

Plantations remain one of the country's and Southeast Asia's best run industries. They have saved the country's economic neck after 1987; palm oil prices rose 30 per cent again during 1988 and rubber increased 20 per cent during the first quarter of 1988. But they are now being squeezed by labour shortages, diminishing land supplies and rising competitiveness and supply both internationally and in the region. Indonesia in particular is undercutting Malaysia with cheaper labour and newer plantation tree stocks. Illegal Indonesian immigrants help fill the gap – but also add to inter-communal tensions. Moreover, just as the general rise in 1989 of world metal prices is finally lifting tin out of the doldrums, land and labour costs are hurting badly.

Yet the issue keeps returning to what the Merrill Lynch analysts (to take just one of many foreign investment analysts' reports) describe as 'rent-seeking philosophy.' This is the reality behind the superficially rosy data from the latest whirl of the business cycle.

Brunei's citizens live in their authoritarian, cradle-to-grave Shell-fare state ruled by a pleasure-loving lightweight. It is, ultimately, a passive economy where entrepreneurs often take no-risk free rides. Within Malaysia's UMNO and the twelve racially based parties joining it in government, political patronage via directly-owned holding companies has played a major role. These firms, in turn, control banks, publishing, industries, mines and plantations. Beyond these mechanisms the newly monied Malays staff the NEP's trustee companies, government corporations and the firms cashing in on newly 'privatised' functions of government, such as telecommunications.

Why must Malaysia, perhaps the luckiest among all the region's countries, suffer this chronic cycle of boom-and-bust, of gathering tension and then, in reply, of authoritarian simple-mindedness? Partly because it cannot escape the commodity trap. Perhaps also, it is because this country, alone among its neighbours, has staked its continued cohesion, even its survival, on one implicit premiss: that non-Malay Malaysians will subordinate everything, and suffer almost anything, in the hope of more wealth. History, culture, religion, language, education, nationalism, mythology or law: in Malaysia these different categories of social reality seem to *exacerbate* Malaysia's divisions rather than to soothe them. In other countries these various ideas, notions or disciplines serve to *unify* people living within a common territory.

The Religious Conundrum

Religion strikes an especially divisive note. Malaysia's constitution defines Malays as, among other things, people 'who embrace the Islamic faith.' This rigid identity of Malays-as-Muslims takes on an ominous element for non-Malays as the world-wide Islamic resurgence has filtered into Malaysia since the 1970s. These trends make a special impact in Malaysia because this extremely multiracial country has adopted one of the most self-consciously 'Islamic' tones of any Asian country in which sizeable Muslim populations dwell. (Besides Malaysia the list includes Bangladesh, Brunei, Burma, China, India, Indonesia, Pakistan, the Philippines and Thailand.)

Some signs are immediately apparent. Malay girls increasingly wear the *telukung*, a light headdress covering the hair. Until forbidden by the government, some women Civil Servants had begun to dress in the full black *purdah* covering all but the eyes.

At another level, *dakwah* or Islamic missionary groups have formed communes. One of these, the Darul Arqam, runs a collective farm near Kuala Lumpur where 'members wear robes and veils of Arabic style dress and try to emulate the life of the Prophet', according to Kamal Hassan, a dean at Malaysia's new International Islamic University. In addition various Malaysian states have strengthened religious departments of their respective governments to enforce rules against *kalwat*, or 'prohibited intimate proximity'.

This results in religious law arrests of adulterers, 'common law' couples and youngsters experimenting with premarital sex. Muslim widows cohabiting with non-Muslim men also face arrest and interrogation. When visiting Malaysia, the writer V. S. Naipal described this trend as leaning towards a 'theocracy', although he omitted to note that Malaysia's majority non-Muslims are exempt from these severe strictures.

The Islamic phenomenon has many causes: the close identity of Malay nationalism with Islam; a reaction to Western values inherent in modernisation; a genuine resurgence of religious sentiment and even a deliberate attempt by UMNO's leadership to head off more extreme Islamic movements. The effect on business is predominantly negative. Non-Malays and foreign investors find the atmosphere less congenial – one of many reasons why investment has flowed south to Singapore or north to Bangkok.

The Educational Time Bomb

Malaysia's prosperity rides not only on resources but also on an adaptable workforce that, whatever the ethnic background, prizes educational achievement. Beginning after Independence and accelerating after 1969, the government has allocated 25–30 per cent of annual spending for education. In addition to keeping six universities, with many branch campuses around the country, Malaysians remit hundreds of millions of US dollars a year to support education abroad for the non-Malays excluded from the de facto quota system favouring *bumiputra*s. By the end of the 1980s, at least 35,000 Malaysians, nearly all Chinese, were studying in the US. Tens of thousands more had found places in Australian, British, Canadian and New Zealand universities.

Of all the simmering issues in Malaysia, none has more conflagratory potential than education. Non-Malay parents resent the Malay-language medium of instruction in secondary schools. By the late 1980s the educational problem, intertwined with high levels of graduate unemployment, had become acute: Malay graduates, accustomed to jobs for life in the government, are not able to find places in private business.

The most complete expression of this close identity between politics, race and commerce lies in the New Economic Policy, which has created enormously powerful trustee agencies spearheading the move to win a bigger share of the corporate pie for *bumiputras*. But the net effect of these moves was to retard the marketplace rather than expand it. Many feudal tendencies are reinforced despite the apparent transition to Western-style corporate management practices. And something like the NEP will remain in place after 1990, continuing its mischief whatever the government's choice of names or labels.

These are the thoughts that come to mind when looking at Kuala Lumpur today, the glass and steel nemesis of a tropical stasis lasting tens of millions of years. They surface again when contemplating Sultan Hassanal in his postage-stamp state. 'When the Sultan puts aside his pleasures, the prevention of a revolution is his main work,' James Bartholomew notes. 'Around him in the Far East he can see worrying precedents for struggles against one-man rule . . . the poorer people of Brunei and some of the better educated might one day find the sight of the élite feathering their own nests too repulsive to bear.'

Ruminating About the Malay Malaise

Botanists say that what is left of Malaysia's rainforest looks much as it did millions of years ago. A few of them even claim that the enormous Dipterocarps and other hardwoods surviving in mountainous pockets amid logged-out devastation comprise the world's oldest continually standing forest. Off the infrequent trails, a vertically defined leafy space closes in. The tallest trees, some measuring 150 feet, stand as sentinels of a lost age. At certain moments, especially in late afternoon, it is not difficult to sense a normally unimaginable length of time.

But this time-out-of-time abruptly vanished a hundred years ago. In Southeast Asia's first rush to wealth, Chinese miners pushed their way into this verdant, steamy retreat looking for tin in the 1870s. They stopped at a confluence of two big brown streams carrying the unappetising name 'Muddy Estuary', for that is what Kuala Lumpur meant in the local Malay dialect.

Within a year most had died from malaria-carrying mosquitoes which bred in stagnant ponds left behind by the mining. Needless to say, this concerned the financiers behind the venture hardly at all. The gamble had paid off, and Malaysia's tin production therefore took stratospheric leaps, riding on price movements following the same trajectory.

In the infinitely more complex rush to riches during the past two decades, 'KL', as the capital is affectionately known, has continued to grow out and up. Until the mid-1960s the town looked pretty much what it was – an administrative centre for a British-devised union of petty principalities. But the new national rulers wanted instant grandeur, a trend reaching its zenith in the 1980s. This rather unprepossessing colonial town watched, thunderstruck, as almost overnight orange-tiled Chinese shophouses and thatched Malay kampong houses were demolished, to make way for the high-rise buildings now soaring into the humid air.

It has all happened very quickly, as any visitor immediately notices. From vantage points within the forests now in undisguised retreat across the length of the peninsula, Kuala Lumpur seems a vision of a high-tech tomorrow. Dominating the Barisan Mountains overlooking Kuala Laumpur is Tan Koon Swan's casino, whose varied complexes, gorgeously lit at night, provide a phantasmagorical interplay of whites, reds and golds as the colours diffuse in encroaching clouds that obscure the capital's concrete needles below, lancing into the sky.

Genting Highlands, as the casino is called, rests on a stack of concrete terraces and is topped by a huge, circular electric sign. In many ways Genting Highlands encapsulates the modern Malaysian experience, especially the gaudy dreams of immigrant Chinese whose relentless energy has made Malaysia so rich, so fast.

But what dreams, and what schemes! Genting comprises a 400-bedroom complex of hotels, a 'love lake' and deafening discos. These all perch within or beside a building the construction engineers said could never be built where the Chinese entrepreneur, Lim Goh Tong, wanted it to rise: on top of a mountain. Engineers were worried about surveying, let alone building, an all-weather road. The legend describes Lim elbowing aside the driver of a bulldozer and lowering the blade himself. Up he went, into the forested inclines.

Lim made his road. He an various politicians or royalty backing him got rich. No matter that the monsoon rainwater cascades down the improbable angles, millions of swift rivulets eroding the land. For me, Genting Highlands best symbolises the peculiarly Malaysian greed and determination to strike it rich, gambling against terrain and weather to build a gambler's haven.

References

Bartholomew, J. (1989) *The Richest Man in the World: the Sultan of Brunei*. New York and London: Viking

Bowring, P. and Cottrell, R. (1984) *The Carrian File*. Hong Kong: Review Publications

Mahathir bin Mohamed (1970) *The Malay Dilemma*. Kuala Lumpur: Federal Publications

Mehmet, O. (1986) *Development in Malaysia: Poverty, Wealth and Trusteeship*. London: Croom Helm

Muzaffar, C. (1979) *Protector?* Penang: Aliran Publications

Stern, J. J. (1984) 'Malaysia: growth and structural change', background paper for a conference on the Malaysian economy. Fletcher School of Law and Diplomacy, Tufts University, Medford, Massachusetts. Unpublished

4

ABRI-CULTURE: DUAL FUNCTIONEERING IN INDONESIA

Number Games

Indonesians, particularly the majority Javanese, have a love of symbolic anniversaries. By the end of the 1980s they (and foreign investors) were indulging heavily in the pastime.

Five years earlier, in 1985, forty years of Indonesian independence had been concluded. Those four decades had also complemented eight *windu*s, the five-year period unique to the Javanese (and Balinese) calendar. In Java's complex culture, the passage of eight *windu*s marks the entry into life's most mature and fulfilling period, a time of measured steadiness and quiet achievement. As for a person, so for a nation, the Javanese reason.

Indonesia's mid-decade point in the 1980s also closed another epoch, this one the conclusion of a twenty-year span of commercial revival after the economic collapse of 1965. The first era of independence, from 1945 to 1965, carries the name Orde Lama, the 'Old Order', while the business and political arrangements in place since then are summed up by the words Orde Baru, the 'New Order'.

Older Indonesians have bad memories of the Old Order. They remember the charismatic but chaotic leadership of Indonesia's first president, Ahmad Sukarno, and they compare the economic disorder of that time with the more substantive, if less exciting, New Order stewardship by General Suharto (Javanese Indonesians often have only one name). Indonesia is thus one of the very few countries to have had just two heads of government since the Second World War. This, by itself, is suggestive of bedrock stability and broad consensus.

Ever since Sukarno was manoeuvred into signing an order transferring executive authority to Suharto in 1966, the same regime has stayed firmly in the saddle. Suharto won a fifth five-year presidential term, indirectly elected by his compliant national congress in March 1988. His principal claim to continued stewardship rests, in his own eyes and in the government's propaganda, on the successful economic transformation of Indonesia since 1965.

New Order, Old Habits

The tumultuous events of 1965 occurred a quarter of a century ago. Yet within Indonesia, Southeast Asia's demographic and geographic giant, the 1990s promise more uncertainty than steadiness. Instead of a widening, deepening economy, feudal habits still weigh heavily on the country's commerce. These habits range from the grip of presidential family monopolies, at the highest level, to obstruction by petty officialdom at the lowest.

Indonesia remains a business and commercial paradox in the region. No other country has anything like the resources and potential of this archipelago of thirteen thousand islands. Yet no other Asean economy is performing, at the onset of the 1990s, more poorly than Indonesia's. Far from economic maturity, the achievement of eight *windu*s may signal mid-life crisis.

For this most populous Asean nation, the 1990s promise not continuity but transition – from one élite to another, and from tired policies of export-led growth to other, as yet unknown approaches. The coming years also portend a shift away from the corrupting dependency on oil earnings and growing demands for a freer, broader and more participatory economy. More than any other factor, the tendency towards bureaucratic control has led to a top-heavy business environment in Indonesia. Technocratic 'fine-tuning', including three large devaluations in less than ten years, has added to the chronic uncertainties caused by conflicting directives, decrees and monopolies.

The Old Order's rhetoric stressed nationalisation and socialist regulation without fiscal discipline. 'I'm not an economist,' Sukarno used to boast, 'I'm a revolutionary.' The resulting fiasco ruined Indonesian business confidence for the better part of a decade. By contrast, the New Order's promise of market-led growth and reform began bravely – yet it has foundered on feudal commercial habits reaching into the highest levels of government. In the 1990s, there is a risk that popular reaction against the commerce of business favouritism could throw Indonesia back to Sukarno-style bureaucratic socialism. This would be a pity: broadly-based, market capitalism has never had a fair go in Indonesia.

The stakes are high. As Southeast Asian scholar Milton Osborne observes (1983), 'the fact that Indonesia's population exceeds 165 million may be well known. But how often is this fact recognised as meaning Indonesia has the *fifth* largest population in the world?' Since he wrote those words at the beginning of the 1980s, demographers reckoned the population had marched well past 175 millions by 1989.

The Archipelagic Reach

Indonesia's size is often forgotten. Its reach exceeds the distance from California to Florida or from Ireland to eastern Turkey. Because Jakarta claims all the water enclosed by a line connecting its furthermost islands, the country's territory embraces 5 million square kilometres – an area one-fifth larger than the United States. Only China, India, the Soviet Union and the United States have larger populations than Indonesia, within whose boundaries lie five of the world's ten largest islands.

In a mere eight *windu*s, not only are the territorial integrity and unity of Indonesia an accepted fact, but the struggle to make these isles and peoples genuinely *Indonesian* has also been won. (The name 'Indonesia' is an invention of nineteenth-century anthropologists and, later, of the anti-colonial struggle. Similarly, the term 'Southeast Asia' is an invention of the Allied Powers' strategic planning advisers during the Second World War.)

The sense of Indonesia as a potential economic giant is shared by most outsiders. From embassies in Jakarta, all the major powers except China (evicted after 1966) monitor business and economic trends in this third point of a triangle joining the numerically largest Asian countries – China, India and Indonesia. Investment and aid totalling billions of dollars pour into Indonesia each year from a consortium that includes the United States, Japan and the World Bank. All donors are mindful of Indonesia's pivotal position between South and East Asia at the juncture of the Pacific and Indian oceans.

Human numbers, strategic waterways, and geopolitics provide only part of the explanation for Indonesia's importance. The other factor is oil: Indonesia's low-sulphur, 'sweet' crude crowns a list of commodity earners including tin, nickel, coal, rubber, palm oil, tea, spices, sugar, coffee and other plantation crops. This spread of natural resources wealth lured Japan into the 1941–45 war. Today it lures different legionnaires from the same country – hundreds of Japanese firms have joined Indonesian bureaucrats and local Chinese businessmen in joint venture businesses. Apart from the petroleum industry, where American corporations reign supreme, the Japanese are the most significant foreign investors in Indonesia.

The Curse of Oil

First drilled in major quantities in the 1920s by Royal Dutch Shell (which still has residual interests in Indonesia), the Sumatran oil fields were a major target of the Japanese in 1941. Today the Minas field near Pekan Baru produces half the country's oil revenue; visitors walk up and touch the main pipeline, which has a diameter of over ten feet. Underneath the metal skin they can feel half the country's export earnings slithering through towards the waiting tankers.

After two global price increases in the 1970s, oil made Indonesia (and many in the Suharto government) stupendously wealthy. Yet the energy resource proved, as elsewhere in the world, both boon and burden, an easy corruptor and spawner of grandiose visions.

These effects first became embarrassingly apparent in the vainglory of the state-owned oil company, Pertamina, during the 1970s. Cattle farms, high-rise buildings, shipyards, refineries, petrol tankers, housing estates and plantations formed just part of Pertamina's swollen empire. Most stumbled into bankruptcy as the profligacy of its chairman, General Ibnu Sutowo, became known to foreign bankers, who anxiously called in their loans during 1975. This precipitated Southeast Asia's first debt scandal of global concern. It was a type of fiscal run; more debt worries were to come to Asean during the 1980s (see Chapter 8).

In the nexus between Indonesian business and power, the crucial patronage issues swivel on a viscous pivot of oil. Although producing less than 3 per cent of the world's total oil supply in 1989, Indonesia remains Asean's largest petroleum producer. It is also the only regional member of OPEC, the Organisation of Petroleum Exporting Countries. Jakarta's decisions to build 'downstream capacity' in the oil industry (that is, to invest in plants using petroleum as a raw material) have added methanol, petrochemical and fertiliser plants to the country's industrial armoury.

If the 1970s were a time of twice blessed boom, the 1980s brought a lessening of the flow. For Indonesia, membership of OPEC has become less of a privilege, more of a burden. OPEC strategies have forced hard decisions on cutting prices and production. During 1985 and 1986, the cartel decided first to reduce production quotas and then, when this failed to halt the oil price erosion, to defend each OPEC country's market share. The upshot for Indonesia was an abrupt switch back to full production policies and generous exploration incentives to foreign companies.

This also failed. OPEC then opted again for production restraint albeit on steadily leaner quotas. Indonesia's daily production dropped from 1.5 million barrels per day (bpd) to 1.44 million bpd, and then down again to 1.19 million bpd. Pertamina meanwhile dreamed up monthly price fixing systems and tried, via the announcement of large but erratic discounts, to attract spot market buyers (the spot market is a 'pick-up' market of oil that is not tied to supply contracts). Neighbouring Malaysia, also an oil producer, cheerfully pumped away, oblivious of OPEC (and Indonesian) entreaties.

General Abdul Rachman Ramly became Pertamina's president in 1984. Thereafter the military-dominated oil monopoly strove to improve ties with the big foreign oil companies, which have production sharing agreements with Pertamina. The Indonesians depend on foreign drilling skills and exploration technology to keep up production, but new fields opening up elsewhere in Asia (in China, Vietnam and Thailand) now threaten Indonesian supremacy in oil production. Though both output and prices fell during most of the 1980s, the American firm Caltex (a joint venture between the Chevron and Texaco corporations) gains half its profits from Indonesian drilling. The largest natural gas producer in Indonesia, Mobil Oil, also derives two-fifths of its global, after-tax profits from Indonesia.

Khaki Commerce

No account of the influence of oil on Indonesian business can ignore the symbiosis between the resource itself, and its military custodians. There has been a long immersion by the brass in the black gold.

The army's grip on petroleum and other areas of Indonesian business life dates from the Indonesian Republic's violent creation after 1945. The struggle against Dutch rule spawned an officer corps drawn from families of rich peasants and petty clerks. After Independence, there were many opportunities to improve their material situation. Despite growing professionalism in more recent years, the Armed Forces of the Republic of Indonesia (popularly known by their Indonesian language acronym Abri) remain enamoured of an elastic, and corrupting concept.

This notion is called *dwi fungsi*, Indonesian for 'dual function'. The dual function legitimises military penetration of business affairs by claiming for Abri a second function besides its traditional role of military guardian. The second, extra function is an activist role in society, that guarantees national stability and resilience. The upshot is a pervasive, and largely extractive, military presence in commercial life.

The Indonesian armed forces are not alone in their commercial zeal. Most senior soldiers in the Asean countries dabble in business, notably the Thais and Filipinos. Moreover, senior officers move regularly into top government positions; in 1988 alone, Abri's former chief of staff General Benny Murdani became Indonesia's defence minister. In that year, the Filipino and Thai chiefs of staff were appointed to the same position in their countries. Soldierly influence appears in the most unlikely places in Asean; Lee Hsien Loong, Singapore prime minister Lee Kuan Yew's son, remains also a reserve brigadier-general and was the army's second-in-command before entering parliament.

Indonesia takes this 'normal', military influence several steps further. Abri differs from other Southeast Asian armies in one key respect: none other claims rights of paternity over the state it protects. Not only do Indonesia's soldiers regard their commercial and political ascendancy as inseparable from the maintenance of national security, but they also see the state as their own, exclusive *creation*. That paternal claim, though accurate, gives a special flavour to Indonesian commerce.

Dwi fungsi also manifests itself in other ways. For example, the Dewan Perwakilan Rakyat, Indonesia's tame parliament, sets aside one hundred seats for the military. Soldiers fill a large number of public company directorships, cabinet jobs and key industrial positions. Most of the twenty-seven provincial governors are Abri appointees. At the next level down of the civilian administration, soldiers have filled as many as two-thirds of the Kebupatan (district chief) slots. The next layer, the Kecapatan, and the next below that and the next, are also staffed frequently by lower-ranking Abri men.

Thus, *dwi fungsi* forcefully backs up this soldierly preponderance in business and politics. Outsiders often imagine that Indonesia's 'khaki commerce' only began after 1965. Yet dual functioneering has a long pedigree in this country. During the 1950s, the military split over the usefulness of the Western professional model; those officers savouring direct involvement in the economy won the day.

Their meddlesome doctrine, the so-called 'middle way', now seems a model of self-restraint by comparison with Abri's later commercial entanglements. In Sukarno's 'Guided Democracy' period, from 1957 to 1965, Abri also explicitly became one of three pillars underpinning the state. (The other two were the communist and nationalist parties, the Partai Kommunist Indonesia and the Partai Nasional Indonesia, respectively. After 1965, the communists were physically eliminated and the nationalists confined to an emasculated role.)

Dual-functioneering became a bedrock norm after Sukarno's departure. One immediate result was a tightening of a grid-lock of Abri commands blanketing the archipelago. An alphabet soup of acronyms, 'Kodims', 'Korems' and 'Kodams', denotes each link of a chain of territorial commands. Parallel to, but ascendant over, the civilian apparatus (in which Abri is well represented), these hierarchical commands reinforce an extraordinarily pervasive military influence.

This is what *dwi fungsi* means in everyday life to most Indonesians. No wonder a perennial joke describes a polite Javanese who, standing in an overcrowded bus, spends ten minutes carefully questioning his neighbour. Only when completely satisfied that the man standing next to him has absolutely no family or business connections to Abri does he ask him . . . to get off his foot.

Some 'standing on feet' was probably necessary to regain economic growth after 1965. It required discipline imposed by a viable national institution to bring down inflation, then roaring at 600 per cent per annum. Someone with authority had to restore elementary communications and reimpose elementary civil peace (many hundreds of thousands of people perished in communal disorders during 1965 and 1966). For many years Abri remained the only force able to guarantee basic order, without which any economic growth is inconceivable.

Is dual functioneering still necessary? The answer to that deceptively simple question will consume Indonesian politics for the remainder of this century and into the next. The question is becoming acute as the end of President Suharto's tenure approaches, most probably at the conclusion of his term in 1993. But dislodging the generals will not come easily.

The military always cautions that Indonesia's commercial and social fabric is flimsy, and easily torn. This caveat sits uneasily beside boasts, in the next breath, about a resilient pluralism. The country's motto, the old Javanese words *'Bhinneka Tunggal Ika'*, is an Asian variant of *E pluribus unum* ('Unity in diversity'). A 'soft' pluralism, of ethnic dances or complex land tenure, causes little anxiety. A robust business and political pluralism is quite another matter, however. Real pluralism would require the military to get out of the way, in both a commercial and political sense.

Technocratic Influence

Yet this is not a jack-booted regime. Since 1967 Suharto and his generals have tried to wear softer shoes away from the parade ground. They brought civilian economists into the government, even if (or precisely because) they have no mass appeal and no independent power base.

These American-educated 'technocrats', a tight-knit group once called the 'Berkeley Mafia' (now a somewhat shopworn tag), frequently make timely interventions with Suharto. They have designed the inflation-beating discipline of the early New Order and created the foreign investment rules that delivered strong growth during the 1970s and early 1980s. Even after 1983, when oil prices dropped sharply, they persuaded Suharto to trim government spending promptly. They have even battled behind the scenes for less nepotism by the presidential family in commercial affairs, although there is a limit as to how far they can interfere. They sensibly shy away from nosing into the key patronage decisions that Abri regards as in-house affairs.

Most Indonesians acknowledge that the army is now changing. They speak ponderously about 'generational transitions', and they are right, up to a point. Suharto, Sudharmono (his vice-president since 1988) and a few others still belong to the '1945 Generation', the men who comprised the improvised army that fought the Dutch. But these veterans form a dwindling band.

After independence was secured, in 1949, Abri accepted no new officers until 1960. In that year, the first graduates emerged from a newly opened academy in Magelang, East Java. They now carry the tag, 'Magelang Generation', and they have been moving into top command positions in recent years. Expressing more wish-fulfilment than certainty, Jakarta's business analysts forsee a gradual retreat by Abri, out of commerce and back to the barracks. Two laws, passed in February 1988 and aimed at inculcating 'soldiership', are cited as evidence of the new mood. Another encouraging sign was the emphasis on professionalism during former Abri chief of staff Murdani's reorganisation of 1983.

Yet all this could be whistling in the dark. Murdani's successor, General Try Soetrisno, has a robust, dual-functioneering reputation. Much of the most open criticism of excessive military involvement in business comes not from the Magelang Generation, but from Suharto's old 1945 Generation comrades.

In 1988, a former Abri deputy commander, General Soemitro, urged more 'openness – so there can be competition among future generations to allow them to rise to the surface.' Another old-timer, General Syamsuddin, accused the government of corruption in the same year, launching his attacks from an unlikely redoubt – his Abri-reserved seat in parliament. Similar noises are coming from General Rajaguguh, a former commander of a staff officer school in West Java. Seminars there during 1987 explored, ever so gently, the limits to the dual-functioneering future.

Despite such intriguing signs, the old meddlesome business habits continue. The more convincing signs of the military mood come in different guises. One was the closure, in 1987, of Jakarta newspapers reporting the business links of Suharto's family. Another was the gaoling, in the same year, of Suharto's fellow 1945 Generation colleague, General Dharsono. A former Secretary-General of Asean, Dharsono was convicted of helping to incite a riot in the Jakarta port area in 1984.

More generally, military-linked companies still prosper from their privileged access to government licences, contracts and concessions while mostly avoiding tax liability altogether. It is hard to give up that life style. The officers controlling such agencies as Pertamina, or Bulog, a monopoly rice distribution organisation, remain close to Suharto. Searingly candid (and confidential) reports by the World Bank, such as an assessment of the military-run Bapindo (Indonesian Development Bank), excite little controversy (see Chapter 10 for details). None the less there is some cause for optimism. Indonesia's generals do not yet form a military caste or *junker*dom on the Prussian model. The army's guerrilla origins still tug at Abri heartstrings.

The strongest argument against khaki commerce may simply be that it has not worked, let alone worked well. The military-dominated industries are anything but models of productivity. At another level, justifications for a strong, military-dominated state since 1965 depend on a claimed need for discipline while the country is integrated into the world economy. Until comparisons with the industrially successful South Koreans became too invidious, that country (where a military-dominated system was consolidated after 1961) was often held out by dual-functionaries as an example to follow. Indonesia lags far behind the South Korean (and most other East Asian) experience with industrialisation.

There is little evidence however that Abri's commercial zeal is loosening, or that market forces are now permeating an economy cluttered by formal, and informal monopolies and by various areas of enterprise off-limits to other entrepreneurs by reason of cosy favouritism and mutual back-scratching. Recent signs seem to point the other way: the Magelang Generation is becoming, so reports claim, irretrievably enamoured of the perquisites bestowed by dual functioneering. After two-and-a-half decades of Suharto's New Order, it still strains belief that the president's successor will be anyone other than a general.

This is where the difference with Indonesia's Asean neighbours becomes most pronounced. In recent years, even Thailand's military has broadened its reach into popular, electoral politics, relying on a decree ordering mass mobilisation 'in support of democracy'. Suchit Bunbongkarn, an authority on the military at Bangkok's Chulalongkorn University, thinks this has happened because the military must now begin to react to other power bases besides its own.

Indonesia is nowhere close to this pluralism. After 1965, Abri's theoreticians, notably the late General Ali Moertopo, coined the concept of the 'floating mass'. After banishing the old political parties, Moertopo wanted the mass of Indonesians simply to 'float' between carefully stage-managed elections. Abri's command structure backs up Moertopo's ideas. There is almost no sign that that system will change much, or soon, at provincial and local levels. It is rather like a lobotomy: the economic body, vastly more robust since 1965, carries an empty political mind.

Cukong Friends

There is another reason why the retired military men staffing government companies show little interest in trimming back Abri's extra, lucrative function. Dismantling the monopoly structures would harm the interests of people other than themselves. Dating back to the early years of independence, the military has built up a pattern of mostly secretive dealings with local Chinese financiers. In popular shorthand, these Chinese financiers and middlemen, business partners and cronies carry the name *cukong*.

The *cukong* phenomenon mirrors the Ali-Baba system in Malaysia (see Chapter 3). It is pervasive in Indonesia, owing to the financial prowess of the relatively small (and therefore vulnerable) Indonesian Chinese community. Most estimates put Chinese numbers at about only 3 million, under 2 per cent of the total population. Chinese traders and financiers are considered fair game by most government officials and local military men; the Chinese, in turn, seek arrangements through which they can purchase protection in exchange for business opportunity. There is much denial involved; the government is ostensibly devoted to promoting the interests of the so-called *golongan ekonomi lemah*, the 'weak economic groups'. This means, in practice, that *pribumi* or 'native' businessmen, as opposed to the Chinese, are meant to be favoured by government programmes.

Starting with Indonesia's most prominent *cukong* connection, it is well known that the Suharto family's longest-standing Chinese business associate is Liem Sioe Liong, now one of the world's richest men. (For an account of Liem's pre-eminent position among the overseas Chinese in Southeast Asia, see Chapter 7.)

Liem, who also uses an adopted Indonesian name 'Sudono Salim', first befriended Suharto when the rising young Javanese commander was in charge of the Diponegoro Division, one of Abri's three most important divisions. Liem sought, and obtained, various monopolies after Suharto became president, including an exclusive grip on the vital flour and clove import businesses (Indonesian cigarette manufacturers use more cloves than the country can grow).

Today the Liem Group probably makes its creator the second richest man in Southeast Asia, if not the world. The richest, by common consent, is the ruler of Southeast Asia's most diminutive country, Sultan Hassanal Bolkiah of Brunei (see Chapter 3). Liem's group includes such stellar names as Metropolitan, Bogasari Mills (the flour monopolist), Indocement (the largest cement plant in Asia) and the textile maker Tarumatex. The group also controls First Pacific (a Hong Kong-based financial holding company), Indosteel (the largest steel complex in Southeast Asia), Indomobil Utama (which assembles and markets Suzuki cars), Sinar Mas Inti Perkasa (a food oil distributor) and the Bank Central Asia (Indonesia's biggest private bank).

The First Family

Assisted by friends such as Liem, the Suharto extended family has become a major force in key areas of the economy. It is instructive to list some of the publicly known business and pedigree political connections.

Suharto's half-brother, Probosutedjo, runs the Mertju Buana group. Probosutedjo also participates in Liem's clove import monopoly and holds supply contracts to Pertamina. When asked about these business favours, Probosutedjo justifies his interests by citing the government's promotion of *pribumi*s, an echo of similar justifications of *bumiputra* favouritism in Malaysia (see Chapter 3).

Sudwikatmono, the foster brother of the president's wife, Mrs Tien Suharto, has a share of Liem's flour and cement monopolies. He also has his own independent stable of companies however, the Subentra Group. When the cement business nose-dived after 1985, the government extended credits worth US$360 million to Liem's group. Liem's competitors were left to sink or swim, without a government credit-line.

Bernard Ibnu Hardjojo, Mrs Suharto's brother, runs the Gunung Ngadeg Jaya Group, which has interests in timber extraction and import licensing. Hardjojo has also become an important partner in a joint cement producing venture with Japanese interests. He is known to be close to another Indonesian Chinese businessman, Bob Hasan. Together they have built up a firm called PT Posopati.

Each of Suharto's three sons (he has six children) also has business interests of the familiar, Southeast Asia duppy variety. The youngest son, Hutomo Mandala ('Tomy') Putra, controls a trading company named PT Humpus. This firm received an exclusive right to market methanol and various acids produced by Pertamina. Reports described Pertamina's 1985 award of the franchise to Tomy as a 'graduation present'.

The president's middle son, Bambang Trihatmodjo, has strong business connections with his brother-in-law, Indra Rukmana Kowara. Together they have created Bimantara, a large holding company controlling over thirty firms that transport liquid gas, make chemicals and ship inter-island cargoes. Indra married a Suharto daughter and comes from a family of *pribumi* entrepreneurs. His father, Eddi Kowara, owns the large construction company PT Teknik Umum; with the Suharto link the company has prospered still further.

Much of the Suharto family business is reported to lie within the Bimantara Group. The group's major money-earners are Trikora Shipping Lines, the airfreight business of Jasa Angkasa Semesta plus various charter helicopter and airport terminal services. Petroleum trading also generates a lot of family cash; the Bimantara Group includes Mindo Citra Upaya Duta and Samudra Petrindo Asia, two major intermediaries in the buying and selling of Pertamina's oil for the US and European markets.

The Bimantara Group has also won control over large construction jobs, such as building the enormous Dumai refinery in Sumatra. The group has also appeared in major telecommunications refurbishing contracts for the government, and in building power stations (see Table 1). Paul Handley of the *Far Eastern Economic Review* reported in 1986 that a Probosutedjo-linked company, Mercu Buana

Raya, had won two major parts of a US$700 million hydroelectric project via subcontracting jobs awarded by a French firm. Bambang and other family relations reportedly also hold a one-third share of Liem's Bank Central Asia.

Suharto's oldest son, Sigid Harjojudanto, also participates in business with Bob Hasan. This includes such industries as the manufacture of tin plate, provisioning offshore oil exploration firms and the establishment of car assembly operations in joint ventures with Nissan Motors of Japan. Ten per cent of Liem's Sinar Mas Inti Perkasa Group is reported to belong to Sigid.

The president's wife, Tien Suharto (cruelly described as 'Madam Tien Per Cent' by regime critics), is often alleged to take too strong an interest in business. The family explains that she is merely adept at 'social fund raising'. Apologists for the regime noted that the First Lady oversees many charitable foundations. These often ask favours from the Chinese business community for her pet projects, one of which is a national lottery.

Table 1

MAIN OPERATING COMPANIES OF THE BIMANTARA GROUP

HOLDING AND INVESTMENT COMPANIES

Bimantara Citra (*Holding company*)
Bimantara Eka Sentosa (*Investments in Plaza Indonesia, Bali Hotel project and Mango Bazaar redevelopment*)

COMMUNICATIONS AND ELECTRONICS COMPANIES

Rajawali Citra Televisi Indonesia
(*Commercial television with Ometraco and BDNI*)
Cakra Nusa (*Telecommunications trading*)
Elektrindo Nusantara
(*Telecommunications equipment manufacturing*)
Settel Technologies (*US – Telecommunications research and investment*)

TRANSPORT AND RELATED SERVICES

Indonesia Air Transport (*Charter services*)
Jasindo Angkasa Semesta and Buana
(*Jakarta airport terminal and spare parts services*)
Handfast Forwarders (*Freight forwarding*)
Trikora Lloyd (*Shipping*)
Walindo Express (*Transport consulting*)

INSURANCE AND LEASING

Bimantara Graha Insurance Brokers (*with Frank B. Hall*)
Tugu Reinsurance (*Reinsurance brokers*)
Tugu Protama (*Insurance*)
Sana Permai (*Vehicle hire-purchase*)

These are only 35 out of 90 Bimantara companies.
SOURCE: *Far Eastern Economic Review* (March 1988)

PETROLEUM AND PLASTICS

Citra Gasindo Prakarsa (*Natural gas*)
Redeco Inti Oilin (*Chemicals trading*)
Redeco Petrolin Utama (*Tank farm*)
Panca Holdings (*HK – Plastics imports*)
Samudra Ferro Engineering (*Refinery engineering with Ferrostal Gmbh*)
Samudra Petrindo Asia (*Oil trading, LNG tanker*)
Permindo Oil Trading (*HK – Oil trading with Pertamina*)

AGRICULTURE AND FORESTRY

Confedd (*Feedmill with Ometraco Group*)
Prakarsa Indonesia Lima (*Palm Oil*)
Indonesia Timber Corp. (*Timber with Bob Hasan*)
Bumi Sumber Sari Sakti (*Palm oil*)

MANUFACTURING

Food Specialties Indonesia (*Milk powder with Nestlé*)
Gelantindo Mukti Graha and Kapsulindo
(*Gelatine capsules*)
Lima Satria Nirwana (*Daimler-Benz assembly*)
Montrose (*DDT plant*)
Indonesia Republic Motor (*Ford assembly*)
Vaksindo Satwa Utama Raya (*Animal vaccine*)
Polychem Lindo (*Magnetic tape*)
Sankyu Indonesia (*Engineering and fabrication*)
Daikin Clutch (*Automotive parts with Daikin Co.*)

The presidential family's influence has become an increasingly common topic of informed conversation although the public media shy away from too direct a reference. The rumour mills even linked one member of the family to a sensational case involving the murder of a Jakarta fashion model, shot at close range in a luxury car in September 1986.

During the 1970s, President Suharto delivered several spirited speeches defending his family against critics alleging business corruption in the First Family. The regime's ire became especially visible when the *Sydney Morning Herald* published an article in April 1986, a few weeks after Marcos had fled the Philippines, leaving behind a bankrupted exchequer. The article alleged the Suharto family had amassed a huge fortune while in power.

Hidden Costs of Business Favouritism

Indonesia's particular form of business culture is often described as having a 'drag effect' on the country's economic growth. Since 1982, Indonesia's growth rates have slowed, averaging 2.4 per cent a year. In this climate the 'overregulated nature of the economy' – elliptical World Bank phrasing for 'insider licensing and monopolies' – has attracted ever harsher criticism.

'What the . . . regulations, licensing and price controls really show', says Arief Budiman (1988), the influential, Harvard-educated chief economist of the Jakarta Centre for Policy Studies, 'is the existence of rent-seeking activities for the benefit of many individuals in the bureaucracy and their partners in the private sector.' Deregulation 'is an alternative Indonesia must take,' he adds. 'Further delay will only bring about worse economic conditions for the Indonesian population.'

The World Bank has been quietly sniping at these distortions for many years. The advice has become more spirited as Indonesia's foreign debt has grown; in January 1988 it reached US$42 billion. The Bank took an indirect line in its criticism. Nothing is inherently wrong about First Family entrepreneurship (indeed, Bambang is said to show particular business flair). What the Bank finds objectionable are the distorting effects on the economy from such large monopolies.

In successive confidential reports on Indonesia's economy, the World Bank has continued to hammer away, saying that import monopolies had 'substantially' raised the cost of imports. One item, tin-lined metal sheet used in the food canning industry, is priced so high that Indonesia has steadily lost markets abroad.

A prime example of this 'distortion' is a 1986 government decree that all plastics raw materials imported from abroad had to enter the country through Panca Holding Ltd, a Hong Kong firm registered originally in the South Pacific tax haven of Vanuatu. According to various foreign reports, Panca's board of directors included Sudwikatmono, Sigid and Bambang. Reports also claimed that Panca's duppying pads 15 per cent on top of the cost of making the final plastics product. No justification existed for the company.

Panca epitomises Southeast Asia's passive 'capitalism'. It collected a mark-up of 5 per cent on top of its middleman's import fee. It contributed nothing; neither bringing buyer and seller together nor rationalising distribution of plastics. In short, Panca was a business drone.

By 1988 the government had promised the World Bank that egregiously greedy drones like Panca would eventually disappear. Yet Panca provides only one example of presidential relations penetrating the lucrative world of business import monopolies, licensing arrangements and franchise dealerships, nearly all of it market-inhibiting clutter so characteristic of the Indonesian economy of the 1980s.

World Bank advisers, ever plentiful in their praise for the country's good macro-economic management, heard recurrent government promises that an attack on import monopolies was imminent. Implementation lagged far behind although an attempt had finally started in 1986 to 'deregulate' 165 separate import items. Even then the move spared the most profitable, crony-connected firms. Another spate of deregulation continued, freeing another 548 separate items by 1987, representing about three-fifths of the value of imports previously restricted.

The new decrees have met many obstacles, formal and informal. There were also many telling exceptions from the list. It was no accident that price slumps had affected many of the previously monopolised product lines. The exempted monopolies still have much clout, commercially and politically.

The exempted monopolies include cotton (a monopoly later abandoned in 1987), flour, steel and steel bars, machine parts, food products and ball-bearings. Many analysts saw Liem's hand behind many of the exceptions but the government denied any ulterior motive.

Nominally designed 'to achieve economies of scale' or to help importers compete in winning large, cut-rate contracts with overseas suppliers, the monopolies pad in extra costs for the Indonesian economy, now struggling in the post-oil era to compete in world markets. The effect of the fabricated steel monopolies on the construction industry overall can easily be imagined, for example.

An added twist to the plastics monopoly scandal is that Panca Holdings also usurped three other state monopolies given the trade in October 1984. After 1986 the three entities were forced to channel their business through Panca, the sole authorised purchaser. And, according to some reports, just to make sure that the cash flow continued smoothly, both Sudwikatmono and Liem made various direct approaches to plastics companies.

Plastics quickly became a favoured business in this nexus of high-level business and political connections. Liem joined Sudwikatmono and other Suharto relations in a joint venture with Japan's Asahi Glass. The purpose? To build a US$195 million plant making plastics. Bambang also took an interest in plastics, setting up PT Polychem Lindo, described by the *Asian Wall Street Journal* as the 'centrepiece of Bambang's diverse business empire'.

Although much monopoly control can be traced to high level contacts between *cukong*s and their government patrons, aristocratic business capital also plays a small role in Indonesia albeit on a much smaller scale than in Malaysia (see Chapter 3). In particular, the family of the late Sultan Hamengkubuwono of Yogyakarta retains extensive holdings in one of the biggest commercial banks, Bang Daging Nasional, and retains shares in companies owning hotels and shopping complexes.

Many voices however doubt the sincerity of the new-found interest in entrepreneurship and the free market. Australian economists Richard Robison and Garry Rodan say (1986):

> the sudden interest in market forces and privatisation has been caused less by conversion to free market ideology than by plummeting oil prices and hence, oil tax revenues. [This] led to dramatic reductions in investment . . . in the major industrial projects . . . at the heart of so much economic activity. Attempts to draft private capital to fill the growing void have proven unsuccessful, largely because private investors had relied heavily upon the state as a catalyst.

As the cascade of oil earnings lessens to a more modest flow, Indonesia's non-commodity producers must become more competitive within an economy that the Australian Indonesia specialist Harold Crouch describes (1985) as a 'bureaucratic polity and a form of neo-patrimonialism'.

The interplay of subsidy and business is a striking feature of the Indonesian economy. Sugar production was raised, via subsidies again, just when the neighbouring Philippines needed to offload an enormous stock overhang. Indonesian consumers meanwhile have had to pay over twice the world price. Even with food items that either sensibly of necessity had to be imported, such as wheat or soybeans, the government's patronage network has raised costs and closed off the trade in agricultural products to private competition.

Loans for perfectly laudible purposes sometimes take circuitous routes to their intended beneficiaries. The National Logistics Board, Bulog, is especially notorious. Its long-serving director Bustanil Arifin, another Abri general, borrowed directly from government banks to implement plans to buy and store rice. By 1987, Bulog owed the banks a staggering US$1 billion. Most government agencies are leaking, loss-making enterprises. Over a third of the entire national economy still belongs to the government sector.

Runs on Rupiahs

During the 1980s, unhappiness with business conditions and macroeconomic management manifested itself in a succession of debilitating runs on the local currency, the rupiah.

In response to oil and other commodity price fluctuations economic affairs coordinating minister Ali Wardhana and his other cabinet colleagues opted for repeated rupiah devaluations to offset drops in US dollar earnings. But rumours of impending devaluations have had a terrible effect on investor confidence, periodically shattered by large reductions in rupiah value *vis-à-vis* the dollar.

In September 1986, finance minister Radius Prawiro won Suharto's approval for a whopping 31 per cent devaluation of the rupiah, the third decreed slice off its value in just eight years. Did the trade ledger show results worth the repeated blows to business confidence? The repeated devaluations did bring better local returns for oil as well as for manufactured items such as textiles and plywood. But the cost in business confidence has been devastating in the 1980s.

'In real terms', the *Far Eastern Economic Review* commented, '[the devaluation] gave marginal benefit to only a few industries [such as plywood and textiles], while tidying up the country's balance sheet. Its major impact was to drastically curtail faith in the government.' These fears continued into 1987, when Indonesian Chinese exchanged rupiahs for a staggering US$1.8 billion in two weeks. Later in the same year, another US$200 million a day in rupiah off-loading occurred, forcing central bank governor Arifin Siregar to dip deeply into his reserves to support the currency. Many local banks made Siregar's job even more difficult. Some converted Bank Indonesia's rupiah notes into dollars.

No amount of exchange rate surgery could disguise the accelerating demands on the servicing costs of Indonesia's foreign debt, however. These rose to 41 per cent of all government spending in 1987, prompting cuts in vital operating expenditure. The transmigration programme, for example, a huge effort to move people off overcrowded Java took a 54 per cent cut in funding. Fertiliser subsidies dropped off by 70 per cent. More ominously, the World Bank and International Monetary Fund estimated that Jakarta's foreign reserves had dropped by nearly a quarter during 1985 to 1986, an outflow approaching US$2.6 billion.

Investment, both public and private, continued to decline during the period. Foreign reserves eroded. Debt servicing rose by 30 per cent in just one year as the lines intersected; as earnings went down, debt servicing payments kept going up. They reached US$5.4 billion in 1985, US$6.9 billion 1987 and US$8.5 billion in 1988. Even allowing for Abri's self-interested myopia, the conclusion was inescapable. Glamour projects had to be scaled down. By acting in enough time to head off truly awesome debt, Indonesia's technocrats stood in contrast to slower moving peers in Malaysia, where the spending spree went on despite the signs of recession.

The turnaround in petroleum earnings forced Indonesia to renegotiate its major liquid natural gas (LNG) contracts. Prices plunged inexorably downwards; in February that year Jakarta returned US$577 million to Japan, describing it as an 'overpayment'. The Japanese had forced a revision of terms in soft market conditions; they had contracted to buy the oil at US$28 per barrel.

The Oil Future

The market for Indonesia's oil looked less bullish as the decade wore on. After cornering Asia's LNG market during the 1980s, Indonesia increasingly ran into more competition, from Malaysia and Brunei. Thailand's newly discovered reserves loomed in the background. Indonesia's biggest customer, Japan, has moved to overcome dependency on Jakarta, which now supplies less than half of Japan's 15 million metric tonne import needs.

Important consequences hang on Tokyo's preferences. Indonesia's undeveloped Natuna field, in the South China Sea, requires enormous investment to extract the 40 trillion cubic feet of gas lying in vast pockets below the ocean floor. Natuna is, potentially, the world's largest LNG reservoir yet American oil firms shied away from Indonesian ambitions to build a 480 kilometre gas pipeline to Singapore which would buy some of the gas for its power stations and export the remainder.

Nor does Indonesia have many options in shifting petroleum sales away from its traditional customers, especially Japan and the United States. Between them they take three-quarters of Jakarta's oil exports. Various one-off supply deals are being struck with other importers, notably South Korea. Even China's oil importing firm Sinochem bought 15,000 barrels per day of Sumatra Light for a duration of six months in 1987, an arrangement which also had diplomatic overtones. (China succeeded, in February 1989, in winning a commitment from Suharto to negotiate on the resumption of diplomatic relations, frozen since 1966.) Many oil importers, notably Australia and China, are becoming oil producers in their own right.

The oil glut in the late 1980s prompted the American Embassy in Jakarta to warn that depleted reserves, increasing domestic use of petroleum products and falling oil exploration could result in Indonesia becoming, by the turn of the century, a net oil *importer*. The embassy report described the oil market in the latter 1980s as a 'full retreat'.

The squeeze between rising local demand and falling external prices is worrying economists. Domestic demand, at about 500,000 bpd, means that the amount of crude oil, condensate and refined product available for export has fallen to about 780,000 bpd at 1980s extraction rates. Increasing domestic consumption, and declining exploration and development of new production fields, adds up to a diminishing resource no matter how world petroleum prices twist and turn in coming years.

Revenue Loss

Declining oil returns force Jakarta to find new sources of revenue. It is not proving very easy. A Harvard Institute for International Development consultancy in the early 1980s devised a new tax regime for Suharto's government. Introduced in 1984, it signals a major shift away from oil dependency and towards income tax. (In a nation this populous, the government has just 600,000 individual and corporate names on the tax rolls.) There is also a shift away from sales levies towards a value ádded tax. Initial returns were disappointing; the old habit of striking a deal with the tax collector remains stubbornly resilient.

In the late 1980s, real government spending declined by between 20 and 25 per cent after deducting debt servicing costs and inflation. The drain on state coffers continues. Subsidies for fertilisers may have brought the country to rice self-sufficiency for the first time since Independence, but the cost of fertiliser subsidies has become too heavy to bear.

Falling petroleum prices have forced cuts in spending on the prestige projects that Suharto has frequently encouraged. He has been attracted to plans that promise to catapult Indonesia into the technological age. His science and technology minister, B. J. Habibie, has sponsored many of these ideas. In cabinet manoeuvres, Habibie is known for wrapping himself in the 'nationalist' mantle while disparaging such 'heartless technocrats' as national development planning minister J. B. Sumarlin or economic coordinating minister Ali Wardhana.

Those meeting Habibie often remark on his irrepressible energy. Anwar Nasir of the *Far Eastern Economic Review*, who interviewed the diminutive minister in 1987, says that 'his obsession with transforming Indonesia into a nation capable of competing in the world of hi-tech by the next century comes through in his gestures; he makes wild gesticulations with his arms (and even legs), and his eyes begin to bulge as he launches a diatribe against those who criticise his vision.'

That vision embraces a wide slice of the technological landscape. Habibie's plans include building a nuclear power station, developing geothermal power, harnessing solar energy and research into supercomputers. But his most lustrous jewel lies in the suburbs of Bandung, a major city in West Java. Here one finds Southeast Asia's premier aircraft industry, a government-owned company known as IPTN.

Begun in 1976 with five hundred staff, Habibie's salesmanship had increased the number of IPTN employees to over 13,000 by 1988. The company assembles helicopters under licensing arrangements with Aérospatiale, Bell Helicopter and Messerschmitt-Bölkow-Blohm (Habibie trained as a Messerschmitt engineer). IPTN also makes two types of fixed-wing aircraft, including the CN-235 passenger aeroplane, under licence from Spain's CASA Industries.

The company flies on the wings of a captive market. Some sceptics say Habibie's dream of a successful aircraft industry 'may never take off', as Nasir puts it. In 1987, out of 242 aircraft sold domestically by IPTN, all but 4 had gone to government entities of one kind or another.

Only 8 IPTN aeroplanes have been sold abroad – to Saudi Arabia, Guam and Thailand. The Thais bought the aeroplanes as part of a barter deal for rice. The

United States Federal Aviation Administration (FAA) has held up certification for the Guam-bound planes. Approval was given only when Air Guam, the ultimate buyer, took delivery of a Spanish assembled CN-235 plane. (The FAA recognises Spanish, not Indonesian, airworthiness certification.)

A foreign airline engineer based in Indonesia had this to say about Habibie's ambitions:

> Hi-tech is more than anything else a body of knowledge. If you have the knowledge but not the equipment, as in India, then you cannot make leaps and bounds. But if you have the equipment and not the knowledge, like Indonesia, you are again in no position to leap-frog in an industry which is at the cutting edge of science.

Habibie and his sceptical cabinet adversaries have quarrelled over this and other high-flying technological dreams. In some instances, Indonesia's indigenous technical and engineering capacity is beginning to reach maturity; a locally-designed airport runway for marshy conditions is just one of many examples. Yet most foreign observers believe Indonesian capability lags behind its Asean neighbours.

As the 1980s wore on, Suharto often seemed disenchanted with the constant nay-saying from his economic advisers. On one occasion, in 1988, he complained in public that certain 'economic analysts', a code word for the technocrats, were 'misleading people with their smartness.' The technocrats took the hint.

For Suharto, rejecting this economic 'smartness' means hanging on to commercially troubled projects such as a colossal steel works in Cilegon, West Java, which one account reckoned had swallowed over US$3 billion in investment since the late 1950s, without ever showing a year of profit on undoctored books.

The tariff-protected steel mill was described by Suharto as 'a sacrifice by the people'. That is an accurate description. Various technocratic smart alecks have tried to wean Suharto off this example of industrial self-indulgence, but without success. Wardhana left the government in 1988, just as some grandiose projects seemed destined to be implemented after being put on the shelf for reasons of financial stringency in the early 1980s. One of these is a US$2.3 billion plant in northern Sumatra to make ethylene and propylene. The project, as noted above, is of gain to the president's family.

Other types of 'smartness' could lead one into trouble. 'Tendentious reporting' became cause for closing *Sinar Harapan*, one of Jakarta's leading daily newspapers. The paper had urged economic deregulation, aiming not a few oblique barbs at the Suharto family. Indonesia's public sector operates 214 corporations, most of them chronic money-losers, or worse. Eight months later, in June 1987, another newspaper went to the wall for criticising Indonesia's inefficient investment policies.

Harbouring Thieves

It was not all negative for business efficiency, however. In April 1985, Suharto approved a dramatic repudiation of the government's own customs service. He approved the award of a contract to do the same work (monitor all imports) to Société Générale de Surveillance SA, a Swiss trade inspection company.

SGS has a daunting task, to clean up one of Southeast Asia's most notoriously greedy customs operations. It also faces some determined bogus trade invoicing, especially from Singapore where exporters of the 5,000 shipments leaving that country each month for Indonesia strive hard to switch goods after inspection. Time sits heavy for Indonesia's 13,000 customs agents, who continue to plot against SGS. In April 1988, they won back a few of their dearly prized prerogatives: Suharto extended SGS's contract but confined its role more narrowly.

Suharto has also sanctioned other changes which, cumulatively, are liberalising the top-heavy and often corrupt economy. As an adjunct to SGS's frontal attack on portside corruption a serious effort is being made to speed up the country's slow-motion ports. Other measures include simplifying foreign investment rules and reducing tariffs. The pace is slow, however, and most of these 'reform packages', as they are invariably described, are essentially reactive. Indonesia has been losing its attractiveness as a destination for foreign capital by comparison with all Asean countries except the Philippines.

Cutting tariffs at the stroke of a pen is one thing. Extricating government businesses hitherto captive to khaki commerce is quite another. Exercises which the government describes as 'privatisation' are moving slowly if at all. In 1986 the sale of an indebted, state-run plantation firm ran into embarrassing problems. Reacting to charges that the sale was fixed in advance, Suharto stepped in to put matters right. Only then did he find that the buyers were *pribumi* businessmen from the influential Bakrie Brothers steel group. Reports linked them to the family of the agriculture minister and also to associates of the First Family itself.

Musical Pirates

Other commercial irritants gave the Indonesians a poor reputation, often (for the size of the slight) disproportionately so. Jakarta's indifference to American complaints about trademark and patent infringements became noteworthy by the mid-1980s, as the local Chinese-controlled, pirated tape industry rolled on regardless, supplying the huge Indonesian market with stolen copies of American, British and other works.

It required a serious threat from Washington to suspend Indonesia's trading access privileges before the government took any serious steps. A new law emerged from the Indonesian parliament, setting tough (5 years' gaol) penalties for selling pirated material. Yet laws have a way of disappearing without trace. Certainly, some shops have continued their trade, oblivious to threatened sanctions.

This point was brought home to an American sports shoemaker, Nike, when it celebrated an Indonesian Supreme Court decision cancelling fake trademark registrations. These had allowed a firm to market fake Nike running shoes. This prompted the firm, based in Oregon state, to challenge the Indonesian pirates in court. The legal battle lasted four years. In 1988 however, reports had surfaced that another bogus variety of Nike shoes were back on sale in corner bazaars.

Bogus Notes of Another Kind

There were even signs that the Indonesian military, whose top-to-bottom interpenetration of business affairs is taken for granted, had become more reckless in its approach. An episode in 1987 showed how ready some Abri officials were to dabble in easy money schemes.

In one example, the Indonesian National Defence Security Council, an army-staffed policy group inside the defence ministry, issued debt instruments in 1985 as part of trade-financing packages. These were marketed around the world by various foreign agencies, some of doubtful probity.

The crux of the problem, however, is that anyone foolish enough to have bought one of them soon learned that Bank Indonesia was resolutely refusing to honour them. The central bank said, sensibly enough, that it and the finance ministry had sole authority to issue sovereign debt notes.

The matter came to light when five men stood accused in New York of attempting to sell these worthless notes, ostensibly valued at US$640 million. Realising their empty quality, they had offered them at a slashed discount to undercover commercial fraud police investigators. The New York police said notes had been peddled originally by a Palestinian, Hassan Zubaldi, who now lives in Damascus.

New York policy also claimed Zubaldi was selling US$3.5 billion of these notes received from Jakarta in 1985. Each bogus note carried the signature of various defence ministry officials. A lieutenant-general, Achmad Wiranatakusumah, had also signed them. So had another Abri general, Chalid Mwardi, Jakarta's ambassador to Syria at the time.

The signature of Ibnu Hartomo, Mrs Tien Suharto's brother, was also on the notes. Reportedly unrepentant, Hartomo said he had signed the notes to generate new money for various 'military projects', which he did not specify. The episode revealed a completely parallel, sovereign debt financing operation, run with military connivance and quite divorced from the treasury and central bank.

The Bright Side

Casting stones at Indonesia's achievement since 1965 sometimes seems churlish. The beneficial changes after that wild, intense time; the improvements slowly coming to the disastrously neglected economy; the proud stewardship of advisers whose ability to put into practice their ideas depended on the willingness of Suharto and his armed forces allies to do so – how can these accomplishments be impugned?

Indonesia rests on centuries of Hindu, Buddhist and Islamic culture, much of it beautifully refined and exquisite. The currently fashionable market mania resists an over-the-counter application to this (or, indeed, to any) economy without addressing the constraints of the local culture.

In Indonesia, the local culture is only partially receptive to Harvard Business School logic. Here the weight of tradition leans heavily towards patrimonial commerce, and tilts away from individual business flair. Commerce remains, as in colonial times, something to which only shifty Chinese are drawn (so the line of local thought goes). How, then, is the capitalist animal – be he (or she) a noodle vendor or a *pribumi* trader – to be nourished?

Urgent Needs, Slow Corrections

The Indonesian economy is slowly changing course, like an oil tanker able to change direction in minute degrees over long distances. There are signs that agriculture will come to provide more external earnings; agri-business has begun to attract sizeable investments from some larger Indonesian companies such as PT Astra, a conglomerate run by the local Chinese billionaire William Soeryadjaya and his family. One project attracting their interest is a US$1 billion joint venture with Scott Paper Company of the United States. The project will create an enormous tree plantation and build a pulp-making plant in Irian Jaya, Indonesia's easternmost province.

Yet agricultural exports, bringing in nearly half the non-oil export earnings still depend on too many services and systems that receive, at best, only indifferent maintenance. Huge investments in irrigation were a case in point: assessments published by the Asian Development Bank say 45 per cent of Indonesia's infrastructure (irrigation systems, bridges, power lines and the like) badly needs repair.

How will this country with a population nearing 200 millions find work for its new generations? The United Nations lauds Suharto's quite genuine commitment to family planning programmes, but the demographic clock still ticks on disconcertingly. Twenty-five million jobs must be found for new labour market entrants before the next century, according to former minister Wardhana. Is this expected to be found within the ramshackle array of inefficient monopolies and an overstaffed bureaucracy?

The government's January 1987 'reform package' marks a start in teasing out cronies from commerce, and bureaucrats from business. In some cases, as with Liem's empire, the business associates of key political figures have already started to move out their assets quietly, already anticipating the end of an era in which Suharto, whose genius has done so much to reunify the archipelago's badly torn fabric, fades finally from the scene.

And the reforms? What will happen after Suharto to the cautious, inching forward towards marketplace economics? Will Jakarta's puny stockmarket, Asean's smallest, finally begin to attract investor cash from a broad cross-section of society? (Fewer than 0.0008 per cent of Indonesians own shares.) Will khaki-tinted monopolies someday cease to clutter the import/export business? Do not expect rapid change: 'In Indonesia you do it gradually,' Wardhana told Raphael Pura of the *Asian Wall Street Journal* in 1987. 'You don't do the whole package at one time, you have to win your battles one by one.'

Will this do the job? In his comprehensive study entitled *Indonesia: the Rise of Capital*, Richard Robison (1986) takes an optimistic view of capital accumulation in Indonesia. He charts the emergence of an indigenous bourgeoisie at a time when 'from both international capital and the free-market ideologues, there is pressure upon a vulnerable Indonesian government to change from an inward-oriented industrial strategy to an outward-looking strategy which seeks . . . to make investment decisions on the basis of efficiency and comparative advantage.'

Within an academic perspective, Robison identifies the key commercial issues confronting Indonesia in the 1990s. 'Demands for a free-trade, free-market approach represent not only a disagreement over economic strategy but a major challenge to the existing structure of political and economic power in capitalist Indonesia,' he notes. These challenges are 'threatening to alter radically the balance of ownership and control' in Indonesia.

They also threaten the formal and informal political and economic relationships which have made possible the emergence of domestic business groups . . . now firmly entrenched in the import substitution sector in auto assembly, textiles, cement, steel and heavy engineering, metal fabrication and pharmaceuticals. Their continued existence has been based upon government intervention involving protection, subsidy, contracts, direct investment and mediation of integration with foreign capital.

Yet the absence in Indonesia of a nourishing, business culture of capitalism does not find mention in this view. One reviewer of Robison's work, the *Far Eastern Economic Review*'s Paul Handley, says 'the point Robison underestimates is that given the money and the chance, the Javanese still have not shown an ability or desire to operate in business in the same way as Chinese, foreign or even some non-Javanese indigenous investors.'

The business acumen of Sumatran Indonesians from the Padang and Minang-kabau areas, for example, is legendary throughout the archipelago. Why do the Javanese lag? 'Most serious of all', Handley continues, 'is that when the leader loses his power, as in 1965, the legitimacy of any of the fortunes being made below disappears. With Suharto the threat of this is worse – as he has used his direct control over all state contracts to benefit a small, select group of relatives and cronies.'

In the recent literature of informal, mass capitalism in Latin America, writers such as Hernando de Soto note that unfettered business freedom has never been achieved in much of the non-Western world. The same observation could apply to most of Southeast Asia, and especially in Indonesia.

'With mercantilism [in sixteenth-century Europe]', de Soto says, 'the state con-trolled economic activities in the interest of national power . . . The government would distribute monopoly rights to produce certain products, to import and export certain goods, and to distribute products and goods in the domestic market. The élite prospered through the manipulation of political power and police actions against those who did not respect their monopolies.' This has a familiar ring.

Intimations of Change

Studies of scholars such as Shahrir (1988) at the Harvard Business School have shown that life under Suharto has improved, at least marginally, for the Indonesian masses. This, it must be stressed, is a considerable achievement. 'Trickle-down economics' has worked, once again. But the question, as in Malaysia, is at what cost? Does the progress so stunningly gained not reflect, after all, the decisions of foreigners, and behind them also, a demand-led economic boom tied firmly to the world trading system?

Despite Suharto's achievements therefore, by the end of a two-decade era coinciding with his presidency the long reach by his family into business has become a prominent nexus in Indonesia's system of business favouritism. The family's link with prominent Chinese has also become a widely discussed, and less widely admired, characteristic of a now ageing New Order. If a freer economy is to emerge, these features need drastic curtailment. Similarly, after eight *windus* of Abri's dual functioneering, Indonesia's economy badly needs new, and narrower, terms of reference for the soldiers.

'The present Chinese business leaders are only stable as long as Suharto's regime is – and they know it,' writes Handley. 'When Suharto is gone, and there is no set mechanism for succession, an entirely new generation of Chinese businessmen will follow . . . despite the widespread affection their father commands, there is little love lost across Indonesia for his children.'

But No Easy Way Out

Like so many other developing countries, Indonesia's investment policies after the 1970s resulted in industries created and capitalised by foreigners (in this case, mainly the Japanese) sheltering behind tariff barriers and producing the familiar array of motor vehicles and consumer durables for the domestic market.

The heaviest burden in tariffs falls on the importer of consumer goods. A former minister of industry, A. R. Soehoed, has argued that 'industrialisation' in Indonesia has led to a 'widening, rather than the deepening, of the industrial structure'. He and other critics argue for an approach that will make industries more deeply rooted in the Indonesian economy.

Deepening Indonesia's manufacturing base does not come easily. Many attempts have been made: local content rules and protection of 'upstream' industries (to make finished and semi-finished products using local resources) have been tried. But the drastic drop in external, mainly oil earnings after 1982 forced a shift towards export sales. A further widening has occurred, without the deepening.

The new wave of investment in industry also comes from foreigners, and also primarily from the Japanese. But the objective now is the export market, especially in Europe and the US. To encourage the establishment of these export-led industries, the strictures against foreign sourced materials have had to be loosened.

Local content rules and 'localisation' strategies, such as rules requiring the hire of Indonesian executive level personnel, have no appeal to outside investors interested mainly in cheap labour to assemble products bound for outside markets. The tariff structure's 'anti-export bias' had to be changed, the World Bank and other advisers said. But that meant direct confrontation with Indonesia's high level duppies.

Quite apart from tariffs, 'the proliferation of import monopolies, duopolies and oligopolies since late 1982 with large and lucrative rent-seeking opportunities has added to the already existing anti-export bias', writes the prominent Indonesian Chinese analyst Thee Kian Wie (1987). Some dismantling of these monopolies has occurred, as noted above. Yet informal arrangements persist in having the same, cost-adding effect.

As Thee notes elsewhere, Indonesia's industrial development for too long remained rooted in import-substituting plants 'unlike its Asean neighbours, where the limits of the domestic market required a reassessment of the virtues of import-substituting industrialisation.' Although overall the pattern of Indonesian industry is not dominated by foreign capital, external technologies determine the product mix via licensing or management contracting deals.

The high number of Abri-run state enterprises does little for efficiency either. 'The government is stuck with most of the state enterprises', say Thee and Yoshihara Kunio in a joint paper (1987). They note the existence of *pribumi* businessmen in shipping, banking, oil-related fields, life insurance, construction, hotel, air transportation and publishing,but they add that 'only a few are involved in industry.'

The outlook for Indonesia's economy continues to depend on commodity markets. With the turn away from inefficient industry producing for the domestic market, Indonesia now depends on decisions by outside investors using comparative advantages, such as cheap labour, to assemble products for sale in third markets.

That approach, while 'efficient', promises as little real indigenous control over the future direction of the economy as earlier policies. Arief Budiman, a notably dissident economic analyst based in Java, contrasts the successful industrial economy achieved in South Korea on the strength of export-led growth. 'Will Indonesia follow a similar course?' he asks (1988). The outlook is not promising. 'What is certain', Budiman says, 'is that the top officials whose interests are embedded in monopolies will not give up their privileges easily.'

References

Budiman, A. (1988) 'The emergence of the bureaucratic capitalist state in Indonesia', in Lim, T. G. *Reflections on Development in Southeast Asia*. Singapore: ISEAS

Crouch, H and Zakaria, A. (eds) (1985) *Military–Civilian Relations in Southeast Asia*. Singapore: Oxford University Press

Osborne, M. (1983) *Southeast Asia*. Sydney: Allen & Unwin, 2nd edn

Robison, R. (1986) *Indonesia: the Rise of Capital*. Sydney: Allen & Unwin

Robison, R. and Rodan, G. (1986) *Financial Institutions and Policies in Indonesia*. Sydney: Allen & Unwin

Shahrir (1988) *Basic Needs in Indonesia: Economics, Politics and Public Policy*. Singapore: ISEAS

Thee, K. W. (1987) 'Industrial and foreign investment policy in Indonesia since 1967', *Southeast Asian Studies*, vol. 25, No. 3. Tokyo

Thee, K. W. and Kunio, Y. (1987) 'Foreign and domestic capital in Indonesian industrialization', *Southeast Asian Studies*, vol. 24, No. 4. Tokyo

5

BOOMTIME IN BANGKOK

Southeast Asia's Newest Star

When Thai deputy finance minister Supachai Panichpakdi warned Bangkok's stockbrokers in 1988 to stop their 'devious machinations', he was simply reiterating a warning that his subordinates had issued, with next to no effect, for many years. No one was listening, and the government knew it.

Following the usual Southeast Asian pattern, the Thai share rally of 1988 enriched a very closed circle of players. But with foreign fund managers being lured to the small but frenetic bourse, what did it matter? There was always room for more money for Thai shares; various 'Thailand Equity Funds' marketed by securities houses in Tokyo, New York or London had proved a great success. Overseas investors now sought shares in Thailand's home market, chasing such favoured listings as Thai Investment & Securities Company, National Finance Company, Bangkok Bank, Thai Farmers Bank, Siam City Bank and, not least, Siam Cement Company, one of Southeast Asia's wealthiest corporations.

These and many other stocks scored big paper gains on the Securities Exchange of Thailand (SET) at the end of the 1980s. Most foreign buyers were coming in, as a local expression goes, on little more than the smell of a Chinese joss stick. In Bangkok they soon learned to ignore much of the share earnings analysis or corporate profile studies to which they were accustomed in other markets. In Bangkok, boomtime quickly became an article of faith for the world financial community which, already receptive to Asian equity funds in Taiwan, Japan and South Korea, followed a herd instinct when reacting to press hyperbole about another 'Asian miracle' in the making.

What a turnaround this bullishness represented from a mood prevailing just two years earlier! At that time most foreign economists had indulged in doom-laden imagery, some even forecasting a collapse of leading Bangkok banks. Soon afterwards, once Thailand had weathered the worst of the 1983–86 commodities price drop, this type of talk vanished like midday ice-cubes on the veranda of Bangkok's Oriental Hotel. The investors' mood swung back; by 1989 the asset-based fundamentals and other investment indices of their favourite stock listings, which only twenty-four months earlier had received the sharpest scrutiny, already seemed strangely irrelevant. It was enough to be in Bangkok, and to be investing in Bangkok.

Although many banks whose shares were now so eagerly sought had come within an ace of folding during the mid-1980s, it was now considered bad form to worry about such things. After all, business was booming once again in this country of 54 million people, with receipts from foreign direct investment, tourism and exports all surging ahead. In the casino-like frenzy of the Bangkok bourse, the god of mammon was once more enthroned, metaphorically at least, beside the ubiquitous Buddha images.

In any event, a much more important 'fundamental' lies behind the whirlwind of trading turnover in Bangkok, a deliberate policy that also underpins other burgeoning share markets in tropical Asia. Throughout the recent expansionary years, SET's management has prevented most companies from listing their shares on the exchange. For all the hyperbole about the SET only 94 stocks are traded. As in Kuala Lumpur or Manila, so also in Bangkok; investor money chases the stocks, not the other way round.

If this were not enough to guarantee high turnover, the 'free float' position of most share listings is. For most stocks, the free float (that is, the percentage of total shareholding traded regularly in the exchange) remains small. Even in normal times these restrictive features would make the SET an easy money-spinner; coupled with Southeast Asia's most buoyant economy, it is not surprising that the SET has become the fastest paced, although not the highest capitalised, Southeast Asian stock exchange.

Foreign Fund Managers Flock to Bangkok

Attracted by this glitter, an increasing number of foreign investment houses have not only bought shares but have also set up shop in Bangkok, encouraged by gushy pieces in the international and regional business press. 'Until last year', said the Australian magazine *Triple A* at the end of 1987, 'Thailand had little good news in its economy. Its trade and current account deficits were consistently high, its foreign debt grew every year, its savings and investment rates were low and the government suffered successive years of revenue shortfalls.' That was not all, said the influential Australian monthly. 'Business was hit by shrinking profits and a spate of corporate failures added to the gloom.'

Yet by January 1989 *The Economist* was writing that 'month by month, Thailand is looking more like [an East Asian business] dragon.' What had changed so quickly to bring foreign fund managers scampering back, lifting their bouts of participation on the Bangkok bourse to over 20 per cent of total traded volume? The gains were so good that even a 25 per cent government capital gains tax on traded shares, normally a strong disincentive, did not deter the foreigners. The new boom also rode on the strength of dropping bank interest rates after 1987, and on the afterglow of success achieved by Morgan Stanley & Company's US$100 million Thai Fund that started trading on the New York Stock Exchange in February 1988. Other securities houses, such as Nikko Securities and Hoare Govett, also rushed in to set up their own Thai funds, channelling perhaps another US$250 million into fresh equity investment in Bangkok.

For all that, deputy finance minister Panichpakdi and a key prime ministerial adviser, Virabongse Ramangkura, were urging even faster expansion as the 1990s dawned. They realised that the SET's turnover, just US$770 million in 1987, still remained small by comparison with Singapore and Hong Kong. Yet plans to add just five more companies to the tiny exchange, including the government-owned Krung Thai Bank and Thai International Airways, were slow in coming. 'Why add more seats at the casino?' reasoned the brokers, who bolstered this good reasoning with even better lobbying.

Mass Capitalism?

The government was prompt to claim that an ever-increasing number of indigenous Thai investors were also finding the capital market impossible to resist, but nearly all activity by locals resulted from institutional investors or Chinese families. To Thai critics the share market also began to seem less impressive as an unambiguous demonstration of the 'popular capitalism' said to be sweeping through Southeast Asia. Using the straightforward measurement of dividing gross domestic product, or GDP, by share market investment capitalised at market values, Thailand's boom does assume more prosaic proportions. The ratio, at just 5 per cent in 1988, falls well under even the mediocre 10 per cent prevailing in India. By comparison, the US figure is 40 per cent and South Korea's is 24 per cent.

Within the rarified world of financial services, Thailand's claim to have built a widely spread marketplace also seems a little threadbare. A few foreign banks (Citibank and Chase Manhattan especially), the Nakornthon Bank and a Chinatown-based firm called the Thai Financial Syndicate between them keep a strong grip on the fund management and hedging businesses, financial services that mushroomed after the baht's qualified float in 1984. (The baht, Thailand's currency, was untied from the US dollar in that year and pegged instead to a 'basket' of currencies, the effect of which was to bring the Thai currency closer to a managed 'float'.)

Looks Good on Paper

To many enthusiasts, these misgivings seemed irreverent carping or worse, mischievous noise from envious sidelines. 'The international discovery, elevation and confirmation of Thailand as one of East Asia's brightest economic prospects has happened in little more than a decade,' wrote the *Financial Times* correspondent in another admiring feature in 1989. This discovery, he said, had happened 'despite an already impressive performance in the 1960s when gross national product increased on average by 8 per cent a year.' A cover story by *Newsweek* magazine ('Asia's emerging superstar') plus regular business coverage by *The Economist* and other major weeklies reinforced the Kingdom of Thailand's reputation as the latest Southeast Asian success story.

Certainly Thailand's macroeconomic figures added up nicely. Runaway human fertility, which had earlier threatened to vitiate economic growth, declined dramatically during the 1980s. Energetic campaigning by Thailand's deputy industry minister, Mechai Viravaidya, founder of Thailand's Population and Community Development Association, had resulted in nearly 70 per cent of Thai couples using contraceptives by 1989, helping to slow population growth from 3.2 per cent per annum in 1971 to under 2 per cent in 1989. The crude birth-rate per thousand population, another common measurement of fertility, dropped from 41 to 25 per thousand persons between 1965 and 1989.

'The Western press, focusing on Mechai's antics rather than his achievements, has unjustly given him a reputation as a kind of condom comedian,' the *World Executive's Digest* noted in 1986. True, Mechai's flamboyant campaigns include dropping condom packages from aeroplanes, painting birth control slogans on water buffaloes and distributing free key chains with plastic-embedded condoms that carry the message, 'In case of emergency break glass'. These marketing gimmicks have enabled Mechai, whom Thais call the 'Condom Man', to place Thailand far ahead of other regional countries whose burgeoning populations, as in the Philippines, are outpacing economic growth.

Within a steadily growing economy Thailand's more moderate increases in human numbers now mean better GDP per capita figures (although the Thai economy's distributional side, as we shall see, fails to impress). Still, even trickle-down economics have made a big difference: growth in Thailand averaged 7.4 per cent per annum from 1965 to 1980, slowing to a still admirable 4.8 per cent per annum during 1980–86. In unadjusted dollars (that is, dollar sums not adjusted for intervening inflation), Thailand's GDP rose from US$4 billion in 1965 to US$41.7 billion in 1986. In the twelve months to April 1989 the economy was growing by over 10 per cent per annum; Thailand's exports rose by 33 per cent during the same twelve-month period, increasing export receipts to over US$16 billion annually.

Those are huge increases by anyone's reckoning. Other measuring rods also show the fast pace. In constant 1970 dollars, the 'value-added' component of Thai manufacturing grew from US$1.05 billion in 1970 to US$7.7 billion just fifteen years later. (The amount of value-added, a key index of any country's industrial progress, calculates the worth of indigenous labour and materials added during the manufacturing process.) The Thais were squeezing this extra value out of burgeoning industries which, at the end of the 1980s, produced 2.7 billion square yards of textiles, 9 million tonnes of cement, 90,000 cars and light vehicles and over 500 million separate pieces of integrated circuitry each year.

This was success, surely. Other measurements, such as the amount of 'manufacturing earnings per employee' (i.e., the wealth generated by industry divided by the number of industrial workers), had shown a 1.1 per cent rate of growth each year during the 1970s. After 1980, however, the same calculation showed a phenomenal increase of 10.6 per cent per annum to 1986.

This growth accompanied – indeed, it was led by – a 9.2 per cent annual growth in foreign trade during the 1980s. And within Thailand's widening spread of exports, manufactured products grew from a minuscule 3 per cent of total exported goods in 1965 to over 33 per cent in 1989. If we widen the Thais' narrow definition of 'manufactured items' to include textiles and machinery exports, then the manufactured segment of exports rises to 60 per cent in 1989. This pointed to a decisive break with the normal dependence of Third World countries on primary goods.

Economists specialising in public finance also liked what they saw in Thailand. A chronic balance of payments deficit in the 1960s and 1970s had given way, in the late 1980s, to a routine surplus – although, as we shall see, this remains a vulnerable achievement. After the boomlet of 1988–89, the government used windfall revenues to prepay foreign debts ahead of schedule. The aim was to bring the debt-service ratio (i.e., the difference between export receipts and debt repayments) down to about 14 per cent. The ratio had gone as high as 25 per cent in 1985, giving Thailand's economic technocrats a bad scare. The late 1980s windfall income also lifted reserves. Was it any wonder that, by 1987, Merrill Lynch advised its clients that 'Thailand has long-term strengths which should enable it to outperform its Southeast Asian neighbours over the next five years.'

Earlier Growth Models

There was just one problem with this kind of talk: it echoed, with uncanny precision, other positive analyses offered a decade earlier, when the Thai economy first attracted international attention. In spite of much progress a slump beginning in 1984 had caught Thailand woefully unprepared and badly managed. The worry is that the same strains could appear again.

'By the early 1980s Thailand had emerged as a rapidly industrialising country with bright prospects for continued growth and industrialisation,' writes Kevin Hewison, a former post-doctoral fellow at the Australian National University in Canberra. His 1987 study notes four reasons for the early optimism: first, local Thai ownership of much of the domestic manufacturing base; second, a relatively constant growth rate; third, an almost minuscule foreign debt burden and, fourthly, regained political stability after upheavals in 1973 and 1975.

This seemed a sound base at the time. It also reflected a different approach by Thailand's economic managers. Before 1958, Thailand tried to copy Japanese and European industries. It made public investments in food processing and textiles. Then it veered towards import-substituting plants during the 1960s, to save foreign exchange and build up infant industries. This strategy won support from virtually all sources of advice, ranging from the World Bank to the Thais' own Board of Investment, and from the National Economic Development Board to the Ministry of Industry and even the central bank.

Protected industries, wherever they are sited, usually have little incentive to export and little self-generated interest in doing so. Thailand's pampered manufacturers were no exception. By the 1970s, however, a need to absorb excess manufacturing capacity had become a major constraint; meanwhile, Thailand's growing trade deficits also required more exporting. Export-oriented growth, which high inflation in the Western markets and exchange rate fluctuations also favoured, thus became the fashion.

Foreign Investment Invasion

Export-led growth has continued as development gospel after the 1970s and remains current orthodoxy. Much of the free trading ideology comes from World Bank advice now championing, after a shift starting in 1979, an ever more accelerated opening of the Thai economy to world market forces. It was also during these years that the first signs of accelerated foreign investment began to appear.

The flow of foreign funds has now become a cascade. During 1987 and 1988, Thailand's Board of Investments had received over 3,000 applications with proposals for investing over US$20 billion. Not all the plans reached fruition, but most did. For example, Taiwanese investors like the Yuen Foong Yu Paper Manufacturing Company have bought into existing Thai firms. Other Taiwanese firms have set up manufacturing plants using family links with the Thai Chinese. Northeast Asian currencies appreciated steadily after 1985; that meant that Japanese and South Korean firms came to Thailand, and elsewhere in Southeast Asia, in search of lower costs than back home. The Taiwanese dollar also became dearer, strengthening on the back of that island's annual trade surpluses of over US$25 billion by 1989. According to one report, the Board of Investments approved proposals involving a total of US$225 million from Taiwanese investors in the first two years after 1985. These figures rose again during 1988–89.

Yet Taiwan's Chinese money (much of which came in through informal Chinatown networks) paled by comparison with Korean and Japanese direct foreign investment, or DFI. Since 1985 the Thais have outperformed all Asean countries in attracting Japanese investment. In 1986, Japanese investments in Thailand increased to 13.6 billion baht, compared with just 2 billion baht in 1985 when Thailand still had the smallest aggregate of Japanese investment in the whole Asean bloc. Nearly 300 Japanese companies have already established plants in Thailand, almost all of them producing for export.

Figures from 1951–76 show Thailand accounting for about 3 per cent of total DFI in Asia by Japanese firms. During the same period, Indonesia was receiving nearly half the DFI from Tokyo. Even in 1985, Japan's US$760 million in fixed investment in Thailand was the lowest in Asean. But thereafter Japanese investment increased so rapidly that, by the first quarter of 1987, investment applications from Japan had exceeded the total number received from Tokyo firms during 1986. The Japanese manufacturers come mainly for Thailand's cheap labour pool, sourced from a population large enough to comprise a reasonable demand base in its own right. The Japanese also find Thailand's easy tolerance of overseas Chinese and other foreigners a mark in its favour although, as anti-Japanese riots in the 1970s showed, this tolerance has its limits. By 1989, twelve major Japanese banks had set up shop in Bangkok, including such familiar names as the Bank of Tokyo, Dai-Ichi Kangyo, Fuji, Mitsubishi, Mitsui, Sanwa, Sumitomo, Taiyo Kobe and Tokai.

The large Japanese presence should not overshadow the American firms setting up in Thailand, firms like Seagate Technology, a California company making computer disk-drives. Seagate has become the largest foreign company employer in Thailand, with 12,000 on the payroll. Other American multinationals, such as International Telephone and Telegraph (ITT) and Data General have also made large investments although the largest single foreign investor in Thailand is the US oil company Unocal, which operates natural gas fields in the Gulf of Thailand.

Meanwhile the US shoe firm, Nike, has combined with Saha Pathanapibul to export sports shoes. West Germany's Adidas also produces footwear in a joint venture with Bangkok's Central Group. Even Arabs have bought into Thailand; in 1987 Bahrain's Arab Banking Corporation became the second largest equity holder in the Union Bank of Thailand, capitalising on a squabble dividing the Chinese owners, the Cholvicharn family.

In 1987 the stock of Japanese and US investments in Thailand had stood in rough parity. Two years later, the Japanese had come out in front. There is an additional wild card: Japanese government agencies do not report as DFI the reinvested profits of overseas Japanese subsidiaries. If they were to do so, the real preponderance of Japan in Thailand could be strengthened by another 25 per cent if not more. Estimates by the US Department of Commerce of international direct investment trends in 1988 used this add-on factor as a rule of thumb.

Resourceful Thailand

For foreign investors, Thailand has more to offer than just a cheap and relatively docile labour force willing (as Malaysian or Singaporean workers are not) to accept continuous, 24-hour work shifts. Plentifully endowed with many natural resources, it is also the only net food exporter in all of Asia, Thailand's agri-business has become a runaway success. Pineapples, tapioca, rice and rubber top the export list of commodities. Rice sales brought in US$174.3 million in 1973; by 1984 the figure was US$1.1 billion.

There there is, surprisingly, the gemstone trade which became the country's fifth largest export earner in 1988. Exported gems and jewellery earned Thailand US$315 million that year. Once utterly dependent on oil imports, Thailand has also come close to supplying all its petroleum needs. If exploration results continue to follow 1980s trends, by the mid-1990s Thailand will become a net oil exporter.

After the commodity crash of 1984–85, Thai commodities regained higher prices, with rice, maize, tin, zinc and rubber prices rebounding. Nor does the country depend on one major commodity, as does Indonesia or Brunei; Thailand's largest export item, textiles, comprises just 14 per cent of export receipts. Stagnating incomes from traditional exports, such as rice and sugar, have found an offset in manufacturing gains. Nor do traditional foodstuffs prevent other agricultural products, such as tapioca and tinned tuna, from scoring export gains.

The Newest NIC?

All these bright trends have led the Thais to dream big dreams. The Western-educated technocrats dominating the central bank, the treasury and the industry and trade departments feel an impending economic transformation in their bones. 'NIC status for Thailand is less than a few years away,' said Thailand's chief economic planner, Snoh Unakul, in 1988. The Columbia University-educated economist was referring to the widely used acronym for 'newly industrialising country', an appellation that, for Thailand, would have seemed wildly off mark until just a few years ago.

Snoh exemplifies the generation of American trained managers who returned home during the 1960s. So does Board of Investment chief Amnuay Viravan, who later became the head of Bangkok Bank, Southeast Asia's largest bank by asset rating. 'Twenty years ago', Viravan said in 1988, 'the private sector didn't care about anyone else. They just went after their own self-interest.' Things have changed, he claimed. 'Thailand is ready for take-off.' Bolstering Viravan's optimism was the evidence of Thailand's unusual commercial resilience during the sharp 1985–86 recession afflicting all of Southeast Asia. During that period, the Thai economy still managed to grow by 3.5 per cent and 4.7 per cent respectively per annum, well outpacing all other Asean countries, even Singapore.

But what is the most important engine of Thailand's undeniable growth? Some analysts had simple answers: '*all* this activity was generated by the stronger East Asian currencies,' said the *Far Eastern Economic Review* in 1988. 'As the baht remained stable against the US dollar, Japanese investors swarmed in.' So did the other foreign investors, eager for Thailand's generous tax concessions which, Thai critics say, are badly distorting the country's tax base. 'The results of the investment boom are substantial,' noted another foreign analyst. 'Export growth zoomed, but imports, strongly weighted towards capital goods, expanded even more rapidly.' Even the most sympathetic free-marketeering economists fear that it is only the extraordinary (but not necessarily sustainable) foreign capital inflows that are keeping Thailand out of chronic deficit.

Rocketing Corporate Profits

Most of this cautionary advice gets lost in trumpeted good news about business performance in Thailand. Breathtaking profit reports attract much more global attention. Several examples will suffice: first, Thai International Airways, and second, Siam Cement Company.

The government-owned Thai Airways emerged from a joint venture with Scandinavian Airlines that began back in 1960. After a cautious start-up, the airline has achieved successively greater profits in every year after 1979. Thai Airways is now flying high on tourism which has grown by 50 per cent annually since 1986. By January 1989, over 4 million visitors had come to Thailand during the previous twelve months, spending nearly US$2.3 billion. Bangkok's new Don Muang airport has also lifted the airline's gains by increasing efficiencies. The airline's fleet will grow from 30 aircraft, in 1988, to 58 aircraft by 1995.

Meanwhile the recent and phenomenally rapid growth of Siam Cement follows a long corporate history in which the company has reported a loss in just one year during the past three-quarters of a century. Regarded often as the 'quintessential Thai conglomerate', the company's name betrays its origin in the concrete and building business back in 1913.

Foreign analysts describe Siam Cement as the closest thing to a 'Thailand Inc.' Siam Cement's holding company oversees a collection of about thirty subsidiaries producing over 5,000 products. Japanese multinationals such as Mitsubishi and Toyota have signed joint venture projects with Siam Cement. Other foreign firms, such as Britain's BP Minerals International, have entered into joint mining ventures. Even though cement and construction still provide 60 per cent of corporate earnings, the conglomerate also makes, under licence, a variety of air conditioners, car engines, plastics, diesel engines, tiles and paper. The 'Thailand Inc.' tag also fits because Siam Cement's board reflects the cream of Thai bureaucracy, a sharp exception to the family-run companies that normally control Thai business. Siam Cement's ownership also reveals a steady monarchical interest, via a 37 per cent stake held by the Crown Property Bureau, the agency that looks after the monarchy's assets.

Both Thai Airways and Siam Cement seem golden enterprises, shiningly successful in a region where even politically well-connected companies sometimes
run into rough financial weather. But do these companies, and thousands of
similarly successful Thai firms, lead an enchanted life?

The Mid-1980s: A Trial Run of Trouble

'By 1985 the Thai economy faced its first major crisis since the late 1950s,'
notes Hewison; 'the initial focus of concern was the mounting debt problem
but the crisis was much broader than this.' It had also begun somewhat
earlier, in late 1982, when higher interest rates and declining commodity
prices pushed Thailand close to an International Monetary Fund austerity
programme.

At this time the banks' liquidity problems slowly became more worrying,
especially as the central bank sought to keep domestic interest rates at a
significant margin above the international (dollar) rates to prevent capital
flight. Business profitability fell sharply. Bankruptcies rose by 27 per cent
in the first nine months of 1985 when compared to the same period in the
previous year.

The mid-1980s slump also pushed Thai farmers to mount roudy demonstrations
against declining agricultural prices; in the first half of 1985 external prices for
maize, rice, rubber, tin and tapioca all fell, despite steady increases in export
volumes. The country's terms of trade began to weaken, slipping by more than
20 per cent between 1980 and 1985. Unemployment rose to over 2 million,
of which a politically significant 10 per cent had university diplomas. Various
government-owned enterprises found themselves unable to lift prices, restrained
for political reasons; meanwhile the country's debt-service ratio climbed to
about 30 per cent while its balance of payments dived deeper into deficit
despite rising remittances from émigré Thai labourers and two devaluations of
the baht.

The oil glut beginning in the mid-1980s also hurt Thailand. Its oil and gas
fields began attracting less interest by the late 1980s. Tough terms brought in
by the Petroleum Authority of Thailand (PAT) in 1983 became unrealistic as
quickly as global prices fell; thereafter the third generation of oil exploration
contracts, known as 'Thai III', sharply cut back at the government's 50 per
cent share of gross oil revenues. Yet even then the incentives failed to entice
the foreign drillers. 'The suspicion of trouble [with PAT] will always be
there,' commented one foreign oil executive. 'In the longer run, you just
don't drill the marginal well.' This contraction of exploration occurred against
a backdrop of steadily declining production. Output fell to 21,000 barrels
per day (bpd) in 1985. These were body blows to Thai hopes to raise oil
production from 40 per cent to 65 per cent of total domestic petroleum needs
by 1990.

Indeed, by the middle 1980s many of the same difficulties troubling Thailand's Asean neighbours to the south had appeared, unexpected and unwanted,
at Thailand's doorstep. And it was not only a darkening commodities picture: after twenty good years the Thai banking system had started showing
signs of having overextended itself. It had begun to falter on the limitations
of family-based management, weak financial information, slothful government

supervision and astonishingly poor repayment performance by the banks' borrowers.

Financial Frights

In the financial sector these limitations showed a troubling penchant for dragging banks close to the abyss of bankruptcy. The Thai experience reflected many of Malaysia's growing pains; the banking industry in both countries waxed fat from two decades of profitable growth before earnings plummeted and non-performing loans quickly multiplied in the ledgers.

Unlike Malaysia however, no serious runs by depositors tarnished any of Bangkok's sixteen commercial banks. For that the Thais should be grateful. Although sorely tested after 1985, the Bank of Thailand's reputation for never allowing a private bank to go under held fast. It was just as well; Bangkok's small number of commercial banks, sixteen in all, started to experience a series of scandals after 1984. These problems soon multiplied, leading to some fully fledged financial emergencies that deeply shook a banking system reporting assets worth Bt850 billion, or US$32.7 billion, in 1988.

The scandals shook Thai complacency. The first glimmers of rough times ahead came in 1984 when the chairman of the Asia Trust Bank absconded. The chairman, Wallop Tarnvanichkul (known in Bangkok's banking world as 'Johnny Ma'), faced accusations of embezzlement and fraud. The central bank promptly guaranteed the bank's solvency. Less than two years later the First Bangkok City Bank's chief executive, reportedly unable to cope any longer with that bank's bad debts, also disappeared. Once again the Bank of Thailand obligingly came to the rescue. In each case the central bank made forced cuts to these erring banks' authorised share capital. Other local investors, hungry for a share of the limited banking business saw a rare chance to buy a bank. (Like the restrictive stock exchange listing policy, the Bank of Thailand does not approve new commercial banking licences.)

Siam City's Travail

Siam City Bank was the next to teeter at the edge. Siam City's former chairman, Boonchu Rojanastien, had by 1985 reported bad debts wiping out reserves and clocking up a Bt380 million deficit. Even this did not deter the central bank, which reassured depositors and saved Siam City's owner, the Mahadumrongkal family, from the ignominy of insolvency. The price of support by Bank of Thailand governor Kamchorn Sathirakul and finance minister Suthee Singhasaneh was high however: Siam City's subscribed capital was shaved by 95 per cent to pay off bad debts and bonus shares were issued to recoup a depleted capital ceiling.

The Thai government's willingness to save profligate bankers from the consequences of their own mismanagement seemed to run true to Southeast Asian form, a response almost identical to Malaysia's central bank. Another parallel could be found in the jostling of various cliques as bad debt problems exacerbated quarrels between shareholder factions. For example, Boonchu Rojanastien, a former finance minister, controlled part of Siam City while the Mahadumrongkals held the other part. Boonchu had claimed, back in 1983, that the bank's bad debts, if written off, would pull Siam City 380 million baht into the red. Boonchu had argued then for a 42 per cent capital increase but the Mahadumrongkal family spiked the move, evicting Boonchu from the bank's chairmanship. Yet in the élite world of Thai business, even Siam City's widely acknowledged capital shortfall did little to cause anxiety: at the central bank Kamchorn said the Mahadumrongkal/Boonchu quarrel was like a dispute between 'husband and wife', and he left the bank to its own devices for over two years.

Problems for Krung Thai

Meanwhile, another set of problems were increasingly dogging Krung Thai Bank, the second largest bank in the country but government owned. Krung Thai's stable of non-performing loans troubled its principal owner, the Thai finance ministry (which owns 76 per cent of Krung Thai's shares). However the ministry's old boy network protected Krung Thai's president, Tamchai Kambhato, under whose administration the bank had accumulated exposure reportedly reaching 10 billion baht (US$340 million at 1987 exchange rates). Krung Thai's chairman was Panas Simasathien, permanent secretary for finance and Thailand's highest ranking Civil Servant.

After Tamchai's departure in 1986, Panas moved to file criminal accusations against him for continuing to extend credit to defaulting borrowers. Soon afterwards, Thailand's auditor-general claimed that Krung Thai had made no provision at all in its reports for doubtful debts, a habit that is standard procedure for Thai banks. Krung Thai never worried much about debts; despite its less attractive interest rates the bank, almost as of right, receives deposits from nearly all Thailand's government-controlled companies. Financial analysts in Bangkok claim Krung Thai's usefulness becomes apparent when government cronies stumble into financial difficulties. It is always nice to know that there is a financial lifeline out there.

This function seemed well illustrated when Krung Thai paid 1.2 billion baht to buy poor quality stocks from brokerages badly exposed during the Thai stock market crash of 1980. The bank held on to the stocks, just managing to break even during the subsequent SET 'bull run' in the late 1980s. But Krung Thai's helpful rescue operations took many other forms; in 1987 it took over managing twenty-two insolvent cooperatives with impressive but doubtful book assets of 20 billion baht. All of the cooperatives were suffering from burgeoning, non-performing loan portfolios. The parallels to Malaysia were only too obvious.

In another imitation of Thailand's southern neighbour, Krung Thai also assumed control of the failing Sayam Bank, once called the Asia Trust Bank, which went technically bankrupt in 1984. Tamchai's successor, Tienchai Sriyichit, seemed content to carry on this quasi-government bail-out role. Shortly afterwards, a Krung Thai subsidiary, International Finance Consultants, also lent 3 billion baht as a credit lifeline to another bank. To many critics, such governmental generosity seemed to put keeping face among the business élite on a higher level of priority than keeping up the health of the financial system.

These alarming events during the mid-1980s forced some improvement in banking reporting standards. After 1986, all banks were required to disclose their bad-debt provisions. However, in the first year of the rule's operation the requirement was waived more than once. The central bank took a relaxed view however; 'what's the use [of the rules] if banks do not have credible balance sheets and income statements?' a central bank official was reported to have asked rhetorically. 'Even if they do issue them, the creditors and the foreign banks will not believe them anyway.' Once again, questions of 'face' appeared to prevail over fiscal discipline.

Looking at the bank scandals in retrospect, it may have been only 'economic prosperity [that] came to the rescue of the country's banks,' as the *Far Eastern Economic Review* commented in 1989. 'Heavy demand for capital ended a five-year liquidity flood in the space of a few months, driving up interest rates three points and helping banks to build profits. Many banks took advantage of this and began wiping off bad debts from previous years that had been enough to collapse nearly all financial institutions.'

Boardroom Bedlam

Lest it seem that only Thailand's banks had become imprudent during the mid-1980s, the story of Mah Boonkrong Drying and Silo Company proved instructive for bemused outsiders. For much of 1987, Bangkok's commercial community watched in fascination as Mah Boonkrong's president, a local Chinese named Sirichai Bulakul, warded off shareholder challenges to his stewardship of a company that had run up debts equivalent to US$85.3 million. The ensuing boardroom row soon became something of a national event.

On one occasion, when Mah Boonkrong's shareholders had an extraordinary meeting, some of Bulakul's supporters went to work. They applied all the finesse of a dirty tricks squad. First they switched off all the lights. Then they shut down the building's air conditioning, a particularly ruthless thing to do in Bangkok. On the face of it these rather extreme delaying tactics seemed to have little bearing on Bulakul's ostensible position in the company's share register. On the face of it, he owned less than 10 per cent of Mah Boonkrong. Business connections via Mah Boonkrong's tapioca shipping business have kept Bulakul in the chair, however. The same connections would keep the company's creditors at bay for a long time.

Risky Whisky

Another example of recession-induced trouble came in boardroom struggles to control the country's whisky distilleries, spawners of Thailand's largest fortunes and the contributor of 1 in every 10 baht of government revenue. The two largest producers, Surathip and Suramaharas, had initially planned a merger, to occur in 1986. It was to have been the biggest and certainly the most high-spirited monopoly in Southeast Asia. Both partners greatly expanded their capacity and both went steeply into debt. Later, when these reached US$1 billion, friendly banks came to the rescue.

At stake was Southeast Asia's most famous whisky, Mekong, a potent spirit celebrated in many Vietnam war novels. The merger also endangered another notorious blend, the so-called 'white' whisky which the Thais make in backyard distilleries; the fermenting molasses gives white whisky its stunning 35 per cent alcohol content. Two families, those of Thalerng Laochinda and of Charoen Srisomburananont, controlled the Surathip Group. In the Sumaraharas Group, Sumeth Techapaiboon's family was easily the most prominent. A bitter struggle erupted between the two families after the failed merger. Price wars brought the once profitable businesses to their knees. The government stepped in with a plan to phase out thirty-two small distilleries, substituting in their place twelve larger ones.

The plan obviously favoured Surathip. With backing from treasury bureaucrats and the biggest banks, Bangkok Bank and the Siam Commercial Bank, Surathip went for the Techapaiboon family's jugular. But that family was not without resources: its arsenal included a middle-sized bank, the Bangkok Metropolitan Bank, controlled by Sumeth's brother, Udane Techapaiboon. Financial observers said that the 'whisky wars' masked a bigger struggle to rearrange the strategic heights of Bangkok's financial world.

Superbike Racer and Santa Claus

These examples of a robustly greedy business culture reflect an increasingly wide open political style since the consolidation of parliamentary politics after 1981. In a uniquely Thai way, the cabinet ministers earn cheers and jeers from the ever partisan, always popular press. For example, prime minister Chatichai Choonhavan has earned the name 'Uncle Chat, the Superbike Racer' because of his penchant for driving motorcycles at high speed through Bangkok streets. (This must happen at night-time; daytime traffic in Bangkok forbids any movement faster than a crawl.) The press has nicknamed foreign minister Siddhi Savetsila 'Sensitive Grandpa', for his wise but easily irritated stewardship of his country's affairs. Finance minister Pramual Sabhavasu has received the appellation 'Santa Claus' for promising an end-of-year treasure trove.

These appellations illustrate the Thais' amusing disregard for politicians, a cynicism amply repaid by many MPs and their military patrons. Yet the system has also produced a few improbable heroes:

Last year I won the 400 metre race at the National Stadium. I'm not 35, I'm 53. Why did I win? Because I eat soybeans every day. When I was in Egypt, I climbed to the top of the pyramids. I don't eat meat, I eat only one meal a day. But my meat-eating Egyptian guides were afraid to follow me because they might not have made it back down. Call me an advertisement for soybeans!

The speaker, Chamlong Srimuang, is a retired army general and strict Buddhist. He also became, in 1986, the governor of metropolitan Bangkok. Until his party faltered in the 1988 elections, at which record amounts of money changed hands, Chamlong's voice was one of the few directed at corruption prevailing among some sections of Thailand's bureaucracy.

'The business élite in Thailand not only has direct and indirect control over numerous firms,' writes Keith Lapor, an economist at St Antony's College, Oxford, 'but have increased their influence and power further through inter-marriage between members of the four most powerful banking families . . . this may explain the abhorrence by many military men of Thai politicians – who are viewed as nothing more than political prostitutes.'

A Thai business analyst, writing for Tokyo's prestigious Institute of Developing Economies, has said that members of one prominent political party's ruling central committee control a total of sixty-nine large companies. He describes another political party leader as a textile conglomerate's chairman. And yet a different type of ersatz capitalist also emerged from the ranks of the military: examples include businesses set up by General Praphat Charusathien and by General Sarit Thamarat, who cornered much of the rice export, government insurance and public works businesses.

This amounts to just a military variation on an older habit among Thai officials who, according to John Girling's unflattering analysis (1981), 'have shown neither the will nor the ability to take over the economy or even the direction of the economy . . . they cannot simply rely on market forces or harmony of interests to provide them with the necessary sustenance; for they must use the power they have, political and coercive, to extract what they can.'

Press and media connections often back up these business and political connections. To take just one example, Kamphol Vacharaphol runs the mass circulation *Thai Rath* newspaper and various television stations in ways that seem to favour friends while disparaging various rivals. In this perfect expression of Platonic justice, Kamphol cultivates important friends who include Crown Prince Vajiralongkorn and industry minister Prachuab Suntrangkoon, who is also an army general.

Another Early Warning Signal: Foreign Debt

The 1980s did more than just confirm the already tight connections between the Thai business, military, political and bureaucratic élite. During that time those connections had been lubricated in part by a surge of foreign financing; as elsewhere in Southeast Asia, Thailand seemed to be acquiring an addictive habit of excessive debt finance.

Thailand's external indebtedness had grown alarmingly during the early 1980s. Total long-term debt, internal and external, rose from US$726 million in 1970 to US$14.2 billion in 1986, a jump from 11 per cent to 35.2 per cent of GNP. Repayments of principal, for both public and private foreign debt, increased from US$23 million in 1970 to US$1.2 billion sixteen years later. Yet it was the external public indebtedness that disturbed many Thais during the years that were being described, usually by foreigners, as 'miraculous'. From just 4.9 per cent in 1970, external public debt rose to 27.4 per cent of GNP in 1986 before falling back to more prudent levels.

A Narrowly Based Success Story

How much of Thailand's success rests on Thai-Chinese dynamism? How much does it depend on foreigners, rather than on an autonomous national achievement? How much do cultural obstacles such as bureaucratic favouritism impede business expansion?

Is not Thailand, ultimately, just one more example of what the Swedish economist Gunnar Myrdal described as a 'soft society', a place where (unlike the 'hard' societies of Northeast Asia or Western Europe the cultural predisposition is always to let someone else do the work? Dozens of writers, Thai and foreign, describe the steward-like, often professional but invariably parasitical Thai bureaucracy's enervating effect on the development of free market capitalism. 'This problem of balancing off economic realism with political demands represents the relationship between bureaucrats and businessmen in Thailand,' says Lapor. In dissecting these issues, it begins to seem that Thailand differs but little from its neighbours.

The vulnerability of Thailand's achievement stands out by the end of the 1980s. Business remained good, even buoyant, although protectionist sentiments in Europe and the US still darken the horizon. Resentment against American pressure over the copyright and trademark law (the same issue also being force-fed to the Indonesians, Malaysians and Singaporeans) has finally prompted the government to submit a draft intellectual property protection law.

The ensuing rumpus in parliament nearly caused the government to fall in 1988. Little enthusiasm exists for the notion that Thais should stop stealing designs and patents fashioned elsewhere. Pirated wristwatches, designer clothes, calculators and personal computers have tarnished Thailand's image abroad. Yet the government has little choice. The Americans have threatened Thailand's neighbours with withdrawal of trading benefits under its Generalised System of Preferences (GSP). The same message reached Thailand. The US takes over one-fifth of all Thai exports; one-fifth of these enter duty free under GSP privileges.

The threats to withdraw GSP privileges went down badly in Thailand, where an anti-American mood was swelling after a controversy over US textile quotas. Washington had also cleared the sale of a portion of US rice reserve stocks on the global market. This harmed the Thai rice trade and depressed prices. All of these were shortcomings in American diplomacy, perhaps, but they also illustrated how much Thailand's export-led strategy remains dependent on goodwill.

Narrow domestic and foreign participation in the share market also belies claims that 'mass capitalism' has arrived in Thailand. So does the endemic poverty of the countryside and the investment attraction of docile labour to assemble products that foreigners have designed and which are destined for foreign markets. That Siam Cement's 4,400 listed shareholders should make this giant firm one of the country's few, genuinely public companies reveals the distance between marketplace pretensions and commercial reality.

Once Again, The Chinese

As discussed at greater length in Chapter 7, the local Chinese community comprises nearly all Thailand's economic élite, a range of enterprise stretching, on the negative side, from heroin traders to timber tycoons whose rapacity has devastated the forest cover that covered nearly 70 per cent of Thailand in 1950. On the positive side, there is no question but that Thailand's tolerance has enabled the commercial dynamism of the overseas Chinese settling there to flower more luxuriantly than anywhere else in Southeast Asia.

Because of comparatively easy assimilation in Thailand, it is difficult to be precise about the size of the Thai Chinese community. Depending on one's willingness to think racially, a woolly approach even with the best intentions, there are between 100,000 'pure' Chinese and ten million 'mixed' Chinese in the country. But it is clear that nearly all the major Thai capitalists in business today betray a strong Chinese origin.

Chinese business expanded sharply during the nineteenth century. Immigrant Chinese sometimes acted as 'tax farmers' (i.e., contracting to deliver certain royalties to the royal treasury in return for a free hand in collecting them from a reluctant peasantry). The rice milling business, coupled with monopolies of rice distribution and trade, also enabled a rapid accumulation of Chinese capital in Thailand. Then the traders moved into banking: Wanglee Bank and Thye San Bank were the most prominent. Most of the 'Thai' banks today are in fact owned by the descendants of immigrant Chinese. Today, also, the Chinese serve as points of entry into the Thai market for Japanese firms.

The Chinese retain control of Thai business through interlocking directo-rates and kinship ties. These create what one Thai writer calls a 'symbiotic relationship' between the Sino-Thai business community, the military and the bureaucracy. The foundation of Thai business and politics rests on this small group, closely tied to the bureaucracy. Keith Lapor also notes the continuing 'clique rivalry in which various Chinese businessmen pair themselves off with different groups of bureaucrats.' The uproar over the wretchedly run affairs of many commercial banks showed how far, and how deep, those connections run.

Even in flexible, tolerant Thailand, a slight tremor of irritation against the Chinese could be felt when these scandals emerged. It has become an article of faith however that the anti-Chinese policies of the 1950s will never be repeated. Introduced by the then prime minister Phibul Songkhram to reduce dependence on Chinese capital and spearheaded by government companies in commerce, utilities and manufacturing, the campaign ultimately created a pampered public enterprise sector in which cosy dealings with the Chinese continue. Various state monopolies were supposed to cut back Chinese influence in such industries as sugar, paper and tobacco. Even the manufacture of playing-cards was passed to a government company.

It all seems a long time ago. Certainly, the Chinese sway over business has, if anything, grown even more commanding in the last thirty years. In Thailand the mere mention of the most prominent Thai Chinese families will also connote the area of trade which their scions have come to dominate. The family of Suree Assadathorn, for example, runs Thai Roong Ruang, a large sugar conglomerate. The late Jootee Boonsoong's family continues his Isuzu truck assembling plant and spare parts businesses. Taaworn Pornprapha's family runs Siam Motors, the sole distributor of Nissan cars. Dhanin Chiaravanont's family runs Thailand's largest argricultural company, Charoen Pokphand, while the relatives of Lawang Laohathai help him run one of the country's largest trading companies. The list is long and formidable.

The joint-venturing habits of Dumri Kontuntakiet, Thailand's most successful tuna processor and aquaculturalist, illustrate these traits perfectly. He is proud of his arrangement with Sumitomo, which has joined him in a joint venture tin-plating factory, an adjunct to his canning operations.

'That's what Thailand has to do to improve the lot of its people,' Dumri told *Newsweek* magazine in 1987. 'Sometimes Thais are not aggressive enough; we have to be tougher because we shouldn't lose this golden opportunity.' Dumri might have been speaking, a Thai government minister grumbled to me later, to a closed door meeting of the Chinese Chamber of Commerce. But, more to the point what are Dumri and his Chinese peers actually doing? As Yoshihara Kunio puts it, in his excellent book *The Rise of Ersatz Capitalism in South-East*

Asia (1988), this type of 'development' is often 'technology-less industrialisation'. '[The Chinese] activities appear quite technologically sophisticated, and they are sometimes hailed as industrial pioneers; but the fact is that they are Japanese compradors.'

Addictive Habits

Up country from Bangkok the Chinese also control another industry – the harvesting, processing and sale of the Golden Triangle's most notorious crop. A Chinese clan network around the world shows the usual business acumen in selling opium. Many of the local Thai authorities either openly sanction or, for reasons of fear, turn a blind eye to the trade. Others, chiefly in the Thai military, conduct a more frontal challenge.

At Chiang Saen, exactly in the centre of the poppy-growing region embracing Burma, Laos and Thailand, the government has built an 'Opium Museum' where tourists pay to see displays carrying warnings against drug abuse. Outside museum confines however the area is still thick with opium warlords such as the legendary Khun Sa, veteran of many battles with the nearby Burmese Army. Khun Sa is a Chinese; his real name is Chang Chi-Fu. He remains one of Thailand's most autonomous traders; only in 1982 did the Thai army dislodge his 20,000 strong Shan United Army from poppyfields yielding 600–700 tonnes of the sticky substance each year. During much of the 1980s growers in South Asia, notably in Pakistan, had eclipsed Chang and his friends but a bountiful harvest in 1989 swung the Golden Triangle back into its accustomed prominence on world markets. With the usual Thai flair, even this notoriety can be exploited for the tourist trade, and an increasing number of the 4 million tourists arriving in Thailand each year now journey to the north, some of them to stand beside a newly built marker which announces that one has reach the fabled 'Golden Triangle'.

Looming Uncertainties

Foreign investment, resilient Chinese entrepreneurship, surging exports, re-bounding commodity prices and bureaucratic business linkages have each helped to make Thailand's economic miracle. But there is another regional trend which could promise less satisfaction. In company with its Southeast Asian neighbours, Thailand cannot escape from what is known as the 'transition issue'.

This takes many forms. Prime Minister Prem Tinsulanonda's long tenure finally ended in July 1988. Taking his place was a disco-dancing diplomat, Chatichai Choonhavan whose Chart Thai party won a prominent place following parliamentary elections in that year. By April 1989 Chatichai had weathered nine difficult months and Bangkok's pundits were reluctant to forecast anything like as long a tenure as Prem, a top-ranking general, enjoyed. Yet the future and stability of Thai business depends on more than the parliamentary process – which involves an interplay of favouritism and patronage among 268 upper house members (of which 215 comprise policemen and soldiers) and 347 MPs in the lower house. Most MPs, in either house, are older men who come from the well-off strata of Thai society.

First Uncertainty: The Monarchy

Leadership changes of another variety also confront Thailand. The country's widely respected King Phumipol Adunyadej, the ninth successive monarch in the two-century-old Chakris dynasty, had his sixtieth birthday in 1987. The King is fit and should live a long time yet.

While his subjects certainly wish him to do so, the succession (though it is impolite to speak audibly about it in Thailand), poses problems that already worry the Thais, accustomed now to a particular style of integrity in the monarchical rule. The King now acts as a check on the military. He can also control to some extent the direction the military will take through the exercise of his approval for high promotions. His preference for representative institutions helps the parliamentary system, crooked though it sometimes is, to persist.

In particular, it is said the Crown Prince Vajiralongkorn may not share the same approach as his father and, in this regard, the Queen might count for a great deal. The King has four daughters, one of whom (the middle one) was considered the monarch's favourite to succeed to the throne during the 1970s. She remains the most admired of the royal children.

The monarchy has come a long way since its absolutism was toppled by a coup in 1932. The royal household's considerable assets are management by the Crown Property Bureau. While subject to great secrecy and sensitivity, the bureau is known to have controlling interests in such blue chip companies as Siam Cement and in Siam Commercial Bank, as well as large chunks of prime business district real estate.

The monarchy's future is just one of many imponderables which include the following questions: will the military allow itself to be eclipsed by politicians whom it continues to hold in barely disguised contempt? How will the Bangkok urban sprawl, likely to become one of the world's fifteen largest cities by 1995, affect mass politics? Will a wave of resentment swell up against the fast-baht mentality of the Thai Chinese?

For all the talk of Thailand's rock-hard stability, this is something less than certain. It is not so long ago that Thailand had the reputation of a Southeast Asian Bolivia, a place where largely bloodless military coups did the business of political succession. A 1971 coup in Thailand had ended a three-year experiment in parliamentary democracy. Intermittent civil disorders had continued until 1973, when the form of democratic government was re- sumed again, only to be abandoned once more in 1976. Two coups occurred before 1980, when Prem took the helm. Two more, both failures, happened after that. The success rate was better before that; between 1932 and 1980 nine coups ousted the government. Thirteen constitutions came, and went, without the public taking much interest. The current constitution dates from 1978.

The late Robert Shaplin, who wrote from Asia for many years on assignment to the *New Yorker*, identified this still changing and fluid political foundation during the 1970s. 'One of the greatest anomalies in Thailand has become the role of the monarchy,' he wrote in 1979, 'which since the 1973 student coup had diminished in the public image. No longer a sacrosanct subject, in the late seventies it had become a source of gossip and, as far as the communists were concerned, an object of derisive propaganda.' The monarchy's esteem has risen considerably since then but the past moods serve to signpost the continuing uncertainties of Thai political life.

Second Uncertainty: The Military

As the quasi-civilian, parliamentary system consolidates there is a tendency to imagine that the Thai military's fixation with direct intervention has gone for good. This seems a wish-fulfilling exercise. During 1988 the government of (former general) Prem Tinsulanonda found it necessary to drop all charges against most of the forty army defendants charged with sedition arising from the attempted coup in 1985.

Shortly afterwards, army commander in chief Chaovalit Yongchaiyuth, supposedly a Prem supporter, issued a statement insisting on a political role for the military and noting that the country's 'deterioration' would lead to a 'revolution' after the army 'had sought prior approval from the public.' No prior approval had been solicited in earlier coups so this attitude, later firmed up in an army document called *Thai Politics from the Military's Perspective*, became more worrying. It was also accepted that Chaovalit was running hard to become the next prime minister; despite the parliamentary system Prem did not sit in the National Assembly. Chaovalit reasoned the same way.

'General Chaovalit's assertiveness reflected the military's view of itself as the protector of the national interest . . . the army declined to accept the unsavoury features of the existing political system, such as the widespread vote-buying and infighting for cabinet positions,' Kusuma Snitwongse noted in 1989. 'Because vast amounts of funds were normally spent on vote-buying during election campaigns, it was understood that politicians hoped to recoup their expenses by attaining cabinet portfolios,' said Kusuma, who is attached to Bangkok's prestigious Chulalongkorn University.

Chaovalit lobbied strongly against devaluation and, in the same year, even propounded an agrarian based, poverty-alleviating economic strategy. His supporters made much of the imbalances of the Thai economy, particularly the fact that the industrial sector was growing ten times as fast as agriculture, a result that widened income gaps between poor farmer and rich (usually) Chinese merchant, and between city (read: Bangkok) and countryside. Soon afterwards the military intervened in the purchase and distribution of rice, for which project it demanded, and received, an interest-free, 120 million baht government loan.

Chaovalit failed to become prime minister. But the opportunities for military politicking in the same vein have not diminished. Under Chaovalit a populist message came through loud and clear. His successors will be tempted to play the same, well-worn groove. Somehow the new, widely touted 'non-interventionist Thai military' still bears an uncanny resemblance to its earlier reincarnation as coup-maker and ultimate power broker. Any businessman with an ounce of sense is still cultivating the soldiers.

Third Uncertainty: Regional Conflicts

> Twenty years ago, America was Thailand's dependable ally and 'Red China' the menace to the north. Today, Thai generals proudly drive their newly delivered Chinese tanks as US military assistance, and influence, continues to decline. One US military officer told me ruefully, 'Thai generals used to come to you and throw their arms around you saying, "we're pals." Now they only do that with the Chinese.'

This extract from the political analyst Eric Guyot's letter to me of March 1988 underscored the many changes now occurring within the Thai military. To their habit of meddling in capital city politics had come another, albeit unwelcome task: defending the country from a well-trained foreign adversary.

Guyot joined other analysts in focusing on two shocks from Vietnam, the cumulative effect of which is to push Thailand closer to the People's Republic of China. Shock number one occurred when the Americans insisted after 1969 that 'Asian nations themselves' would have to look after their own defence. Shock number two occurred when a newly reunited Vietnam invaded neighbouring Cambodia in December 1978. 'Within a matter of weeks, the Thai armed forces, which had last officially fought a foreign war in 1845, now faced the world's third largest military machine,' Guyot said.

The odds looked none too pleasing. 'From the Thai perspective, its ancient [Vietnamese] enemy had defeated the French in eight years, the Americans in eight years too, and had just fought China for 17 days, arguably emerging the victor.' The chilling prospect of tangling with Vietnam resulted quickly in an informal alliance with China, one that persists to the present day. Yet the Thais do not take their country's stability necessarily for granted, and neither should investors in Thailand. Quite apart from the now receding fear of invasion, the Indochinese wars have deposited more than 325,000 refugees in Thailand – mostly Cambodians but also about 80,000 Laotians and nearly 5,000 Vietnamese. Diplomatic fumbling by Thailand in this arena of conflict could make, overnight, a hash of economic forecasts.

Fourth Uncertainty: Will the Domestic 'Demand Base' Be Rich Enough?

Both the Thai Chinese and the foreigners have concentrated their money in light industry, stepping into agro-business, notably an enthusiasm for prawn farming, as well as toy making, jewellery and disk drive manufacture. Despite the enormous gains made in manufactured exports, something close to one-half of Thai exports comprise foodstuffs or beverages.

This type of footloose, light industry creates little follow-on opportunities for local workshops, however, while they add to imbalances in purchasing power between Bangkok and the countryside. Even during the time of the boom urban unemployment had climbed well beyond the officially acknowledged 4 per cent; in 1988 the number of new 'job market entrants', as the jargon goes, came to 850,000 youths. Most Thai analysts believe unemployment has growth both absolutely, in overall numbers of workless people, and as a percentage of the total workforce.

The troubling prospect of the 'graduate unemployed' has become more serious since an unofficial freeze in 1985 on expanding the bureaucracy any further.

Although foreign firms add many semi-skilled employees to their payrolls, more substantive economic effect is elusive. An analysis of the employment generating effects in an Export Processing Zone in Malaysia (see Chapter 3) finds an echo in various Thai studies. In short, there is not very much. Despite foreign investment approvals increasing after 1986 by nearly 100 per cent each year, little heavy industrial expansion has occurred.

At the end of 1978 a confidential report of the World Bank, leaked to the press, revealed that one-third of all agricultural households in Thailand, or about nine million people, still lived in conditions of absolute poverty. The report criticised not only the rich landlord interests but also the invariably corrupt bureaucracy, for failing to confront Thailand's poverty. This truism remains; a land reform programme dating from the 1970s has become stymied by powerful landed interests, one of many reasons (see below) for Thailand's dismal agricultural productivity. Meanwhile, the absolute number of absolute poor has grown.

The preface to another World Bank study, this one in 1980, said that 'analysis of economic change in Thailand over the past two decades clearly shows that rapid and sustained growth has lifted a very substantial proportion of the population out of absolute poverty but [also] that a significant proportion of the rural population, particularly in the outer regions, has been left out of the process of economic change.' Elsewhere it emphasised that 'Thailand should not, and indeed, need not follow the type of development strategy that enables the bulk of the population to improve their standard of living only through the slow "trickling down" of benefits from the top.'

A full decade later, that cautionary advice has not been heeded, despite the trumpeted arrival of another 'miracle' and claims that, by the 1990s, Thailand will have become a 'fully industrialised state', to echo a prediction by the National Economic and Social Development Board. Yet the gap between urban incomes and those in the countryside has widened, not narrowed, since the boom.

If he is lucky, a farmer might make one-eighth of the income of even an odd-jobbing labourer in the city. Appalling slum conditions characterise life in much of an increasingly polluted Bangkok. 'Income distribution surfaced as one of the government's most important challenges during [the late 1980s],' according to the *Far Eastern Economic Review*. 'For wage earners and Civil Servants, not to mention the rural sector, individual incomes were not keeping pace with higher commodity and consumer goods prices, partly because of the continued flow of unemployed and underemployed people from country areas.' For long-term market expansion, the Thai demand base remains rooted in the one and only city worthy of the name: Bangkok.

The Parasitic City

In the 1960s, Keith Buchanan, a New Zealand geographer, coined the phrase 'Parasitic City' to describe social transformation in Southeast Asia. The expression, and the reality spawning it, remain the same nearly thirty years later. Over 75 per cent of corporate tax revenues come from the metropolitan region. Almost every per capita index of progress – telephones, light bulbs, doctors, hospital beds, motor cars and the like – show a Bangkok weighting that, literally, puts the rest of the country to shame. Yet the pace of urbanisation overall in Thailand is laggard by contrast to other Asian nations rushing headlong towards fully fledged industrialism. For impoverished peasants, Bangkok is the only manufacturing Mecca. A lengthening procession of Thai and foreign advisers have preached the need for regional development but the tide towards the capital city seems irreversible now.

The Fast-baht Crowd

Meanwhile the boom has elicited all the worst aspects of Southeast Asian vulgarity. In 1988 the *Asian Wall Street Journal*'s Helen White described housing developments with

> cherubim-laden arches and Venetian style bridges. Ornamental urns and balustrades adorn homes named 'Pandora', 'Mercury', 'Hermes' and 'Ulysses' . . . many well-to-do urbanites, enriched by Thailand's steady economic growth in recent years, have opted to broadcast their wealth with ostentatious homes; apart from pilaster sensations, some builders . . . offer such exotic styles as 'Victorian Princess' or 'Bavarian Castle'.

A World Bank paper of 1980 said it all: 'Growth has been accompanied by a widening disparity of welfare among population groups and among the different geographical areas in the country.' What, one might well ask, has changed in the intervening, boom years? The picture of Thai development begins to look increasingly skewed and partial, weighted towards the middle earners of just one albeit fast-growing city.

Fifth Uncertainty: Disappearing Forests

On 10 January 1989 the Thai government of prime minister Chatichai Choonhavan issued an unprecedented directive, abrogating with immediate effect all timber concessions. The move followed crippling floods during the previous November in southern Thailand when avalanches of mud and timber debris from denuded hillsides swept through valleys killing at least 500 people and devastating farmland. 'In three days we saw the equivalent of a thousand years of erosion,' said a member of the Thai parliament.

The floods, the worst recorded in Thailand, provoked strong public anger about the 71 million cubic feet of timber removed each year by logging companies working 301 concessions. 'Thai officials and journalists say they have been wary of probing logging controversies, fearing rich and powerful timber interests might resort to violence to silence them,' said a Reuters report from Bangkok. For a while a bolder approach seemed to be working but the Chatichai government's brave measure led quickly to two problems.

First, Thailand's need for wood continued unabated, resulting in imports of lumber increasing from 700,000 cubic metres to at least 3 million cubic metres a year. Deforestation in Burma and Laos promptly accelerated to meet the demand. Two days after the Thai ban, cash-hungry Laotian authorities repealed a prohibition against exporting raw logs to Thailand, a measure imposed just a month earlier to slow down deforestation in that country.

Secondly, the government's prohibition cannot be fully enforced. An immediate problem arises from charges that many of agriculture minister Sanan Kachornprasart's cabinet colleagues have become rich from the timber trade. There are many more beneficiaries: military officers retain profitable business ties with Chinese loggers and the forestry department itself is notoriously corrupt. In 1989 a retired supreme court judge, Niyom Tiwtanont, spoke out against the 'corruption that riddles all aspects of the timber trade.' He described forestry officials and their logger friends as a 'provincial mafia.'

In addition, the ban ignores the thorny problem of the immediate unemployment it has caused. Hundreds of thousands of Thai labourers and farmers practising shifting cultivation depend on depletion of the forest. They will evade the ban which, for intimate commercial reasons, is being poorly enforced anyway. Meanwhile the continuing deforestation, as in the Philippines, poses a clear and present danger to Thai agriculture, threatening also many hydroelectric, hydraulic and irrigation works.

'Thailand is losing its forests rapidly,' said the International Union for Conservation of Nature and Natural Resources in 1989. 'Destruction of valuable watersheds is affecting runoff and causing excessive floods and erosion. Siltation of reservoirs is becoming a serious problem.' At the very least, Thailand is losing its timber resource, once a money-maker. At the very worst, Thailand is endangering much of its infrastructure and degrading land quality. The prescription for many rural families is more poverty; they will not fit easily into the glowing projections of a wealthier domestic 'demand base' for Thailand's industries.

Sixth Uncertainty: The Wrong Skills

The Thais have increased primary school enrolment to 97 per cent of all targeted children. Whereas in 1965 only 2 per cent of the tertiary age group was enrolled at a tertiary institution, twenty years later this had risen to 20 per cent. But in spite of these gains, 'another factor which surfaced was the poor supply of skilled labour and professional workers,' the 1988 *Asia Yearbook* notes. 'The most severe deficiencies were in science and engineering,' it adds. Revealingly, the allocation for education, as a percentage of total government spending, has been static since 1965.

It is not simply the static spending that is so worrying. Reports from the government's Office of University Affairs show low, static percentages of graduates taking degrees or diplomas in science and engineering. During the 1970s the figure rose from 12 per cent to 14 per cent of total graduates. But then, despite the large increase in university rolls, this figure has held constant ever since – in sharp contrast even to the comparative figures elsewhere in Asean.

Let's All Be Lawyers (or Civil Servants)

Of 6,225 graduates in science and engineering in 1984, for example, only 300 Thais took a degree that year in any area of the natural sciences; by 1988, not one Thai had completed a PhD in physics, for example. In a review of graduate unemployment, Thai educationist Achara Vorasirisonthorn has written that 'natural science graduates find it much more difficult to gain employment . . . as Thai development policy puts little emphasis on research in new technology, most of which is imported.'

Worse still, UNESCO data on the percentage distribution of Asean students by field of study shows fewer Thai students entering these fields today than in 1970 (see Table 2). It is difficult to disagree with the dissenting Thai economist Pakdee Tanapura; he says 'the history of successful industrial capitalist development . . . illustrates that it is *not* [Tanapura's italics] the resource base that determines the wealth of a nation but rather the quality, development and distribution of the manpower and labour force.'

Table 2 Percentage distribution of university students by field of study in five Asean countries: 1970 and latest year available

Country	Year	Total students	% in science and engineering
Indonesia	(1971)	252,000	18.2
	(1982)	616,000	15.2
Malaysia	(1970)	14,500	30.7
	(1981)	67,368	34.2
Philippines	(1971)	688,000	14.0
	(1981)	1,336,000	33.8
Singapore	(1970)	14,000	44.5
	(1982	31,000	57.4
Thailand	(1970)	55,000	13.6
	(1987)	217,000	9.5

SOURCE: UNESCO

Seventh Uncertainty: Infrastructure

Thailand has also fallen behind in providing for a strong foundation for sustained growth. Its communications system is close to collapsing under the strain of sudden growth. Although the proportion of imported energy has fallen within the country's overall energy consumption, it still stands at about half. But falling global oil prices have undercut the attractiveness of incentives to foreigners to search for new fields; most firms have postponed exploration plans. Moreover, many estimates of Thai natural gas fields have had to be scaled down; doubts centre on the recoverability of some of the finds.

By the late 1970s Thailand began planning for a huge project, the Eastern Seaboard Development Programme. The plan was aimed at redistributing investment to the east of Bangkok and the cost, set at US$4.5 billion at 1981 prices, would have covered new port, roads and communications with a natural gas pipeline.

After doing its sums again in the early 1980s however, the government realised that the cost would exceed 'more than ten times the average cost for new industrial investment', as the World Bank noted in its *World Development Report* for 1988, while adding new foreign load indebtedness. As a result, the programme was scaled down radically, with total expenditure only half that originally planned.

None the less, a badly needed new port at Laem Chabang was expected to open in 1991, despite cancellation in 1988 of a US$460 million fertiliser plant on the east coast. The port will ease horrendous congestion at Bangkok's existing port. 'The worst of the country's utilities, such as telecommunications, cannot even begin to meet the new demand,' according to the *Far Eastern Economic Review*. Thailand has a very low 1.8 telephones per 100 inhabitants; by contrast the figure is 6.3 in Malaysia and 27 in Singapore. These are becoming severe constraints on developments, even within the export-led, urban-centred model the Thais have chosen.

Eighth Uncertainty: Laggard Farmers

Food and food products accounted for half of all Thai exports in 1984. This is an increase over the 1973 figures. Yet, despite its importance, even those steady supports of Thai agriculture, tapioca and pineapples, did not have a guaranteed future by the close of the 1980s. Tapioca arrives in Rotterdam in crude form, where it is ground and processed into cattle forage. Thailand's tapioca competes with French grain, an irritant to that country and to other grain exporters, notably the US and Canada. Since 1981 an import quota of 5 million tonnes has prevented Thailand from expanding its tapioca exports; the quota may rise higher after 1992.

The lucrative Thai pineapple canning industry, which began when US companies escaped Hawaii's rising costs in the 1960s, has surged ahead as political instability in the Philippines prompts multinational growers like Dole and Del Monte to look for new sources of supply. Thailand has gained both their attention and investment. Canned pineapple became, by the late 1980s, the country's seventh largest industrial export. Thai pineapples accounted for one-third of total world trade in this fruit.

Yet of fifteen major companies doing business in pineapples, the *Asian Wall Street Journal* in 1988 reported only three making money in the middle of a boom: Thai Pineapple Canning Industry, Dole Thailand Limited and Siam Food Products Company. The others were simply coasting on special promotional privileges extended by the government. Under-capacity plagues the industry. The companies buy pineapples, not from their own plantations, but from over 50,000 small farmers who have ploughed up their sugar cane to make way for pineapple.

More generally, economist Uwe Parpart has identified (1986) the persistence of 'low-productivity agriculture' as a 'millstone around the nation's neck and the principal barrier to successful future economic development.' He writes that, 'population, total rice production and harvested cultivated area have all roughly quadrupled – with no increase in average productivity in 60 years!' Thailand remains fundamentally a rice economy but 'despite crop diversification in the past two decades, rice cultivation continues to dominate the agricultural sector.' Parpart's analysis of average yields, in his own words, 'reveals the danger . . . of low-productivity expansion of cultivated area.'

Vulnerable Miracle?

Thailand remains one of the best places to do business in Southeast Asia. Less interference? Undoubtedly. A more diversified economy? Unquestionably. More cooperation with local Chinese entrepreneurs? Self-evidently. The government knows the game, and plays it well, allowing few racial, political or religious obstacles to trip up or harass unwary investors from abroad.

Yet Thailand, at the end of the day, remains as firmly locked into the demand-led phenomenon of Asean prosperity as any of its tropical Asian neighbours, no matter how much more successfully its exporting business was performing as the 1990s began. Even the macroeconomic picture appears less solid on closer examination.

First, the terms of trade – how many units of exports are needed to pay for a unit of imports – continue on a historical negative trend against Thailand. Poor longer-term prospects for commodity prices, as seemed likely in 1989, imply that Thailand has to move faster to reduce dependence on agriculture.

Secondly, there is an unvarying gap between the savings rate, rather reasonable, and the rate of investment. During all the 1980s however, both savings and investment have fallen. Investment as a percentage of GDP dipped below 20 per cent in 1986, one of the lowest Asian rates. This means too much reliance on foreign money.

Thirdly, and throughout all the headlong boom, Thailand's exports have not covered its import bill. In 1987, for example, its export receipts of US$14 billion came US$1.2 billion short of the import bill. Only tourist spending, about US$2 billion a year, plus hard-to-quantify amounts remitted home by nearly 150,000 Thai workers abroad, brought the account into overall net surplus.

These are both slippery foundations on which to base a sustained economic drive. Tourism, as is all too well known, depends disproportionately on the sex trade. As a February 1989 conference in Bangkok made plain, it is simply a matter of time before the fatal AIDS affliction begins to become apparent. The result will be quick and catastrophic for the Pattya, Phuket and Bangkok sex trade.

Already there are signs, such as the imposition of special fees for tourists, that the golden goose may be endangered by petty depradations. The crush of tourists at the major Thai temple sites may soon qualify as an affront by itself. *The Economist*, commenting on tourist impact, noted that 'piped music and marching songs blare out over loudspeakers' in many temples. The social costs of catering to tourism, which now earns much more than rice exports, are becoming more onerous.

Similarly, remittances from overseas workers are vulnerable. The Middle East, for long a destination for Thai menial and semi-skilled workers, has become less buoyant. The Gulf States have cut back on foreign workers, especially those from Southeast Asia, preferring to use Pakistanis, Bangladeshis and others of the same religion. The cut-backs in new project starts in the Gulf countries, the consequences of stagnating petroleum markets after 1985, have badly cut back this source of remittances.

Yet these external payments, just as in the Philippines, have a vital effect on rural welfare; the best appointed homes in the countryside invariably belong to families with one or more members working abroad. Another destination for many Thais is Japan, where menial work offers, by comparison with Thai wage scales, rather large salaries. Thai women in their tens of thousands also work as 'hostesses' and 'entertainers' in Tokyo nightclubs.

A fourth cause for worry on the macroeconomic side is fear that the government may start listening to advisers urging higher foreign borrowing to accelerate the rush to NIC status. While Thailand opted during 1987–88 to prepay some of its external debt, the government has not lost its habit of spending more than it earns. The budget deficit in 1987 came close to 4 per cent of GDP; in 1988 the politicians opted for an 11.1 per cent increase in government spending. Having brought debt-servicing down by the late 1980s, Thailand may thus soon face an upsurge of new interest payments. But is the overall strategy correct?

In 1980, after all, inflation had peaked at 20 per cent while foreign debt had been growing at nearly 30 per cent per annum in the three previous years. It is even more likely that the current government, an interesting hybrid between military and civilian control, might react more precipitately to 'preserve prosperity' by reckless borrowing. If not, can a regime currying civilian support find the political will to raise taxes? 'Traditionally', Merrill Lynch's chief Asia economist Sanjay Chaudry says, 'tax collection has not been among Thailand's most successful industries.'

Finally, and not least, if the international economic environment worsens again the Thai miracle may seem little more than another *ningas cogon*, a Filipino expression meaning 'prairie fire' or 'flash in the pan.' The vagaries of world trade rescued Thailand after 1986, notably a 40 per cent drop in oil prices during that year plus significantly lower international capital market rates. 'If these developments had not occurred,' Merrill Lynch told its clients in 1988, '[Thailand's] position would be quite near to that at end-1985 – dismal.'

Free Riders After All

The modern Thai economy results from changes initiated in the middle of the last century, when the Siamese monarchy reacted to colonial encroachment by the colonial powers, notably the British and the French to the west and east, respectively. Two kings, Mongkut and his son Chulalongkorn opened their closed society to world trade, and started rapid administrative change. Alone among all the territories now comprising Asean, Thailand escaped colonial rule.

No one denies Thailand its many achievements, which taken together have pushed economic growth rates to levels only dreamed about in other areas of the developing world. This has occurred with close cooperation from successive teams of World Bank advisers. The Bank's guidance since 1980 has been steady, and remarkably consistent, in its broad outlines. So too has the willingness to listen on the Thai side. Former finance minister Sommai Hoontrakul's long stewardship became synonymous with World Bank-minded 'restructuring'. His former deputy, Suthee Singhasaneh, continued this free marketeering bias after Sommai's departure in July 1986.

Yet the dynamic is other peoples' markets. These days the main impetus for growth comes not from the Thai 'natives' but from Japanese, Korean or Taiwanese investors who set up in Thailand because of wage scales which, as of 1989, amounted to less than one-sixth of the equivalent rate in Taiwan and to just *one-sixteenth* of the remuneration given for the same work in Japan. These days, Thailand's growth comes from a government now willing, in the face of fierce domestic criticism, to throw away nearly all the foreign equity participation constraints once part of the stock in trade of Thai nationalism. 'It just isn't possible to do much more,' a Nomura Securities analyst told me in Bangkok. 'How can they relax exchange controls more than they already have?

How can they give more tax breaks than they have already?' The Thais, in short, have sold the farm.

Korean Comparisons

In the sense that such an economy becomes self-generating in its technology, in its skills, in its applied research, Thailand still presents a question mark. 'Like Singapore,' Kunio says provocatively, 'Thailand does not have dynamic industrial capitalists of its own; technologically they are dependent on foreign companies.'

If, as I argue, *this* is more appropriately the measure of transition out of dependence, passivity and economic subjection, then the Thais have not yet passed the test. On present trends they may need to wait many more years before industrialisation on even the South Korean model occurs.

Has reliance on foreign investment per se, as contrasted to foreign debt finance, helped or hindered Thailand's ambition to become a self-generating industrial country? Lapor has compared South Korea's industrialisation with Thailand's economic growth since the 1960s and concludes that the Thais have made the wrong choice. He finds that the sums coming into Korea as DFI 'contributed only a small share of total capital formation.'

Both countries began with import substitution policies to build up their industries – that is, encouraging local manufacture of products available on the world market, and protecting the new 'infant' manufacturers from foreign competition by high tariffs. Thirty-five years ago, South Korea and Thailand stood in roughly the same position.

Since then, various economic measurements show a widening gap between the two economies. The numbers of Koreans or Thais employed in agriculture or industry, or the amount of energy consumption per capita, or the proportion of Korean or Thai students taking science and technology courses, or the industrial content of the two countries' exports – all these measurements suggest that South Korea has become a self-reliant industrial economy while Thailand has not.

One reason for this result is government efficiency and patrimonialism. Lapor contrasts the South Korean government's machinery to Thailand's, saying that the 'ability of the government to follow a rational policy has been prevented in large part by the presence . . . of powerful interests which have resulted in the virtual impotence of the planning process.' It is not a matter of the Koreans running a spotlessly clean administration; revelations in the Korean press during 1988 and 1989 showed that considerable corruption permeates that country. But corruption does not, per se, impede the development of a modern economy. The Japanese system of business vividly illustrates this point as well. Perhaps the *effect* of illicit payments on overall economic planning, rather than their mere presence in an economy, spells the crucial difference. Thai patronage may be of the more 'free-riding' variety without contributing much in return.

In the final analysis, therefore, Thailand's 'economic miracle' does not seem her own creation. In the past, the ideas, money, skills and markets came from local Chinese monopolists and financiers, or from *farang* (the Thai word for Western) countries like Britain, France or America. The taking of that role today appears increasingly to be the prerogative of Japan, of which more is said in Chapter 12.

It does not require clairvoyance to imagine the events that, in retrospect, will be seen as knocking reality back into Bangkok's boom. A sharp deterioration of

the domestic and external accounts; a resumption of foreign indebtedness; higher
inflation; a move to 'distort' domestic economic policy by adopting 'nationalist'
(i.e. anti-Chinese) policies or by resorting again to price controls and domestic
protectionism – all these could derail this latest Southeast Asian success story. We
might join the Thais in hoping the train stays on track, but we must acknowledge
that the engine speeding ahead in front carries a bogus maker's plate. It may be a
powerful dynamo, but it is not 'Made in Thailand'.

References

Girling, J. (1981) *The Bureaucratic Polity in Modernizing Societies: Similarities,
Differences and Prospects in the Asean Region*. Singapore: ISEAS

Hewison, K. (1987) 'National interests and economic downturn: Thailand', in Robison,
R., Hewison, K. and Higgott, R. *Southeast Asia in the 1980s*. Sydney: Allen & Unwin

Kunio, Y. (1988) *The Rise of Ersatz Capitalism in South-East Asia*. Singapore: Oxford
University Press

Parpart, U. (1986) 'A strategy for the agro-industrial development of Thailand', *Bangkok
Bank Monthly Review*, December

World Bank (1988) *Thailand: Toward a Development Strategy of Full Participation*. Washington, DC

World Bank (1988) *World Development Report*. Washington, DC

6

SINGAPORE: THE EXCEPTION THAT RULES THE PROOF

Success Story

The Republic of Singapore evokes powerful and contradictory emotions in South-east Asia – an odd reaction, one might have thought, to a small city-state of just 2.7 million people. Yet the ambivalent response stems from deeply-rooted insecurities over the island's remarkable success.

Singapore forms an exception to the region in nearly all respects. In a predominantly rural archipelago it is overwhelmingly urban. It has achieved standards of living far in excess of its neighbours. The Asean bloc's 300 million non-Singaporeans live in resource-rich countries, as Chapter 8 makes clear, but Singapore needs even to import its own water. Neighbouring countries wax fat from commodity cropping and petroleum, but Singapore lives by its wits. Above all else, others in the region rarely forget that Singapore is the only predominantly ethnic Chinese nation among them.

In Singapore these characteristics result in a type of unconscious double life, in a state of mind intensely alert both to regional subtleties and to global trends. In its external political policies, Singapore insists on belonging to the region and plays a superbly agile diplomatic game. In business strategies however it wills itself apart. Manifestly successful during the last two decades, Singapore has entered the small group of East Asian countries that, thanks to the world trading system, have become industrial states.

This chapter, while in no way gainsaying that achievement, focuses on its vulnerability. Singapore's honest government, remarkably steady leadership, relatively successful attempts at nation-building and its obviously free economy stand as perhaps the brightest achievements of Southeast Asia's fast growth period over the past two decades.

Yet the achievements remain more vulnerable than is commonly assumed. In an almost tragic sense, Singapore remains hostage to its neighbours. If they succeed, Singapore succeeds in double measure. If they fail, Singapore will be dragged down also, if only because of its proximity to them. That, at least, is the underlying assumption.

For twenty years beginning in 1965, Singapore's GDP expanded by an average increase of nearly 8 per cent. Yet the fear remains that, just as Chinese millionaires lose their fortunes overnight, so also may Singapore lose everything in a few bad turns of the wheel. Against that prospect, Singapore's US$13 billion worth of gold and foreign exchange reserves (a June 1987 valuation) helps only to lessen the most obvious insecurities. The country does not lend and does not borrow. It is Asean's prudent shopkeeper.

This awareness of external vulnerability lends the edge to pronouncements from Singapore's leadership at National Day speeches and at openings of parliament. The world is an insecure place, Prime Minister Lee Kuan Yew stresses. We do not have the luxury of resting on our laurels. Relentless change is the order of the day. The formulae for past success do not guarantee future prosperity.

Crossroads or Revolving Door?

Behind these relentlessly dour pronouncements lies an unspoken fear: no amount of success can eliminate the possibility that, one day, global economic depression and regional instability may intersect at the Singaporean crossroads. The metaphor of a road junction is apt. Foreign banks and companies tend to think of Singapore as a parking-place rather than a nation. They value it as a place through which the ciphers of Southeast Asia's finance and trade most easily pass. Today, as a hundred years ago, the country's strategic position is self-evident. When founding a British colony on Singapore in the early nineteenth century, Stamford Raffles immediately perceived the entrepôt possibilities of this swampy islet at the mouth of Johor.

Singapore's financial services reflect the advantages of that good position, as well as its excellent communications, an English-speaking workforce and an honest administration. The financial sector has grown very rapidly over the past two decades, far faster than elsewhere in Southeast Asia. Ten per cent of Singapore's workforce is now employed by the finance and banking industry. The sector now accounts for one-quarter of the country's GDP, only a little less than the wealth generated by manufacturing industries.

If the notion of a crossroads or a junction seems apposite, another metaphor is that of the revolving door. Every day, tens of millions of banking and service transactions give Singapore's economy a spin. The economy also revolves around buy and sell orders from commodity traders and from numbers of another kind – tourists. Annual tourist arrivals are now more numerous than Singapore's population.

From afar, Singapore epitomises the Southeast Asian success story. Yet it is, in fact, only the second richest regional country. Singapore's US$12,500 per capita income in 1988 came to only half the figure for the Brunei sultanate across the South China Sea. These statistics are misleading, however; wealth circulates sluggishly among Brunei's people, who number just one-tenth of the size of Singapore's population. Brunei's élite receives wealth; it does not generate it. Singapore, by contrast, remains a dynamic dot in a lethargic sea; Brunei aside, Singapore's standard of living ranks second in Asia after Japan.

Within the region, Singapore's success draws much envy. The self-confidence of the island republic's younger generation sometimes approximates to arrogance. Irritation arises readily because the island's wealth rests on the commercial energy of its predominantly Chinese (76 per cent) population. This flat, humid pancake tucked into a socket of Johor coastline did not become a success by making 'duppy' money, although its banks are happy enough to take it on deposit. Singapore, demonstrably, has 'made it'. Against the many patrimonial tendencies in the region the Singaporean spirit makes a striking contrast. Its demonstrable devotion to the free market makes it, in Southeast Asia, an exception that proves the rule.

A Glance at the Recent Past

The future did not beckon so invitingly to Singapore when, in 1965, Singapore's shopkeepers pondered the fate that had severed their island away from its two-year federation with Malaysia. The event is said to have brought Lee Kuan Yew to a rare display of tears.

No one at that time had a very clear idea of how Singapore would earn its living if cut off from the Malayan peninsula. There were even fears that contact or trade with Johor might be hindered. Although these anxieties proved unfounded, to many foreign correspondents (who so often get it wrong) Singapore's future looked distinctly unpromising.

Lee's key associates at the time included S. Rajaratnam, who became Second Deputy Prime Minister, and Goh Keng Swee. Together with Goh Chock Tong, later First Deputy Prime Minister and with Tony Tan, who joined the cabinet in his early forties, these men devised the outward-looking, export-oriented policies that have worked so well. The post-1965 experience has vindicated their most extravagant hopes with growth rates faltering only two decades later.

1985

In 1985 Lee's People's Action Party (PAP), comfortably entrenched in 77 of 79 parliamentary seats, fell victim to a very sharp economic reversal. Singapore's GDP actually shrank that year, a shocking deceleration for a business community grown wealthy on warehousing, onward shipping, oil rig maintenance, construction, oil refining, light manufacturing and financial services. As Lee later acknowledged, Singapore had become lulled by its own success, and by the sense that world trade, tourist flows, manufacturing investment and commodity prices would remain constant.

By the mid-decade point it was becoming clear that these 'givens' had lost their axiomatic quality. Lee, always a sceptic even in buoyant times, had his doubts proven when the recession building up after the last spurt of a commodity boomlet in 1984 came home with a vengeance. Adding insult to injury, the government's policies, as Lee was candid enough to admit, compounded the problem.

The government's high-wage policy, enshrined for half a decade, was diminishing the country's attractiveness to outside investors. A 1986 report prepared by Lee's son, trade and industry minister Lee Hsien Loong, said that Singapore 'had reached a developed country's income level before having become a fully developed economy.' As far as local investment was concerned, the PAP's habit of preferring state enterprise over private initiative was also looking wrong-headed.

Self-criticism comes rarely in Southeast Asia. Yet at mid-decade point the unheard-of happened in Singapore: the government admitted it was wrong.

Tony Tan stunned a social gathering of senior Civil Servants by quoting from the American historian Barbara Tuchman's *The March of Folly*. ' "Persistence in erroneous policy, or a policy which has become erroneous because of changed circumstances, is the cause of folly in government",' Tan intoned. According to Robert Cottrell of the *Far Eastern Economic Review* in 1985, Tan then told the assembled bureaucrats that they had 'to develop a sense of when a government policy should be modified or reversed' and to 'bring unpleasant facts to the attention of political masters.'

Originally the aim behind raising labour costs had been to force the pace of industrial diversification. The rises were achieved via increases to the compulsory employee pension fund contributions by employers and through the imposition of employer-funded worker retraining schemes. Other devices were used to lift an already high rate of savings.

With the possible exception of a few economically inert Gulf oil states, Singapore's 43 per cent national savings rate probably topped the world ratings in 1985. It remained, in 1989, a good ten points ahead of Japan. One of Singapore's key savings mechanisms is the Central Provident Fund, a pension fund which receives money from a levy on employers which, until 1986, was pegged at a hefty 25 per cent of employee salaries.

The PAP government realised that it had pushed labour costs far too high. 'A high rate of savings is necessary in the early stages of a country's growth,' Tan said in 1986, but he acknowledged that the savings mania had gone too far. For the recession-hit country, 'enforcing a high rate of compulsory savings, which cannot be reinvested rapidly, will lead to a further contraction.'

Some economic warning signs had become too insistent to ignore. During the late 1970s and early 1980s, manufacturing investment had grown rapidly but declined sharply afterwards. Spending on industrial research and development (R & D) was running at under 0.6 per cent of GDP whereas, in Japan, it regularly exceeded 2.3 per cent of GDP during the 1980s.

Industrial and manufacturing profits also fell by 31 per cent between 1980 and 1984. During the same period, the country's overall 'cost structure' (which includes everything from the price of a telephone call to the burden of compulsory pension contributions) had risen to a point 'where we are no longer cheap', as one government paper candidly admitted in 1986.

The rationale for pricing Singapore out of some down-market industries had been clear enough when instituted earlier in the decade. Tan, Goh, Lee and finance minister Richard Hu believed that industry built on cheap labour and component assembly hardly amounted to the commanding ground of late twentieth-century industrialisation. Instead, they saw Singapore's future lying in high-tech enterprises.

'Information' and 'services' became the favoured watchwords. The government wanted no more smokestack industries and other down-market factories for Singapore. Coupled to an intense educational bias toward technological training, the government's high wage policy would pluck Singapore from the low-value-added groove into which so many other Asean countries had slipped.

For a while this approach seemed to succeed. Singapore telecommunications executive Chia Choon Wei said in 1986 that 'a recent study of world trade places Singapore sixteenth in the world and second among all developing countries as exporter of services.' He described Singapore as an 'information distribution centre', and forecast that information services would become the republic's future economic mainstay. The installation of a state-of-the-art, fibre optic telecommunications system enabling advanced data processing via the telephone system was also seen as necessary groundwork for an impending 'Information Age'. This move to a new stage of industrialism was accompanied by investment in new medical service laboratories and in 'science parks'. Technology-intensive pharmaceutical plants also began to establish themselves in Singapore.

These plans had to take reduced priority after the 1985 recession, however. In that year alone, the country lost nearly 100,000 manufacturing jobs. By the end of 1985 the economy was contracting at nearly 2 per cent per annum while capital formation had plunged by 13 per cent over the previous year. Worker layoffs in construction increased. Even the service sector looked less promising. During the first half of the 1980s, the competitiveness of Singapore's services had declined by 25 per cent vis-à-vis Hong Kong.

Entrepreneurs' Lament

Another factor became evident. Singapore's adherence to unobstructed entry of foreign investors was now seen as having stifled local entrepreneurship. Biting criticism came from small-business entrepreneurs who, as part of a government sanctioned exercise in 1985 and 1986, delivered the sharpest of all reports from business groups convened to deal with the crisis. Here was the authentic voice of local business people whose investments had spawned the great bulk of Singapore's 70,000 small businesses. Ninety-five per cent of these employ fewer than 50 workers.

'Singaporeans have been traditionally entrepreneurial,' the report said. 'But an economic policy which stresses the role of foreign investment in manufacturing inevitably forces the local entrepreneur into a lesser role.'

The report said favouring outside investors had led to local enterprises being snuffed out 'by foreign producers and suppliers through predatory pricing launched from protected home bases.' This claim won support from the Singapore Chinese Chamber of Commerce which said that 'the government appears to be favouring foreign multinational companies to the detriment of local indigenous companies.'

Since 1985, some Singaporean entrepreneurs have continued to claim that this alleged government preference for the big battalions creates local passivity to world trading and investment currents. Instead of risk-taking, Singapore's indigenous business class has developed 'a low tolerance for failure', in the words of the small business group.

The group also found that the school system in Singapore is partly responsible for this 'risk averse' attitude. 'The educational system overemphasises grades and performance and, one suspects, also conformity,' it said. 'The pressure-cooker atmosphere from primary school level to university leaves little time for innovation and creative activities . . . Singapore's very economic success has contributed to the paucity of young entrepreneurs.'

Although these words reflect the distrust with which some Chinese Singaporeans regard the PAP's English-speaking cosmopolitanism, the message did have an impact. By this time Lee and his colleagues had already decided to break with past policies and they needed some grass roots 'cover' for their next move. But the voices from below had also contributed to the needed change.

Reversing Gear

Soon after Tony Tan's December 1985 speech the government moved quickly to cut the provident fund levy. Internal debate also centred on whether the Singapore dollar should depreciate *vis-à-vis* the American currency. Although that was decided in the negative, other changes won approval.

The tax on company profits fell from 40 to 33 per cent. Rates for government corporation-charged services, from warehousing to port fees, also went down, while the Central Provident Fund levy on employers dropped to just 10 per cent of employee salaries. Some domestic pump-priming was occurring at last.

As the *Far Eastern Economic Review*'s deputy editor Philip Bowring noted, however, it was still hard for the PAP leadership to turn away from its 'desire both for virtuous thrift combined with a natural caution in investment. Having forced the populace to save, there was a deep responsibility (not one found in many governments) to safeguard the value of savings.' For Singapore, opening the demand-led, Keynesian floodgates to stimulate economic recovery did not come easily, even in the worst recession of its post-Independence history.

Lee's oldest son, Lee Hsien Loong, took an active part in formulating the new policies. Hsien Loong, also a brigadier general at the age of 32, spoke to me shortly afterwards about some new investment policy directions. The wealthy Government of Singapore Investment Corporation needed, he said, 'to take a more active role overseas and use some of the money which we have, not just to accumulate interest but also perhaps to buy companies – not real estate, but companies with skills and perhaps attract some of them to come back and set up here.'

Singapore's new commercial strategies place little trust in the region's own internal business dynamism. Quite the contrary; after the mid-decade rebound, Singapore's altered blueprint gave next to no priority to investment in neighbouring Asean nations. The younger Lee, known widely as 'B-G', seemed clear-headed about chances for substantive economic cooperation within the Asean grouping. He told me that 'even in Singapore there are pressures to attempt to protect our own business people . . . cooperation within Asean is best pursued in a low-key, tactful and discreet fashion.'

After changing direction in the mid-1980s, Lee, his son and his PAP colleagues opted to accelerate investment in business computerisation by tax advantages and to encourage more 'information products' such as business consultancies. More money should go into 'sunrise' industries, they decided, and less into 'sunset' businesses such as ship repair, oil refining and warehousing.

The main direction of the new service economy now lies outside the Asean region, reflecting the PAP's preference for linking Singapore to the global networks of finance, commodities trading and transportation. For all that, there are still 'critics who feel the extra-regional emphasis may be mistaken . . . Singapore is not only a gateway to Indonesia and Malaysia, it is at the crossroads of East Asia, the dynamism of which seems assured, and South Asia,' as Bowring notes.

The Financial Centre of Asean

The improvements in business performance after 1986 have been helped by Singapore's financial industry which rests on decisions in the 1960s to create the Asian Currency Unit (ACU) offshore holding accounts. Singapore consistently has discouraged, however, attempts to use its dollar as a trading currency in its own right, preferring instead to manage domestic money supply and keep the local dollar pegged to the US dollar.

By 1988, 125 foreign commercial banks jostled for space in Singapore, giving Shenton Way, a premier drive along the south coast, a Manhattan-like appearance. Sixty-three foreign merchant banks also established branches in Singapore, from which they now chase offshore business such as the restructuring exercises forced on Malaysian corporations by the New Economic Policy.

Singapore's finance industry has grown explosively during the last twenty years. At first hesitantly, but then quickening after 1973 oil prices made its Malay neighbours rich, the republic's banking and financial sector still rest mainly on the offshore ACU market. By 1988 banks in Singapore had a colossal US$210 billion on call in ACUs, compared to US$30 million enticed into the first ACU accounts when the market started exactly two decades earlier.

The development of a sophisticated financial sector occurred in other Asean countries as well. Yet Singapore managed to escape the financial scandals plaguing Malaysia and Thailand. By 1987 the Monetary Authority of Singapore (MAS) had approved a secondary market for government securities. Very slowly, MAS moved to issue about US$17 million in government securities over five years – a major change from the once tepid public bond market.

As the financial sector grew, Singapore's leaders began to take a tough line against 'little Singapore' sentiment. Monopoly minded professions such as banking, the law or stockbroking at varying times sought to restrict foreign participation. Yet the government was moving the other way, especially after the Pan-Electric débâcle savaged the Singapore stock market in 1985.

The Pan-El Shock

The government forced open the share brokerage business after the collapse of Pan-Electric Industries ('Pan-El') revealed weak financial underpinning for many brokers involved in 'forward contracting'. By 1989 the Stock Exchange of Singapore (SES) had approved a number of joint ventures between foreign companies and local brokerage houses, including arrangements with Morgan Grenfell, New York's Bankers Trust, the Kuwait Asia Bank and even the Australian brewing company, Elders Pica.

'Forward contracting' acquired an infamous reputation after Pan-El, a many-sided manufacturing firm quoted on the Singapore and Kuala Lumpur share markets, drove the market to near-collapse. A forward contract is a form of share financing in which investors sell shares coupled to an agreement to buy them back at a specified, or unspecified, higher price. Pan-El shares traded via forward contracts in thousands of lots during 1985.

Speculative interest in Pan-El began with the company's decision to borrow heavily to support expansion schemes. Many of these deals took the form of cross-investments in family firms controlled by the Malaysian Chinese politician and tycoon Tan Koon Swan, who indirectly owned about one-quarter of Pan-El.

Although Pan-El owed foreign banks about US$225 million at the end of 1985, it had also committed itself to buy another US$50 million in forward stock-contracts. Tan's personal companies siphoned off funds from these Pan-El loans. By the middle of 1985 however, creditors were starting to demand repayment.

To no avail. Pan-El's first default occurred in November 1985. This led quickly to a suspension of trading in Pan-El shares. Later the company went into receivership, leaving behind a tangle of contingent liabilities spreading out from Pan-El and Tan's own companies. The SES management panicked, opting for an unprecedented, three-day closure. So did the Malaysian stock market.

This probably hastened the débâcle. Virtually every other share price crashed when the markets reopened, as fears about multiple exposure to Pan-El's forward contracts grew. This event opened, in turn, a floodgate of anxiety about the financial health of other Malaysian companies, most of which are quoted in Singapore as well as in Malaysia.

The Singapore police finally arrested Tan in January 1986. He pleaded guilty in August of that year to a modified charge of abetting a criminal breach of trust. He then went to prison for two years where he later, in his own words, 'found God'. His creditors had less success in finding all their money.

The foreign banks were deeply shocked. Pan-El spelled the end of a rash of lending to Singaporean and Malaysian corporations. Many loans, with shares as sole collateral, had proved to be poor risks. At the time, semi-permanent damage seemed to have been done to Singapore's squeaky clean reputation. Questions also surfaced in the foreign press about the competence of the SES supervisory authorities.

If issues of competence were important however, they might just as easily have been directed at the judgement of the foreign banks themselves. Most of the bigger foreign banks in Singapore, especially US and British banks, had extended credit to Tan for many months after the traditional Chinese old-boy network had begun to hum with doubts about Tan's creditworthiness. The whispers were becoming audible from the stockbrokers who, when the crisis broke in December 1985, defaulted on nearly US$300 million in forward-contract obligations.

Although caught off guard, Singapore's government rebounded quickly. Tighter laws put the formerly autonomous SES under the control of the monetary authorities. A forced capital increase for the brokerage industry also materialised, as did a US$75 million financial 'lifeboat' demanded from all resident banks to prevent complete ruin from Pan-El's default. The moves saved the exchange although some brokerages went to the wall. One of these was a firm controlled by Pan-El director Peter Tham Wing Fai, who later went to prison on conviction for an unrelated act of stock forgery.

For Singapore the fiasco dealt a bad but temporary blow to its ambitions to become East Asia's pre-eminent financial centre. Its reputation was salvaged, but it had been a close shave. Furious rows erupted between the Singapore Society of Accountants and Coopers & Lybrand, the international accounting firm. The Society brought disciplinary proceedings against Coopers, which had audited Pan-El. Coopers responded by bringing a defamation suit against the Society.

Stephen Duthie, writing in the *Asian Wall Street Journal* a year after Pan-El's collapse, said that the 'passage of time has done little to erase nagging questions about the Pan-Electric débâcle. Chief among them is why Singapore's financial regulators, the company's many creditors and its three independent auditors failed to take action before [Pan-El] self-destructed.' Particularly bitter about the fiasco were the banks the government had encouraged to keep credit lines open to Pan-El right to the bitter end.

An assessment by the *Far Eastern Economic Review*'s Singapore correspondent Nigel Holloway was more phlegmatic. 'Many of the changes made after the death of Pan-El would have occurred anyway,' he wrote. 'But the collapse gave both regulators and traders a good kick in the backside, from which some never did recover.' He said also that 'it was a needed kick, because Singapore, which aims to become the Switzerland of Asia, was not adapting quickly enough to the more competitive world financial climate.'

The SES persisted in clearing away the damage caused by Pan-El. It introduced electronic share-trading using computerised, automated quotation systems already operating in the London and New York stock exchanges. The result moved the concept of continuous, twenty-four hour trading closer to realisation, and gave Singapore a head start over Tokyo, Honk Kong and Sydney.

The rebound by the SES after Pan-El developed considerable momentum: before the October 1987 crash the average daily trading volume had risen to US$34 billion. This was twice the figure prevailing before the Pan-El affair. With trade of this higher magnitude the SES now matched the Sydney, Zürich, Paris and Frankfurt exchanges although it still lagged behind the Big Five – Tokyo, Osaka, New York, London and Hong Kong.

Home Truths or Awkward Facts?

There is little point in begrudging Singapore's self-evident success. The problem is that outside praise sometimes seems uncritical. Some awkward problems are worthy of note.

The most obvious of these is a geographic location that creates insecurity as well as opportunity. In the minds of many Singaporeans their country remains a Chinese island surrounded by Malay seas. In this context 'Malay' is used in its broad, pre-Independence sense. For many Chinese the designation 'Malay' includes everyone from turban wearing, fundamentalist politicians in neighbouring Malaysia to the opaque Javanese of Indonesia.

Another awkward issue is the future cohesion of the PAP. Since the Socialist party withdrew from Singapore's parliament in 1966 the PAP has commanded this city-state without effective opposition. The party is commanded in turn by a man now synonymous with Singapore. 'Harry Lee', as the last colonial British generation used to call him, has also become the best known Southeast Asian leader. By the time of his 65th birthday on 16 September 1988, Life Without Lee had become an ever more open issue.

Before the Pan-El fiasco and mid-decade downturn, Lee had hinted broadly that the time had arrived for a transition to the new generation. Daily management had already gone to Goh Chok Tong, Tan and Hu, although no one had much illusion about where ultimate responsibility lay. 'The master controls are still with me,' Lee said in April 1986. 'If I see things heading for a crash, I will use the override.' By 1989 however he had agreed to surrender the premiership to Goh.

The prime minister has a reputation for blunt delivery. A Cambridge University graduate of very considerable intelligence, Lee easily commands the most impressive mind in Southeast Asia. One of Lee's biographers, James Minchin (1987), supplies an anecdote that reveals the prime minister's toughness of approach.

'A former Singapore newspaper proprietor . . . was having an audience with Lee and apparently not toeing the line,' Minchin recounts. 'Lee leaned over, grabbed him by the collar and said "I'm a thug, you're a thug, and as one thug to another, you'll do what I say".'

Some observers see this occasional, private irascibility becoming more public as Lee's twilight years approached. He seemed reluctant to do what he has urged upon himself – to transfer power to subordinates and to let them work without having to look constantly over their shoulder.

Some of Lee's thinking has caused controversy in recent years. His views on human genetics have led him to endorse plans to encourage more breeding by university graduates. The argument was that more issue from 'intelligent' women would stock the island republic with the right genetic material.

Given a paucity of Singaporean resources, other than drive and diligence, the motivations behind the plan seemed understandable although the élitist elements in the plan touch some raw nerves. Lee had become increasingly concerned that Singapore's 1960s birth control programme generally had been too successful. Singapore's demographers began to forecast a shrinking population early in the twenty-first century.

A falling birth-rate would slow economic growth, Goh Chok Tong also reasoned aloud in his speeches. The average age would rise from 27 years to 43 years in the first decade of the twenty-first century. The number of young men to defend the country would decline. Living adjacent to a fast-breeding Malaysia and Indonesia, the racial arithmetic looked troublesome to some. Singapore's minority Malays, who comprise about 15 per cent of the population, also have a higher rate of reproduction than the majority Chinese.

In 1983 the government created a 'Social Development Unit', an interesting euphemism for a state-sanctioned dating service designed to help university graduates meet on vacation cruises and resorts. The government also began a plan to help the children of graduate mothers gain preference at schools for their third child, but public opposition prevented its implementation.

That did not dampen the PAP's demographic zeal. 'At least two. Better three. Four if you can afford it' became a familiar slogan. The country's annual budget put aside an increasing number of incentives for bigger families, especially tax rebates. The 1989 budget extended a tax rebate of about US$10,000 to the fourth child. Plans were drafted to enable better-educated foreigners to marry Singaporeans while rules designed to prevent Singaporeans from marrying migrant workers or domestic helpers, were tightened.

Meddling Foreign Journalists

Some of the foreign reporting of Lee's interest in these issues may have darkened the PAP's already dim view of the foreign media. Senior ministers began disparaging interference by 'James Bond journalists', to use one description used in parliament.

'Interference' came to include most attempts, however well intentioned, to report trends in Singapore's internal affairs (a job not made easy by government officials' refusal to speak to the foreign press). The ensuing quarrels over the 1980s have not put either party in a particularly positive light. The self-righteous reaction of some of the affected media provoked logical circumlocutions from the PAP that were worthy of medieval metaphysics. In Southeast Asia, one wag has noted, Singapore not only is the exception that proves the rule but is also, for the foreign press at least, 'the exception that rules the proof'.

In the late 1980s Lee's government drew a bead on the foreign media, imposing indefinite restricted distribution for varying periods on *Time*, *Asiaweek*, *The Asian Wall Street Journal*, and the *Far Eastern Economic Review*. For the *Journal*, distribution dropped from 5,000 to 400 copies after that newspaper's editor refused to publish a letter from a Singapore official. The *Review* was given a choice of seeing its 10,000 circulation slashed to 500 copies. Its publisher chose instead to suspend circulation in Singapore altogether. The *Review* also cancelled a printing contract in Singapore for the magazine.

The Singapore authorities judged the *Review*, the *Journal* and others to be 'engaging in the domestic policies of Singapore.' In reaction to the action against the *Journal* the Paris-based International Federation of Newspaper Publishers telexed information minister Yeo Ning Hong. 'Depriving most of your citizens of a major source of information about international business [is] a severe blow to your country's justified credibility as an international financial centre,' the federation's president Sir Gordon Linacre said, 'and [casts] . . . serious doubts on your government's commitment to freedom of expression.'

From Washington, a Voice of America editorial, reflecting US government opinion, said 'by punishing the *Journal* the [Singaporean] government actually punishes the business community, depriving it of timely financial news from a trusted source . . . Singapore long ago proved capable of prospering in free market competition against much larger economic rivals. Surely it can compete in the marketplace of ideas.'

In one sense this feuding occurred in an unlikely arena. In most respects it is hard to imagine a society more accessible than Singapore's to the outside world. 'Lee's island is more open to foreign influences than almost any other place on earth,' foreign correspondent Nigel Holloway noted. 'Exports and imports each year generate three times more cash than the domestic economy taken by itself. There were three million visitors in 1985, to an island with a population of 2.6 million. TV is full of American pulp. The BBC's World Service is boosted and rebroadcast locally on VHF radio.'

The trouble is, liberal or 'Western' influences come in along with those publications and programmes. These are less welcome. 'Because we are now bilingual,' Lee told a Washington audience in 1988, 'Western lifestyle seeps into our life, [leading] to a more individualistic type of society [where] the government's duty is to allow individual fulfilment.' Yet in a hostile world, 'Who will guarantee you three square meals a day, a safe roof over your head and that you will not be attacked and captured and destroyed?

'Ask the foreign correspondents, how do we guarantee that?' Lee said. 'But they are not interested. They are interested in purveying their set of values. They start off with those premises, particularly the Americans. They come from the most wealthy civilisation. They believe that if we follow them, we will become wealthy like them . . . now the strange thing is that the Japanese have not followed them and are getting wealthier. And those who followed the Americans are getting poorer.'

There prime ministerial retorts had a fair measure of bite in them. And, to be absolutely honest about it, some among the foreign press have found it difficult to feel warm-hearted about Singapore. Some have tired of its bland newspapers and its rather forced cheerfulness.

There is something quite disagreeable about a small country becoming so successful, especially when the formerly patronising colonial power and nearby 'white' Commonwealth countries, Australia and New Zealand, have slithered down the per capita GDP stakes during the past two decades. Averaged out, Singaporeans earn more per capita than New Zealanders. They are gaining fast on the Australians. No wonder that the dismissive jokes implicitly acknowledge this success. Singapore, as one remark puts it, 'has all the ambience of a supermarket checkout lane'.

It should be noted that Lee's media watch extends beyond the Western press. When in 1987 a series of articles in Kuala Lumpur's *Star* newspaper suggested that Lee had been less than forthright in explaining the reasons behind housing minister Teh Cheang Wan's suicide in December 1986, the prime minister promptly issued a libel action against the newspaper. The *Star*, owned by the Malaysian Chinese Association, does not circulate in Singapore.

An Unhappy Episode

Teh's sad end illustrated the continuing temptations of power, even in Singapore. Once praised as a PAP trustworthy stalwart, Teh figured in allegations of corrupt favouritism in government housing contract awards.

His suicide note accepted responsibility for 'this unfortunate incident.' The note said that, 'as an honourable Oriental gentleman I feel it is only right that I should pay the highest penalty for my mistake.' The government later said that Teh had accepted two payments equivalent to US$235,000, from real estate developers. Prime minister Lee said other officials had not been involved.

Malfeasance was also hinted at in foreign press revelations about collusion between Singapore defence officials and Bofors, Sweden's leading weapons manufacturer. In 1987, evidence appeared in Stockholm that Bofors had been shipping weapons via Singapore to Iran, in defiance of Swedish law. The reports said Bofors had been certifying the Singaporeans as the end-users of the arms and that Singaporean officials had connived in this deception. Bofors parent company, Nobel Industries, admitted that 'unacceptable re-exports of defence materials had occurred.' It was not clear that this necessarily impugned Singapore's government however, even if end-use differed from that noted on the invoices.

Lee's occasional visits to the US prompt press questioning there about his attitude to the media. The often grim-visaged political veteran remarked in April 1988 that Western correspondents assume that 'all politicians are venal', an attitude that Lee did not want to see gain ascendancy in Singapore. Lee sets high standards. It mattered little that Tan Koon Swan was president of Malaysia's biggest pro-government Chinese political party when the Singapore authorities prosecuted him after the Pan-El débâcle. Tan spent 16 months in gaol and, upon his release, was immediately rearrested and extradited to Kuala Lumpur. There he faced new charges, notably a US$9.2 million criminal breach of trust arising out of alleged mismanagement of funds.

Trading in a Protectionist World

Lee's disagreements with the foreign media coincided with a display of outrage following a US decision, in 1988, to exclude Singapore from the Generalised System of Preferences (GSP). Since 1975 the GSP has exempted from import duty about 3,000 products from more than a hundred developing countries.

Within Asia, Washington also dropped Taiwan, Hong Kong and South Korea from the programme. The reason in all cases was that GDP per capita now took these Asian economies well beyond developing country status. By contrast, Singapore's Asean partners (excepting Brunei) still enjoyed the preferences.

The net effect of the US decision was to add an extra US$70 million in tariff charges, a burden affecting 10 per cent of Singapore's exports to the US. Although anticipated by Singapore's manufacturers, the GSP revocation went down badly. Finance minister Richard Hu and his cabinet colleagues also resented American demands that the Singapore dollar and other NIC (newly industrialising country) currencies had to appreciate against the American dollar.

Singapore's reaction to the withdrawal of GSP preferences was easily the most audible of the four Asian NICs. The reason was simple: Singapore had expected its GSP privileges to remain intact as a result of a bargain reached eighteen months earlier with Washington.

An unpublished 'record of understanding' of bilateral consultations on the GSP on 22 and 23 September 1986 shows that the 'US delegation stressed that it would recommend a favourable GSP package . . . if a new Copyright Act were passed . . . and protection granted to US [copyright] works by the end of 1986.'

The confidential paper shows that the American delegation had also promised that 'sixteen out of eighteen waivers in Singapore's request list would be granted.' The record noted various items of uncertainty on the Singapore side. The 'US side noted the Singaporean delegation's concern but expressed the view that regardless of the outcome with respect to this item, the results would be very positive for Singapore.'

Singapore kept its part of this bargain. A copyright law was passed. When the GSP decision was announced, Singapore's trade union congress staged an unusual protest rally outside the US embassy. One union leader called the GSP revocation 'shameful and irresponsible.'

Yet American unease over its Asian trade imbalances had been clear for some time. A major study in 1987 by Morgan Guaranty Trust Company of New York, entitled *The Asian NICs and US Trade*, included Singapore among the 'Four Dragons', another piece of journalist's shorthand for the Asian NICs. Between them these countries accounted for over 20 per cent of America's US$170 billion trade deficit in 1986.

The economic policy implications became increasingly obvious. Washington leaned on these countries to allow their currencies to appreciate against the US dollar. It exerted pressure to break down their restrictive trade practices. It battled with their *laisser-faire* attitude to protecting intellectual property (copyright, trade marks and patents). By 1986, the Americans had forced one of the Dragons, Taiwan, to float the Taiwan dollar. South Korea began to loosen its own currency, the won. Singapore however has held fast to policies designed to prevent the use of the Singapore dollar as a trade, and therefore traded, currency.

Although Singapore felt penalised for its success by the American decision, the GSP revocation speeded the diversification of its industry. More worrying was the likelihood that the US move would jeopardise Singapore's standing with the European Community and Japan. By the end of the 1980s Singapore was sending duty-free exports worth 700 million annually to these two trading destinations. 'He doth protest too much' was the American reaction to Singapore's complaints. A later expulsion, in 1988, of an American diplomat also soured relations.

The US GSP decision occurred at an historical moment when Singapore had started to become one of Asean's chief beneficiaries of the yen's dramatic appreciation against the US dollar that started after September 1985. Nearly all the major corporate names of Japanese manufacturing came to Singapore. Aiwa Company and other consumer electronics firms opened new plants. At the end of the 1980s Japan had become Singapore's largest external market, displacing the US.

The effort employed by Singapore to head off recognition that it had become a rich, exporting 'Dragon' came as no surprise to those countries which already had withdrawn Singapore's special entry privileges. In July 1985, New Zealand had decided to delete Singapore from its own GSP system. This so provoked foreign minister Suppiah Dhanabalan that he won Asean approval to insert condemnatory language about the decision (an insignificant move in so far as it affected Singapore's trade) into the closing communiqué of an Asean foreign ministers' meeting that year.

This harsh response badly upset the New Zealand delegation and helped set the atmosphere for a decision, bound to be taken anyway, to repatriate a battalion of New Zealand troops stationed in Singapore. None the less, the episode marked a small but not insignificant example of a certain loss of interest among old friends in 'going to bat' for Singapore. Perhaps, given the growing Japanese presence in the region, a gradual attenuation of old associations was inevitable. The Japanese investment thrust into Southeast Asia is discussed in Chapter 12.

Political Uncertainties

Singapore stands like a sentinel at the gates of Southeast Asia. Its 'guns' in an age of demand-led commerce are the trading houses, financial flair and Chinese entrepreneurial drive. The island relies on its wits and is loathe to put a clamp on trade, for what ever reason.

Although a tin cartel grouping Indonesia, Malaysia and Thailand has wanted to cut back severely on tin smelting in the region, as part of a forlorn hope to restrict supply, Singapore would not shut down its smelter. Singapore has also been reluctant to make cargo switching after customs inspection a crime; freight handlers claim this makes it easier for smuggling operations from Singapore to reach into adjacent Malaysian and Indonesian territory. Environmentalists also dislike Singapore's unwillingness to sign the Convention on International Trade in Endangered Species (CITES), which prohibits trade in animal products of endangered species.

Internal Politics

The PAP's uncertainty about its prosperous but ungrateful ward – the Singaporean people – grew during the late 1980s. Stung by the PAP's 12 point drop in public support to 62.9 per cent in the 1984 general election, Lee mulled over various ideas, including altering the basis of the franchise and changing the method of determining parliamentary constituencies which the republic inherited from Britain.

In 1987 a bill went to Singapore's parliament creating 'teams' of candidates to run in what the government called 'Group Representation Constituencies', or GRCs. Half the 79 MPs have now become representatives for 'team MP ' districts. The idea is that voters will choose among a list of three MPs, an exercise that merges three constituencies into one. Critics say one result will be to increase the odds still more against opposition candidates winning a place in parliament.

The government counters that the GRCs will ensure that Singapore's minority Malays and Indians have a voice in parliament. Lee warns that a sense of racial disparity could arise from a lack of minority representation in parliament, and more Malay and Indian faces will presumably join the Group MPs. The government's detractors however say that two opposition MPs in parliament were two too many for the PAP, and that the GRCs will eventually eliminate an opposition presence.

The PAP's apparent displeasure at overt opposition extends beyond its increasingly chilly attitude to the foreign press, discussed also in Chapter 2. In May 1987, twenty-two mainly young people associated with the Catholic Church were arrested and charged with planning a Marxist conspiracy endangering the state. Held under Singapore's Internal Security Act (ISA), similar to Malaysia's legislation, most of the accused were freed in December of that year.

In April 1988 however, a Singapore newspaper printed an open letter from some of the freed detainees, alleging torture and other maltreatment during their detention. The government promptly rearrested the nine signatories. In March 1989 the authorities prevented a British barrister, Anthony Lester, from continuing to represent one of these detainees, angered apparently at Lester's out-of-court remarks back in Britain about the ISA. Singapore also moved at this time to abolish ISA-related appeals to the Privy Council in London; the Council remains Singapore's final court of appeal in most other cases.

It must be clearly understood that these controversies did little or nothing to dampen international business confidence in Singapore. The government's cold-eyed handling of allegedly revolutionary dissenters may even have won it more favour from foreign firms. Singapore scores at the top of nearly all international political and business risk surveys.

If restrictions on the media create one caveat over the sincerity of Singapore's embrace of free market principles, its attitude to the labour market creates another.

Notwithstanding routinely tight labour market conditions, the PAP has set its face against allowing foreign workers to stay in the republic for more than short periods. In 1987 the government reportedly approved plans by several firms, including a subsidiary of the US National Semiconductor Corporation, to bring several hundred Chinese workers to Singapore, a sensitive decision given knee-jerk suspicions of China by Indonesia and Malaysia.

Notwithstanding such unorthodox solutions, Singapore continues to phase out foreign workers in accordance with a long-term objective. New measures emerged in November 1988 to stem the flow, now reduced to 16 per cent of the country's labour force. Each employer has to pay about US$120 a month as a levy to the government. The new rules also restrict the number of foreign workers to no more than 40 per cent of the workforce in any factory or on any construction site.

The toughened approach caused strains with Singapore's Asean neighbours, especially with Thailand. Thai naval ships, buses and even special trains raced against a 31 March deadline to remove over 10,000 Thais working illegally in the country, mainly on construction projects. After that date the overstayers faced gaol sentences of at least three months and three lashes of the cane. Apart from the Thais, labourers have entered Singapore illegally from Sri Lanka, Pakistan, India, Malaysia and the Philippines.

Thai prime minister Chatichai Choonhavan was reported to have mused at a cabinet meeting about whether 'instead of sending [transport] ships, we should send warships to Singapore.' Thai deputy foreign minister Prapas Limbabaandhu reportedly told Singapore officials that 'if Thais are continuously treated like that, the overall relationship will be affected – Thais are not familiar with caning.'

The availability of cheap, migrant labour has enabled Singapore to complete major projects on time, such as a new terminal at Changi international airport and an underground mass transit system. That the government should crack down hard on illegal workers at a time when Singapore's construction industry was begging for more labour showed the PAP's determination to move the country beyond labour dependent growth.

The labour shortages, the ethnic sensitivities, the row with Asean neighbours – these were just a tiny slice of a large 'if' hanging over Singapore's prospects in the 1990s. After a rush of wealth lasting two decades, Singapore's future now seems to offer two broad possibilities. Either the island will become Southeast Asia's pre-eminent financial and high-technology manufacturing centre, or it may have to reconcile itself to becoming just another offshore adjunct of Japanese manufacturing.

Many internal issues will influence the outcome, of course – political stability, good communications, sound technical education and the like. Yet external questions also arise, including two major issues to be decided in the next decade. These include the issue of Hong Kong's future after 1997, and the pace of liberation in Japanese financial markets.

Hong Kong's Future

Hong Kong's future matters because Singapore aspires to the British territory's current prestige as a world financial centre. The countdown to the 1997 passing of Hong Kong back to Chinese sovereignty ticks away. Singapore's financial policymakers are already preparing for a time when Hong Kong, one of the most dynamic market economies in the post-Second World War era, begins to lose its lustre. Here the 'if' hangs on Peking's intentions. If China does what it says it wants to do – to preserve Hong Kong's capitalist economy within a still nominally socialist system – then the territory's commercial resilience will survive. After the June 1989 Tiananmen Square killings this seemed in doubt.

This course of events is by no means guaranteed. By 1989, China's often contradictory, market-minded policies were coming, once again, under severe domestic criticism. In China's cities, the annualised inflation rate climbed past 30 per cent. In their 1984 agreement with Britain, the Peking authorities promised to let Hong Kong continue, much as usual, until AD 2047. If Hong Kong's already commanding momentum as the leading Asian financial centre continues, Singapore's loftier ambitions may be thwarted.

Hong Kong's 6 million people, 98 per cent of them Chinese, reside within a territory of 1,000 square kilometres that is mostly rocky outcrop. The industry of the immigrants however places this foreboding abode in seventeenth place out of all the world's trading countries, and thirteenth place if the centrally planned economies are excluded.

Hong Kong has become the world's third largest financial centre, after London and New York. It operates the third largest container port after New York and Rotterdam. Its shipping registers include 12 per cent of global merchant fleet tonnage. If Hong Kong's private shippers combined their operations they would create the world's second largest merchant fleet.

By the late 1980s almost 45 per cent of Hong Kong's exports were going into China's hinterland, much of it quietly re-exported onwards from Taiwan. Before the communists took power in China, Shanghai had been the most important Chinese manufacturing centre. Hong Kong took the lead after 1949, first as a fabricator of light consumer goods and then, fuelled by the opening of America's market (which took 40 per cent of Hong Kong's exports during the 1980s), as a major and diversified manufacturing base.

Hong Kong, like Singapore, is a tiny territory without natural resources that has blossomed into a key trade hub. In both territories the government has concentrated on infrastructure, on low-income housing and on specialised training. Subject to this state-led enterprise, both territories practise non-interference in the marketplace. In both, the most important elements are an unqualified free flow of capital and a lack of customs duties.

Singapore wants to overtake Hong Kong. Singapore's quick banking growth and its expansion of financial services in many respects mirror Hong Kong's phenomenal growth. But there are important differences.

Although both city-states gain about a fourth of their GDP from financial services, Singapore's banking and finance growth has been 'top–down'. Rather than Hong Kong's casino-like spontaneity, Singapore's regulators have proceeded in a more controlled way, creating a financial market with the ACU device.

The Monetary Authority of Singapore, headed by Goh Keng Swee since 1980, tended to take an aloof attitude to the sector it regulated, behaving as incorruptible, but rather unapproachable, mandarins. The approach has its advantages. Singapore has not had a banking failure since the 1930s, in striking contrast to a stream of financial fiascos in Hong Kong. Yet Singapore is also seen to levy too much tax on foreign banks, by comparison with Hong Kong.

Another impediment results from the comparative immaturity of Singapore's financial market. This applies especially to the still weak bond market. In 1986, government bonds maturing in less than ten years had a tiny market, almost exclusively confined to the captive government pension fund. That had to change. Only a few major bond dealers, such as Crédit Suisse First Boston, had even set up offices in Singapore. American consultants advised on the presentation of government securities, supervisory needs and a clearing house system.

Yet a restrictive approach to the expansion of this market limited bond dealerships to just four domestic banks. This snuffed out the foreigners' hopes despite the certainty that the Singapore government would immediately achieve one of the world's highest traded ratings. This go-slow attitude contrasts with the approach of the Singapore Monetary Exchange, or Simex, which has expanded strongly on the back of the ACUs.

Whither the Yen?

The second issue for Singapore is even more imponderable. What will be the future unit of account for Southeast East Asia's trading economies? Conventional wisdom has seen the Japanese yen driving all before it. A wave of Japanese investment rolling into Southeast Asia after 1985 seems to make those predictions plausible. But Japan's gigantic reserves of capital had not, by 1989, led necessarily to liberalised banks. The yen has still not become much of an offshore, traded currency.

Nor has the sea change in global exchange rates yet displaced the US dollar as the pre-eminent currency of account. Indeed, the dollar began to strengthen again in 1988 and 1989, presaging a period of comparative exchange rate stability after the tumult of the previous five years. To be sure, some offshore yen accounts have built up, notably in Europe, but the transformation of Tokyo into the dominant world financial centre still lags. If this should occur, Singapore could find that its appeal remains simply as a base for regional banking operations while the big banks increasingly plot strategy, and buy foreign currency, in Tokyo.

Apart from financial trends, there are many industrial imponderables. Singapore has made a conscious decision to solicit foreign manufacturing investment without attempting to force the local equity ownership in the new enterprises. Its hopes have been pinned on the transfer of foreign technology via new investments. This approach, reaffirmed after the mid-decade recession, has won much growth.

Foreigners have generated three-quarters of all manufacturing investment in Singapore since 1975. This is an extraordinarily large percentage and a very different result from that achieved by Hong Kong's indigenous capitalists. The figures available now suggest that outside interests own perhaps 90 per cent of Singapore's industrial capacity. Increasingly these interests are Japanese.

This approach may inhibit local manufacturing expansion, as the grumbling local entrepreneurs have claimed. Nigel Holloway noted in 1987 that 'Singapore has much that is modern and internationally competitive, but alongside this exist old-fashioned businesses which employ far too many people.' When I spoke about the issue to Lee the Younger (about whom it was being said that 'the son also rises') he said that 'dependence on the multinational is inevitable.'

Outsiders often overlook that Singaporean business often has a 'mum-and-dad' style of management. Similarly, educational standards still have some distance to go. 'The telephones and the airport are the equal of any metropolis,' Holloway notes, 'but more than half of Singapore's adults have no better than primary education. Twenty-three per cent have received no formal education at all.' Is this the future Southeast Asian information metropolis?

Whither the State?

The extent of public ownership in Singapore also surprises outsiders. Foreigners tend to assume that Singapore's devotion to the free market has led to avoidance of state ownership. Nothing could be further from the truth. In many areas of investment, Singapore's public sector takes a commanding lead.

Government-owned companies in 1988 included three finance ministry holding companies, eleven manufacturing companies, five petrochemical firms, twelve trading houses and the country's largest bank. Six ship repair enterprises, three aviation companies and five corporations working in housing and construction also belonged in the government's stable. So did printing, tourism, property management, farming, health services, and even business consultancy firms.

All in all, there were 450 government firms in 1987, capitalised at over US$5 billion. The government explains the large public sector away by arguing that it has had no choice but to lead the way into heavy industries. This is an accurate explanation; after all, local entrepreneurs have failed to emulate their Chinese cousins in Hong Kong. (Hong Kong Chinese comprise mainly migrants from neighbouring Guangdong, while Singaporeans are usually Hokkiens.) Singapore's best known tycoons, such as Lee Kong Chian and his descendants, usually create banking empires. Very few homegrown, Singaporean multinationals have emerged although there are some exceptions (see Chapter 8).

By the end of the 1980s, the government had committed itself to privatising over forty of its companies. This will create nearly US$3 billion in new stock and add a much wider spread of listings in the SES. Those state firms targeted include entities in which the government has a holding of 60 per cent or more, such as the Development Bank of Singapore, Neptune Orient Lines, Sembawang Shipyards, Singapore Airlines and Keppel Corporation.

Privatisation has squared well with the sentiment of lower ranking PAP politicians; the younger Lee has also thrown his weight behind it. Yet state corporatist ideas are taking a long time to die in Singapore, and the listing on the SES of previously government-owned companies does not, by itself, create entrepreneurial capitalists. By April 1989 the government was ready for another privatising push, this time targeting the Singapore ports authority and even, in an echo of British prime minister Margaret Thatcher's policies, some segments of its public housing empire.

Government-owned companies plus seven public utilities still account for 45 per cent of GDP, however. During the mid-1980s the country's largest seven statutory boards earned about US$750 million a year, 22 per cent more than the earnings of the island's ten most profitable listed companies.

Privatisation is not simply achieved, moreover. Some of those government firms are proving hard to sell. These include the country's five refineries, which have faced hard times after the oil price slide beginning in 1985 and as refining overcapacity has emerged in Southeast Asia.

Politics and Confidence

Finally, and no matter what its growth rates show, Singapore's attractiveness to outside investors still depends upon the calibre of political management in adjoining neighbours, Indonesia and Malaysia. Singapore's almost manic insistence on dealing with the global economy masks this deeper concern, one felt on the local stock market every time racial tension or political uncertainty clouds the prospects of these large neighbours.

In an interdependent world it is not unusual to feel the effects of a neighbour's blunder or lament the spillover effect of foolish policies by other governments. For Singapore's intensely trade-dependent economy, however, this type of vulnerability is acute. Not only do global trends beyond its influence make business forecasting difficult but, at a deeper level, business confidence depends on factors outside the PAP's control.

Foreign minister Dhanabalan articulates these constant worries. 'Once confidence is lost, what is going to happen?' he asked. 'It is not only a question of foreign investment, it is also a question of our own people. Our good people can go to almost any part of the world. If confidence is destroyed they will leave the place and they will not come back.'

No wonder the country's approach to the world suggests a gloom-prone pragmatism resting on cold self-interest. Ominously, 'B-G' Lee reminds Singaporeans that 'overnight, an oasis may become a desert.' He means it. His father observes that the 'world of states shares many characteristics of the world of beasts.' He means it. The island spends nearly US$1 billion each year on defence and has created a small but efficient arms industry.

By the beginning of 1989, Lee the Younger was advocating a new 'national ideology' to counter Westernisation. In a series of speeches he voiced fears that the country's old, workaholic habits are disappearing as its people become wealthier. 'Within one generation, or at most two, the spirit of Singapore will disappear, the society will dissolve and the nation will be no more,' without a non-Western ideology reinforcing hard work.

Is not this taking things too far? Perhaps. Lee and the PAP know well that nothing can be taken for granted. Asean coherence may be fleeting. On matters of commercial substance, regionalism (as Chapter 11 explains) is illusory. The world is full of dangers but, after Lee's departure, will Goh Chok Tong manage these uncertainties with the same measure of toughness and agility shown during Lee's thirty-year stewardship?

These are never particularly popular points to make in Singapore. But they explain why, in essence, the leadership feels so acutely that the country's glittering success remains hostage to its region. It always will be so. In gloomier moments, when the uncertainties of political succession at home and in neighbouring capitals seem especially troubling, the fabulous achievements appear so fragile, so vulnerable. Singapore may not be, as one migrating Singaporean told me at the airport, 'just a bubble waiting to pop', but it does not take anything for granted. Perhaps, ultimately, that is why it has been so successful.

To sum up, this exceptional Southeast Asian country operates, in the last analysis, on its own heady self-assurance. By controlling information at home to reinforce that confidence, the island's governors still 'rule the proof'. Yet an Asia far older than Singapore encircles their glittering but vulnerable achievement in a seductive, dissembling embrace. Like the Indonesian islands just visible from the skyscrapers on Shenton Way, the fatal charms of Singapore's neighbours lie ever ready to unravel the island's convincing success.

Living with that sense of abiding insecurity has prompted the Chinese of Singapore, and overseas Chinese minorities elsewhere in Southeast Asia, to make hay while the tropical sun shines. Chapter 7 considers that remarkably energetic minority.

References

Cottrell, R. (1985) 'Singapore reconsiders', *Far Eastern Economic Review*, 13 December
Minchin, J. (1987) *No Man is an Island: a Study of Singapore's Lee Kuan Yew*. Sydney: Allen & Unwin
Morgan Guaranty Trust Company (1987) *The Asian NICs and US Trade*. New York

7

CHINATOWN

The Chinese Puzzle

Of many mistaken notions about the Southeast Asian marketplace, none exceeds the error of overlooking, or underestimating, the persistence of Chinese business strength. Those searching for signs of the magic of impersonal market forces usually find the famous 'hidden hand' of Adam Smith attached to the arms of about 20 million ethnic Chinese.

The great majority of overseas Chinese living in archipelagic Asia are descended from poverty stricken migrants coming less than a century ago to *Nanyang*, literally the 'South Sea'. Motivated by a consuming commercial drive, these refugees from the squalour and insecurity of warlord-ridden China swept into their new lands like a tempest. Their windstorm of ambition coincided with the opening up of those vast island territories, nearly all of them colonies, to the stiff breezes of the expanding world economy. Barely 6 per cent of the region's 300 million people, these migrants dominate every national economy.

It is not an especially onerous tutelage, despite wild chauvinist claims or racist cant from 'native' apologists. Chinese businesses mostly fit a 'mum-and-dad' retail trading mould and work to razor-thin margins. Nor do the *Nanyang hua-chiao*, the 'overseas Chinese in the South Seas', spread themselves evenly throughout the region. In small, successful Singapore and Brunei they comprise three-quarters and nearly one-half of the respective populations; elsewhere these percentages drop to more diminutive fractions as in Indonesia or the Philippines (see Table 3.)

Everywhere however the immigrant Chinese have generated powerful business and financial interests, with credit lines often stretching back to Taiwan, Hong Kong and Macao. Since the 1960s these links have gone further afield, to Australia, Canada and the United States as the third or fourth generation spirits away its profits to lands offering the impression of rock-hard stability. True, Chinese migration has been a factor in these English-speaking, New World countries since the 1860s; but the financial position of these minorities (all Asians still form less than 2 per cent of the US population, for example) has never been stronger.

High Turnover, Quick Return

In the Asean region therefore, 'Chinatown' means much more than the old, rather shabby Chinese quarter wedged into the downtowns of nearly every Far Eastern city. 'Chinatown' now serves as a byword for a special type of powerful commercial dynamism. As many never tire of telling, much of this Chinese energy remains incredibly shortsighted while some of it is greedy to a breathless degree.

There are good historical reasons for the rapacity: the fast-extractive impulse simply mirrors the restrictive and even intimidating attitudes adopted by native Southeast Asian rulers towards Chinese commercial success. More often, however, the varying layers of government 'cooperate' with the Chinese, but at a cost progressively more burdensome as payoffs to key political personages rise into the higher strata.

At its essence therefore, 'Chinatown' in Southeast Asia also connotes a steamy, secretive place, a below-decks engine room powering the region's economic miracle. Down there, in the muck and mess of politics and money, amid boilers and grease, the real motors turn over, far removed from the economists' crisp charts and smart uniforms on the ship's bridge.

In the modern Southeast Asian economies the Chinese still work, by design or force of habit, in the bowels of these glamorous ships of state. Descendants of noodle vendors or tin miners have become a rich, if outrageously *nouveau riche* tribe, their wealth secreted away in the bulkheads or thrown at passing tax havens. For them it is a matter of indifference that their business engine room also propels the vessel forward; it is as if the engine operators worked simply to harness the power they generate to their own living quarters. If this vulgar commerce, the staff of life and gossip to the Chinese, results in others getting rich as well, then so be it. Slipping out of the metaphor let us put the point directly: determined Chinese immigrants have done more than any other group to make the economies of archipelagic Asia some of the world's fastest growing.

Table 3   Overseas Chinese in Asean

Country	Chinese	% of total population
Philippines	600,000	1.4
Indonesia	3,250,000	2.5
Thailand	3,500,000	8.5
Malaysia	3,687,000	35.5
Brunei	46,700	46.7
Singapore	1,580,000	72.0

SOURCE: Limlingan (1987)

Straight Talk at the Banquet

On a two-week business visit to Malaysia you are at your eighth (or is it ninth?) Chinese banquet in Kuala Lumpur. It may be the seventh (or is it the eleventh?) course. You have long ago lost count of the speeches. Then, stealthily, an over-full silence envelops the private room as torpor descends on your fellow diners, all of them Malaysian Chinese businessmen.

Crimson from French cognac (the Hong Kong and Malaysian Chinese make these two countries the world's first and second largest markets for the stuff), your hosts launch into elaborate toasting. Down goes more of the liquid, the colour of gold, tumbler by tumblerful. And then, rather oddly and imperceptibly, a new phase of the evening begins.

At this late hour, before the guests slink home in their BMWs or Mercedes, money-minded home truths start to drip out. Your urbane, Berkeley- or Oxford-educated Chinese host across the table becomes conspiratorial, eager to trade some just-between-you-and-me observations. A 'neutral', largely ignorant foreigner plus oceans of brandy and a late night venue; this is the witching hour of Chinese chauvinism.

Awkward Opinions

What comes tumbling out is usually a torrent of disdain for the business sense and political ethics of the 'native' peoples amid whom these Chinese transplants have prospered so brilliantly. One of my hosts on these occasions pulled out a notebook, touching gold pen to Italian paper. He first drew lines and then some bar charts, all meant to correlate prosperity in each Southeast Asian country to the varying percentages of Chinese among the wider populations.

His Courvoisier-laced hypothesis was easy to grasp: without the Chinese traders, middlemen, transport operators, financiers, wholesalers, warehouse owners and retailers the region's commodity wealth (four-fifths of the world's natural rubber, one-half of its palm oil, three-fifths of its copra production and so on) would count for little. Indeed, it would never get to market. To listen to these after-midnight confidences, only the industriousness of *hua chiao*, the Chinese word for themselves, makes the wealth possible.

The trouble is that some of that wild talk seems plausible, even without the brandy. Always remembering the exceptions – the poverty stricken Chinese farmers in Perlis, the out-of-work tin miners in Perak and the perennial poverty among Sarawak's Kek fishermen – the Chinese can fairly claim the dragon's share of business success.

Social surveys, private or government alike, show them commanding incomes four or five times the size of their place in the population charts. The countries where the Chinese comprise the majority or a near-majority, or where they simply feel secure, have achieved the highest growth: Singapore, Brunei and Thailand. This should not be taken too far; Brunei's golden path is oil while Malaysia's natural resources have delivered the bounty. Yet the obvious correlation suggests more than mere coincidence.

To enter the world of overseas Chinese business is to transport oneself into an arena where the commercial markings seem familiar enough but where the manner of moving towards them seems utterly foreign. Geomancy (the positioning of build-ings, houses or an executive's desk according to 'lucky' points of the compass); fortune-telling or postponing investment decisions because the numerology looks bad – these all influence 'rational', marketplace behaviour. One Chinese tycoon prefers to sign contracts on the seventh day of the seventh month of the seventh in the series of twelve zoologically named years in the Chinese calendar.

In Chinese business, one rarely mentioned point of reference is to decide where businessmen or women 'fit' in the sometimes muted, often shriekingly audible row between business groups favouring Taipei or Beijing. China's desire to woo back the overseas Chinese, or at least to relieve them of their wallets, has become more evident since the Four Modernisations campaign began in China during the late

1970s. More than 5,000 foreign firms have invested directly in China since 1978, a direct challenge to the Asean region's faltering effort to win new investment. Many of these are fronts for overseas Chinese. The motherland's siren call still turns their head.

A Recent Exodus

Pockets of Chinese traders, farmers and miners have lived in the region for over 600 years, yet the largest migration happened mostly in recent times, and often within living memory. The influx from 1880 to 1920 was without precedent; compare the current, nearly 50 per cent Chinese share of Brunei's population to an 1889 census showing just 80 Chinese amid a native Malay population just touching 15,000 people. Even in Singapore, the 'natives' outnumbered the Chinese until well into the late nineteenth century.

The immigrants came via the southern port cities of Canton, Swatow, Hai-kou and Amoy. Some set their sights on Australia, South Africa, California or Hawaii, but they comprised a modest handful. 'On a world-wide basis', says Filipino-Chinese scholar Victor Limlingan in a 1987 Harvard Business School study, '96% of all overseas Chinese live in Southeast Asia (including Hongkong and Macao); 65% of all overseas Chinese are in the Asean countries.' They have remained tightly knit in part, as Lynn Pan noted in a 1989 *Far Eastern Economic Review* article, because of the '[Chinese] immigrant's nurturing of his language and because of his bottomless appetite for forming clan associations.'

The economic impact of these people, whose roots lay in two southern Chinese provinces, Fukkien and Gwandong, has been astonishing: in the century elapsing since the second, and the last wave of Chinese migration beginning in the 1880s, they have moved into command positions in retailing, professions, importing, commodity trading, mining, fisheries and, crucially, in finance. 'The Westerners colonised the tropics by exporting capital and establishing estates, mines and commercial enterprises while Chinese colonisation relied on brains and brawn,' notes Lennox Mills, a noted scholar of the region.

'The typical Chinese immigrant was a penniless labourer who worked with concentrated energy until he had saved enough to forsake manual labour for some form of business,' Mills adds. 'If Horatio Alger had chosen to place his success stories among Chinese rather than Americans, he could have found a plethora of examples for his favourite theme of poor boy from the farm makes good in the big cities.' (The stories of Horatio Alger appeared during the last thirty years of the nineteenth century in the US, and invariably portrayed a rags-to-riches success by some poor immigrant boy, armed with pluck and little else.)

A Less than Enthusiastic Welcome

Nowhere did this happen without large adjustment problems. Throughout Southeast Asia a spectrum of racial edginess exists between resident Chinese and non-Chinese peoples. The gamut of reaction runs from the slam-down-your-shutters mentality corroding the confidence of urban Chinese in parts of Java or Sumatra (where they are widely despised) to the apparent indifference of Thais to the 15 per cent Chinese minority dwelling amid them.

In both Indonesia and Malaysia, and in the Philippines during the 1950s, some quite specific policies were tried to ease out Chinese middlemen. In some countries, policies were introduced aimed at usurping them altogether, especially in 'commanding heights' financing or commodity wholesaling.

In Malaysia a quota discriminating in favour of Malays operates with government sanction and coercion: the stated objective is to make the bare majority of Malays 'masters of their country again', although language this provocative rarely finds its way into politicians' speeches. *Bumiputra* and *pribumi*, as noted earlier, are the words, in Malaysia and Indonesia respectively, that mean an indigenous or 'native' person, as opposed to a Chinese or (as in Malaysia) an Indian (a South Asian Indian) as well.

Thailand: Easiest for Chinese

If Indonesia's or Malaysia's racial business policies stand at one end of the spectrum, Thailand's tolerance must take the opposite datum point. For centuries the Thais and immigrant Chinese have coexisted with remarkably little strain, with neither religion (Buddhism), social customs (drinking and gambling) nor culinary habits (pork-eating) creating distinctions. In Muslim Malaysia or Indonesia and Brunei, these divergent habits count a lot against the Chinese; in Buddhist Thailand or Roman Catholic Philippines they fit much better into the dominant social ethos.

In Thailand these and other attributes have blended perfectly into the local ethnic tapestry, with Sino-Thais considering themselves Thais without a hint of the second-guessing that keeps so much Chinese capital chasing fall-back positions around the world. In Thailand most estimates attribute 90 per cent of commercial and manufacturing investment to Chinese ownership. Over half Thailand's banking and finance also operates under Sino-Thai control. A 1983 study showed Filipino Chinese owning nearly two-fifths of the largest 259 of the one thousand biggest Philippine corporations. The larger Chinese population in Malaysia does not translate to overwhelming control, largely because of that country's discriminatory New Economic Policy.

The Chinese 'question' has become muted in Bangkok. By the end of the 1980s, both of Thailand's deputy prime ministers, Bhichai Rattakul and Chaitichai Choonhavan, cheerfully acknowledged their Chinese ancestry. Many prominent Thai Chinese have made their surnames sound 'Thai'; this is a gathering habit among the 6 million Chinese within Thailand's population of nearly 60 million. As Paisal Sricharatchanya, Bangkok bureau chief of the *Far Eastern Economic Review* wrote in 1988, 'the Sino-Thai community today has emerged as the dominant economic group, controlling a lion's share of practically all key business sectors.'

They also comprise the ascendant student group in the best Thai educational institutes, such as Thammasat and Chulalongkorn universities. Sino-Thais come close to monopolising the medical and engineering faculties, without apparent resentment. Sporadic nationalist reactions during past Thai regimes this century made little long-lasting impact on communal feelings, and today the only restrictive entry practices seem to persist at the Chullachomkhlao military academy, which insists on excluding cadets born of first or second generation immigrants.

This largely amicable coexistence, enhanced by frequent intermarriage, may not endure indefinitely however. The rapacity that led to the wrecking of Thailand's forests and coastal resources usually carries a Chinese face, say Thai critics, an allusion to overwhelmingly Sino-Thai interests in the companies that have almost logged out Thailand's vast forests.

Other local chauvinists see a Chinese hand behind the biggest banks and finance companies, prompting occasional mutterings from younger military officers. Ambitious generals, such as Chaovalit Yongchaiyut, occasionally also make veiled appeals to 'indigenous' feelings *vis-à-vis* the Chinese; up to the end of the 1980s however, these undercurrents normally become stilled once the aspiring soldiers reached power.

Thailand's reliance on Chinese diplomacy also grew as the need for a protective shield against Vietnam added up to much less suspicion in Bangkok of Chinese motives than in Jakarta or Kuala Lumpur. China's Four Modernisations deliberately seek overseas Chinese capital: the agribusiness Charoen Pokphand Group, run by a Teochew clan group, is just one of the many Chinese companies to respond.

Muddling Through in Malaysia

Even in Asean countries thought to be 'tough' on local Chinese, the treatment varies enormously within different districts. In peninsular Malaysia's east coast states of Kelantan or Trengganu, the Chinese feel a highly vulnerable minority. And so they are. Pork-eating, *mah jong* gambling, liquor and womanising happens only behind tightly shut doors.

In Malaysian places with more even racial balances however, these anxieties become less acute. In eastern Indonesia, predominantly Christian communities make it easier for Chinese to live and let live; among the more orthodox minded Muslims of North Sumatra, however, the degree of social isolation, and even of occasional danger, becomes almost palpable. Desecration of Chinese graves sometimes jolts towns in Java. And during the aftermath of a failed coup in Indonesia in 1965, entire communities of Chinese were expelled or murdered.

These tragedies happen only in moments of extreme instability. More often the modus vivendi between native politicians and immigrant Chinese businessmen is all too apparent – a line of business protection reaches back to the most powerful people in government.

Indonesian Chinese: The Region's Wealthiest

The close links, described in Chapter 4, between Southeast Asia's richest Chinese, Liem Sioe Liong, and Indonesian President Suharto illustrate the point very nicely. Liem financed Suharto's regiment when the future president needed that support; ties of loyalty reaffirmed over the years have since resulted in Liem becoming pre-eminent in large slices of commerce.

By the mid-1980s too Liem was leading investor groups back to China, with plans to fund a US$700 million oil refinery in Fujian, Liem's birthplace, well under way. Liem thus mirrors at the macro-level of regional business a prudence no different from that of a smalltown Chinese retailer.

Although Malaysia's New Economic Policy has catapulted thousands of Malays into business positions, the 'functional', as opposed to 'symbolic' or 'notional', company directors are still overwhelmingly Chinese. Behind the wall of 'native' Indonesian names, the same situation occurs in Jakarta boardrooms. The small, Chinese slice of humankind in Indonesia (less than 3 per cent) probably controls over 60 per cent of wholesale and 75 per cent of all retail businesses. The children and grandchildren of Teochew or Hokkien immigrants control over three-quarters of all the paid-up investment in finance companies. Altogether, about half of Indonesia's Chinese live in Java, with another quarter residing in Sumatra and the rest scattered throughout Borneo and among the lesser islands.

Different Kinds of Chinese

In all these countries the question of identity always provokes confusion. Curiously, at the highest and lowest income levels a tendency exists to identify strongly with the particular country of residence, especially in Thailand and the Philippines. Shopkeepers, however, still think of themselves as 'Chinese', no matter how many generations established in Nanyang. The patterns of Chinese 'dialect' groups also fit into pre-conceived occupational tracks; Malaysian car mechanics always seem to be Kecks while Borneo businessmen speak the Fukkien dialect. These differences mean a great deal socially, but only among themselves. For outsiders the appellation 'Chinese' still says it all.

Broadly speaking, the Chinese in Thailand and in the Philippines have an easier time of it than their ethnic counterparts in Malaysia and Indonesia. The finely cut racial and demographic balance in West Malaysia makes for insecurity among the Malays; this combines with an ever more orthodox conception of Islamic practice. Religion reinforces Malay communal feeling, so much so that the symbols of Islam, perhaps the most self-consciously universal religion, can become dangerously akin to anti-Chinese provocation.

In Indonesia the reasons for a much more corrosive anti-Chinese sentiment have, perhaps, a more complicated pedigree than the simpler Malay fears of becoming 'strangers in their own land'. It is often forgotten that the Javanese comprise the largest group of ethnically and culturally compact Asians outside the dominant Han Chinese, Japanese and the (more heterogeneous) Indian Hindus.

With their syncretic, Hindu-Buddhist background overlaid with nominally observed Islam, the Javanese now number nearly 70 millions. They provide the largest bulk of the 100 millions now living on Java, the others being the Sundanese, whose cultural identity comes close to Javanese forms. Java and the Javanese feel they comprise the heaviest counterweight to the Chinese in archipelagic Asia. They also remember the Dutch colonial government's use of Chinese as tax collectors.

Ali on the Lookout for Baba

Yet edginess about the overseas Chinese remains a complicated phenomenon. Relying for political mileage on what a noted scholar of overseas Chinese, Peter Gosling, calls the 'myth of the merciless monopsonistic middleman', powerful people in government collaborate in a variety of business deals which in Malaysia go by the name of Ali-Baba, with Ali the Malay becoming the 'sleeping' or 'blind' partner of a business, but giving it the necessary 'native' front. Baba, the Chinese businessman, goes about his tasks, relying on Ali's protection – since Ali gains financially from the deal – and the arrangement continues for as long as it is to everyone's satisfaction. *Ni yao shen ma, wo men yu shen ma*, goes the old Mandarin Chinese expression. 'Whatever it is that you want, we have it.'

Another twist for the Chinese lies in the habit of implementing 'national' language policies in Asean countries. This often increases social isolation. But this forms just a slice of an array of government moves to weaken the business strength of the Chinese; in Malaysia and Indonesia arguments favouring positive discrimination for the *bumiputras* stress that Chinese economic power will always win the day against the natives in any open, free market competition. This argument blithely ignores divisions among the Chinese themselves; it may even guarantee their commercial supremacy.

Linda Lim, an authority on the subject, writes that 'discrimination against Chinese in education and employment may force them to resort to more self-em ployment in order to survive, in effect locking them into small- and medium-scale entrepreneurial activities, especially in commerce, and thus preserving their dominance' (in Lim and Gosling (eds), 1983) – exactly the opposite from that intended.

The point is that government policies *reinforce* racialism in Southeast Asia's ostensibly market economies, distorting those self-same markets by forcing quotas and placing 'no trespass' signs over large sections of the economy. The overall result, as might be imagined, accelerates a less likeable tendency in Chinese business practice: short-term results, quickly turned over or taken out. It also leads to the 'nest-egg' mentality, a cause of enormous capital flight to safer havens in Australasia, North American and Western Europe.

Perhaps the best way to grasp the extent of overseas Chinese power in Asean commerce results from comparing their share of capital investment to the amounts invested by the largest foreign investors. One Harvard study showed resident Chinese in Asean controlling two to three times as much total investment as the Japanese, the region's largest outside investor; this advantage grew to four to five times the amount of invested American funds.

Even in the countryside, where Chinese penetration lags far behind their urban commercial success, immigrants from south China had come to own 80 to 90 per cent of the rice mills in Thailand and the Philippines by the 1950s before government action forced them to divest these businesses. The result was predictable: a precipitous drop in efficiency before the rigour of controls relaxed and, indirectly, the Chinese moved back in again.

Trying to Explain the Sino Magic

What precisely accounts for this amazingly rapid and formidably strong business success? Writing about Malaysia thirty years ago, Victor Purcell described 'their close-knit communal business tie-ups and connections, their extensive hold over the wholesale and retail business, their control of transportation, their powerful banks and their own wealth [which] are such as to constitute an impregnable barrier against any substantial encroachment by other communities in their economic preserves.'

These words from Purcell, then the doyen of overseas Chinese studies, might seem a trifle sweeping today, as government power has forcibly readjusted the pattern of wealth in some Asean countries. Malaysia's NEP stands dominant, although the Malay business élite does its share of free-riding. In the Philippines a 'Philippines for the Filipinos' campaign in the 1950s also put Chinese business on the defensive, but this became history against the long years of the Marcos decline. Moves at the same time also animated anti-Chinese business sentiment in Indonesia, where Chinese arguably still feel the most isolated, disliked and threatened.

In business flair the Chinese cannot be equalled, even among other migrant groups. 'The contrast in economic performance between the Indians and the Chinese – who both came to Malaysia as mining and agricultural workers – is a persuasive argument that what contributed more to the success of the overseas Chinese was more that *they were Chinese* than that they were a minority group,' Limlingan says boldly.

This need not reflect badly on Southeast Asia's 'natives', nor should it conjure up a picture of indolent locals outwitted by crafty Chinese laundrymen. The same successful dynamic worked wonders in the United States: in the 1920s nearly all Chinese men there laboured in restaurants, or worked as domestic servants, cooks or agricultural coolies. By the 1970s however, just a generation or two further along in time, 30 per cent of American Chinese held professional level occupations, *double* that of the 'white' population at large.

Community Values

The key factors for Chinese business success seem to have been broader economic transformations occurring in their new countries, plus their immigrant status and tight clannish system. Chinese social groups – clubs, chambers of commerce and the like – place enormous emphasis on credit-worthiness. In every Chinatown across the Asean region the chamber of commerce acts as a catalyst for trade, lobbying, Chinese language dissemination, group charity, welfare of widows and orphans, burial ceremonies and even fire protection.

Linda Lim says all Asean stereotypes invariably characterise the overseas Chinese as 'mainly urban, commercial, successful and prosperous.' But Chinese work as market gardeners in Thailand and Malaysia, smallholder rubber growers and dealers in Borneo and some West Malaysian states. They belong to families working for generations as fishermen, and in many rural towns across the wide region they work as lorry drivers and forwarding agents. In Malaysia and on some of the Indonesian islands, notably Belitung off Sumatra, Chinese have mined tin or farmed wide tracts of tidal salt flats since the 1730s.

These older communities were overwhelmed by the flood of new Chinese migrants beginning a century ago. In Malaysia, Chin Kee Onn's sensitive book *Twilight of the Nyonyas* (1985) vividly portrays the vanishing world of the 'Nyonya' or 'Baba' Chinese communities along the Malacca Strait, groups which lived harmoniously among local Malays, intermarrying and evolving a unique language, culture and – especially – cuisine.

Yeap Joo Kim's *The Patriarch* (1984) also describes a Straits-born Chinese, 'KSE', who came from an old Sumatra trading family which intermarried but remained, at the core, Chinese. In Islamic Indonesia and Malaysia these tales now pluck nostalgic responses; nationalism and highly politicised communalism have consigned the Baba and 'Straits' heritage to the cultural scrap heap.

The retreat was also forced by brasher immigrants from Canton or Fukkien whose swift moves into urban retailing and financing spawned the stereotyped 'Chinaman' of Southeast Asia. And these migrants also became syndicate operators and commodity traders who, like the European Jews also, were thought to control the destinies of nations.

The power of every cliché lies in its being partly true. The same applies to the 'myth' of the omnipresent Chinese trader and financier. Though statistically only a slice of the perhaps 20 million *hua chiao* in Asean fit the sleek stereotype, the economic power of those at the top remains awesome. Linda Lim charts what she calls 'interlocking business and social interests at the highest corporate levels' in Malaysia and elsewhere.

Lim's work begins with the words, 'the Chinese are a particularly acquisitive race' and proceeds to note that 'Chinese economic monopolies in Southeast Asia evolved in direct response to a set of historical, social, economic and cultural forces operating at a particular time.' Once established, these monopolies tend to perpetuate themselves however, and like an armadillo they present vengeful defence if social networks are threatened.

To what specific formulae can we attribute Chinese business dynamism? The key Chinese commercial concepts revolve around rapid, high turnover to keep cash from 'sleeping'. An often hostile external environment plus antagonistic or exploitive local governments make flexible and rapid liquidation of investments a primary concern. 'The period of danger is the "sleeping period", where cash may never awake from its deep slumber . . . a willingness to trade a smaller margin for a shorter sleeping time gives rise to a turnover orientation,' Limlingan says (1987).

This means ordinary rates of return fail to attract the Chinese if the length of return on investment is longer than normal (but would be normal to Western investors). This 'fast-in, fast-out' mentality marks the Chinese business approach throughout Asean.

It also prevents many from realising greater potential, especially in manufacturing or large, market-share decisions where the Japanese have surpassed the local Chinese. Foreign distributors often find that their credit-giving becomes the main, rather than the ancillary concern of local Chinese who ostensibly have signed up as product distributors. But the product is dumped instead to realise quick cash gains, which the Chinese then re-invest at greater return, a system that puts product distribution companies unwillingly into the financing business.

The 'no-sleeping' rule for Chinese capital can even lead to absurdity. Chinese clients borrow from a non-Chinese commercial bank, only to put the cash right back in again on deposit with the same bank; they prefer to absorb the interest-differential to have instant access to ready cash. The businessman (or woman – many Chinese family fortunes have grown from masterful women) then moves to back this up by a gentler credit-line back through various clan networks (Hokkien, Fukkien, K'ek or whatever).

These networks often as not radiate out of Hong Kong or Taiwan. The ideal 'deal' becomes a self-generating cash-cow which no longer requires any paid-in investment. Better still, the business becomes self-financing, a style of commerce Filipino Chinese like to call *ginisa sa sariling taba*, 'frying in its own fat'. Hence the attraction of money-lending. And this 'constant turnover' leads also to low-margin, high-volume business capturing an ever wider slice of the market. Once accomplished the business is left, cooking in its own juices: noodles or nutmeg, copper or carburettors – the approach remains the same, regardless of the commodity or service.

It was once a truism among business economists that this style of business, enriching and nimble to be sure, did not however allow the Chinese to move into the 'serious side' of commerce. Trading was one thing, producing for trade quite another. Just as Chinese individuals could not move beyond being middlemen, so the complacent rationale went, so also would the various territorial 'Chinatowns' such as Penang and Singapore remain forever stuck in their entrepôt ruts. Buying and selling, loaning and borrowing; but never producing. How wrong these mostly Western analysts were.

Chinese Gain From New Policies

Ironically, the Chinese drive into bigger business pastures resulted from government pressure in Malaysia, Indonesia, Thailand and the Philippines. All of them began trying to squeeze Chinese from their retailing niche. Lim says that 'Chinese middlemen in nearly all Southeast Asian countries face policies to limit and replace them,' yet the Chinese responded by raising the stakes.

Convinced that their capital would go into terminal 'sleep' if kept in hitherto normal niches, the Chinese began searching for other opportunities. In this quest they exploited a superficially changing business climate, brought about by policies requiring at least a façade of 'native' commercial involvement. Malaysia's New Economic Policy, Indonesia's *pribumi* favouritism and the 'Philippines for the Filipinos' campaign all sang the same refrain.

This search for new business horizons received much impetus from 'projectitis', the malady already described, to which cash-rich Asean governments feverishly succumbed in the 1970s and 1980s. In Jakarta and Kuala Lumpur, industrialisation programmes mimicked Marcosian vanity in the Philippines. Thailand's public-sector ventures also created massive plans, huge price distortions and market-defying differentials.

Tariffs, import licensing and export monopolies were devised to ensure commercial 'success' of these heavily capitalised ventures. Complicated subsidies, ostensibly to encourage certain infant industries, became available. Chinese businessmen such as Robert Kuok, Tan Khing Ing, Harry Rahardja, Liem Sioe Liong, and hundreds of lesser names saw their chance. The Kwek family in Malaysia geared up Hong Leong Industries while the Overseas Chinese Banking Corporation and Malayan Banking empires belonging to Khoo Teck Huat also rode the industrial expansion.

Kuok's sugar refining expanded to reach Fiji and Australia, while United Motor Industries provided a jumping-off point for Malaysian Chinese Eric Chia's interests in government-linked trading and production entities such as the Malaysian Overseas Investment Corporation, which experienced severe management difficulties in the 1980s. Chia also won a board seat on the government-owned Heavy Industries Corporation of Malaysia. These men were the comparative 'Old Money' Chinese, alert however to new business opportunities.

Some newer Chinese entrepreneurs soon joined them. Whether in rubber trading (Lee Yan Lian), services and hotels (Khoo Kay Peng), gambling (Lim Goh Tong) or timber (Wee Boon Peng), adroit Chinese accommodated themselves to the pro-native policies.

Far from ejecting the Chinese, restrictive government policies pointed the shrewder ones towards new sources of money becoming available via 'development finance institutions' owned by government, but operated on predictably feudal lines, favouring clients and penalising free operators. All that was necessary was sufficient *bumiputra* cover and tight links to native bureaucrats, such as those nurtured carefully by Chinese in Johore and other Malaysian princely states.

Even the array of guarantees for foreign investors, the so-called 'pioneer industries' exemptions, also worked to Chinatown's advantage. The pioneer schemes prompted huge capital laundering and recycling, as Chinese money went to Hong Kong or Taiwan and came back again in the guise of 'foreign investment', often in league with Japanese multinationals.

Indonesian Chinese businessman William Soeryadjaya (like many of his ethnic Indonesian peers he has shed his Chinese name) is often seen as a beneficiary of this process. He took over a failing, state-owned motor assembly enterprise and then brought Toyota into the business. Similar stories abound throughout Southeast Asia.

Chinese Corporatism

Another factor was at play. New ideas about corporate organisation were filtering through to the family-dominated, abacus-and-teacup businesses. The 1970s witnessed a growth of interest in corporate conglomerates – vast business empires which, through economies of scale, would dominate markets. These ideas received reinforcement from the demonstrable success of Japan's *sogo shoshas*, the multi-faceted trading houses that had links going straight to the ordinary consumer and back to the production line.

Bruce Gale, a student of Malaysian Chinese business, puts it this way:

Traditionally the Chinese in Southeast Asia owed their commercial success to . . . economic individualism, family loyalty and a keen eye for the need to adjust to new political circumstances. Small retail establishments, as well as large, Chinese-owned corporations, remained essentially kinship-based. Control and ownership were closely linked.

'In recent years however, a new type of commercial organisation has arisen in Malaysia,' he added, 'shifting the balance of power within the local Chinese community and challenging well-established patterns.' The new form of business involved mobilising capital from thousands of Chinese artisans and professionals, and using that money to create new holding companies and cooperatives.

Some of these new firms took the form of investment holding companies run by racially-based political parties: the most prominent examples were the Malaysian Chinese Association's Multi-Purpose Holdings Berhad, and the Malaysian Indian Congress's Maika Holdings Berhad. By the end of the 1980s, both had run into serious trouble, as dispensing patronage took priority over the management of the companies.

On each of these new corporate flagships, almost without fail, the 'immigrants' brought influential 'natives' to the boardroom. As noted, before his downfall Tan Koon Swan, president of the Malaysian Chinese Association, put Mohamed Noah Omar, the father-in-law of two Malay prime ministers, into the Supreme Corporation board. Another director, Tunku (a princely title) Mohamed Besar Burhanuddin, linked Tan to the Negeri Sembilan royal family. The Malay business élite bestowed various honorific titles ('Tan Sri', 'Tun' or 'Datuk' are the most favoured) on their Chinese partners.

Coupled to the commodities boom and to buoyant global trade, the two golden decades were especially profitable for the many lucky Chinese entrepreneurs who made this decisive jump. Pre-eminent among all the Chinese pushing into industry must be the Liem Group of Indonesia, whose owner, Liem Sioe Liong, ranks as perhaps the world's richest man after Brunei's Sultan Hassanal Bolkiah.

The Cukong's Cukong

Liem started his business career as a poor Fujian immigrant to central Java in the 1930s. His group now embraces over forty-five companies, including Bogasari, an exclusive wheat-importing and flour-making concern; Cold Rolling Mill Indonesia Utama – Indonesia's first cold rolling steel mill, and Indocement, the biggest cement-maker in Southeast Asia. Liem's financial reach is more awesome. Through Bank Central Asia and various insurance companies, Liem has branched out into First Pacific Bank, Asia's most footloose and talented banking group now buying into Philippine and other regional banks.

Liem's ties to President Suharto go back to the time the Chinese immigrant made an acute business decision to keep on supplying the Indonesian revolutionary army with food, even when it could not pay. When Suharto came to power after 1966, Liem reaped the windfall, becoming (though Javanese favour the word *cukong*) a 'crony' when he won an exclusive right to import cloves from East Africa.

This was then a business worth US$120 million each year because of the Indonesian passion for clove cigarettes and because of chronic supply shortfalls in Indonesia, the original source of the spice. Yet another import monopoly buttressed the Bogasari deal while the grievously unprofitable steel mill, a lemon since former President Sukarno's days, became 'profitable' when Suharto approved tariffs plus exclusive import rights to specialised steel and metal product companies controlled by Liem. Steel prices rose, the mills became money-makers for the first time, and Liem's group became richer by a quantum jump. As the 1980s drew to a close, Liem continued his quiet divestment, moving assets out steadily via First Pacific's buy-outs.

Not all Chinese-Malay relationships stay as steady or as long as the Liem/Suharto bond. Their quiet collaboration contrasts sharply with another Ali-Baba association, also at the highest level, but one which collapsed amid strident recrimination during 1986–87.

A Royal Tiff

'Arrogance, distrust and misjudgement may all have played a part in the break between Malaysian entrepreneur Khoo Teck Puat and his financial advisers,' wrote Raphael Pura and Stephen Duthie in the *Asian Wall Street Journal* in April 1987. Reputedly one of Southeast Asia's richest men, Khoo's empire fell apart when Brunei's sultan Hassanal Bolkiah, discussed in Chapter 3, pounced on his son, Khoo Ban Hock, who had served as chairman of the National Bank of Brunei, 70 per cent owned by the Khoo family.

Chinese magnates invariably edge towards acquiring banks: for the Khoos the reason had became clear when reports alleged that the National Bank of Brunei (NBB) had lent around 90 per cent of its funds to Khoo-owned companies – which owed US$466.3 million to the bank. It was an illustration of one of the oldest Chinese corporate games which had badly backfired.

At a certain point in the career of any Southeast Asian tycoon, a bank becomes vital to continuing the financing of roll-over expansion. But Brunei's sultan had different ideas about the proper use of the NBB; he wanted it to become more of a central bank, or at least to have it perform many central bank functions, much as the Hongkong and Shanghai Bank presides over money supply in Hong Kong.

Khoo may have had other ideas. One day in November 1986, the sultan's men suddenly arrested Khoo's son, together with a British accountant and two other ethnic Chinese bank officials; with Khoo's son in a prison in Bandar Seri Begawan, Brunei's capital, bargaining began in earnest. The sultan also froze all the NBB's assets including all interbank transactions between the bank and over forty correspondent banks abroad. The multi-millionaire's son faced charges of conspiring to defraud the bank, tampering with financial records and giving false assurances about the bank's affairs.

The Brunei bank débâcle also revealed the hands of several foreign banks, one of which came under attack for financing Khoo in return for the then 70-year-old tycoon's help in beating back a corporate raid. In August 1986 Standard Chartered Bank, still a major banking force despite Britain's relative decline in Far Eastern influence, gave Khoo a US$37.4 million credit line for the NBB, just eight days after Khoo's 5 per cent holding of Standard Chartered's shares had been disclosed in London, helping to spike a takeover bid by Lloyds Bank. Reports even circulated that Standard's corporate defence tactics had involved financing Khoo to buy the beleaguered bank's shares, although the bank vigorously denied breaching banking rules and asked for a Bank of England inspection.

The credit seems to have received no publicity at the time it was extended. In Brunei, the local Standard Chartered branch had listed the credit to NBB as local lending, while the NBB itself reported the loan simply as offshore borrowing, according to reports.

Moreover, suspicions in Brunei remained strong that Standard Chartered knew very well that bad blood between the two immensely wealthy men would spill over into litigation and arrests. Apart from Standard Chartered, American Express Banking Corporation also had its fingers burnt: when its assets were frozen the NBB owed it Br$70 million. All in all, the National Bank owed almost Br$500 million to thirty-two banks, mostly in London and New York, as well as to over 30,000 local depositors and to the Brunei government.

To further complicate the story, fierce rows broke out between Brunei officials and Khoo's choice of financial adviser after the arrests and freezing of assets, Shearson Lehman Brothers, whose ideas for repaying the loans over three years were described by Brunei's finance secretary as 'worse than any we have received before' from Khoo. In early 1987 Shearson suggested fresh borrowings (described as 'refunding their deposits') from NBB, plus exempting Khoo's indebted companies from immediate liability and a freeze by the Sultan on all his litigation against Khoo – in Brunei, Hong Kong, Malaysia and Singapore.

The Sultan would not bite. His officials declined even to talk to Shearson Lehman, whose corporate tie to American Express Bank caused suspicion. Nor were the creditor banks prepared to cooperate, despite pleas in person by

Khoo, supported by two-hour slide-show presentations in darkened New York boardrooms.

'I have never defaulted on a loan,' Khoo reportedly told the stony-faced bankers. 'I have never failed to uphold my financial obligations. It is my unshakeable intention to continue to fulfil all my responsibilities. I will stand behind my companies. I will service my debts.' To add to Khoo's misery, Singapore's finance ministry launched its own investigation into Khoo-owned firms holding deposits in the NBB.

By 1987, the old patriarch, his estimated US$1 to 1.5 billion financial empire teetering around the globe (he had interests in the US, Britain, Australia, Malaysia, Hong Kong, Singapore and Brunei – to name the largest host countries), retreated to a London exile, From this distance he watched a Brunei court sentence his son to prison in 1987, a woeful end to grand ambitions and perhaps Asia's strongest ever collision of financial wills between 'native' and immigrant, a shattering end to the grandest 'Ali-Baba' arrangement fashioned during the two golden decades.

Foreign Bankers Beware

Like many other Western banks during the 1980s, Standard Chartered showed a knack for over-enthusiastic lending to Chinese tycoons. Its exposure to Khoo family interests seemed more than matched by outstanding loans exceeding US$125 million to one of Sabah's most diversified millionaires, Hiew Min Yong, whose 'imprint was all over Sabah', as John Berthelsen and Raphael Pura wrote in the *Asian Wall Street Journal* in 1988. 'He was involved in property development, publishing, sawmills, brickworks, aquaculture, hotels and plantations,' they added. 'Today however, the empire has collapsed and the millions of dollars creditors lent him have vanished.'

Hiew's working style proved too much, even for his political protectors in Sabah. His main patron, former Sabah chief minister Harris Salleh, fell from power in 1985; it was not too long before Hiew began to feel the heat, especially as the prices for timber, a crucial contributor to Hiew's cash flow, began to tumble. The new state government declined to give Hiew any new timber rights. A US$10 million luxury hotel opened in Hiew's home town of Tawau – but few guests came.

Hiew reportedly took all of this badly. Before his arrest in 1988, Standard Chartered had tried without success to recover its money; Hiew ignored bankruptcy proceedings in an effort to revive his businesses. He moved around in the company of bodyguards. Bankers claimed his operatives terrorised many of his 250 creditors. One of Standard Chartered's branches in Sabah was vandalised, and its Sabah manager was beaten up. Vehicles were set on fire and lawyers were intimidated.

Standard Chartered's problems with Khoo and Hiew illustrated its wider failure in lending aggressively to mainly overseas Chinese in Southeast Asia. These portfolios performed so badly that the bank, in 1986, had to write off £71.3 million in bad debts in the Asia Pacific region. The bank and other creditors reportedly found they held identical security for different loans – an old trick in Southeast Asian circles but a surprise for the 'blue eyes' competing frantically with each other to lend to men like Hiew.

Other Alarums and Excursions

Other instances show how the absence of a strong business protector can harm Chinese business interests. In one case a 68-year-old Indonesian Chinese business-man, Oen Yin-choy (alias James Semaun), had run Hong Kong's Union Bank until it wobbled towards collapse in 1985 and needed saving by an injection of public money. Thereafter, he moved out to California, leaving an investigation under way in his wake.

This did not cause immediate problems: Oen né Semaun also ran a bank in Jakarta and another one, the Trans National Bank, in California. Similar to the Khoo collapse, a pattern of double-back lending by these banks to Oen's companies emerged from the Hong Kong investigations. Reports in April 1987 said these amounted to US$102 million, with most loans in default and some blatantly fictitious.

Again, as with Khoo, much more than half of Union Bank's portfolio comprised these sweetheart loans. Even the criminal charges in Hong Kong (the US justice department filed for extradition) echoed Khoo's charge-sheet: false accounting, misrepresentation of the bank's affairs and publishing a false financial statement. Oen cut his losses to go into retirement in San Francisco; investors in Union Bank and in the Indonesian bank suffered badly. The loan books yielded a dismal harvest: the *Journal* reported one US$8 million loan in which Oen's bank took '19 plots of [rice] paddy' as collateral, and a US$10 million loan for which 'four plots of vacant land in West Java totalling about four hectares' was accepted as security.

Chinese Credit Lines

This pattern of overseas diversification appears frequently in stories about Chinese tycoons, both successes and failures. The failures tend to attract more notice once creditors lose confidence – which happened with increasing frequency during the 1980s. The collapse of Hong Kong's Overseas Trust Bank (OTB) in 1985 showed how far-reaching these financial links are.

Chang Mieng Thien, a Malaysian Chinese, built up his wealth by adroit trading in rubber and adroit manipulation of ethnic Hokkien Chinese, who were persuaded to join their fellow clansman in his financial lending. Chang eventually came to control the large United Malayan Banking Corporation, sold in 1980 to a Malaysian Chinese political party. His overseas links included the large Toronto Dominion Bank, which took equity in UMBC; another was the Bank of Oman.

The Chang family remained, however, family-minded. Assets went to Canada and Australia as part of the inveterate 'rainy day' mentality; this left Chang assets in Asia only feebly supported. Chang's son Patrick, took over the OTB when his father died in 1982. But the family tie, so strong and intensely loyal, cannot compensate for lack of managerial flair. Borrowing short and lending long caught up with OTB, with the June 1985 collapse triggering panic runs on OTB linked banks all around Asia, and massive stock losses in Chang-related listed companies.

The Chinese Juggernaut in Perspective

The overseas Chinese hold the patent to no magic formulae of business success, as the spectacular stories of collapse and financial ruin above illustrate. Nor do they possess an exclusive patent to commercial aggressiveness or acuity; the 'myth of the lazy native' has long been dispelled, while the general success of other migrant communities in Asean – Arabs, Sikhs, Gujaratis and other stray Asians – hardly raises query.

Southeast Asian 'natives', such as non-Chinese Filipinos, often become dazzlingly successful in the US or Australia; even back home the business record of non-Chinese, in the Philippines and elsewhere in the region, excels whenever government intervention or paternalism is restrained. Ask any Indonesian about the Sumatrans from the Padang west coast, or the Buginese from Sulawesi; see if the Penang Malays have not won a proud niche in the commercial history of their island.

Rigorous business research supports this view. In a book appearing in 1985, Japanese economist Yoshihara Kunio showed results from an exhaustive sample back in 1971 of 250 Philippine-based manufacturing companies. These included 87 foreigners (chiefly Americans at that time), 80 Filipino-Chinese and another 80 non-Chinese Filipinos.

By comparison with other regional countries, it seems that Philippine culture did not, *at that time*, despise genuine business flair or reject risk-taking. Kunio's dated data showed that, in 1971 at least, the American colonial history might have produced a local élite less contemptuous of entrepreneurship than elsewhere in Southeast Asia – where the élite, free-riding Malay, Javanese or Thai circles, still influenced by royal court etiquette or its attenuated forms, preferred to let others soil their hands in trade.

In the Philippines however the intervening martial law years of Marcos savaged much of that entrepreneurial attitude, while the élite families displacing the Marcos 'cronies' after the 1986 'revolution' showed no hesitation in perpetuating the monopoly prerogatives so stifling to genuine market capitalism.

Renewed Nervousness

Respected or reviled, the Chinese minority throughout island Asia is going through many changes. The economic climate is uncertain, and many seek, almost desperately, to place golden nest eggs in Western countries and then, when the time seems right, to go and sit on them. Archipelagic Asia remains stuck in its feudal ways, complacently retracing the familiar steps of parasitic patronage.

Yet more mighty currents are washing through the region – chiefly the slow emergence of China, and the likelihood that the migrants so protective of their 'Chineseness' while in the archipelagic diaspora, may return, literally or via their cheque books, to help finance Mother China's entry into the third millenium.

By the late 1970s Hong Kong was shifting away from its older role as entrepôt trader and light manufacturer and towards something new: land speculation. The colony's rabidly free-marketeering philosophy gave it a global distinction, and this sentiment fastened on the suspenseful game of deciding, rather as in a game of 'chicken', who will bail out first from property investment, taking (naturally, naturally) a hefty capital gain on the way out.

In no other Asian city in the late 1980s did as much money go into real estate investment; for several years it seemed that an iron rule of return had been established – urban land or property would always turn a trick; doubling your money, the 25-year-old millionaires said, just depended on whether you wanted to 'wait just a few weeks or stretch it out for a whole month.' And these views came from veterans of the mad Hong Kong boom and bust during 1980–83.

Yet these distractions before Hong Kong's return to China had many implications, few of them very pleasing, for Southeast Asia's free-riding economies. If – admittedly a big 'if' – China keeps its word about preserving Hong Kong's capitalist structures, the offshore credit lines may begin to be thrown inland, with China taking an ever greater share of that investment.

This could become a trend coinciding with greater insecurity, flatter economic performance and tougher political times for the overseas Chinese in Nanyang. Already the Peking authorities have learned much about attracting money back from the overseas Chinese; Liem Sioe Liong's refinery plans for Fujian are just one of many projects under way as the *Nanyang hua-chiao* seek to ingratiate themselves with a changing homeland.

For example, Malaysia's sugar baron Robert Kuok has invested M$320 million to build Peking's new Shangri-La Hotel, to which is attached a major commercial office building complex. Singapore's Chinese are not far behind, as Lee Kuan Yew's son, Lee Hsien Loong, has led investors back to the motherland.

Peking even recruited Goh Keng Swee, the mentor of Singapore's economic success after independence, to serve as an adviser on China's 'special economic zones' mushrooming along the southern seacoast. Nor are the Thai Chinese far behind: one joint venture between Sino-Thai business and the Chinese government is the Shanghai-Ek Chor Motorcycle plant, a US$21 million firm partly financed by Bangkok's Charoe Pokphand Group.

Chinatown's Corporate Future

For the better part of a century, the savings, acquisitiveness and 'sleepless' financial wizardry of the overseas Chinese have generated enormous entrepreneurial dynamism in Southeast Asia. The business acumen of the Chinese, although vulnerable to family quarrels and to preferences for short-term gain, has weathered many political challenges.

It is difficult to understand the tenacity of overseas Chinese commerce without a grasp of the new corporate structures now changing the face of Southeast Asian business. Even in areas where Chinese business involvement is expressly precluded, the interaction between Chinese-controlled business and gigantic state-owned patrimonial companies forms the stuff of high drama in contemporary Southeast Asia.

Paradoxically, every effort to dislodge the Chinese in one area of business leads to their consolidation in another. The move into local industry, producing for a protected market and working under Japanese licences, illustrates this resilience. Nowadays an increasing number of Chinese family companies are venturing into industrial and service businesses reaching into the international arena. It is to these and other, non-Chinese wellsprings of wealth in Southeast Asia that we now turn.

References

Chin, K. O. (1985) *Twilight of the Nyonyas*. Singapore: Federal Publications

Kunio, Y. (1985) *Philippine Industrialization: Foreign and Domestic Capital*. Singapore: Oxford University Press

Lim, L. Y. C. and Gosling, L. A. P. (eds) (1983) *The Chinese in Southeast Asia*. Singapore: Maruzen Asia

Limlingan, V. (1987) *The Overseas Chinese in ASEAN: Business Strategies and Management Practices*. Manila: Vita Development Corporation

Mills, L. (1979) *Southeast Asia*. New York: Praeger

Yeap, J. K. (1984) *The Patriarch*. Singapore: Federal Publications

8

WELLSPRINGS OF WEALTH: SOUTHEAST ASIA'S COMMERCIAL CRUCIBLES

The various contests for business favouritism in Southeast Asia increasingly occur within a range of commercial crucibles, such as corporate empires and stock exchanges, that were unknown, or insignificant, a mere generation ago. In important new areas of business like aviation, electronics, financial services or tourism, the super rich of the Asean countries have added to the wellsprings of their earlier wealth: trade finance, trading houses, plantations and raw commodities.

Literally millions of small and medium-sized businesses have appeared since political stability became the norm after the late 1960s, adding to the increasing complexity of business and to its range. And millions more investors have become addicted to wagering large sums in the region's rapidly growing capital markets. It is no longer just the overseas Chinese. At the same time that playful share market habits have gripped Southeast Asia's burgeoning moneyed classes, the enormous expansion of student enrolment in courses of higher education is propelling more graduates into business and commerce.

It all seems to be purposeful and suggests that Southeast Asia's market economies are finally coming of age after relying for so long on outsiders' markets and money. Yet many doubts persist. How much of this headlong change merely disguises a continuation of older business and political habits that are indifferent, or even hostile, to the free market?

Asean Share Markets: Much 'Aduh' About Rather Little?

'Singapore and Malaysia, why bother?' asked the *Asian Wall Street Journal* in a provocative opening paragraph in early 1988. Why indeed? The utterance 'aduh!' in Malay societies marks feelings of dismay or unpleasant surprise. For millions of Southeast Asian investors, large and small, this word came to dominate their audible reaction during much of the 1980s to share market slides right across the region.

For much of the decade investors had a shaky ride. In Malaysia and Singapore, 'free falls' (that is, a bottoming out of the market without any buying support) followed the October 1987 collapse of Wall Street equities. This collapse followed hard upon a more localised crash in December 1985, when a system of 'forward contracts', in which shares were traded on promises to pay in the future, inflated the Singapore exchange on little more than speculative air (discussed in Chapter 6).

Meanwhile, in Manila, a moribund stock market (absurdly divided between two exchanges) had slowly revived after Marcos left. The pace picked up during 1987, fuelled by gambler funding from Hong Kong, but then succumbed to rumours of *coups d'état* and to uncertain prices for the narrow band of Philippine commodities. Across the South China Sea, in Thailand, the Bangkok bourse continued to draw investors, as we have seen in Chapter 5. Yet it remained narrowly based and thinly traded, for all the excitement generated among foreign investors. Only Jakarta's exchange remained in the doldrums; Indonesian business almost never seeks finance by raising share capital, preferring to rely on well-tested, and subterranean channels of local Chinese credit. And in Brunei, who needed a local share market when Singapore beckoned just across the sea?

1987 and All That

Despite an impressive rebound, the worldwide 1987 stock market collapse badly affected the region's equity markets whose vibrancy is too often mistaken by outsiders for vitality, or as a signpost of entrepreneurial flair and investor know-how. The bad taste lingered for months after the crash: most rights issues (when shareholders receive preferential purchasing privileges for new stock) did very badly in Singapore and Malaysia after October 1987. This afflicted even such gilt-edged securities as a US$182 million issue, announced just before the crash, by Singapore's government-owned Neptune Orient Lines. When the issue was floated after October 1987, Neptune's underwriters had to slash the share price by more than 50 per cent.

Other share issues in the region were also badly squeezed by the October crash. Singapore's Sim Lim Finance took a hammering, as did a share increase by Malaysia's Roxy Electric Industries; although blessed with pedigree political linkages to various politicians, Roxy had to cut its US$36.3 million new issue price by 24 per cent. Pilecon Engineering of Malaysia, another well-connected firm, chopped 35 per cent off its post-October new issue in order to attract buyers. Yet they were slow in coming to these major companies.

Singapore's exchange however proved surprisingly resilient in the near-panic, even after it had dropped more traded value after October than any other Asian share market. From its own all-time index of 1505 points in August 1987, the Stock Exchange of Singapore (SES) plummeted to 779 points during the following month. After November 1987, the market took another battering as hysterical rumours reached Singapore of brewing racial conflict in Malaysia; fears of Chinese–Malay ethnic conflict 'across the Causeway', as the bridge connecting Singapore to southern Malaysia is known, precipitated a one-day fall of 12 per cent in the SES index.

To the growing band of foreign fund managers setting up shop in Singapore and Malaysia after 1980, these alarums and excursions in the latter part of the decade seemed an improbable denouement. Most of the major investment funds from Europe, Japan and the US were ecstatic about the high-yielding stocks they found in the early 1980s, even if some blunders marred their forecasting. In Malaysia, for instance, the London securities firm of James Capel gave its clients a breathless but mistimed endorsement of Malaysia's Multi-Purpose Holdings, the mismanaged business vehicle of the Malaysian Chinese Association, then under Tan Koon Swan's growing influence.

Signs of foreign interest had multiplied quickly in that halcyon decade following the second oil price rise in 1979. A newly unveiled Malaysia Fund sold well on the New York Stock Exchange just a few months before the October crash. Brokers rushed for placings in its initial US$60 million offering, twice the amount of capital raised by the first Asean fund of its kind, the Bangkok Fund. Delighted by the capital inflow into Asean share markets, the Asian Development Bank started to plan for the creation of stronger capital markets, including mutual funds (a concept that has done poorly in the region) and even sectoral or single-industry funds (such as special funds for plantation or mining stocks). As Chapter 10 explains, these ideas were fresh and innovative by comparison with the rest of the bank's operations.

Second Thoughts About the Bourses

Taken together these trends reflected signs that East Asia's most rapidly emerging capital markets were now centred in the Asean archipelago. Apart from Hong Kong, Asia's fastest growing stock markets during the first half of the 1980s were indeed the hectic, if peanut-sized bourses of Manila and Bangkok. Not far behind came the Singapore and Kuala Lumpur markets, known collectively as the 'Causeway market' because of a common historical and interactive history (over a third of the listings on each exchange are cross-listed on the other).

Before the October 1987 crash the Asean exchanges, including Hong Kong, had a combined capitalisation of US$150 billion (see Table 4). Yet a large caveat must apply to our wonderment at such a large figure; much of that figure, about half, had accrued in the eighteen months leading up to October 1987. Although much of that capitalisation melted away after 1987, foreign institutional investors continue to nibble at these nascent markets. The Asian Development Bank's Asian Development Equity Fund, launched in 1988, has found ready buyers in Japan and Europe.

All this seemed very satisfying to the region's business boosters, intent upon proclaiming the victory of mass capitalism in this part of East Asia. And indeed, as Asian share market specialist Anthony Rowley points out (1987), most countries of any size in Asia now have a functioning stockmarket. Yet Rowley and others also caution that this fact alone is not to be confused with either size or significance in the global market.

A closer look at the nature of listings, the thin markets traded, the comparatively tiny number of investors, the paucity of listings, a preference for glitzy, speculative free-fliers and the periodic absence of participation by major capital funds within host countries all point to some large question marks over claims of self-generating, mass capitalism.

Table 4   Asean share markets' capitalisation (January 1985)

Category	Indonesia	Malaysia	Philippines	Singapore	Thailand
Companies listed	24	281	154	308	96
Annual turnover (US$ million)	2.4	2,341	79.9	3,937	421
Market capitalisation (US$ million)	105	28,416	942	38,040	1,732
Share market capitalisation as a percentage of GNP	0.1	63*	2.9	68*	4.3

*domestically incorporated companies only

SOURCE: Asian Development Bank

Compared with Japan's capital markets, now the largest in the world, the Southeast Asian share markets are diminutive and, as Rowley comments, *'terra incognita* for most foreign investors. Even Hong Kong's share market, capitalised in 1988 at over US$40 billion, comes to less than 3 per cent of Tokyo's (or Osaka's) capitalisation in the same year. Yet Hong Kong dwarfs the Asean exchanges by almost the same magnitude, belying claims that this slice of tropical Asia now figures as a major, independent capital market force. 'What stands out', says Rowley, 'is the relative insignificance of other markets in Asia. [The] markets are often tiny in relation to the size of the economies they operate within.'

Immature Markets

The signs of capital market immaturity are still strongly evident. The panicky closure of Singapore's exchange in December 1985 revealed weaknesses in the stock-trading and brokerage house networks. In 1986 Hong Kong analyst Robert Cottrell noted that 'for all the volatility of the Hongkong market, even the great crashes of 1973 and 1982 did not produce breakdowns of the system' as had happened in Singapore in 1985. Together with virtually every other analyst, Cottrell had to eat his words soon afterwards. Hong Kong's exchange, in a dismal act of cowardice, ordered a three-day cessation of trading to weather a hurricane of sell-orders during the October 1987 crash. It was all for nought; when the exchange reopened the daily traded values plunged by 33 per cent.

The immaturity of Southeast Asian share markets is apparent in other ways. Industrial listings fall well back in the queue. Buyers want property and financial companies instead, banking on high cash turnovers rather than longer-term profit and strength. These hothouse favourites usually become speculative sweethearts on the strength of a tiny percentage of free-floating shares. Southeast Asia's hugely oversubscribed new share issues say more about an engineered paucity of new stock listings than about 'fundamentals' or about confidence in future profitability of the newly quoted company. Local Chinese, state-backed trustee funds or foreigners invariably comprise the players in these casinos. Money moves in and out at a fast rate. Pension funds, municipal governments or insurance companies look elsewhere for safe capital gains and steady return.

All in all, there is a 'preponderance of financial and property companies among the listings . . . especially in Asean markets,' Rowley notes. This prompted a reaction, by the late 1980s, back to the more solid, plantation stocks. These remained some of the best buys in the regional exchanges, often undervalued by outside investors as much from ignorance as from conscious decision. Malaysian listings such as Consolidated Plantations or Harrisons Malaysia Plantations Berhad, gave solid earnings in most years and escaped the manipulations of most property stocks.

Yes, We Have No Fundamentals

At a deeper level the much-vaunted entry by foreign funds into the Asean exchanges ignores a fundamental facet. 'The façade of internationalism . . . is deceptive in some ways,' Rowley says. 'Beneath this façade lies a fundamental difference of approach, of culture and of market structure. One manager of a major US investment group bluntly told a Manila investment seminar in 1986 that fiscal fraud in many Asian countries 'is almost a national pastime,' Rowley reports. 'In some countries, insider dealing is accepted as part of the culture – the culture of making money. Small investors do not mind too much whether company directors are making money from dealing on the inside, provided those on the outside can make something.'

It is not as if share markets are a new phenomenon in the region: efforts to start one in Indonesia began in 1912, and Manila has had a share exchange since the late twenties. The Singapore and Malaysian bourses began as one exchange, sited in Singapore in the 1930s. But in the Philippines the Marcos years overwhelmed the advantage an early start had given to the Manila exchange. After the departure of Marcos the World Bank's International Finance Corporation helped create a US$250 million capital fund to direct equity investment towards light industry. Political uncertainties caught up with these markets, repressed for many years in the later Marcos era and reacting too buoyantly in 1986. Rich Hong Kong Chinese put their spare cash into the fifteen actively traded shares in Manila.

Manila's two exchanges also rely on bullish news for some minerals in the late 1980s, especially gold. With a capitalisation just 6 per cent of the size of the Hong Kong market, Manila rides high or low on the prices of just two minerals, copper and gold. Over one-third of the companies listed on the Manila or Makati exchanges are mining firms; in addition, there are communications companies, such as Philippine Long Distance Telephone Company, which have dual listing – in both the Philippines and in New York.

After Aquino came to power the share market went for a wild bull ride. Philippine share prices had suddenly become the cheapest in all of Asia, with very low P/E ratios (the price/earnings ratio divides the market price of a share by its annual dividend earnings). Underpriced stocks took off, based on steadying prices for the two key minerals plus buoyant corporate earnings rising by 55 per cent on average in the two years after Marcos left. Some upward moves in vegetable oils, notably coconut oil, also titillated investors. But political unrest, anchored ultimately in an insurgency that would not go away, made the markets here an especially good example of the Asean casino syndrome.

Manila's lesson in the Aquino years shows that money can be won from the market, but only by those with steady nerves. 'Quick in, quick out' – that old business adage – is being reaffirmed. Moreover, the new government squandered any chance it had to widen the base of the Philippine brand of oligopolistic capitalism. Aquino repeatedly promised to privatise almost 300 government-owned corporations; after two years of such undertakings fewer than 5 per cent had been privatised.

Some of the larger government-owned companies, such as the Manila Electric Company or the Philippine National Oil Corporation, seemed ideal for divestment schemes which would float the shares, as part of the sell-off, on the stock exchange. Here, at last, was a chance to widen the stockmarket and give the fixed-income Filipino middle class a chance, literally, to take stock. But the opportunity was missed, lost in contests for patronage and in efforts by prominent families to regain, as in the electricity utility, what was 'rightfully theirs'. (See Chapter 2.)

With excitement for Manila running only fitfully, the spectacular success of Bangkok's Securities Exchange of Thailand (SET) won more admiration from foreign investors, as Chapter 5 explains. In sheer vitality the Thai market was beginning to outshine its regional rivals towards the end of the 1980s, with all eyes on such meteoric listings as Siam Food Products and Siam Cement Company, both of which trebled their market value over 1985–87. The Bangkok Bank, Asean's biggest bank, also lifted the trading index as did most other financial stocks. Overall the SET's own index jumped by almost 100 per cent in 1986, at a time when the other regional bourses had slumped despondently.

Baubles, Bangles and . . . Bangkok

Was Bangkok the gilded exception to its neighbours? Undervalued share prices plus, by Southeast Asian standards, reasonably high dividends, made Bangkok the darling of the Asian bargain hunters and brought in many outside investors. In 1985, Merrill Lynch created a precedent by registering a Bangkok Fund which put US$25 million into Thai shares. The Thai Industrial Finance Corporation at the end of 1986 set up a rival fund, the US$30 million Thailand Fund, a joint venture with the International Finance Corporation and Vickers da Costa, the sharebrokers for Citibank. These were easily placed.

Yet on closer inspection the SET also seemed to suffer the same basic problems as its lesser Asean competitors: tiny capitalisation and sparse listings (less than a hundred in 1988 valued at about US$2.8 billion). This meant Bangkok's SET was worth almost exactly *one-thousandth* of Tokyo's quoted shareholdings; it was also fifteen times smaller than Singapore's capitalisation.

Like Kuala Lumpur and Manila before it, Bangkok has long dreamed of hoisting a second trading board; yet in all of Asean only Singapore had done so by 1988, and then only with mixed results. Secondary trading boards in advanced share-trading centres normally offer facilities for venture capital, a willingness to invest in the anticipated accrued value of ideas plus enterprise over a longer time. That strikes few responsive chords among Asean investors although the Asian Development Bank has tried hard to get the notion rolling.

The idea of the second boards was to attract more equity financing for expanding companies, which rely too much on bank borrowing. Moreover, the Thais retain time-consuming, bureaucratic procedures for permission to remit share market earnings abroad; informal rules also keep the proportion of any one stock owned by outsiders to well below 50 per cent. Ultimately, the Thai share market remains secondary to Thailand's exceptionally agile commodity and tourism-based economy and, as such, the equity market is also subject to swift vagaries of world trade and fashion. The share market 'fundamentals' in Thailand are as good, or as vulnerable, as that.

Abortive Paper Markets

The same vulnerability afflicted plans to build up commodity trading markets in various Asean countries; fundamentals still depend a great deal on the confidence of outsiders, especially those accustomed to dealing in the long-established US and European markets. But foreigners need to be sure of the regulatory, trading structure in Southeast Asia's much publicised new markets. Apart from stocks and trade in 'physicals' (i.e., buying and selling for actual immediate delivery of a particular commodity), Southeast Asian countries have tried, with mixed success, to create a succession of 'paper' markets – that is, promises to deliver a unit of a particular commodity at some future time.

The rationale for futures trading as it has evolved in the Americas and in Europe is to enable traders and suppliers alike to better determine future prices and to hedge against abrupt changes in price; only rarely does a futures contract become a contract for physical delivery). But when it does, usually by speculative 'cornering' buying, it can batter a market unless there are strong back-up guarantees.

The rudest shock hitting any of these nascent Asean commodity markets came when, in 1984, the entirety of Kuala Lumpur's buoyant palm oil market came crashing down. This followed massive defaults by traders who, the day before, had controlled over 90 per cent of all open positions on the Kuala Lumpur Commodity Exchange (KLCE).

The most prominent operator behind the default soon appeared: Malaysia's Kentucky Fried Chicken franchise holder Loo Cheng Ghee. Drawn by buoyant prices for palm oil, Loo helped engineer a ten-fold increase in prices over six months. He was joined by many brokers in an effort to bid ever higher for all available product and then, when forward contracts had brought all the available product into their hands, to squeeze suppliers (who had firm contracts for delivery to foreign buyers) for every last penny.

The crisis itself erupted when the KLCE's clearing house refused to register deals that seemed to lack real money to support the promised contract price. By forcing a compulsory settlement of over six thousand defaulted contracts however, the clearing house bankrupted a trail of brokerage houses. The day after the defaults, real trading virtually ceased: on 29 February, the 1984 leap year's extra day, only twelve lots changed hands. The market had collapsed. Malaysia's Palm Oil Growers Association said the clearing house 'had destroyed the good name of Malaysia.'

Certainly the fiasco permanently altered the view of the London-based International Commodities Clearing House, which held 30 per cent of Kuala Lumpur's clearing house. The default also badly harmed the KLCE's reputation in overseas markets; so did well-publicised claims that a client of one foreign-based trader denied ever having given various buy and sell orders. One Singapore broker told me he had heard only of two, insignificant instances in which commodity trading clients had denied giving instructions. None of this gave Asean's markets a very good name and it wrecked the KLCE, launched with fanfare only a year before. The embarrassment was compounded for Malaysian primary industries minister

Paul Leong who was in Europe attempting to induce traders to come to the KLCE when the crisis broke.

Mice That Roar?

The erratic share markets, the bumpy ride on the nascent commodity exchanges and the poor development of secondary markets for more long-term investment financing – all these caused little surprise to businessmen familiar with the region and knowing the limits to its hectic growth. Southeast Asia's tremendous expansion bucketed a lot of money into its capital and commodity exchanges, but the wealth did not much deepen or diversify those markets. It is similar to a leaking pipeline of small diameter through which a suddenly trebled amount of water must flow. The leaks sprout into jets. The spillover gushes out more rapidly. In truth, Southeast Asia's money and commodity markets lag far behind the rest of the world in their sophistication, range, spread, volume and (often) probity.

Despite the fast changes, the region has found it hard to break the grip of the old financial centres. Despite strong currencies in Singapore and Malaysia, central bankers (and outside traders) were reluctant to see the Singapore dollar or the ringgit denominating trade invoices. So also with the baht, Thailand's currency, and all the more so, because of frequent devaluation worries, for the Indonesian rupiah.

A simple comparison makes the point. *All* the economies of the developing world, not only those in Asia, still generate less than one-third of the combined gross domestic products of the 'rich man's club' of the Organisation of Economic Cooperation and Development (OECD) members (the countries of North America, Australasia, Western Europe and Japan). The International Finance Corporation however estimates that the aggregate capitalisation of all the developing countries' stockmarkets comes to only 2 per cent of advanced country market valuations.

Even by comparison with other regions, Southeast Asian share markets are relatively underdeveloped. For example, Brazil's market in 1985 reached US$43 billion capitalised value, strides ahead of Singapore despite the island republic's pre-eminent position in its region. Yet another caveat must be put alongside Asean's equity markets. 'Foreigners have been encouraged to think of Asian economies as being 'open' and 'flexible', Rowley writes (1987). 'This is because many Asian nations, especially those in East Asia, have demonstrated a willingness to keep their economies open to trade and to external, direct, investment,' he adds. Yet 'if they had shown half this flexibility in allowing foreigners to invest in their stockmarkets, they would have received much bigger inflows of foreign equity by now.'

But Qualified Praise Is Due

None of this can gainsay the astounding growth of regional share markets in Southeast Asia. There were even more signs by the late 1980s that Indonesia had finally decided to remove regulations shrouding Jakarta's deathly quiet share market where, on particularly busy days, a couple of thousand dollars' business earns the press description 'hectic'. Moreover, in the wake of the October crash, foreign investment fund managers eyed the commodity price rebound which, while not as sustained as the golden years preceding the 1985 crash (see Chapter 9), still bolstered plantation companies and an increasing array of manufacturers.

As the 1990s dawn, there are signs of healthier balance in investor calculations about the region. After the 1987 crash, just about everything outside a narrow range of companies with strong earning fundamentals suddenly looked 'exotic' again to foreign investors. Yet they had not (as some panicky bankers had advised after the December 1985 fiasco in Singapore) run for cover. The issue, as always, is relative. And as a relative business risk, Southeast Asia looks better than most developing regions. And not least, or so the argument goes, since the Southeast Asians are learning all the time, moving two steps forward and, while sliding back, never dropping further back than before. Slowly but surely, capital markets are taking hold.

Banking: Whirlwind Growth

The Asean banking industry showed a faster, asset-backed growth over 1965–85 than any other economic sector in the region. The combined banking assets grew from US$600 million at the beginning of those two decades to US$350 billion by the end of the twenty years. This growth blossomed as widely as it went deep: thousands of new depositor branches opened although the number of banking licences generally was restricted in all the Asean countries.

The old colonial banks such as Hongkong and Shanghai Banking Corporation or Standard Chartered, retained their strong market position, often in trade finance or credit extension to commodity growers, but banks such as the Bangkok Bank (with US$10.3 billion in assets in 1988 it is the Asean region's largest commercial bank), Malayan Banking Berhad (US$5.3 billion), Thai Farmers Bank (US$4.5 billion) and Overseas Chinese Banking Corporation (US$3.7 billion) rapidly expanded also. See Table 5.

Big Banks . . . and Bigger Banks

These figures look impressive. They *are* impressive. Yet the region's financial sector performance, which included explosive growth also in merchant banking, financing companies, leasing operations and even (laggardly) venture capital services, have to be measured against weightier achievements by the sharper side of the East Asian Edge – in Northeast Asia, to be exact, where the Japanese, Taiwanese and Korean banks have grown at astounding rates. This is not to disparage the Asean banks however, which have quickly risen from the status of a Chinese pawnshop to become major financial players.

By comparison with even the middling Japanese provincial banks, even Bangkok Bank seems a modest banking force. In a list compiled by the PA Management Group in Australia of the top 200 Asia Pacific banks (see Table 6), Bangkok Bank only comes 68th. The second largest regional bank, Bank Nasional Indonesia 1946, ranks just 94th while the third largest, Bank Bumiputra, achieves only the 96th position. The rest of the Asean big banking league assumes a similarly more modest placing; of all Asean commercial banks in the top 200 list (thirty-seven

Table 5   The top ten Asean banks in 1988 (US$)

Bank	Assets (less contra items)	Capital plus reserves
	Billions	*Millions*
1. Bangkok Bank	10.27	470
2. Bank Negara Indonesia 1946	7.26	276
3. Bank Bumiputra Malaysia	6.66	600
4. Development Bank of Singapore	5.88	784
5. Malayan Banking Berhad	5.28	395
6. United Overseas Bank	5.22	622
7. Thai Farmers Bank	4.47	338
8. Krung Thai Bank	4.05	169
9. Overseas Union Bank	3.72	329
10. Overseas Chinese Banking Corporation	3.70	505

SOURCE: PA Consulting Group, Australia

in all), only three were placed in the top 100 and only fourteen in the top 150. Over half fell into the bottom twenty-five.

By contrast, all but fourteen of the top seventy Asia Pacific banks were Japanese. The top twelve were Japanese, with Dai-ichi Kangyo, Sumitomo and Fuji Banks taking the top three billings respectively. The remaining fourteen comprised, in order of asset-backed importance, one Hong Kong bank (the Hongkong and Shanghai Banking Corporation, ranked 13th), one mainland Chinese bank (the Bank of China, ranked 21st), four Australian banks (Westpac, the ANZ Banking Group, the National Australia Bank and Commonwealth Bank Australia), an Indian bank (the State Bank of India), two South Korean banks (Bank of Seoul and Korea Exchange Bank) and four others from Taiwan (two), Australia (one) and South Korea (one). All the rest of the top seventy were Japanese.

Where's the Money Going?

Asset-backed strength is just one measure of the position a bank holds. In Asean, what signs were there that the region's banks and their millions of

Table 6   Top 200 Asia Pacific banks, 1988

Bank	Southeast Asian rating	Asia Pacific rating
1. Bangkok Bank	1	68
2. Bank Nasional Indonesia 1946	2	94
3. Bank Bumiputra Malaysia	3	96
4. Development Bank of Singapore	4	104
5. Malayan Banking Berhad	5	108
6. United Overseas Bank	6	109
7. Thai Farmers Bank	7	111
8. Krung Thai Bank	8	117
9. Overseas Union Bank	9	118
10. Overseas Chinese Banking Corporation	10	119

SOURCE: PA Management, Australia

new depositors were using the financial system in creative new ways, increasing savings and developing new lending instruments to marshal domestic savings?

In many more innovative banking services the Asean banks and bankers lagged behind. Despite a heady start in Europe and the US during the 1970s, venture capitalism took a long time to get started. At a Bangkok seminar in the late 1980s, an Asian Development Bank official, Ivan Zimonyi, said 'there is an urgent need to increase the flow of risk capital to innovative entrepreneurs in Asia', but the lack of indigenously derived technologies to cultivated cramped the chances. Most foreign investors bring their own technology with them, bag and baggage.

Family-based businesses, the norm in Asean especially among local Chinese, invariably reject outside investors. Outsiders have an awkward habit of requesting financial information, an embarrassment in a region where three sets of books are kept (one for the tax department, one for creditors and one for the family). Almost no serious market research precedes loan applications. Thinly traded share markets also inhibit risk capitalists from buying equity; so does the emphasis on quick returns, endemic in local Chinese business culture. Venture financiers like the Singapore-based Elders Pica Growth Fund Ltd, partly owned by an Australian brewery or the Bangkok-based Business Venture Promotion Ltd, are still a rarity.

In many ways therefore, bank lending remains very traditional, with Chinese urban banks, especially in Singapore, working as a custodian for Asia's richest families while becoming also the repositories of mass earnings. Government-owned banks have also accumulated vast assets, relying on their link to power and on ethnic solidarity. Malaysia's Bank Bumiputra has deliberately styled itself the flagship of that country's New Economic Policy, aimed (as explained in Chapter 3) at giving Malays a better deal. Most government departments keep their savings in Bank Bumiputra, as do many other corporations. These government-influenced banks include Krung Thai, Thai Farmers, Bank Nasional Indonesia 1946, Malayan Banking Berhad and the United Malay Banking Corporation.

A Vogue for Private Banking

In parallel with growing personal fortunes, many Asean banks have created private banking departments. So have outsiders such as the Rothschild family or Banque Indosuez. Their business comes from uncertainties clouding the region: persistent tensions with local Chinese business clans and the impending 1997 changeover in Hong Kong. Singapore's personal banking business still rests largely on one device: the Asian Currency Unit (ACU), free of tax, free of identity and easily convertible.

Overseas Chinese hold ACUs by the billion, usually in US dollars. Singapore's monetary authority in 1987 said ACUs totalled US$36.5 billion. Many more millions have gone from Chinese families into Australian banks from Chinese wanting to migrate to Sydney or Perth; similar advantages adhere to Canadian banks. Other foreign banks have followed fast: the Swiss remain pre-eminent in the exclusive, personal services side, such as Bank Julius Baer in Zürich, but their competitors in Luxembourg, the Cayman Islands and Hong Kong have also won much new business from restless clients seeking nest eggs outside Southeast Asia.

Hong Kong Jitters

The problems facing Hong Kong as a result of that territory's real estate mania in the early 1980s precipitated a series of rolling liquidity crises around the region. The Ka Wah Bank's collapse, a major one, receives fuller treatment in Chapter 7. Again, the pre-eminent position of overseas Chinese money in Southeast Asia was made apparent, albeit in a negative way.

The September 1983 run on the Hang Lung Bank, and on four smaller Macau banks, precipitated a mad run on dollar accounts in Hong Kong – and nervousness in Asean banks tied by the Chinese networks to Hang Lung's owners. One American bank president received frantic calls from Hong Kong staff to have dollars sent by airfreight. The overseas Chinese, often using informal credit lines escaping clear definition in bank ledgers, retained a clear hold on Asean financial resources (see Chapter 7) although as in Malaysia, campaigns to 'indigenise' the banking sector achieved some notable successes.

Nor were the gains in the Asia Pacific available to everyone: paralleling the growth of the market were some closures. In 1987, the financial world was stunned to learn that two major merchant banking subsidiaries of Lloyds Bank and of the Royal Bank of Canada were closing down in response to Asia's syndicated loan market slump. This type of re-thinking affected other financial services: Merrill Lynch quietly pulled out of Kuala Lumpur in 1986, unimpressed with the wildly oscillating but thin share market there.

Looking Ahead

By the end of the 1980s, Asean financial markets had entered a new stage. The stagnation of the loan syndication market, which had led the expansion of the banking industry in the 1970s, followed the explosive growth of sovereign debt. New financial instruments, such as the floating rate note and other exotica such as NIFs (note issuance facilities) took centre-stage. A large number of banks, domestic and foreign branches, chased the market.

Overshadowing all of this however was the impending liberalisation of Tokyo's financial market. Euro-yen business could bypass Singapore and other centres. Japanese banks which have arranged loans through their Singapore or other Asean branches will in future be able to book loans in Tokyo offshore accounts – this could savage bank loan assets in Asean. Interbank business could also suffer. Banks have their 'economic hinterlands', to be sure, but as the yen displaces the US dollar as the unit of Southeast Asia's foreign commerce, large-scale trade financing could go more often to Japanese subsidiaries.

Thus the dominance in Asean of foreign (US, British and Japanese) banks, may continue; in this major league lending and creation of new (the FLN) instruments, the region's banks are way behind; even the Development Bank of Singapore, that country's largest, cannot keep up because of the small asset size relative to such giants as Dai-ichi Sangyo or even the Hongkong and Shanghai Bank.

On the other hand, fears about Hong Kong's future could deliver a windfall to Singapore; by the late 1980s a steady exodus (led, ironically, by Hong Kong Chinese bank executives) pointed to a dimming future after 1997. (Australia and Canada operate 'entrepreneur' migrant schemes, accepting Hong Kong Chinese so long as they bring large amounts of capital with them: migrants going to Canada, for example, usually bring about US$400,000 as their ticket of entry.) This points to a passive gain for Singapore, to be sure, but a likely gain none the less in the race to become the region's pre-eminent financial centre. Ultimately, it will come down to gut instinct. As Hong Kong economist George Hicks comments, 'it is hard to imagine international financial circles trusting a communist country with a major financial centre.'

Something New: Asean's Multinational Corporations

Another of the region's commercial crucibles is the government-run or -controlled investment holding company, a device serving a variety of political, fiscal and personal purposes.

The Singapore government's investment holding arm, Temasek Holdings Ltd, rivals in size the various funds created for the public and personal wealth of Sultan Hassanal Bolkiah, Brunei's ruler. In Malaysia, holding companies like Multi-Purpose Holdings, Maika Holdings, Permodalan Bersatu Berhad and the UMNO-dominated Fleet Holdings vie with the Malay trustee company Permodalan Nasional Berhad in buying shares with public finance. Many of these funds risk close proximity to 'crony conglomerates' but, on the positive side, they act as midwives to the formation of new multinational corporations.

These large firms represent an extension of the colonial era trading house or single commodity company, aiming to win control over a slice of the regional trade: palm oil plus palm oil products; rubber plus rubber products or banking plus consumer finance come most readily to mind. The aim is to take both upstream and downstream control. Asean's best known conglomerates are Malaysia's Sime Darby, Thailand's Siam Cement, Indonesia's PT Astra Group and First Pacific International and Singapore's United Industrial Corporation (UIC).

Not all succeed. Malaysia's brash, oil rig servicing company, Promet Berhad, seen as a front-running multinational in the early 1980s, disappointed outside creditors such as the Royal Bank of Canada, Lloyds Bank, the National Bank of Abu Dhabi, the First Interstate Bank of California and Banque Nationale de

Paris – just some of many foreign banks holding unsecured debts against Promet totalling over US$110 million in 1987.

Yet let the success stories also speak. 'In a region where connections are at least as important as acumen in determining business achievement, the Singapore conglomerate UIC holds some valuable cards,' the Hong Kong financial writer John Mulcahy observed in 1987. 'From chairman Lee Kim Yew, brother of Singapore prime minister Lee Kuan Yew, to chief executive and principal shareholder Oei Hong Leong, heir to Indonesia's Wijaya family palm oil empire, UIC's links are impressive.'

UIC typifies the match in Southeast Asia between connections and competence: from a mere detergent maker in the early 1980s its diversified earnings had grown five times within the decade. 'Among the partners with whom UIC has established relationships are Thai businessman Tridhosyuth Devakul, who boasts familial connections with Thailand's royalty; enigmatic Hongkong corporate raider Joseph Lay; the Soviet Union (through 50% joint-venture company Singapore-Soviet Shipping) . . . and Australian financier Kevin Parry,' said Mulcahy.

The Richest of Them All?

The First Pacific empire may be the richest of all the new, Asean multinationals. Suharto associate Liem Sioe Liong owns the group, which comprises two quoted companies, one in Hong Kong and one in Amsterdam, each with a set of subsidiaries. From Hong Kong, First Pacific International Ltd acts as a holding company for securities and trading businesses; First Pacific Holdings, also from Hong Kong, runs banking and financial service companies, including California's Hibernia Bank. First Pacific reaches into most of Southeast Asia, making large acquisitions in the Philippines where it controls paper companies, manufactures soap and runs an investment and securities firms. Three of Liem's five-member 'board of executive managers' are Filipinos, including his managing director, Manuel Pangilinan. The other members include Suharto family members and associates.

Astra Group's Growth

The Soeryadjaya family's PT Astra Group also showed the same diversification, linked at each step to confidants of the ruling regime. The Sime Darby Group, based in Malaysia, is another example. One report put Sime Darby's US$1.2 billion assets, in 1982, at twice PT Astra's size, but both conglomerates were increasing their turnovers by US$500 million more each year. The Liem Group probably dwarfed them all in asset-backing while most of the so-called 'new' multinationals still reflected their traditional, tightly held Chinese family business character. Sime Darby however deliberately opted for the Western 'managerial' model of organisation.

Another Crucible: Industrial Whistle Stops

Penang's experience as a leading export zone shows both the labour-absorptive temptations and the ultimate irrelevance of a special Asean approach: the free trade zone (FTZ). The smallest Malaysian state and the only one with a predominantly Chinese population, Penang became Britain's first Far East possession in 1786. Two hundred years later, this 285 square kilometre island, described in tourist guides as taking the 'shape of a swimming turtle', had begun to run into problems with its 15-year-old success story.

That story rode on its FTZ, one of Asean's earliest experiments with the concept. Basically the FTZ and the similar 'bonded warehouse' programmes operate within a tax-free, customs-free island enclave within the wider, national economy. Outside investors set up cheap, easy-to-build factories within a fenced-off, isolated estate. Their materials come in duty free and go out as wholly or partly assembled products exempt from excise or other tax. The attraction for the host country, and for the investor, is the local labour used. Penang's wealth once flowed from performing a service function not unlike Southeast Asia's only other Chinese-run island, Singapore. But Penang remained in Malaysia, and by the end of the 1960s it had pioneered the Free Trade Zone concept.

The zone quickly became an important prop for Penang's one million inhabitants, of whom nearly 70,000 people were working inside. For every investment in the zone that backfired, usually caused by bad market timing (as when Hong Kong computer plastic frame makers Atlas-Intak opened a US$32 million factory in 1984) there have been many more successes. The FTZ has been widely copied throughout Asean: witness the equivalent schemes operating in Cebu, Bataan, Jakarta, Medan, Surabaya, Singapore and in Thailand. The Penang FTZ expanded from just 36 factories in 1970 to 259 fifteen years later. By the mid-1980s Penang had become the world's largest exporter of 64 kilobyte silicon memory chips, supplying over half the world's demand.

Penang economists Kamal Salih and Mei Ling Young (quoted in Clad, 1985) rightly claim that 'the impact of the industrialisation strategy on the growth of Penang's economy has been tremendous.' Much of that credit went to the Penang Development Corporation (PDC), one of the comparatively few Malaysian state corporations doing an outstanding job. The PDC displayed surprising resourcefulness, by luring to Penang a West German company which, in turn, won an astonishing victory over Japanese interests by securing a contract to make steering column parts for Malaysia's self-styled 'national car'. (See Chapter 3.) The move, described to me by Penang governor Lim Chong Eu as 'Penang's business politics at its best', shamed and astounded Mitsubishi's engineers, who had no choice but to accept a decision taken by Malaysian prime minister Mahathir Mohamad himself.

Spilling Over?

One of the fondest claims of the FTZ idea is that it has acted as a catalyst for indigenous industries. But has this been true? The amount of *indigenously* generated, industrial expansion in Penang has been surprisingly skimpy: my researches showed only about 1,000 workers engaged in under twenty small factories. The conclusion was obvious: the FTZ works as a self-contained island, importing nearly all its raw or semi-finished materials, assembling them with Penang hands, and moving them on again. The value-added comes almost entirely from the labour component. Penang ideas, Penang inventions or Penang-conceived marketing ideas play next to no role.

For all its success therefore, Penang's FTZ shows this very glaring gap. Other questions also hung over the experiment. For a start, most of the workforce had semi-skilled assembly jobs; three-quarters worked in electronics or textile factories where, for the time being, advances in labour-displacing robotics had not made inroads. That would change, and change quickly before the end of this century. Secondly, the PDC travelled too far down the familiar, monumental road; one especially obtrusive example was a 67-storey office tower named Komtar, claimed as Southeast Asia's tallest building and for many years sadly lacking in tenants.

Claims that the zone was acting as an 'inddustrial catalyst', were not entirely off-beam. Some entrepreneurs did respond to the various, sub-contracting possibilities opening up as the FTZ expanded and as the foreign firms needed work done in a hurry. One example was Eng Hardware Engineering, which serves almost as a textbook case in down-market industrial development. Eng Hardware makes precision-stamped parts for the semiconductor companies; over ten years it had grown from a backyard foundry to a US$2 million operation employing one hundred people. But these numbers were insignificant compared with the data showing that the FTZ after two decades employed seventy times as many people as the few, locally-owned support industries for which the FTZ became an indifferent midwife.

In an era of rapidly changing industrial processes and marketing, even the zone's continuing attractiveness to foreign investors could not be taken for granted. All over Asean, industries moved away to Bangkok – which held out the smoothest investment incentives. In the Philippines, bad placing of the Bataan export zone, on the west side of Manila Bay, kept it in the doldrums. Once dominated by American electronics, especially semiconductor manufacturers, even Penang began to lose some of its 'footloose industries', so named because of their light overheads and penchant for following the easiest investment packages.

On-off policies by the federal government in Kuala Lumpur scared away some investors, although the gains more than balanced the losses by the end of the 1980s. The readiness of the US, Japanese and West European semiconductor industry to continue investing in Asean was evident, even during the slower years of the late 1980s. In Malaysia for example, thirteen US manufacturers working there, primarily but not exclusively in Penang, invested another US$236 million during 1987–88 in response to steady growth in the electronics market, and exports from Malaysia alone increased by 27 per cent over 1986, worth nearly US$2 billion, keeping the 21 per cent of Malaysia's workforce employed working on these assembly lines.

By the end of the 1980s the electronics industry had become the steadiest of Malaysia's business performers. During the commodities slump of this decade it rose to become the country's largest single earner of foreign exchange and, by 1987, it accounted for 37 per cent of total manufactured exports and 16 per cent of total exports. But all of this, to make the point again, depended on outsiders' investment, outsiders' markets and outsiders' technology. Instead of Mahathir's dream of a vibrant, self-generating industrial takeoff, using Malaysian resources and concepts, the opposite had occurred, with the country ever more hostage to footloose foreigners, and to outside market trends. Penang had shown the way. It was a story which, to a varying degree, applied elsewhere throughout Southeast Asia.

No 'Open Skies'

Aviation became a bright spot on the business horizon during Asean's two-decade flight into golden business weather. Philippine Airlines, known as PAL, initially did well although by the time Marcos left the new government frankly described it as 'too expensive to run', with local fares frozen for short-sighted political reasons at 1979 levels. The government also aimed to privatise PAL, a forbidding task that spawned yet more years of report writing and missions by merchant bankers to Manila.

Privatisation proceeded with Singapore Airlines (SIA) and Malaysian Airlines System (MAS). One hundred million SIA shares were two-and-a-half times oversubscribed in 1985, with 40 per cent of the public issue (which represented 16 per cent of SIA's issued share capital) going to US, Japanese and European investors. Since its founding in 1972, SIA has never reported an annual loss; only twice have profits even dipped over the preceding year.

In Asean, Thai International and SIA became the two biggest aviation stars. Thai regularly announced US$50–60 million pre-tax profits, with SIA doing better still: its 1987 US$213 million profit stood highest in the region. SIA's chief claim to distinction lies in rapidly turning over its aircraft; in the mid-1980s its planes had an average age of just 30 months; for aircraft operated by International Air Transport Association (IATA) members the average age exceeded 10 years. The policy boosted its image, saved fuel, increased safety, cut maintenance costs and added extraordinary gains each year from aircraft sales.

Emerging from the 1971 split of the former Malaysia-Singapore Airlines, MAS also performed well. Its share capital in 1985 expanded another 30 per cent after a public issue of 105 million shares, another Asean privatisation. MAS, SIA and the other Asean lines profited from the general expansion of the Asia Pacific travel region: Pacific Basin air services grew exponentially during the two-decade rush to wealth, generating by the 1980s about US$10 billion in revenues each year, including US$2 billion from carrying air cargo.

But these airlines operated in a vastly different business environment from the older, more established carriers. It was not by accident that the *Far Eastern Economic Review*'s 1986 feature on Asian aviation was entitled 'The myth of open skies'. Contrary to America's freely competitive business arena, the Asian carriers gained from bilateral air agreements with dozens of countries that limited the number of carriers and even the minimum fares charged. The net result was to protect these airlines from competition.

The free market applied more to the marketing side, with IATA ticketing and standard agents' commission safeguards going by the board. Even so, the older airlines scrambled to increase their business in the Asean and East Asian area. In 1986, for example, the US carrier United Airlines bought Asia Pacific air rights belonging to the cash-strapped Pan American Airlines. For these United paid a price equivalent to twenty-two times Pan Am's annual earnings from its trans-Pacific routes.

MAS's experience showed how easy it was to reach one stage, and how hard it became to advance to another. During the hard-hit 1980s MAS's balance sheet showed impressively good returns, reaching its highest ever after-tax profits of

US$40.5 million in the recession clouded year of 1983/84. Generous taxation decisions by the government – which only took US$1.7 million the next year from even larger earnings of US$44 million – allowed MAS to generate enough cash to expand.

But to where? Despite the fabulous expansion of Asia Pacific travel, MAS faced tough times for its push into the Tokyo, US and European markets. Malaysia raised the battle for an extra daily service to London into a major bilateral row with Britain and, at a less audible level, quarrelled with Japan over its intransigence in refusing to give MAS more passenger pick-up rights at Tokyo for onward passage to the US. Within Asean, each airline follows *dirigiste* policies, pushing up domestic fares to carry the overseas services.

'Free trade' therefore only applies to the Asean airlines' ambition to elbow their way into the already profitable European, US and Japanese markets. Longer-range aircraft coming on the market during the 1990s will be reducing the appeal of intermediate stops between, say, the Australian and European markets. Southeast Asian carriers are fighting to postpone that day. But within the region, except for bilateral, minimal services between capital cities, competition has gone by the board. The excuse is a lack of passengers – few Indonesians went to Manila; fewer Filipinos went to Bangkok (except as a stopover on the way to employment in the Gulf States) and so on. But by pinning their expansion on more distant markets, Southeast Asian carriers deprive themselves of the chance of a more vibrant, intra-Asean market. Although passengers gain from the competitive ticket sales to and from the region and other metropolitan destinations, in a business sense the Aseans' airline success can also be described, in essence, as a 'free ride'.

Shipping: No Open Waters

As the 1980s drew to a close the shipping market, in Southeast Asia as elsewhere, suffered from a vast 'tonnage overhang' – in short, too many ships. What was needed, as the *Far Eastern Economic Review*'s Yearbook said in 1988, was 'a less romantic view of ships' in Asean. Vessels needed, the *Review* said, to be viewed as 'seaborne trucks which must be kept working to earn a living.' But this required a 'sea-change' in investors' attitude, away from 'the short-term grasping for capital gains', an approach largely responsible for the financial disasters beginning in the late 1970s.

Some exceptions remained, but they did not belong to the Asean region. Hong Kong's Tung Group drove its container fleet mercilessly into profitability after coming perilously close to bankruptcy. Another Hong Kong firm, the Wah Kwong Group, culled its fleet right back to thirty ships, and stayed above water on the back of the charter trade. Within Asean however, and notwithstanding its archipelagic character, attempts to coordinate shipping investment failed on the rocks of mismanaged economic nationalism. In 1987 shipping specialist Nick Seaward observed that, 'despite the fact that Asean has pinpointed shipping as one area in which regional cooperation would be worth pursuing, nearly all the countries of Southeast Asia still seem hell-bent on knocking each other out of the shipping and port business.'

Rust Bucket Labour Market

A freer market applied to the men who worked these ships, both within and outside the region. Southeast Asia for most of the two decades flooded the sealanes with cheap labour. Yet the late 1980s, according to *Lloyd's Maritime Asia*, witnessed the Philippines' 130,000 registered officers and ratings being whittled down to just over 55,000 of whom fewer still found work. On board, labour-saving devices plus fierce resistance against cheap Asian labour from the International Transport Workers' Federation began to reduce this presence still further.

In 1986 alone, Filipino seamen sent US$206 million home, where entire villages depended on these remittances. During the heyday of the trade nearly fifty-five nautical schools were operating in the Philippines, many of indifferent quality; by 1982 only eight were still functioning. Indonesian ratings also suffered from the industry's continuing squeeze – and also from a realisation that Burmese or mainland Chinese crews could be acquired for even less than their own, scanty rewards.

Investment Incentives: Another Distortion

Southeast Asia's commercial crucibles continue to depend on government favouritism both direct, and indirect. In the indirect category fall many of the investment incentives designed to lure outsiders to set up plants in exchange for another form of free-riding. 'Tax holidays' in more honest language mean abdication of revenue from foreigners by host country treasuries. Within this meaning many foreign companies also became cronies in a strict, free-market sense.

As the 1980s wore on, significant second thoughts began to surface however about the spillover gains from much of the foreign investment, not only from the FTZs. A look at direct investment during the 1980s showed a falling off in the attractiveness of the Asean region; in fact, much of the apparent overall boost in world investment towards Asia resulted from the demands of its biggest country, China. See Table 7.

Table 7   Direct foreign investment in Asia, Asean and China

Country	1982	1983	1984	1985	1986	1987
China	389	595	1,227	1,634	1,598	1,550
Total Asia	3,601	3,692	3,824	4,247	4,054	4,020
Asean countries						
Indonesia	205	270	221	270	221	203
Malaysia	1,256	1,179	778	684	452	403
Philippines	14	98	9	−11	86	167
Singapore	1,260	931	862	959	574	876
Thailand	175	327	394	159	219	848

SOURCE: International Monetary Fund

The investment approach using give-away tax policies and free-hand profit repatriation is now causing second thoughts. Yale University international economist

Gustav Ranis writes (1986) that 'India and the People's Republic of China . . . both seem to be realising [that] fascination with what is likely to remain a relatively small export-oriented enclave can be misleading and costly.'

Despite the open-house policies therefore, exemplified by Penang's long flirtation with footloose industry, the 'capital goods industries such as machinery, metal products and the domestic production of parts are still relatively undeveloped', as Miyohei Shinohara, chairman of the Tokyo Institute of Developing Economies, commented in an Asian Development Bank journal in 1986. And 'attempts to encourage ancillary industries with 'local content' policies have, in general, not been very successful because they have resulted from "top–down" pressure . . . [foreign] firms seem to recognise local content rules as being little more than political pressure,' he says, while noting the exceptions in the electronics industry. Crystal production for the semicondutor industry has advanced – yet (and this proves the point) always at someone else's direction and with someone else's expertise.

Free-market, *laisser-faire* attitudes are a long way from this direct government meddling in industrial expansion. 'In every East Asian country, except Singapore and Hong Kong, free trade – on the import side – is hardly a description of reality, as amply testified by dozens of studies of effective protection,' notes Australian National University economist Hal Hill (1987). 'Industry [in East Asia] has grown as much in spite of, as because of high-level, government intervention.' The free market, at the level of investment choice in industry, remains stunted.

Corporate Management: Form and Substance

It was not only investment money that washed through Southeast Asia's six market economies during the golden years that began in the late 1960s. An entirely new commercial structure to the region emerged, with the imposing new banks, businesses and bourses taking both Western corporate form and management substance straight from Western models. Hitherto sleepy, commodity trading houses, backyard foundries or Chinese, mum-and-dad retail shops were transformed almost overnight into the industrial or merchandising conglomerates outlined above, each sporting fancy corporate logos and swelling to employ armies of briefcase-carrying executives.

The transition from the archetypal, high-ceilinged colonial office, ceiling fans twirling lazily overhead, to corporate conglomerates headquartered in soaring steel towers thus occurred with astonishing rapidity. Southeast Asia's squat, unimaginative caterpillars were turning into globally competitive butterflies imbued with Western management ethics. Or were they?

Tan Koon Swan, the Malaysian Chinese corporate king whose career led him from gambling house management to a Singapore gaol cell, talked to me about his studies at Harvard Business School. It had certainly made a great impression on him. The talk in the late 1970s, at Harvard and in the other great business schools, centred on conglomerates and Tan imbibed deeply.

Tan's public and private lives ran on parallel tracks. His family-based Supreme Corporation remained in the family with another confidant, Peggy Chang, running much of Supreme's financial side. But Tan the corporate man also emerged in his public dimension. This occurred via his creation of Multi-Purpose Holdings Berhad, an investment holding company that, he promised, would revolutionise the way the Chinese did business in Malaysia, putting them once again at the front table opposite the Malays. Multi-Purpose soon won a listing on the stock exchange, and the gilded promises of wealth reached every envious, back-street Chinese trader, feeling in retreat since the Malays had taken decisive command of government back in 1969. The appeal had special force for those whose ancestors came from China's Hainan island, the origin of Tan's father, a street hawker.

Tan's sad fate simply illustrated the intersecting lines of overreaching political and financial ambition and poor economic trends. Had he tried his experiments in a more buoyant time, Tan would have been more likely to succeed, just as Mahathir's state-funded white elephants had the bad luck of poor timing. But the point remained that 'Western management', in most cases, took second place to the drive and cleverness of 'big men' in the nexus of politics and business.

In the Family Way

Apart from the bigger firms, what was the commercial climate in which smaller businesses – the vanguard of mass capitalism – were working? Precisely because of the prevalence of monopolies and family-linked commerce, the truest test of a real interplay of market forces and entrepreneurial drive lies in the success or failure of thousands of small commercial entities.

In Asean's self-styled market economies these businesses face enormous problems. Studies from the region itself point to poor business acumen, management and prospects. 'Discrimination against small- and medium-scale industries is likely to lead to a "low-level equilibrium trap",' an Institute of Southeast Asian Studies report (ISEAS) said, somewhat mystifyingly.

Its author, Robert Clapham (1987), described this 'trap' as a no-win situation in which investors face 'depressed demand, a high degree of competition because of low barriers to [business] entry, low levels of profitability and a lack of access to formal finance.' Businesses cannot be improved because 'day-to-day survival absorbs all entrepreneurial energy.' This is a very different picture indeed from the popular image of mass capitalism thriving throughout East Asia.

Book-keeping Illiteracy

For example, business attitude testing among potential Malay small entrepreneurs applying for business 'start-up' loans showed some disturbing signs. 'Characteristics important for entrepreneurs, such as personal independence and willingness to accept risks, are very poorly developed,' another report from the ISEAS says (1986). These 'negative characteristics' included 'an autocratic . . . and distinctly paternalistic attitude'. The ISEAS report also says that 'gaps in knowledge' appear in 'all areas of business', with scant understanding of such basics as 'book-keeping, costing, financing, procurement, quality control, sales and marketing and personnel management.'

Small traders in Indonesia fare even less well. They 'keep no written records at all . . . and have no accurate conception of their production costs, a lack of fundamental business know-how that in many cases is so serious that even the many positive characteristics of the new entrepreneurs are not sufficient to compensate.' The report makes woeful reading: '[Small businesses] stand as marginal enterprises on the threshold of economic collapse, not just in their first year but for several years thereafter.'

Looking at the small engineering industry in Indonesia, for example, another study, this one by the World Bank in 1984, found that 'only low standards prevailed with respect to work procedures', with 'virtually no quality control or inspections carried out.' The reports, which cannot be taken as blanket censure of bottom-line business in island Asia, still put a question mark over the real progress made by everyday capitalism in the region.

Product Piracy: Another Free Ride?

Slipshod attitudes to basic business procedures have a mirror image in the indifference to business ethics of the most elementary kind. From pirated music cassette tapes to fake Rolex watches, the Asean region has excelled at pirating the trademarks and characteristic surface appearances of up-market products and producing them at down-market costs and quality. Gucci bags, designer shirts, Yves St Laurent scarves, Dunhill wristwatches, IBM computer software programs or branded Italian shoes – all these were copied with abandon in virtually all Asean countries.

As Chapters 4, 5 and 6 explain, intellectual property theft became a major issue in the 1980s. Tough American pressure, linked to a possible withdrawal of GSP trading privileges in the American market, forced Indonesia, Thailand, Malaysia and Singapore to enact copyright protection laws which, depending on how well they were enforced, made the practices illegal. But all the laws had loopholes, including those in Brunei and the Philippines, enabling most ethically lightweight manufacturers to behave with impunity. In Malaysia, a new ostensibly tough copyright measure coming into force in 1987 contained a provision blocking Kuala Lumpur from signing the international copyright conventions. The upshot was that foreign intellectual property still had no protection. The government connived in the evasion of royalties: for example, the state-owned Radio Television Malaysia network stopped paying royalties for copyright works in 1970.

This attitude to trademark and copyright protection was one of the least agreeable characteristics of these self-avowed market economies. The US was especially incensed. By the late 1980s the Americans increased the pressure. Allen Wallis, undersecretary for Economic Affairs under the Reagan Administration, said that US companies avoided investing in Asean because brand name and trade confidentiality received no protection there. The absence of such safeguards in Indonesia became cited, regularly, as the biggest obstacle to up-market US investment there.

Singapore's efficient and determined Civil Service made a real effort to enforce the ban on selling pirated music and video-cassettes, and that success was, to a lesser extent, achieved in Kuala Lumpur as well – where two-thirds of the consumer music recordings, according to the local phonogram and videogram federation, had been pirated. In both countries, trade and industry department officials received search and seizure powers. Yet in a strange but deliberate inversion of the new copyright protections, Singapore then changed its law again, to allow local entities to print fake editions of publications banned from circulating in the republic.

Elsewhere, penalties for stealing copyright or trademarks were drastically increased. In Indonesia the law provided for fines equivalent to US$60,000 and gaol terms of up to seven years. But, as in Hong Kong and Taiwan, the authorities usually looked the other way, especially in Thailand or Indonesia (where estimates put the annual number of pirated music cassettes at 30–40 million, making this country the largest exporter of pirated music in the world).

Apart From (Someone Else's) Ships, No Free Labour Market

If the small businessman showed gaps in competence or ethics, how free was Asean's labour market during the region's great boom? In Singapore as in most of the other countries in the region, trade unions have deferred to government dictate and, as a result, organised labour has had little real interplay contracting for wages or better conditions. In most countries, trade union membership steadily declined as a reflection of the hostile, anti-union mood – good for business but a gap in the fabric of contractual labour freedoms.

By the late 1980s, membership of Singapore's National Trade Union Congress had fallen to below 15 per cent of the island's workforce, a drop from a figure of 30 per cent in the early 1970s. The trades union federation in Malaysia also went into decline – less than 8 per cent of the workforce was unionised as the 1980s drew to a close. In Thailand, only 6 per cent of non-agricultural workers belong to unions; many of those which still have influence, as in the workforce of Thailand's government-owned railways, fall prey to military manipulation. The same applies to Indonesia, where the government has near-total sway over the trades union federation there, the FBSI. Only 2.9 million workers, out of a population of 170 million, belong to unions.

Finally, each Asean country firmly resists unqualified movement of labour, the surest sign of an impending, region-wide economy. Virtually all the regional governments tax their citizens each time they travel outside the country, penalising movement just as much within the region. Moreover, the labour-short countries only accept workers in a rigidly regulated way, as in Singapore, or allow them to slip in through the backdoor as helpful new figures in the racial arithmetic – as in Malaysia's acceptance of poor Indonesian plantation workers, ethnically similar to the Malays. At the level of business executives, 'indigenisation' policies to replace foreigners make no concessions to any particular foreigner's Asean background.

Business Education: How Good Really?

The explosive growth in Asean business during the 1970s and 1980s has prompted a great increase in the numbers of students entering business schools. The rising prosperity allowed more people to continue formal education, and the largesse spilling over from government coffers, whether gained from earned or borrowed money, found its way most speedily into spending on education; here the minority Chinese and the majority indigenous populations shared something in common. Each cultural tradition, whether Mandarin, Confucian, Buddhist, Christian or Muslim, gave emphasis to education and the acquisition of skills.

But what skills? Thailand's 54 millions still had only ten public universities from which to choose – often no choice at all for the great majority failing its examination entrance tests. The government promoted a university carrying the name

Ramkhamhaeng ('open admission') University, which swept 750,000 students on to its books in the first two years, while the government's Sukhothai Thammathirat Open University enrolled 140,000 home students although its modestly equipped library, slightly over 10,000 volumes, meant a book per student ratio of 1:14. Yet even these paper mills could not cope with the demand for 'business' and other courses, and private institutions finally received permission to open university level courses. This began in 1969; there were twenty-one institutes operating in 1987.

Indonesia's recent infatuation with business schooling reflects the huge rise in privately run 'universities' there, from none at all just after independence to about 600 in 1988 enrolling 675,000 students. Most of these institutions offer budget-rate education and deliver a highly variable result. But the glut of rote-learning graduates has reached its zenith in the Philippines, where nearly 850 private 'institutions' pump out graduates. It is a barhopper's truism in Manila that every hostess has 'a college education', often in 'business administration'.

Sadly, these courses seldom direct themselves to the business needs of commercial firms; rather they disguise a poverty of ideas about post-graduation employment with resonant course prescriptions offering 'strategic management', and other, similarly worded courses. In one respect the country's private universities do cater for business: the three largest private institutions and many smaller institutes operate strictly for profit. The shares in each are widely traded. The University of the East's enrolment alone by far exceeds student numbers at the three 'best' institutes for business and commerce: the government-funded University of the Philippines, plus the privately run Ateneo de Manila University (a Jesuit school) and De la Salle University.

In all these countries, as Asian education specialist Albert Yee pointed out in 1987, 'the relatively young private universities in Asia have concentrated on meeting the demand for diplomas . . . merely servicing the demand for academic certification cannot be more than an extension of secondary schooling and represents a deterioration in the basis for gaining higher education. In the long run, diplomas themselves are worth little unless backed by an ethos and institutional identity worthy of being called a university.'

*

The foregoing observations are meant, as I have stressed, to provide a corrective to glib assertions that the region has appended itself, rather undeservedly, to East Asia's 'economic miracle'. Rather than focusing on the unquestionable evidence of enormous expansion, I have sought to peer beneath the corporate fabric, the business school enrolments, the booming stock markets, the raw investment data, the expanding free trade zones and other measures of progress to see how far the ethic of free, untrammelled marketplace capitalism has gone.

The basic contention is: the 300 million people residing in marketplace Southeast Asia became the beneficiaries of a free ride made possible by the expansion of global trade, freer movement of capital and, especially, the opening to all comers of the enormous US market. A primary engine for that free ride came from the explosive growth in demand for Southeast Asia's commodities. Unrivalled in its resources of both 'hard' and 'soft' commodities, Southeast Asia remains vulnerable, still, to the whims of the outside markets that have dominated archipelagic Asia for nearly five hundred years. In this way also, the two-decade boom, now increasingly at risk, represents a continuation of the past.

References

Clad, J. (1985) 'Penang's road to growth built on shifting foundations', *Far Eastern Economic Review*, 19 September

Clapham, R. (1985) *Small and Medium Entrepreneurs in Southeast Asia*, Research Notes and Discussion Paper No. 49. Singapore: ISEAS

Cottrell, R. (1986) 'Singapore's sharemarket', *Far Eastern Economic Review*, 23 August

Hill, H. (1987) 'Fifth column', *Far Eastern Economic Review*, 26 September

Institute of Southeast Asian Studies (1986) *Small and Medium Business Improvement in the ASEAN Region: Marketing Factors*, ed. Kenneth James and Narongchai Akrasanee. Singapore: ISEAS

Mulcahy, J. (1987) 'UIC goes multinational', *Far Eastern Economic Review*, 3 February

Ranis, G. (1986) 'The export-led model of industrialisation', *Asian Development Review*, vol. 4, No.2

Rowley, A. (1987) *Asian Stockmarkets: the Inside Story*. Hong Kong: Review Publications

World Bank (1984) *Indonesia: Policies and Prospects for Economic Growth and Transformation*. Washington, DC: East Asia and Pacific Regional Office

Yee, A.H. (1987) 'A private look at Asian education', *Asian Wall Street Journal*, 27 March

9

COMMODITIES: GLUTTED CORNUCOPIAS

Commodities: First and Foremost

Southeast Asia wants, quite literally, to outgrow its past. This is proving difficult. At most corners of this resource-rich archipelago, the evidence of nearly five hundred years of cash-cropping reaffirms the region's basic source of wealth: commodities.

'King Commodity' has long been a byword for the business side of Southeast Asia and continues to be its commercial alter ego. For half a millennium the exploitation of raw materials, including minerals, had determined the political and economic face of the region. Even Europe owes its Age of Discovery in large measure to Western competition to control a spice trade centred on obscure islands lying within present-day eastern Indonesia.

Buccaneers from Portugal, the Netherlands and England reached the East Indies, as they were known, hungry for pepper, cloves, nutmeg and cinnamon. These spices drew adventurers and merchant-pirates half way around the world. Against the awesome profits from the spice trade their perilous voyages, lasting two years or more, seemed a tolerable challenge. Scurvy, malaria and increasing hostility from the natives did little to dampen their greed: financiers from Leiden, London or Lisbon could realise 700 per cent return on capital from a single journey.

One by one, the European powers cornered the spice crops while enforcing ruthless monopolies of sale and distribution, mostly in league with local rulers. After several hundred years of this, other commodities began to become more important. By the close of the eighteenth century, labour-intensive plantation crops such as sugar, coffee, tea and, later, rubber, palm oil and cocoa began to overshadow the smallholder-grown spices. Economies of scale favoured the new plantations as much as the new factories processing the tropical products in Europe.

A new commodity era then followed as colonial barons amassed plantation and trading fortunes. Most of the names still gracing the region's commercial firms – Guthries, Harrisons, Inchcape – came from this new breed of capitalist and entrepreneur. In one form or another therefore, tropical commodities came to connote the very riches of the Indies.

Commodities Today

They still do. The Asean region's two-decade-old boom owes much to the flow from the world's most abundant commodity cornucopia. And seemingly endless products have flowed down this funnel of wealth.

In 1960, Malaysia grew just a fraction of the world's edible oil. Two decades later it had become the world's most productive palm oil producer, widening its small market niche into the size of a large wedge. By 1989 Malaysia and Indonesia combined produced 90 per cent of global palm oil supplies and nearly 45 per cent of all the world's traded vegetable oil. Twenty years ago, most Indonesian villagers would not have recognised an oil palm. Now their country relies on this umbrella-shaped, viscous plant for 20 per cent of export earnings. Another achievement resulted in the east Borneo state of Sabah, which rocketed to Asian pre-eminence in the growing of cocoa. Some of the world's highest per hectare yields are now being won from Borneo plantations. Elsewhere in free-market Southeast Asia similar marvels have occurred.

The same quick returns hold true in Thailand, where tapioca has become that nation's biggest agricultural earner, just ahead of rice exports. Europe's winter-bound dairy herds eat the stuff by the shipload. And produce from the land also complements an increasing harvest from the sea: Thai canning factories produce more tinned tuna than any other country.

Similar commodity windfalls have enriched Brunei and Indonesia, both beneficiaries of oil and natural gas production, and of timber and forest products as well. The Philippine sugar lands on the Luzon and Negros islands once bestowed great wealth on favoured families. Rubber plantations in Sumatra and on the Malayan peninsula fuelled the colonial prosperity of the 1920s. At one point, Malaya fed more revenue to London than all other British colonial possessions combined.

These same plantations are still profitable. Singapore, too, though an entrepôt, mainly Chinese-inhabited appendage to British-ruled Malaya and northern Borneo for its first century after colonial rule, profited mightily from the commodity cornucopia. Even today, the island republic's trade relies heavily on commodities re-exported through its busy harbour. The commercial power of commodities business can be noted by the effects of its sudden absence; a major cause of economic ruin in Indochina after the Communist victories there in 1975 was the abandonment of once immensively profitable rubber plantations.

Still a Regal Earner . . .

Commerce in commodities still accounts therefore for a large part of Southeast Asia's recent growth. Yet for all the regal returns, King Commodity earns little adulation. Quite the opposite occurs: Southeast Asian economists tend to treat the region's continuing dependence on commodities like a family resentful of its dependence on largesse from an aged aunt. Her income may still support the household but her presence has become a source of embarrassment.

To put it another way, renditions from 'Down on the Ol' Plantation' evoke little sentimental response these days in Southeast Asia. For most economists, plantation-style cropping conjures up embarrassing colonial vignettes instead: docile labourers plucking oil palms or bug-eyed natives watching as colonial planters in pith helmets mark out spacing for rubber trees.

Southeast Asia's commercial catchword these days is 'diversification'. Governments want to diversify away from dependence on erratic commodity earnings, and to become industrial powers instead. Although increasingly important, the region's nascent industries still lack the impact that commodities have on world markets. Manufacturing, invariably described by economists as the 'secondary sector', still takes second place behind the primary, or commodity sector.

Singapore economist John Wong and most other regional analysts have few illusions about this. 'The continuing export of commodities has provided the main engine of economic growth for the resource-based Asean economies,' Wong says flatly (quoted in Kintanar and Tan, 1986). The chairman of Tokyo's Institute of Developing Economies, Miyohei Shinohara, acknowledged in 1988 a 'relationship between the rapid growth of manufactured exports and relatively high growth rates' in Southeast Asia, but he says 'it is a complex one.'

This complexity results, as noted in earlier chapters, from the borrowed and footloose nature of Southeast Asian industrial growth. Southeast Asia's politicians aspire to a factory-filled future, despite the fact that many of the region's manufacturing enclaves amount to little more than electronics firms sunning themselves on a tax holiday.

. . . But Prices Badly Faltered in the 1980s

Given recent history, it is not surprising that the 'Four Farms' (the four largest Asean countries) dabble in dreams of industry. By continuing to depend on commodities they know too well that they condemn themselves to a business life of troubling uncertainty.

It is an insecurity repeatedly underlined by the commercial experience of the 1980s. By mid-decade point a deep anxiety was already running through Southeast Asia about the prospects for most commodities, including petroleum, tin, rubber, coffee, copper, nickel, rice, pineapples, vegetable oil, copra, tea, sugar, timber and even in minor products such as the formerly all-important spices.

The problems arose from sustained declines in demand or huge stock overhangs (that is, large stockpiles which depress prices). Decreasing seasonal off-take by once reliable customers such as the Soviet Union also drove prices down still further. (The centrally planned economies, know as CPEs, often appear on the market at predictable times during the year.) Chronic oversupply of many products, such as vegetable oils, exacerbated the 1980s recession.

Although prices have recovered from the slide between 1984 and 1986, longer-term trends are pointing to an unmistakably downward price movement for most commodities until the turn of the century. Changes in the nature of industrial processes also presage major changes in the nature of demand for Southeast Asia's raw materials.

The End of the Golden Weather?

More than any other event, the mid-decade downturn signalled the end of a twenty-year rush to wealth. The recession's causes were complex but in the closing months of 1985 its commodity prices took as hard a collective hammering as they had ever taken, with every prominent export crop experiencing weakening, stagnant or abruptly contracting markets.

Prices for agricultural commodities, metals and minerals without exception 'declined sharply, leading to a collapse of commodity markets', as Asian Development Bank (ADB) chief economist K. N. Kohli noted in an internal paper in 1987. Commodity Production Agreements (CPAs), which had been designed to buttress producers against these sharp trends, simply buckled under the weight of sell-orders from Rotterdam, Kuala Lumpur, Singapore or Chicago commodity traders.

Like stock markets during the global October 1987 crash, the price of many commodities dropped in 'free fall' as CPS stabilisation funds either went bankrupt or failed to cushion buying support. For nearly all its plentiful spread of commodities, Southeast Asia seemed caught in 'quasi-permanent surplus', a piece of trader jargon meaning 'too much of a good thing'.

For example, Indonesia, Thailand and Malaysia, the region's three largest natural rubber producers, have been confronting the inevitable glut resulting from excessive rubber-tree planting in the late 1970s, when demand forecasts had shown exponentially rising demand. Meanwhile, rational commodity procurement within the region is lagging. After the February 1986 'People Power Revolution' in Manila, Philippine businessmen sought orders from neighbouring countries, especially for cheaply priced sugar. Yet import monopolists from other Asean countries prefer to buy their product from Papua New Guinea or even from Australia.

Competitive widening of acreages mark just one example of a triumph of narrow, national interests. In another example, Malaysia criticised tin producers for ignoring production quotas. Yet Kuala Lumpur's politicians also thumbed their noses at OPEC, to which Malaysia does not belong. On this occasion they benefited from other producers' self-restraint by increasing oil production to 510,000 barrels per day. This is not a censorious comment; during the 1980s commodity producers have worked overtime to protect export earnings. Indonesia did the same when it came to observing coffee quotas; the Thais looked both ways when it came to protecting tin earnings.

When Boom Goes Bust: Sabah's Experience

The implications of the 1980s commodities collapse have gone far beyond the bleak figures at the back of the financial pages. In rural areas among Southeast Asia's 3,500 mile arc of islands, where two-thirds of the region's 300 million people live, the downturn has had catastrophic effects.

To select a concrete example, the commodities downturn hit business in Borneo like a tropical hurricane. Both Sabah and Sarawak are important timber producers; the bottoming out of their raw log, lumber, veneer and pulp markets exacerbated the effect of happy-go-spending habits entrenched during two decades of extravagant growth. About three million people, mostly subsistence farmers or jungle-dwellers, live in these two states, which comprise 60 per cent of Malaysia's territory. Nearly 30 per cent are Chinese however, living in small town shophouses.

Crashing timber prices in Borneo after 1982 proved a harbinger for other commodity prices throughout Southeast Asia. Oil prices followed suit a few years later, halving revenues. The timber recession was the first to expose profligate habits acquired during easier times. Sabah especially had supped long and deep at the fount of prosperity; as in all binges, however, the morning-after caused plenty of headaches. A local banker employed vivid, if slightly exaggerated imagery when describing business sentiment to me in 1986. 'We're dealing with the business equivalent of *The Day After*,' he said, referring to a then topical American film depicting nuclear catastrophe.

While this was overstretching the problems, it set the tone for a rapidly contracting economy, one which had been, quite literally, the world's fastest growing during much of the 1970s. Yet the sliding prices for timber, dipping petroleum earnings, falling tourist numbers and glutted town property markets quickly became the most vivid signs of a business slump unprecedented in scale and severity during Sabah's short, twenty-year history within Malaysia's thirteen-state federation.

By the mid 1980s, signs of overambition crowded the wide avenues of Sabah's capital, Kota Kinabalu, an old colonial seaport grown to 300,000 people. Empty office blocks and deserted shopping complexes stood as mute reminders of a decade's profligacy. Empty building space in Kota Kinabalu, known as 'KK', reached a million square feet – as much vacant space as in Manila before Marcos fled the country in February 1986.

Sabah's Lament: Into the Valley of Debt

Sabah's story echoed tales from all over Southeast Asia. Export price setbacks dealt harsh blows to its highly open economy; foreign trade accounts for an astonishing 250 per cent of the state's GDP. When a new government took power in KK after 1985 it discovered debts of hitherto unimaginable amounts.

Financial information reaching the new cabinet showed financial extravagance outclassing even the wildest Philippine debt-financing. Caught by a revenue squeeze, the state treasury not only presided over an empty exchequer but also was forced to avoid being sucked into what one official called a 'fiscal whirlpool' left behind by Sabah's previous government, formed from the Berjaya Party. Debt-servicing was gobbling up more than two-thirds of Sabah's operating budget.

The cause of this debt was distressingly familiar: a bad bout of projectitis, made worse by padded costings and cost overruns. A former state premier, Harris Salleh, had grand plans to expand Sabah's economic base. These looked good on paper, but they relied on heavy borrowing from foreign banks to finance a clutch of natural gas, methanol, iron fabrication, pulp and paper, hotel, tourist and office building projects.

When the commodities downturn hit full force the resulting financial disaster hung like a pall over this wildly beautiful patch of northern Borneo. Multi-million dollar government loans to local agencies rapidly became non-performing, with many defaults going back to 1975. Bizarre state guarantees for loans to golf clubs, or to luxury condominium towers, also littered the books.

Many projects inspired by Harris, especially a natural gas utilisation scheme and a plant for making pulp and paper, generated only tiny cashflows many years after completion. Servicing the loans for these two projects, which cost US$1 billion each, suddenly burdened Sabah's small population with interest payments amounting to US$100 million annually.

The enormity of Sabah's debt, which gradually became apparent, dwarfed the politicians who inherited the government. 'Frankly,' one minister told me, 'the scale of the thing is terrifying.' Four state corporations owed US$200 million to the government, the largest part of about US$314 million in outstanding loans to various agencies. Even the state's electric power company owed US$40 million. 'It was a nightmare,' the brother of the new state premier told me in KK.

All in all, by 1985 Sabah owed over US$1 billion to foreign banks and to domestic creditors, a per capita debt *twenty-five times higher* than in the Philippines, then the Asian pariah of the banking world. Nor did the state's financial liability stop there. Sabah's finance minister, Bernard Dompak, discovered that the sum total of domestic and foreign debt, of committed equity capital, of non-performing but disbursed loans given by the state amounted to over US$2 billion.

'Public debt between 1978 and 1984 increased at more than 13% per annum,' one of Dompak's advisers reported privately. Between 1983 and 1986, foreign debt rose each year by 43 per cent. For the one-fifth of Sabah's people who survive by collecting jungle produce or by working on subsistence rice farms, debts of this magnitude seem remote. For every other Sabahan the burden was, and remains, real enough.

What went wrong for this showcase state? Sabah's growth during the two decades beginning in the late 1960s was phenomenal: 'measuring the size of its gross domestic product, Sabah's economy by 1983 was two-and-a-half times larger than it was in 1971,' the Malaysian prime minister's chief economic adviser said at a closed seminar in Kuala Lumpur.

Beginning in the 1960s, sales of oil, gas and wood products pumped hitherto unimaginable amounts of money into Sabah's coffers. Yet only the severity of its boom-and-bust-cycle sets Sabah apart from the rest of Southeast Asia. Ruined by debt, ravaged by the cronies of successive governments, deforested of its chief resource and selling gas on fixed contract to Japan, Sabah in the 1980s became a mute reminder of a faltering rush to wealth that had been based on a plentiful flow of money down the commodity cornucopia.

Falling Prices Hurt Many Others

Elsewhere in Southeast Asia the commodity surplus problem was no laughing matter by the mid-1980s. 'While many commodity prices have been declining,' Kohli of the ADB remarked, 'the reduction in the past several years is unprecedented both in coverage and severity.'

High stocks and excessive production paralysed the sugar market, especially the inefficient producers in the Philippines. The situation in the Philippines amply merited the description 'disastrous' because the 1980s slump pitched hundreds of thousands of sugar workers, always a breadline group, into a growing chasm between local production costs and world prices. Laid-off workers became recruit-ment gains for the communist New People's Army watching the decay from the hills. On Negros island, a preserve of ethnic Chinese landowners, the insurgency closely paralleled the collapse of the sugar industry.

Social distress became obvious in other ways. The Malaysian government depends on votes from Malay rubber smallholders. By 1985 the falling price of natural rubber had eroded their standard of living, one cause of rising receptivity to various strains of Muslim fundamentalism in parts of Malaysia.

Most of Southeast Asia's people live in the countryside, where living standards are acutely sensitive to even small changes in commodity prices. Yet Southeast Asia's often impressive improvements since the 1960s relied too much on cash-cropping and too little on adding more processing facilities and using transport and raw materials more efficiently. The drift to already swollen cities tended to be event-driven, as when raw material prices dropped.

Even the prices for various 'star' commodities wobbled badly during the 1980s. To take one example, cocoa prices zoomed to US$1,500 a tonne in September 1986 before plummeting down by nearly 50 per cent just six weeks later. Stocks bought by the cocoa buffer fund for price support ballooned overnight to 75,000 tonnes, which depressed prices still further rather than buttressing them. Regional countries refused to join the cocoa cartel, free-riding instead on its production controls.

Star Commodities Also Falter

Of all commodities, apart from petroleum, vegetable oils had seemed the region's biggest commodity earner. But behind even this golden crop rose the worrying spectre of increasing world oil-seed production, reaching over 200 million tonnes annually in the late 1980s.

Droughts also hurt production. In the Philippines the copra and coconut oil business went into an especially bad slide, hurt by poor quality control, by declining market shares (palm oil fetched better prices than coconut oil), by a notorious default in a US$30 million order in 1987, by poor weather and, not least, by a negative image in consuming countries for being the fattiest of all 'Tropical Fats'.

In just one season, prices ranged between US$170 and US$600 a tonne. Crash and climb, crash and climb: the same violent oscillations afflicted the tea and timber markets, with the former crop, grown in Malaysian and Indonesian highlands, dropping to a historical low of about one US dollar a kilogramme in 1987. Much the same sort of news wrecked earlier demand forecasts for the so-called 'hard' commodities, metals and wood.

No one would quickly forget the chaos overwhelming the tin market in 1985 when panic selling drove prices from US$15,000 to US$4,500 a tonne in a matter of a few weeks. In a brave but doomed defence of floor prices, the International Tin Agreement's buffer stock fund bought tin until it went bankrupt, which almost brought down the London Metal Exchange with it.

These events mirrored a strange, solo act by Malaysia five years earlier when its public exchequer had financed a 'mystery tin buyer' in London, believed to be the Malaysian government following another failed dream to corner elusive markets. Adding insult to injury, the American Strategic Stockpile continued to unload the metal throughout, infuriating Jakarta, Kuala Lumpur and Bangkok with every market-depressing sale.

Disappearing Forests

Two problems surfaced in the timber trade, a get-rich-quick perennial in Asean's feudal business practices. Southeast Asia's rapidly dwindling forests fed the trade, the wood going out either in processed form (plywood) but just as often as rough-cut timber or even as whole logs. Two constraints appeared: supply and competition from other countries whose industries relied on regenerating forests.

The alarms sounded by the world's conservation lobby are by now too familiar to require much labouring. Citing headlong and heedless logging in South America and in Southeast Asia especially, groups such as the Geneva-based International Union for the Conservation of Nature and Natural Resources (IUCN) have warned that all the region's hardwood forests will be logged out by the turn of the century.

Depletion rates support that bleak view. The implications for watershed management, for the climate, and for soil quality, for flood control, for fisheries, for genetic diversity are tirelessly repeated and tiresomely familiar. A few forest plantation projects funded by World Bank money have started, and some local quarters voice alarm.

Southeast Asia's forestry departments are singularly corrupt, and use their elaborate reafforestation provisions in the concessions given to logging interests as one more 'negotiable' in the elaborate systems of patronage extending back into those self-same departments and beyond into higher levels of government.

Apart from depletion, Southeast Asia's timber industry faces hard competition. Reports surfaced after 1986 describing sales of logs from the Soviet Union to Japan, normally the most prominent buyer in Southeast Asia. European suppliers, using improved trans-Siberian railways, have also started seizing market shares. The disinclination to replant logged over forests means that the mechanisation in Europe and the Americas of renewable forests (where trees can be coaxed to grow faster) may confine Southeast Asia to a relatively thin portion of the market.

Back to the Futures

During the great economic expansion of the 1970s and early 1980s, regional countries became interested in cornering another side of the burgeoning commodities trade. Rather than allowing exchanges in faraway Rotterdam, London or Chicago to determine raw material prices, the Asean countries moved to create their own commodity markets especially for 'futures trading', the buying and selling of contracts for delivery of a particular commodity at a future time. This is known as 'paper' trading, as opposed to trading in 'physicals'.

In the past, the arrival of sailing ships back in Europe or China, or their loss at sea, largely determined scarcity and supply of tropical Asia's coveted commodities. These days, however, the market must cope with abrupt oscillations that foreign merchants would have found unnerving even fifty years ago. These result from tremendous changes in electronic communications which enable trading to dip and surge like the tremulous lines of an oversensitive seismograph.

In the storage and transmittal of electronic information the same changes
so radically transforming Southeast Asia's capital markets have also reworked
commodity trading. Delivering the product itself now occurs within a thicket of
hedging and speculative trading in markets where the anticipated price of delivery
becomes an object of trading fascination in itself.

Margins now change with lightning speed, hostage to speculators operating in
an ever-widening arena. Genuine 'twilight trading' in all the major global markets
has arrived; New York, Chicago, Kansas City, Singapore, Tokyo, Rotterdam
and London remain 'wired' twenty-four hours a day, obliterating time zones.
The erosion of Sunday holidays has eliminated the weekend 'breather' period,
making never-close markets a reality for the first time. As is the practice, these
global futures contracts are rolled over, re-sold often scores of times before being
liquidated. Only rarely does a futures contract become deliverable. Indeed, that
is not its purpose.

Increasingly the Southeast Asians went to locate this activity inside the region.
Bringing futures markets closer to the region's producers, so the theory goes, will
create a new brokerage industry to educate producers in the intricacies of 'hedging',
limiting one's exposure by buying short and selling long, or the other way around.
Malaysia's creation in 1983 of a futures contract in palm oil was one of the boldest
steps in this direction. London experts in the complexities of running a clearing
house were brought to Kuala Lumpur where they designed rules for a new market,
the Kuala Lumpur Commodities Exchange (KLCE).

Commodities trading has always had more than a fair share of adventure to it;
some even call it the world's most byzantine business. The swings and abrupt
turns of commodities markets make the business attractive to hoarders with low
overheads in bull markets. In Southeast Asia this type of character is often lured
into the ring. A bull market overtook the KLCE in 1984 which propelled the
volume of paper trading to thousands of 'lots' per day, each lot being a purchase
or sale of one tonne of crude palm oil.

In these circumstances the bold attempt to corner the palm-oil futures market, as
mentioned in Chapter 8, succeeded in driving up prices as refineries became frantic
for delivery. The reaction by the KLCE authorities helped to crush confidence in
the embryonic exchange for many years afterwards while confirming Southeast
Asia's 'casino' reputation among European and US traders.

Following OPEC . . . into the Sunset

In the face of these varying but generally pessimistic trends, what is Southeast
Asia to do? Relying on raw materials seems misguided. Commodity cornering,
a favoured goal during the 1970s and early 1980s, now seems opposed to the
longer-term play of global market forces.

The attractiveness of cartels was understandable however; the successes of
OPEC had an enormous effect on Southeast Asian opinion in the 1970s, as they
did elsewhere in the developing world. In countries producing commodities as
divergent as coffee or coconuts, tin or tea, dreams of engineered supply squeezes
became the vogue.

Unworkable price stabilisation schemes emerged, one by one, usually in league
with Southeast Asian producers. These horribly complex balancing acts between
producers and consumers promised guaranteed supply and steady prices. Most

of the commodity production agreements edged towards bankruptcy. The International Tin Agreement, as noted, plummeted into bankruptcy in 1985. One London analyst described the ITA's twenty-two producer member countries as 'at each other's throats' during a month-long orgy of mutual recrimination. In the Association of Tin Producing Countries, or APTC, Malaysia came in for much criticism, especially for its mysterious tin-buying efforts.

Southeast Asian reliance on CPAs has often led to surplus choked culs-de-sac. The International Coffee Agreement, for example, has come under great strain as member countries refuse to accept cuts to their production quotas even if large producers, such as Brazil, fail to meet their quotas at all. The tin cartel's failure is self-evident. Other CPAs, such as the Asian Rice Trade Fund, have never left the drawing board. Even a reasonably successful grouping like the International Coffee Organisation, meeting in 1987 and again in 1989, could not agree on minimal production quotas to sustain prices. The International Tropical Timber Organisation, sited in Japan, never moved beyond a consumer-dominated grouping.

Even the more successful CPAs have had a trying time during the 1980s. To take one example, the global AIDS scare has enabled Indonesia, Malaysia and Thailand to become macabre beneficiaries as demand for surgical latex, essential for the manufacture of condoms, increased sharply. Demand brought latex prices to their highest point in many years. Yet even these, sharply increased prices did not enable the International Natural Rubber Organisation, the rubber trade's CPA, to reduce its 360,000 tonne rubber stockpile by more than just two thousand tonnes. INRO's rubber mountain resulted from brave but ultimately doomed price support spending after 1985.

As the Southeast Asian countries enter the 1990s even a global Common Fund for Commodities, which finally won enough pledge money to start operations in 1987, does little to brighten their faith in commodities. In the Uruguay Round of trade talks under the auspices of the GATT, a global approach to reducing tariffs for all tropical products has fallen far short of the 'fullest liberalisation' promised by the GATT's Punta del Este declaration. Seven categories of tropical commodities worth about US$60 billion in 1989, stood to benefit. But no rapid market opening could be expected at the dawn of the 1990s.

In one sense the CPAs simply reflected a mood common in the immediate, post-OPEC years of the 1970s. In this era the Club of Rome had predicted acute shortages of most resources by 1990. Yet this supply-minded 'resource diplomacy' soon foundered on many inconvenient trends leading, by 1988, to the lowest real prices for agricultural commodities and basic metals in thirty years.

Longer-term Trends

To sum up: just about *every* commodity has crashed during the 1980s, dropping to levels among the lowest recorded in the past several decades. In all these cases, Kohli says, 'the basic reason has been that supply greatly exceeded demand – contrary to predictions less than a decade ago by . . . organisations, including the Club of Rome, that there would be major shortages of all commodities during the 1980s and beyond.'

Proof of the false prophecy lies in the trends noted above. It remains to explain why reliance on commodities proved a disappointing gamble.

As an initial factor, supply grew rapidly with technological innovations in production. Bio-technology promises higher yields in most crops, including those directly competitive (soya beans, for example) with Southeast Asian products. Heavier investment in substitute materials at the same time has reduced need for products once thought irreplaceable, such as tin, copper and aluminium.

Mining and smelting of these minerals occurs in Indonesia, Malaysia, Thailand, Singapore and the Philippines. Metals especially have become vulnerable to advances in composite materials. Fibre optics development now enables cable-makers to cut the weight of their product twenty-fold. Even in food commodities, substitution has become a worry. As the *Far Eastern Economic Review* noted in 1988, 'the danger for Malaysia and other Far Eastern vegetable oil exporters, as always, lies in the increasingly easy substitution into competing products.'

Other production changes bode ill for Southeast Asia's nickel, copper, bauxite, coal, tin and iron mines. Metal fabricators in the industrial countries now produce directly for end-use manufacturers, cutting demand for raw ingots. Longer-term changes in industrial materials also promise further drops in metal usage. Ceramics are replacing metal in many engine parts; tougher plastics are also reducing motor vehicle weight.

Meanwhile, Southeast Asian governments have added to the commodity sector's overcapacity, becoming fiercely competitive among themselves in the process, despite a decade of talk about Asean economic coordination. Heedless of impending gluts, a race ensued to build fertiliser and methane plants in Malaysia and Indonesia. Aluminium plants were planned throughout the region, with enormous investment implications.

On the demand side, dietary changes are reducing demand for some Southeast Asian products, such as coconut oil and other allegedly heavily saturated fats. Distortions to the marketplace also result from decisions by the rich Western countries to ensure stability of supply and to protect influential political constituencies, especially the farmers.

High farm product prices have prompted large increases in domestic supply which, also unsurprisingly, have ensured tariff barriers discouraging enough to protect home suppliers. By way of example, the incorporation of Greece, Portugal and Spain into the European Community has created an olive oil lobby in Brussels, site of the European Commission's headquarters. Vegetable oils from Asean now face the prospect of stiffer entry hurdles.

All these factors were surveyed by *The Economist* magazine in April 1987. Its succinct report: 'the world has a commodities glut. Technology has boosted agricultural yields and made metals redundant for many of their old industrial uses. Foolish policies of price support in rich countries have increased the food surplus.'

The 1990s: Vulnerable Markets, or Reborn Hope?

Shortly after these words were written an upturn in commodities became apparent, with strong price increases in mostly industrial raw materials (metals and rubber) although some food commodities, notably coffee, bounced back. Was this a major corrective to a long-term, downward spiral for Southeast Asia's commodities?

A boom in stainless steel, a major nickel user, began in early 1989, but generally the 'hard' markets also remain vulnerable. This judgement applies with even more force to the tin market, crippled by a large stock overhang and by the development of new mines, such as Neves Corvo in Portugal or various new workings in Brazil, which operate more cheaply than the marginal Malaysian mines.

The fall of the US dollar after 1986 also lifted prices. (The markets denominate nearly all commodities in US dollars.) The strengthening of the dollar at the end of the 1980s also gave little hope for dramatic new gains. Nor did improved industrial growth rates. In vegetable oil the availability of soya remains the key to the market, a key determinant outside the region's control. Non-Asian soya crops continue to expand, as do oil seed crops in India and Pakistan, two of Southeast Asia's biggest buyers which are now intent on self-sufficiency in vegetable oils. All this portends less demand for Southeast Asia's so-called 'golden crop'.

Nor will sugar prices rebound quickly: stockpiles in 1989 amount to 30 per cent of global production. Consumption habits in some countries are turning away from refined sugar while production is growing in others; in China, sugar production increased fourfold during the first half of the 1980s. Apart from these supply issues, other global trading phenomena, such as discounted selling and 'counter-trading' (a type of quasi-barter), are also adding to uncertainty about commodity price trends. Interestingly, the authorities in Singapore decided in 1987 to permit counter-trade firms to do business in that city-state, a sign that this commercially astute country recognises that traditional commodity dealing is now changing.

In short, much of the evidence suggests a long-term trend against the once regal position of Southeast Asian commodities. Globally, as the World Bank's commodity forecasts reported in 1987, the 'exports of the non-fuel primary commodities by the developing countries are projected to show less overall change [to 1994] than imports.' In its recurrently published *Outlook for Primary Commodities* the Bank acknowledged (Duncan (ed.), 1984) that, 'with industrial activity continuing to grow, there may be periods in the next few years when prices for metals/minerals commodities will increase sharply. But given the excess capacity which pervades these industries, any such price increase should be short-lived.'

Downstream Processing: A Way Out?

Malaysia stands out in its success in redirecting crude palm oil exports away from distant Europe (or to neighbouring Singapore) and into its own refineries. These now produce a range of products, and exemplify the admonishments by economists to go 'downstream', and to add more value to raw commodities inside Southeast Asia. In Indonesia, plywood factories sprang up in the early 1980s after government edicts forbade the simple export of felled logs from Borneo and Sumatra. Plywood factories however create a voracious domestic demand for logs.

In the Philippines, sugar juice had long been sent to become molasses and alcohol; newer, more interesting refinements making more complex ethers and esters also emerged during the 1970s. Throughout the region, the mostly overseas-Chinese-owned and -operated metalworking shops have also become increasingly sophisticated engineering shops, able to do precision machine tooling work. These are real accomplishments.

Yet Southeast Asia's slow pace in achieving more downstream processing, more product diversification, more control over marketing and distribution has surprised many outside economists. A private adviser to the Malaysian prime minister, the Japanese business economist Kenichi Ohmae, has harped on this theme, giving (as noted in Chapter 3) pep talks to astonished Malaysian ministers.

The growth of regional multinationals such as Sime Darby Berhad or PT Astra Holdings in Indonesia shows a slow receptivity to this message. Founded eight decades ago by two British planters, Sime Darby employs over 30,000 employees in 200 companies located mainly within Southeast Asia. It remains based on cocoa, rubber and palm oil plantation earnings but has diversified into insurance, travel agency work, heavy earth-moving equipment, footwear, car tyres and vehicle hire. Nearly all of these are companies whose shares are traded on local stock exchanges.

Diversification, for Sime Darby, is meant to avoid too much dependence on plantation earnings. Even though its plantations subsidiary in Malaysia, Consolidated Plantations Berhad, gets higher productivity out of its Tamil workforce than any other firm; none the less the commodities mainstay means vulnerability. PT Astra, by way of contrast, has branched into palm oil from a solid base in distributorships of manufactured products, especially motor agencies.

In one case, a plan to add value to a major local product collided with government inertia and conflicting advice from the World Bank. Sugar planters, self-interested to be sure, have promoted at varying times a plan to use Philippine sugar-based alcohol as a substitute for lead additives in petrol, almost all of which is imported. Even the plan's opponents accept that alcohol-laced petrol would save foreign exchange, revitalise often moribund sugar mills and create new employment. Not least, the proposal, if implemented, would reduce lead poisoning of millions of poor Filipino children living on the kerbside.

Two years of haggling resulted in no action, however. Government papers reaching the trade and industry secretary, José Concepcion, claimed that 'all the private sector – consumer, sugar planter, miller, gasoline producer and distiller – would support the National Alcohol Programme.' In essence the 1986 version of the programme aimed at substituting, over three years, the dangerously high amounts of tetra-ethyl lead added to Philippine petrol with anhydrous alcohol made from sugar juice.

From a public health viewpoint, the case for reducing lead additives seemed self-evident. Studies suppressed during Marcos's time showed children living next to Manila's major roads having lead levels which, in Western countries, require immediate hospitalisation; one Philippine study says 7.2 million Filipino children, almost all of them living in urban areas, have absorbed dangerous amount of lead, a condition that can result in gross mental retardation or in lung and kidney damage.

With the sugar industry in chronic depression by the late 1980s, the idea had strong support. Fuel alcohol would come from the juice and molasses distilled in forty-one mills. With greater amounts of alcohol, petrol would burn better. Lead levels would fall from 0.16 grammes per litre (gm/l) to just 0.028 gm/l in most petrol grades.

The case looked overwhelming: less foreign exchange, better health for children, more use of local product, better efficiency in engines, employment generation and the saving from bankruptcy of many sugar mills. The lead content of local petrol had become a national scandal, surpassing by as much as five times the maximum permissible limits for lead additives in Europe or America. By Japanese standards, Manila's traffic belches out fumes with lead levels three times higher than in polluted Tokyo.

Why has this type of downstream processing of raw material not succeeded? First, the government stands to lose a little revenue: US$18 million in 1986.

Secondly, the price of oil remains a crucial constant. Even at 1987 oil prices the plan made economic sense but it died still-born when they dropped still further. Finally, the World Bank, intent on closing down inefficient sugar mills, has little time for a plan to keep many of them functioning. The denouement for this attempt to diversity sugar production was as follows. The sugar stayed in the molasses and the lead remained in the petrol. Caught between World Bank methodology and demands of another kind, Corazon Aquino's government reacted in a predictable way: paralysis.

Outlook

For the remaining years of this century, 'primary commodity prices will . . . remain depressed, much below those prevailing during 1970 to 1983,' says Kohli. The habit of drinking deep at the commodity fount has proved seductive – and costly.

Yale University economist Gustav Ranis (quoted in Tanzi, 1987) has identified the basic problem of depending too much on commodities for export earnings. 'In a broader sense, the relatively easy availability of earnings from traditional exports helps a country to avoid difficult policy changes needed to move a system from import substitution to export substitution.' By contrast, those relatively poor in natural resources, such as Korea, Taiwan or Japan, have had 'relatively little option but to gradually shift from a land to a labour-based expansion path.'

Southeast Asia's commodity producing countries had the luxury of time, the luxury of a choice. They have used the time which commodities earnings give them to create industry, to be sure, but it is of the import substitution variety. The result of the first wave of post-war regional industry caters almost exclusively to captive home markets.

During the most recent decades industrial growth expanded to create a new generation of steel, fertiliser, car assembly, chemical and refinery plants. These rely on foreign debt finance, foreign technology and foreign markets. More recent changes have switched priorities, to be sure, and now concentrate on light assembly plants aimed at export markets. Southeast Asia still processes only a tiny fraction of its commodities, preferring instead to lure footloose industries and their imported components with tax holidays and cheap labour.

Recent trends suggest that the time-buying advantage of commodity reliance has now passed into history. As commodity prices fall over time, the cost of manufactured goods is rising in relative terms. The 'gross terms of trade will continue to move sharply against primary commodity exporting countries such as Indonesia, Philippines and Malaysia,' recent ADB reports stress.

To be sure, the commodity bind is not iron-clad; the GATT round directed at liberalising agricultural trade holds out a promise of major reform. But no one pretends these will come quickly or that, once achieved, the Asean countries will necessarily be able to command bigger market shares than cheaper unit cost producers now emerging in Latin America and even elsewhere (New Guinea, Solomon Islands) in the Asia Pacific region.

This logic also applies to the richest commodity of them all, petroleum, which no longer promises the fabled riches it once delivered. China, Vietnam and (when it discards its chronically failing government) even Burma may increasingly offer cheaper oil prospecting in the 1990s than is now possible within the established Asean oil producers.

There are signs that the dangerous depletion of resources, notably in timber, have belatedly elicited public alarm. 'We have almost no forest left,' said Thai prime minister Chatichai Choonhavan when announcing two decrees in January 1989 that banned, with immediate effect, all commercial logging (see Chapter 5). The Bangkok *Nation* newspaper said that 'these courageous and far-sighted measures set Thailand apart as a leader in forest conservation among the many tropical countries facing a similar dilemma.'

Indonesian forests, heavily logged and burned in Borneo and Sumatra, also became political issues in Jakarta. Philippine senators drafted bills to try to save the 1 million remaining hectares of primary forest still left in the 7,000 island archipelago; thirty years earlier forest cover had amounted to 52 million hectares. Entrenched timber businessmen fought back however, and large doubts hung over the resolve, and the administrative capability, of these countries to conserve their forests. Meanwhile, however, the export-earning imperatives point toward accelerating depletion of fixed resources, of which increasing amounts must be allocated toward satisfying local demand. Indonesia's rising population is using an ever-rising proportion of the country's petroleum, for example.

In varying and often complex ways therefore, the food, agricultural raw materials, minerals, metals and energy products flowing from Southeast Asia's commodity cornucopia are hostage to unfavourable trends on the global marketplace. Development economists needed to look ahead toward new strategies to ensure Southeast Asia's continuing prosperity. So did the region's key financial institutions, such as the Asian Development Bank.

In an internal bank paper entitled 'An assessment of the impact of falling commodity prices on bank operations', Kohli reviewed the bleak future of primary commodities and said that 'the bank, being an agent of change, will need to anticipate rather than react to events . . . in future the bank will have to be more aggressive in investigating and seizing opportunities for lending.' As Chapter 10 illustrates, there are well founded doubts about the ability of Asia's largest development finance institution to take this in-house lesson to heart.

References

Duncan, R. C. (ed.) (1984) *The Outlook for Primary Commodities, 1984 to 1995*, World Bank Staff Commodity Working Papers No. 11. Washington, DC: World Bank

Kintanar, A. and Tan, L. E. (1986) *ASEAN–US Economic Relations: an Overview*. Singapore: ISEAS

Tanzi, V. (1987) 'The public sector in the market economies of developing Asia', *Asian Development Review*, vol. 5, No. 2

10

DEVELOPMENT BUNK

An Asian Birthday

On 24 November 1986, the Manila-based Asian Development Bank (ADB) became 20 years old. On that date also, Masao Fujioka, a finance ministry bureaucrat from Japan, began his second five-year term as the president of this little known bank, the world's largest regional financial institution. The multi-billion dollar bank marked the occasion with a glossy history book boasting that it had become the 'most successful regional organisation in Asia'.

There was much to be proud about. The institution, beginning in 1966, has given nearly sixty large loans a year to its twenty-eight developing country members, known in bank nomenclature as 'DMCs'. Much of this money has gone to countries like Taiwan or South Korea, helping their economies to become fully industrialised by the 1980s.

Less successful DMCs also have gained from the ADB's largesse. Southeast Asia's roads, railways, ports, airports, telecommunications networks and electricity plants have benefited from the bank's 'infrastructural' loans although the richer Asean countries no longer draw on ADB funds. Many hundreds of loans have been successfully devised and implemented. Although loan volume slowed in the mid-1980s, by the end of the decade the ADB was again pushing out large sums, mainly to India and China.

With the admission of China as a member, and India becoming a borrower, the number of people served by the ADB has increased to 2.5 billion, Fujioka tells financial gatherings around the world. The ADB has become, he says, 'a bank for half the world'. Apart from maverick North Korea, every Asian country belongs – albeit with varying degrees of participation.

All the world's advanced capitalist countries, whether located in Asia or not, sit on the bank's board of governors. These countries, together with the DMC members, choose a board of directors that meets once a week in Manila, where the bank's new US$171 million headquarters building opened in 1989. Member countries have both a basic vote and a proportional vote when it comes to deciding the bank's affairs.

Twenty per cent of total voting power is divided equally among the member countries, but the remaining 80 per cent is proportionate to each member's relative share of subscribed capital. Some of this is paid in directly but most remains on call in a promissory note. Forty-seven countries now belong to the ADB.

Signs of Age

The bank likes to claim that its performance has both vindicated hopes of a 'safe' regional role for Japan and for speeded development throughout Asia. Indeed, a major US Treasury report on the world's multilateral development banks (MDBs) in 1984 called the ADB 'the best of the regional MDBs'. But how true are these claims? One-ninth the size of the World Bank, the ADB entered its third decade dogged by controversy, troubled by slipping loan levels and haunted by a backwash of loan repayments threatening to outpace new loan approvals.

The ADB is no longer immune from sceptical second thoughts. Unfortunately for Fujioka, the bank's birthday party also coincided with an erupting crisis of confidence among the members of his staff, a problem of morale that has continued to plague the bank. Quarrels pit many among the bank's six hundred professional staff against each other or against the Japanese-controlled management.

These wrangles often run along predictable national lines as the full extent of America's diminished importance in Asia becomes clearer with each passing month. Although the US and Japan hold equal shares of the bank's capital, Japan gives more to the ADB's soft concessionary aid funds and this gives it the more commanding position. So does the tremendous financial power of Japan, now the world's second largest economy and likely to become the most powerful of all by 1993. Inside the bank, Tokyo's voice (though politely muted) is thus ascendant.

Although all the bank's presidents have been Japanese, many Westerners at the bank do not like what they see in the Fujioka era. 'The glimpse of the possible future of regional economic leadership to be seen in the Japanese management of the ADB – the only international financial institution in which Tokyo controls the majority of top jobs – doesn't give most of the bank's 47 members cause to take heart,' notes Jonathan Friedland (1988) in *Institutional Investor*. He says that

> President Fujioka, though generally credited with running a tight financial ship, is strongly criticised by Westerners at the bank for his inflexible, highly personal and thoroughly Japanese management style . . . To put it as politely as possible, Fujioka remains a deeply controversial Chief Executive Officer among the bank's multinational cast of economists, loan officers and engineers.

Often intensely personal controversies arise from policy differences. Robert Wihtol, author of a 1988 study of the bank, highlights the most obvious problem: in many eyes the bank has become a mindless, intellectually dishonest loan pump:

> The Asian Development Bank has come under growing criticism in the 1980s for emphasising the quantitative aspects of its operations, particularly the annual expansion of loan approvals, while at the same time disregarding developmental, technical and economic aspects of its projects. This tendency was evident in the 1970s but has become more pronounced in the 1980s following the strong push by Masao Fujioka, who took over the presidency of the bank in 1981, to increase lending at a time of stagnation or decline in the demand for ADB loans.

Poor Little Rich Bank

That this rich but relatively unknown bank should become a source of controversy is somewhat surprising. As Asia's largest bank its liquid portfolio alone was US$4.5 billion in 1988. In recent years it has been the largest buyer of bonds on the New York, Tokyo and European markets. Fujioka's bank borrows with unvarying triple A ratings from the capital markets. It enjoys a sound reputation for, if anything, overly conservative financial management.

Lending to the bank comes easily. Yet staff, speaking usually on condition of anonymity, claim that the bank's lending itself comes too easily as well. Allegations regularly surface in the press that the end result of ADB loans disproportionately benefits Japanese contractors and suppliers. It is even claimed that most of the ADB's borrowers have little interest in the loans, for which bank staff have claimed they must often invent supporting data to justify in the first place. Michael Haas, a University of Hawaii scholar, describes these criticisms in a new study of the bank (1989):

> The reason for [an ADB] loan appears to be that a commercial firm is considering foreign investment but there is insufficient source of electric power, too few roads to haul commodities to port, inadequate port facilities and the like. The loan, then, provides infrastructure that the corporation requires. As soon as a project is completed, the corporation derives its profit, while the cost of the loan is passed on to the indigenous population through increased taxation, higher rates for electricity and other devices that favour élites over the masses.

The bank's problems have grown since this internal criticism first became audible in the mid-1980s. To be sure, little or no existential despair seems to trouble most bank staff, whose Mercedes, BMW and other luxury motorcars enter the Philippines under duty-free privileges. None the less, a report to Fujioka from the US management consultant Hay & Associates showed that work morale and *élan* had plummeted by the early 1980s.

It remains at rock bottom although there are various compensations. By one count, bank staff owned 360 Mercedes vehicles in 1988. In this poorest Asean nation, ADB professional staff enjoy the same invidious perks as diplomats.

Some nationals on the bank's ten-tiered, tax-free payroll enjoy salary differentials as high as 20:1 compared with home country wages. Some even pay a portion of their salaries to officials back home, a reward for being put forward for a ADB post. Apart from the cars, Manila has other temptations. Bar girls and swimming pools are just some of creature comforts making bank jobs highly prized. Few staff members, especially from the DMCs, are prepared to jeopardise this life style. For the compliant, fixed-term appointments remain a rarity.

The cost for acquiescence is small, almost trifling. Just say 'yes' and don't get in the way. In the words of one senior officer, 'there's a tremendous pressure to put out loans. But as long as you get the loan through you will be rewarded, regardless of the impact of the project [on the borrowing country] or even if the receiving institution is bankrupt. They [the bank] will find a way to get you if you don't succeed.' Another staff member, at director level, said 'all the glamour comes from putting new loans on the books, rather than making the current ones work.'

Mid-life Crisis

Claims such as these, and reports that the ADB now faces a 'mid-life crisis' (in its early twenties?), make a sharp contrast to the bank's public relations image. This depicts a slightly fussy but benign Asian uncle, dispensing goodies in a plodding but prudent way. Fujioka's defenders say that, in his first years, the president simply sought to lift slackening lending by tough but informal quotas although the president has stoutly denied imposing crude, simplistic 'quotas'.

Yet the president has come in for criticism for indulging in precisely this alleged approach. More seriously, disgruntled bank staff have ferreted out internal papers that show serious doubts at board level about the viability of projects rushed for board of directors' approval at the annual 'bunching' time toward the end of the calendar year.

Some documents point clearly to departures from bank policies, just to get more loans on the books. A large, US$115 million loan for a coal-fired power station in Tamil Nadu, India, contravened bank strictures against loans to power utilities that depend on government subsidies. (The bank has long argued for market rates for power consumers, turning down loan requests from subsidised power utilities.) An ADB manual propounds this market-minded approach: 'subsidies . . . must be excluded from the computation of internal cash generation or self-financing capacity.'

So much for dogma. The anti-subsidy stricture has yielded, however, to pressure from the management to push out more loans. The successful recipient of the bank's revised thinking on the matter was receiving, in 1985, a full 40 per cent of its revenue from government subsidies. 'It's no secret that an exception is being made here', a senior bank official stated just before the huge loan was approved.

Senior ADB management dealt with the problem by inventing new bottles for old wine. Far from a direct subsidy to electricity consumers, the Indian government largesse was just a 'form of social cross-subsidy paid to the farm sector' said one ADB vice-president. It was only 'incidental' that this 'cross-subsidy' operates via artificially low electricity rates. No wonder the expression 'intellectual dishonesty' arises in ADB staff complaints.

Even more seriously, one staff member, pushed out of the bank in 1986, claims he was instructed to distort and invent facts to suit the loan proposal. Others say that, in contravention of the bank's charter, the bank's management uses overtly political reasons to justify lending. A senior ADB economist told me that 'about one-third of the projects are cooked in one way or another'.

'As many as one-third of the [ADB's] loan projects have been approved, it has been alleged, on non-economic grounds unrelated to the notion of policy-oriented loans,' says Haas.

At best [he explains], the loans often reward government ministers who are making domestically unpopular but economically necessary decisions. In other cases, it is alleged, the payoff is to a particular corporation (writing the specifications so that only one firm can do the job), with a sidepayment to the government minister who agrees to the terms of an unneeded project, such as the dredging of a harbour into which no ships have ever or will ever dock.

A Question of Quality

Even perfectly acceptable projects seem to suffer from the loan rush. A hydro-electric project wins board endorsement as a 'classic example of a clear, simple, neat and necessary project'. Yet delays in lining up co-financing by the bank lead to the borrower being charged a 'commitment fee' of nearly 1 per cent on the loan while co-financing lags behind. The cost to the borrower: US$1 million.

Board reports describe another borrower as 'technically bankrupt' but new loans are still approved. In another case, the Indonesian finance minister tells an ADB executive he was unable to recall whether a poorly run state bank in Jakarta, Bapindo, has received a necessary capital injection from the government.

In this specific case the ADB's new loan of US$75 million completely depended on this new capitalisation. The executive involved reported to the board that 'satisfactory clarifications' had been received. Unfortunately for him however, the ADB had received a World Bank report on Bapindo just two months earlier, a paper that painted a damning picture of Bapindo.

'In its present financial, organisational and managerial circumstances, it is not clear that Bapindo is sustainable', the World Bank said. 'Certainly it is not creditworthy – if it ever was.' The World Bank appraisal of Bapindo also said that 'it is already clear that the write-off and losses far exceed Bapindo's own resources.' This then was the borrower to which the ADB was so keen to lend.

Other examples abound of apparently poor quality loans. A loan for an oil mill project in Burma vitally depended on certain crucial 'constants' such as reliable raw material supplies and minimal capitalisation of the cooperatives planning to borrow ADB money. Bank staff say they were told to ignore inconvenient or contradictory information that might imperil the loan. A similar episode occurred in a foodgrain storage project for Pakistan.

Staff papers also show that new loans have proceeded despite borrowers' non-compliance with earlier bank loan conditions. A staff member familiar with the report of a private consultant, brought to Manila by the ADB to measure compliance with the bank's loan 'covenants' (conditions), said most borrowers have treated the ADB's loan strictures as a 'joke'. At one meeting, ADB vice-president Gunter Shultz, a West German, complained about 'serious defects in project administration'.

Yet lending to persistently underachieving DMC borrowers continues, even to countries like Nepal where state corporations have sold off ADB-financed fertiliser to India on the sly. An agricultural bank in the same country was discovered by ADB staff to be 'a bankrupt institution' making an 'imaginary profit'. This contrasts with earlier praise, in public loan documents, for the borrower's collection record, 'one of the most outstanding among the regional development financial institutions'.

In another example, background board-level papers to successive lending to a Korean fisheries project complained of 'inadequate research being done' before loan approval. Follow-up reports said that 'the major part of the project has so far been a complete failure'. A later bank report said that the same project – designed to give berthing places for hundreds of fishing vessels – rests on an 'assumption [that] is no longer valid . . . information available concerning actual port usage indicates . . . no boats are based there.'

Members of the board of directors, speaking privately, acknowledge that some ADB loans are 'padded' with non-essential project components, simply to lift overall loan sums. The go-ahead for loans also depends on procurement 'balance' within the board, and even on support for particular personalities in borrowing governments, as Haas notes. Notes of board meetings show that directors worried about projects being 'pushed through prematurely', a result that 'would erode the bank's credibility'.

This sort of unease in the mid-1980s prompted bank management to convene rarely used 'fail-safe' project review meetings to try to iron out problems. Frustrated staff even 'leaked' documents to various members of the board of directors in an effort to halt projects endorsed by top management. Fujioka promptly appointed a panel to hunt down these and other culprits, headed by ADB General Counsel C. P. Jhong.

Notes from one ADB board meeting record the president as 'greatly concerned at the systematic and large-scale leaking of internal documents.' Stung by criticisms of quality, Fujioka hit back in another board meeting at 'unwarranted criticism that the bank is trying to reach a lending target at the expense of quality.' This is 'untrue', he said, because a US$2.6 billion loan 'target' had been underachieved by 33 per cent. Logic of this kind makes even the bank's Western-educated Japanese staff raise their eyes heavenwards when discussing their chief.

In 1986, an unprecedented two-man panel investigated particularly bitter charges of falsification of financial data in a loan to Burma. Security mania became the norm in 1987 and afterwards, following critical articles in the foreign press based on internal bank papers. The bank has imposed drastic security measures, including visitor passes valid for one floor of the building only.

ADB vice-president Stanley Katz, an American, has warned staff that 'disciplinary action' would be taken to stop 'leaks', an unusual word to describe the passing of bank papers to the bank's owners. 'This is a very open organisation,' Katz claims, 'but we don't like the board [of directors] to get half-baked information that will stack the deck against a project . . . if I caught anybody breaching the procedures for the provision of information, I would sack him.' One board director questions this mentality, calling it the 'mushroom principle'. By this he means that management 'keeps the board in the dark, and covered by dung.'

Despite Fujioka's rhetoric that 'the bank continues to improve its reputation as a sound development financing institution producing high quality projects', the doubters have a solid case. World Bank reports during the 1980s back up assertions that ADB loan quality is declining. The deteriorating performance is in step with a 'general decline' of multilateral loan quality during the past decade.

'[The ADB's] agricultural loans were . . . less successful than those in other sectors', the ADB itself has admitted. Nearly a third of the bank's projects were yielding, by 1986, a 'less than satisfactory income'. 'While the ADB has increased its rural lending and adopted a rural development policy emphasising both growth and poverty alleviation, it does not automatically follow that bank projects are more effectively narrowing income gaps [or] increasing employment', says Wihtol (1988) in his study of the bank.

'A major conclusion [of his study] is that the change in the bank's development policy has led to only very limited changes in project content . . . with little tangible impact on rural poverty', Wihtol says. His conclusion finds support from a group within the board of directors, which argued that 'investment in projects of direct benefit to the poor have economic returns equal to, or greater than, other kinds of projects.' This type of reasoning goes against the prevailing wind at the bank.

Boardroom Wrangling

Criticism from the damning, if sometimes one-sided internal documents have stung the ADB's management into rebuttal. But controversies over loan quality have formed a backdrop to the ever more visible quarrelling between the Japanese and the Americans over the bank's future. Records of board meetings show steadily rising Western disenchantment over Fujioka's leadership, even to the point of the French director provoking a vote, which was defeated, over the president's salary.

After a change in British directors, Whitehall also enquired into the sacking of a British engineer who became too vocal in criticising a US$3 million contract to replace an internal bank telephone system that had had only three years of use. Another row with board-level implications broke out when the bank's first 'performance auditor' clashed with Fujioka.

In a letter to the president in February 1987, the auditor, a Swede, complained of obstruction in carrying out his assignment, which was 'to make a performance audit of the bank's investments during 1979 to 1984.' He told Fujioka that, 'after many difficult compromises between generally accepted audit standards and consideration of individual persons, I managed to present a report which reflected most of the main findings. One was that the bank during the early years of the period suffered a loss of US$100 to 200 million in [the] form of safe market revenues.'

The official, who later lost his position, also said in his letter that his 'conclusion [about the alleged loss] was confirmed by the staff of the [bank's] Treasurer's department, [yet] I was informed that you . . . were not interested in getting any similar investigations made in the future.' Asked about these charges, ADB treasurer Alan Gill has replied that 'safe market revenues' is not a viable concept and said the figures sent by the Swede to Fujioka were inaccurate. Whatever the situation, the dispute has done further damage.

At the interpersonal level, board-level atmospherics at the ADB are not the best. During much of President Ronald Reagan's administration, the US director at the ADB was Joseph Rogers, a free-marketeering ideologue who enjoyed delivering sermons to the board. According to most participants, he also enjoyed riding roughshod over Fujioka, lecturing the reticent Japanese on the need to lend more to the 'neglected private sector' and less to 'socialist failures' like Burma. Past Australian and West European directors have also lacked an appreciation for Asian niceties and 'face' although Fujioka has not been without allies in the Western camp such as the departing British director, for example, who conducted his own, private review of project quality.

Criticism of Fujioka has become very personal in some publications. 'Set up to serve the world's most populous region, the Asian Development Bank is dominated by one man,' said one report in a major New York newspaper. Other reports have poked fun at the alleged 'cult of personality' growing up around the president. In a fawning prose owing much to socialist realism, ADB press releases describe Fujioka's 'untiring efforts' and 'remarkable statemanship' in the ADB. 'Unmindful of jet-lag after long journeys from abroad', says one handout, 'he often drives straight to the office to clear urgent papers.'

Procurement is the Game

Behind this bad personal chemistry lie other, more significant issues. An internal bank paper notes that Japan's share in total bank procurement of goods and services was about 50 per cent in 1983. A board-eyes-only paper says Japan's share of procurement was only a little over 26 per cent in the same year. Which is accurate? There is no way to check.

Criticism of loan purchasing that favours Japanese suppliers occasionally surfaces inside bank documents. A July 1979 internal evaluation of that no-boats-in-the-harbour Korean fisheries project said 'diesel specifications have been written precisely around' a type of Japanese engine. It also complained that the bank's procurement procedures were not being followed.

In 1984, controversy over a US$15 million contract to Japanese firms for twelve rice mills in Burma raised the issue of favouritism again, especially after an initial decision awarding the job to a West German company was rescinded. This controversy received coverage in the *International Herald Tribune*.

Another example lies in the alleged rejection by bank management of an internal treasury department report. The recommendations urged liquidating some 'Japanese Samurai' bond holdings well ahead of maturity. Such an action, while profitable to the bank, would not have pleased the Japanese institutions issuing the instruments. These examples underline the unease about extensive, if informal, pro-Japanese policies at the bank.

Improved gains for Japanese industry are a prime reason behind Japanese enthusiasm for greater ADB lending to India and China, a trend that disturbs Indonesia, now the bank's largest borrower. Jakarta, which host an ADB representative's office, has become so capital hungry that it now pleads for all project expenses, even local costs, to be picked up by the bank's loans.

Fujioka's push for more lending to China suggests grand plans. He urges the ADB to become an Asian 'resource centre'. Vice-president Katz says the bank is becoming 'an instrument of development not just a purveyor of capital.' In response to American pressure, new sections to promote co-financing and private sector lending have also been created.

One successful plan, co-managed with Nomura Securities in Tokyo and Morgan Grenfell in London, is a US$100 million Asian Equity Development Fund, with ADB underwriting. The fund began operating from Luxembourg and bought in most Southeast Asian securities markets. Less successful was a much touted move by the ADB into equity operations (that is, bank purchases of stock in companies undertaking development projects). After three years of operation, the bank had placed just US$7.03 million in Asian ventures.

A Question of Control

Despite Japan's enormous financial, investment and trade influence around the world, the ADB remains the sole international organisation in which the Japanese enjoy pre-eminence. Even on paper the Japanese edge is clear, if slight: its approved ADB capital subscription of US$2.784 billion exceeds the US$2.744 million subscribed by the US; none the less the voting share held by both countries remains the same (a little over 18 per cent).

The ADB is now on the frontline of commercially strategic trench warfare in Asia. Questions of control mirror a contest between two tendencies. The first leans toward the creation of an exclusively Japanese sphere of economic influence in Southeast Asia; the second allows for the maintenance of a pluralism enabling European and American business influence, while never to approximate again to its colonial era ascendancy, to retain a wide sway.

The 'Japanese factor' at the ADB now turns on two issues: the direction of bank policy generally and, more specifically, the outcome of Tokyo's campaign to overturn the voting parity Japan now has with Washington.

Even in such apparently 'neutral' areas as development policy the Japanese hand is visible. Wihtol says 'there is evidence of considerable Japanese influence on the bank's rural development policy, derived from Japan's concern with its food security and emphasising the need to increase foodgrain production in Southeast Asia . . . [Given] that the main objective of the Japanese approach is increasing agricultural production, it has detracted from the degree of emphasis placed by the bank on a more directly poverty-oriented approach.'

Haas makes a similar point: 'The paucity of [ADB] loans to industry seems to suggest that the ADB wants developing countries of Asia to produce raw materials for developed countries elsewhere but are not to take over the processing and manufacturing of their own natural resources except to make parts for assembly into products finished in the First World.' In a privately circulated paper, ADB chief economist K. N. Kohli has argued for a 'qualitative change in orientation by the bank' urging it to 'anticipate rather than react to events', but his ideas have made little headway.

On the second point, the US made a stand during 1988 to resist a demand for another capital increase to the bank. The Asean countries especially fear that another increase would deal the Americans out of their parity position. This would occur, they reason, because the US Congress would balk at higher capital subscription commitments to a bank that does little to further US commercial interests.

Two weeks before the bank's twenty-first annual meeting in Osaka in May 1987, the Sub-committee on Foreign Operations of the powerful US House of Representatives Appropriations Committee heard testimony criticising the ADB. At about the same time, Australian federal senator Janine Haines accused the ADB of 'unfair allocation of project contracts'. She said it 'has been suggested that granting [loans] apparently has become an end in itself' for the bank.

Just before the Osaka meeting, the *Australian Financial Review* claimed ADB connivance in bias against Australian suppliers for a bank-financed livestock project in Indonesia. The Belgian government made preparations to withdraw an unused US$1 million technical assistance support fund that the bank had never used. Bias against European sources of supply was hinted at. Yet the rich countries except Japan invariably close ranks against efforts by developing member countries to build in preferential procurement policies for DMC suppliers. (The World Bank gives DMC suppliers 15 per cent and 7.5 per cent for goods and services contracts, respectively.)

It is clear that the ADB does not need any more capital for its operations. The issue is control, not finance. Each capital increase has negative effects, as Haas explains (1989):

Continued increases in [the ADB's] capital have been voted over the years, although nearly half of the capital is unutilised. As the increases require more capital commitments from developing countries, the latter are thus compelled to make loan applications so that their funds will be put to some use. This vicious cycle [sic] leaves the leadership of the bank in the role of promoting increased lending for its own sake, according to many critics.

Sour Grapes

Many critics of the ADB have self-interested motives. The success of the Japanese in manipulating the bank's procurement procedures evokes self-righteousness that masks considerable envy. Much of the sniping comes from the losers in the arrangement, especially from Western manufacturers of capital goods. It must also be said that many Western country board directors are sleepy veterans of their respective treasury departments, drifting toward retirement on one last perk and unwilling, or unable, to play the system as well as Japan, Korea or even West Germany.

To give him his due, Fujioka galvanised a bank staff that had also become more than a little sleepy over the years. Fujioka's announcement in June 1989 of an early retirement prompted considerable regret among some member countries which valued his energy and dynamism while caring less for accusations that the ADB had tried to move too much money, too fast, under his stewardship.

Paradoxically, the ADB is right to claim for itself the mantle of 'the most successful regional organisation in Asia'. The reason is clear. The ADB plods on alone across the field; it has no contenders. In the bank's commemorative book, *A Bank for Half the World*, the author says cleverly that 'nothing else has got half as far or looks half as strong' as the ADB. He is also right: the boasts on the bank's age of majority are thus backhanded, if unintentionally so.

The truth is that the ADB, for all its faults and inertia, remains the closest approximation of a regional business grouping in Southeast Asia. The Asean association also began in the same year as the ADB's operations and it also, has been prone to generous portions of self-praise.

These cannot disguise a lack of truly regional economic dynamism however, a failing now glaringingly apparent after two decades. Asean's member countries have achieved often stupendous growth rates yet this owes almost everything to faraway markets and almost nothing to demand inside the region. Contemplating the regional vacuum, Southeast Asian business people have recurrent cause to ponder an old Chinese adage: 'hollow drums make the most noise.'

References

Friedland, J. (1988) 'Preparing for the Pacific century?', *Institutional Investor*, April
Haas, M. (1989) *The Asian Way to Peace: A Story of Regional Cooperation*. New York: Praeger.
Wihtol, R. (1988) *The Asian Development Bank and Rural Development: Policy and Practice*. London: Macmillan Press in association with St Antony's College, Oxford

11

RELUCTANT REGIONALISM

Swords into Bonus Shares

In the middle of the 1960s, two quarrelling Malay countries decided to patch up a rather bitter family feud. When Indonesia finally called an end to its three-year campaign of *konfrontasi*, or 'confrontation', against neighbouring Malaysia, it also backed out of an imbroglio ruining an already battered economy and humiliating its poorly performing army.

That quarrel, now almost forgotten in the wider region, originally became inflamed in 1962. In that year Britain decided to incorporate its two northern Borneo territories of Sabah and Sarawak into the existing Malay federation of coastal islands and princely states lying a thousand kilometres west across the South China Sea.

Linked together with the Borneo jungle possessions the new creation, called Malaysia, quickly provoked a hostile reaction from an Indonesia ruled erratically by its charismatic president, a man named Sukarno. But the failure of *konfrontasi* could only be acknowledged in the aftermath of a failed *coup d'état* in Jakarta in 1965. Indonesia's new military rulers, taking over gradually but irreversibly after that year from the ailing and outmanoeuvred Sukarno, realised that his campaign to disassemble Malaysia was hopeless.

That recognition marked the beginning of the modern phase of the Southeast Asian market economies. More than any other factor, this new mood among Malays became the basic precondition for two decades of business calm that followed. The regional peace regained had consequences therefore going far past the elimination of border tensions: burying this hatchet also made possible, for the first time since the Second World War, the achievement of commercial stability throughout most of tropical Asia. Only mainland Indochina, convulsed then as now by battlefield conflicts, lost the chance for peace and plenty.

False Starts Towards a Regional Club

It was only logical that this new regional order would gain a framework, and a name. The first attempt at formal regional association occurred when Malaya (as Malaysia called itself in the pre-Borneo merger days), the Philippines and

Thailand created the Association of Southeast Asia in 1961. This grouping promptly drifted into irrelevance however; Indonesia's Sukarno rightly viewed it as an anti-Indonesian pact.

Another try at grouping tropical Asia came in a shortlived but grandiose scheme that aimed to put inside one association all the region's major Malay states. In other words, this time Indonesia would be allowed in but Thailand, with its strikingly different Buddhist culture, would stay out. The plan, floated in 1963, took the name Maphilindo, an acronym formed from the first letters of Malaya, the Philippines and Indonesia.

Yet this organisation also never had a chance; Jakarta's confrontation with Malaysia began shortly afterwards. Moreover, the very notion of Maphilindo carried an implicitly anti-Chinese tone, one that denied Singapore, dominated by its large ethnic Chinese community, any participation in the new club. That, indeed, was one of the objectives: Indonesia's first vice-president, Mohammad Hatta, revealed Jakarta's feelings when he criticised British plans to include Singapore within the Malaysian federation.

Any country that included Singapore 'would inevitably become a second China,' he said. 'The Singapore Chinese would then be able to extend their [commercial] power through the entire area.' Although Singapore's expulsion from Malaysia soon afterwards alleviated most of the gloomier Indonesian worries, the persistent dislike by the region's native peoples of the overseas Chinese continues to colour attitudes to Singaporean commercial success. (See Chapter 6.)

An Enduring but Overrated Framework

After these failures the region devised a framework that has shown much more longevity. The Association of Southeast Asian Nations, now known universally as Asean, emerged as a by-product of the stability regained after the ending of *konfrontasi*. Asean had a modest beginning: the Indonesian foreign minister, Adam Malik, simply brought up a new idea for regional association during a meeting in July 1967 with his Thai counterpart Thanat Khoman. Malaysian deputy prime minister Tun Abdul Razak also participated in the early talks.

The idea quickly gathered momentum. A joint communiqué from Jakarta and Bangkok also won assent from Kuala Lumpur, Manila and Singapore; these governments then created the present grouping in August 1967, although it would take them nine more years before they would agree upon an anodyne accord, the Treaty of Amity and Cooperation in Southeast Asia, with which they have clothed their loose and still wary association. Even then it required the shock of communist victories in Indochina to force these countries to take the next steps forward, including a long list of self-conscious 'regional' initiatives which, as we shall see, have come to very little. After all, the Southeast Asians themselves never tire of noting that Asean 'exists merely to strengthen national identity, not to diminish it.'

Still, the change in the regional mood after the late 1960s was palpable. Instead of the normal invective, sharpened by mutual ignorance and colonial myopia, a habit of chummy golf course meetings became the norm among Asean politicians. What the Americans call the 'buddy system' has helped to entrench a habit of keeping counterparts reasonably well informed. The buddies formed a remarkably durable cast of characters, including Malik, Thanat, Razak (who later became Malaysia's prime minister), Singapore's long-serving foreign minister Sinnathamby Rajaratnam and, not least, another veteran, Philippine foreign minister Carlos Romulo.

All this helped consolidate an environment increasingly conducive to business expansion. As cooperative habits spread, other squabbles, such as Thai-Malaysian border problems or an awkward Philippine claim to the Malaysian state of Sabah, were smoothed over. But – and this is the key point – they did not invariably find complete resolution, an omission that will cause renewed bilateral problems in the years ahead as Asean runs short of direction.

Regional Realism

Most descriptive writing about Asean turns on what the organisation is *not*. Although the grouping stresses economic cooperation it basically remains an instrument for discussions among essentially autocratic governments reluctant to surrender any power to regional institutions. There is a high degree of artifice involved in the workings of Asean; Y. C. Sit, a Malaysian at St John's College, Oxford, calls this a 'deliberate ambivalence' that runs through the grouping at every turn. Asean's members shy away from a formal alliance, yet their anti-Vietnamese bias has dominated their stance since 1979. Ambivalence, or hypocrisy?

The Asean countries also boast about their various collaborative connections, especially in economic and business affairs. An overabundance of meetings by ministers and officials result in press releases suggesting decisions of commercial substance, yet this is far from the truth. The Asian business community knows that substantive economic integration in Asean lags far behind the rhetoric.

The American analyst Donald McCloud has identified (1986) the basic historical reasons why enthusiasts for Asean economic integration on a par with the European Community face recurrent disappointment. At Independence

the states of Southeast Asia found little to bind them together. Although many regional leaders spoke of the prominence of regional politics and the importance of cooperation among neighbouring states, the bonds with Europe and the allure of global politics were stronger . . . Further, the traditional regional political system offered few models for interstate cooperation . . . subjugation by force had been the primary means for dealing with neighbours and the standard relationship was Superior to Vassal.

McCloud has become a regional optimist, however. Despite this unconducive past he argues that 'in less than four decades since [their] independence, these states have developed a creditable record in cooperative ventures' within an evolving sense of regional identity 'notably missing at the time of the first arrival of the European colonial powers.' John Holdridge, a former assistant secretary of state for East Asia and the Pacific during the Reagan administration, is another convert, and he writes about Asean in glowing terms.

'In contemporary East and Southeast Asia', Holdridge said in 1987 'the birth and maturation of Asean has been one of the outstanding developments. Asean has provided its members with a framework . . . for acting together to achieve economic advantage for all.'

The Myth of the Evolving Regional Market

But has it really provided such a framework? In nearly all Southeast Asian countries the local business community takes a wholly different line. The smartest money consistently has bet, and won, on the side of economic nationalism, even if these include *dirigiste* fallacies long discredited in advanced industrial economies. The reason for this preference is clear: under the guise of national industrialisation policies, tied to import controls, tariffs and a spread of incentives, local Chinese and their political patrons have prospered mightily. In many instances the result has erected new walls around already highly pampered industries, all in the name of self-sufficiency and industrial maturation.

'A genuine regional marketplace would deprive the *towkays*, *cukongs*, *taipans* and *cronies* of their natural arena,' said a Thai deputy finance minister to me in an unguarded moment. Real intra-regional competition is the last thing the Asean 'duppies' want. What is the point of being in power, a Filippino politician asked in a famous aside back in the 1950s, if not to get rich? What indeed? Maintaining a privileged stranglehold is precisely the point of winning power and influence; moves to develop a competitive regional economy would severely undermine that.

That explains why business interests linked in particular to the Indonesian, Malaysian and Philippine political leaderships have never shown enthusiasm for even the modest, straightforward and low-cost economic initiatives coming out of various Asean meetings. These include ideas for the harmonisation of automotive component manufacturing within the region. Over the past two decades, commit-tees have devised schemes for Asean diesel engine manufacturing collaboration, for Asean soda ash and superphosphate plants. Yet nearly all have foundered on the blunt fact that, as Singapore's prime minister Lee Kuan Yew noted back in 1977, 'it is easier to deal with Asean's external partners than to sort out the intra-regional arrangements between Asean members themselves.'

As Southeast Asia's most successful foreign investors – the Japanese – know full well, there has never been much chance of strong, sustained moves towards a supra-regional economic community in Asean. From the grouping's inception until the present day, the Southeast Asians have taken a leisurely view of their new creation and its possibilities. 'Unless we consolidate ourselves in economic cooperation,' Rajaratnam said in 1973, 'it will be difficult for others to regard Asean seriously.' His words still hold true.

Bureaucratic Smoke and Mirrors

From the first years, Asean's principal rationale has been as an arena for meetings. An annual gathering of foreign ministers complemented an officials' standing committee which met for two to three days every two months. Then, after 1976, a tame and largely functionless secretariat was set up in Jakarta. It has had little or nothing to do since then. Nor has it had much with which to do even that: the secretariat's budget has hovered at US$2 million a year, a oddly parlous situation for the under-worked officials sitting inside their grandiose headquarters building.

Bureaucratic clutter of the worst kind has seized hold of Asean like a virulent form of tropical virus. In each member country, National Secretariats for Asean have blossomed inside the foreign ministries. These civil servants provide the second tier of authority after the politicians' golfcourse chats.

It is not only cynical foreigners who distrust the process. For example, the Malaysian analyst Zakaria Ahmad, deputy chief of Kuala Lumpur's Institute of Strategic and International Studies, has called the Asean system 'slow and tedious.' Similar comments slide from the lips of the very diplomats who have commandeered Asean, a double irony but wholly consistent with the 'Asean way'.

No Substance but Plenty of Suitors

Just as the region's boom was stuttering into recession during the mid-1980s, Asean had become a saleable commodity in its own right. To financial and business analysts around the globe, the Southeast Asian grouping looked up-and-coming, another East Asian 'success story'. A spate of 'Asean newsletters' began to emerge; once Western politicians learned how to pronounce 'Ah-si-ahn' they tossed the word around in speeches acknowledging this hitherto ignored flank of the overall 'East Asia Edge'.

As in other aspects of Southeast Asian marketing, this rise to international stature resulted primarily from outside attention. On the inside, meanwhile, the Asean label was losing whatever magic it had earlier possessed becoming, instead, a catch phrase. How far expectations had slipped within the region is illustrated by an increasingly sceptical press. On the eve of Asean's twentieth anniversary, a *Far Eastern Economic Review* cover-story carried the cruel heading, 'Who cares?' next to the Asean logo.

Even optimists like McCloud seem to accept that Asean's early promise has dimmed: 'economic cooperation or integration through such agreements as an Asean free-trade zone has not developed,' he says (1986). Although 'low-level economic adjustments have been made, Indonesia . . . has blocked significant progress.' A hard look at Asean's record shows that persistent economic realities belie the proclaimed achievements. Boasts about regional integration amount to a type of tailored trickery worthy of *The Emperor's New Clothes*. In this Hans Andersen story the vain king at least had ruled sovereign; by contrast, Asean near the beginning of the 1990s resembles a sleepy collection of do-nothing potentates parading in pantomime once a year.

Michael Leifer, a noted Southeast Asian analyst at the London School of Economics, says that Asean's 'declared primary goals of promoting economic growth . . . through regional cooperation have been realised only to a very limited extent.' In his 1989 study entitled *ASEAN and the Security of Southeast Asia*, Leifer notes that 'by 1987 trade among the six member states, whose combined populations comprise some 300 million, had amounted to no more than 17% of their total trade.'

Leifer remarks that the so-called PTAs, or 'preferential trading arrangements', only account 'for around 2% of that intra-Asean trade.' Even pro-Asean enthusiasts such as R. D. Palmer and T. J. Reckford, whose book *Building ASEAN: Twenty Years of Southeast Asian Cooperation* appeared in 1987, have acknowledged that 'one basic problem is that Asean trade is largely directed toward trading partners outside the region . . . trade among Asean countries only amounts to about 14% of total Asean trade.'

A Diplomatic Merry-go-round

In the time-honoured fashion, Asean has sought to fill its commercial emptiness with purposeful activity elsewhere. In particular it has puffed out its diplomatic agenda to fill the economic void. Asean's foreign ministers now meet their main external aid donors, who are called 'dialogue partners'. Foreign ministers from Australia, Canada, the European Community, Japan, New Zealand and the United States flock to these annual fêtes, all proclaiming the usefulness of 'keeping in touch'. And, to be fair, there has been much to talk about in regional security, especially in the aftermath of Vietnam's invasion of Cambodia in 1979.

Nor did these sessions entirely pass without achieving accords having economic substance. For example, real work has gone into an Asean ministerial 'trade preferences negotiating group' which lobbies the dialogue partners for improved trade access for such common Asean country products or commodities as textiles, semiconductors or vegetable oils. Similarly, a Japan-Asean Forum on Synthetic Rubber has also helped the Southeast Asians anxious to preserve their natural rubber exports to Japan.

Yet, once again, the 'externality' of these steps is readily observable; serious efforts for *internal* market-widening in Asean, which would have created a huge pool of over 300 million customers, have foundered year after year. Always eschewing bold moves, the Asean governments have opted instead for a type of near-paralytic caution. For example, a much ballyhooed 'common rule of origin' trading principle, aimed at giving margins of tariff preference to raw materials imported from Asean neighbours, turned out to be a bogus victory: each Asean member had already promised to do the same thing under the GATT.

The real trade concessions have come, not from within Asean, but from without: Australia, the European Community and America have extended to the Southeast Asian economies some of the world's most generous GSP terms. Only Japan has been reluctant to give concessions. In the mid-1980s, the Americans contemplated negotiating an 'Asean–US Initiative' similar to special trade arrangements reached between the US and Israel. Although the idea did not proceed because of internal Asean jealousies, Asean's exporters gained from America's GSP list of 2,800 duty-exempt items. Many of those gaining were Japanese-managed or -licensed firms, set up in Southeast Asia to avoid country-of-origin trading restrictions.

Still on the diplomatic front, Asean's ministers started after 1984 to make provision for various one-to-one, 'dialogue' chats. Every dialogue partner was welcome to sit in for round-table talks, except the European Community – an exclusion prompting EC Commissioner Claude Cheysson to remark tartly, when we met in 1985, that the 'Asean countries have now decided to run their own little club, to which they will now issue cards.' The core issue for the decade after 1979 was Cambodia, and the Vietnamese-armed intervention in that country. Trade and economic questions fell far down the list.

The business interests in the various dialogue countries, initially excited about regional commercial prospects, began to watch Asean in growing disappointment. They had hope for the possibility of an evolving, integrated market, the first such experiment in Asia. But these hopes soon proved forlorn. The track record for

Asean's internal regional business development should have warned even the most optimistic outsider.

A Record of Failure

Consider that record. Back in 1969 the grouping had set up an Asean Fund to administer US$1 million set aside by each member each year. The plan became moribund almost immediately. In 1977 another approach was tried when Japanese prime minister Takeo Fukuda offered US$1 billion to another development fund. He coupled this with an initial donation of US$20 million to finance a new breed of industrial projects. There were no takers.

These flops did not deter other moves. An under-used and under-publicised Asean Cultural Fund was next to emerge, again funded by the Japanese. Then an Asean Industrial Projects programme was unveiled in the 1970s; after a decade of operations only five projects had received finance. By 1989 only two of these, both of them fertiliser plants, had gone into operation.

Undaunted, Tokyo offered scholarships in 1980 and then, in 1983, it unveiled a Japan–Asean Cooperation Promotion Programme focusing on trade promotion. Then another Japanese prime minister, Zenko Suzuki, blessed a fund for 'human resources development' to which his government gave US$25 million. Quarrelling among Asean's member countries slowed the idea, which had puzzled the intended recipients anyway. Again most of the money was never spent. Publicly the Japanese retained their composure; privately they lamented the lack of even pro forma willingness to inject regionalism into the region.

Internally, within the region, the mania for meetings also produced little real commercial or business gain. Even the much-vaunted moves to improve regional financial and banking services came to comparatively little.

The Asean Finance Corporation

One such experiment was the Asean Finance Corporation, or AFC. Created in 1981 by the Asean Five (Brunei became the sixth member in 1984) the corporation was incorporated in Singapore and capitalised at US$100 million. This time the apparently serious intent and the obviously serious money made available by governments also prompted 140 private banks to pledge funds equivalent to the entirety of the AFC's authorised capital.

Seven years later, only fourteen Asean joint ventures had received money from the AFC, an operational performance of two loans a year. 'The AFC's performance through 1985 was poor, characterised by excess liquidity, slow rates of growth, high provision for doubtful loans and declining profitability,' researcher David Schulze noted in 1988. The total AFC assets at the end of 1986 'were actually US$5 million less than at the end of 1982.'

The AFC's profit-and-loss accounts by the end of the 1980s showed 'a rather dismal picture', Schulze continued. 'Total provision for bad loans accounted for nearly one-third of the AFC's total assets in 1986', a position that 'casts significant doubt on the quality of loans the AFC has been able to make.' Schulze concluded that 'ownership diffusion – no group owns a controlling interest – has resulted in a lack of commitment.' He added, harshly, that the AFC 'has yet to prove that it can either significantly increase the total volume of loanable funds available to Asean or to function aggressively as a merchant bank.'

The Bankers' Acceptance Scheme

The same lack of commitment characterised the next brainstorm from the Asean economic ministers. This time they gave their imprimatur to a plan for bankers' acceptance notes, known as ABAs, intended to facilitate a growth in Asean's intra-regional trade. Once again, the results were dismal. 'The failure of the ABA . . . stems from the low volume of intra-Asean trade and, hence, low demand for these instruments,' Schulze remarked.

The ABA idea had emerged initially as part of an Indonesian/Thai scheme using US$6 million in start-up capital to underwrite the use of any Asean local currency when used to buy goods from another Asean country. But not only was the market 'too small to be priced competitively,' as Michael Haas, a University of Hawaii researcher remarked in 1988, but 'cut-rate equivalents were available from New York banks as well.'

Similarly disappointing results have dogged an Asean Reinsurance Pool created in the 1980s. An emergency 'rice reserve scheme' also fizzled out, after price fluctuations and after the attainment by Indonesia of self-sufficiency in rice production and even, in some years, of a surplus. Under the scheme, each Asean member had undertaken to put aside 53,000 metric tonnes of rice in national stockpiles. The idea centred on the willingness of surplus production countries, such as Thailand, to sell to shortfall countries at preferential margins. The scheme was never used.

A Lack of Energy

Yet another disappointment has plagued the efforts to improve electricity sharing among the Asean countries. Despite the archipelagic nature of the area, an Asean grid would make much sense. First suggested back in 1968, the plans have not developed although various bilateral, and even one trilateral, power-sharing agreements have emerged. Still, the 'missed connections' outnumber these achievements: 'Asean has a lacklustre track record in energy cooperation,' says Serafin Talisyon, a Filipino specialist.

'The Asean Petroleum Sharing Agreement took a decade to be formalised,' he says. It also 'provides cause for healthy skepticism because it stipulates conditions which effectively give priority to exporters' pre-existing commitments . . . the major decisions by Asean economic ministers on energy have been to establish one committee and working group after another.' Enticed for several years into aiding ostensibly Asean-wide projects, such as a forestry project involving nationals from all the region, foreign donors quickly concluded that the individual Asean countries had no real intention of regionalising the projects.

Swaps

With each failed proposal hopes that Asean promised to become a vibrant economic grouping became ever more suspect. The closer one examined the efforts of pan-Asean business regionalism, the more obvious the chimera appeared. That is not to say that all the plans have failed; a currency swap arrangement became useful during the early 1980s, when the Philippines experienced an acute shortage of foreign currency.

Largely because of chronic balance-of-payments imbalances, Manila's central bank repeatedly used the swap – which committed each Asean central bank to set aside US$40 million. This money would fund currency swaps equivalent to a maximum of US$80 million whenever Manila experienced severe foreign exchange shortages. Even though the regional credit line stayed open for only three months at a time, the Philippines' neighbours did help, however minutely, during that country's acute foreign exchange crisis from 1983 to 1985.

Serious Proposals Ignored

As these examples suggest, Asean's chief productivity index is measured by generating paperwork. Each ministerial meeting sees a plethora of plans, which thereafter sag quickly into oblivion for want of interest by the business community and want of political will by their political patrons. Most businessmen distrust government-sponsored commerce, however ambitious its ambit; those that took the bait, as when Malaysia's prime minister became infatuated with Japanese-style business groupings, often found themselves out of pocket. The best thing was to carry on as normal.

Some businessmen have tried to be serious, however. Back in 1982 the former head of the Asean Chambers of Commerce and Industry, Anand Panyarachun, urged immediate steps towards making regional business a reality. He urged the free import and export of raw materials for designated 'Asean projects' and identical treatment to all investors from other Asean countries.

He also called for a 'liberal' approach to employing Asean nationals in predominantly Asean projects wherever sited and urged zero tariff costs for all Asean Industrial Projects. He argued for steps towards a common external tariff rate, for common financial instruments to give lower-cost financing for intra-Asean trade, for an Asean Payments Union and an Asean Export-Import Bank. He also suggested eliminating all restrictions preventing Asean banks from opening branches in other Asean countries. His was a voice in the wilderness: nothing has happened to these proposals since 1982.

Industrial Complementation Fizzles Out

More than any other plan, the fate of 'Asean Industrial Complementation', or AIC, illustrates the enervating lack of will at the top. The idea was that each member country would specialise by producing component parts for a larger product, with entry guaranteed by preferential tariffs. Years of negotiations occurred before just one project, a plan to make automotive assembly parts, got under way.

What were the results? By 1985, annual trade under all AIC categories totalled US$1 million, a tiny fraction of external trade. This trivial result came almost entirely from the manufacture of a type of engine drive belt.

The AIC negotiations became preoccupied with the automotive proposals. Faced with uncertainties about marketing the final product, Singapore withdrew from a promise to build a diesel engine plant under the AIC scheme. Although the attitude of this intensely business-minded city-state mirrored the real feelings among business firms about the prospects for the AIC idea, the remaining Asean governments persevered with fitful planning for a regional motorcar manufacturing scheme.

At first there still seemed to be some chance of success. 'Further discussions among the . . . principal automotive manufacturers and their Asean franchise-holders were held in Jakarta in November 1983,' according to an account by T. Pawitra, director of PT Star Motors, a large franchise-holder in Indonesia for German cars. Yet 'meanwhile,' he said, 'Malaysia had decided to produce its own automobile, a serious blow to the complementation schemes.'

Never to be discouraged for long, Asean's economic ministers soon plunged into yet another idea, this one called 'Asean Industrial Joint Ventures', or AIJVs. The notion was that joint venture partners would win from their home governments a promise of preferential market access for products *not already being manufactured*. At last this seemed a way of avoiding the entrenched monopolists and licensees. Or was it?

After 1983, the joint venture project proposals centred on such exotica as plans for the production of 'rack-and-pinion steering mechanisms' or 'constant velocity joints'. Other proposals surfaced for joint venture manufacturing of motorcycle cables, high-quality security-grade document paper or even for building cattle slaughterhouses. Each idea had to win approval from Asean ministers, a major effort since Asean's cumbersome decision-making process requires a complete consensus, even on small details. Thus, once again, most of the joint venture plans slipped away, or became plagued by delay and investor second-thoughts.

Praise Where Praise Is Due?

None of this litany of misadventure has inhibited a growing army of respectful, and mainly foreign academicians from praising Asean to the skies. The American chambers of commerce created various US/Asean business councils while foreign governments promoted technology exchange committees. Both the US and the European Community signed multilateral economic cooperation agreements, as did Japan, although these contained very little of substance.

As the Asian affairs analyst Hans Indorf remarked in 1987 'topics discussed during the first US-Asean dialogue still appeared on the agenda for the seventh dialogue in 1986 . . . America's relations with Asean are positive yet only minimally productive.' An economist at West Germany's Kiel Institute of World Economics, Rolf Langhammer (1988) meanwhile has taken a hard look at Asean's commercial and trade pretensions.

Asean Trade Diplomacy: How Successful Really?

Langhammer claims that 'due to the large discrepancies between Asean and the European Community with regard to domestic market size, the Asean countries have been . . . free riders, receiving concessions negotiated by the "Big Three" [that is, the European Community, the US and Japan] . . . rather than being equivalent negotiators.' Langhammer and other analysts are now taking the view that the Asean region has grown passively, benefiting from currents in the world economy that luckily flowed in Southeast Asia's direction during two indulgent decades.

Much of the outside world's commercial misunderstanding about Asean results from a bewildering number of groups and programmes, committees and communiqués. It all looks very busy and purposeful. Some of the activity makes a difference; most does not. Various committees of the Asean economic ministers discuss collaborative ideas in finance and banking; in industry, minerals and energy; in trade and tourism, and in transportation and communications.

'Discuss' seems the operative word. One specialist claims that, in a typical year in the 1980s, 'eight permanent committees were supported by nine subcommittees, and seventy-three "expert/working groups"; . . . in all, two hundred and sixty meetings and project activities took place during 1984' alone.

For all this bustle however, the Asean economies have moved further away from one another over the last decade. Only in trade access diplomacy have there been real gains, but this has nothing to do with harmonising internal markets. The GATT, the temporary success of commodity cartel agreements, and the round of talks fostered by the UN Conference on Trade and Development in the 1960s and 1970s – these and other exercises have given Asean external cohesion.

Yet even its external links often have less substance than meets the eye; for example, a 1980 Asean–EC cooperation agreement simply promises that each grouping will 'consult' with the other before taking trade measures that might affect the other grouping. No exclusive economic ties are created. In trading with Europe, every matter of real trade substance is negotiated bilaterally, between the EC Commission in Brussels and each jealous Southeast Asian country.

Even the GATT's so-called negotiation 'counters', which are expressly designed for multilateral trade diplomacy, have been haphazardly used by the Asean countries. This applies even with such obviously common issues as a threatened EC tariff on vegetable oils. Restrictions from Brussels on textile exports, another important Asean area industry, were revised only after bilaterally negotiated 'self-restraint agreements'. So much for the claims of 'one Asean voice' abroad.

The lack of real regional, commercial consensus becomes apparent in other issues. Asean's influence may be wildly overstated. Langhammer describes trade deals in which Brazil, South Korea and Hong Kong were also striving for continuing access to Japanese, US and EC markets. Initially these countries appeared to do less well than the Asean Six in gaining duty-free exemptions for their exports.

On closer examination however, Langhammer found 'there is no evidence that Asean as a *unit* revealed better collective lobbying power than other suppliers, which lobbied individually.' Even the supposed model of coordinated Asean trade diplomacy, a multi-fibre self-restraint agreement limiting textile imports into the EC, now appears to be little better than the result of a zero-sum game.

In this game of access therefore, some Asean country producers gained and others lost, in almost equal measure. But Asean per se won neither privileged nor permanent trade access; by comparison, other regional economic groupings dealing with Brussels, such as the European Free Trade Association (EFTA) countries or the Lomé Convention states (which comprise most of the ex-colonies of EC countries in Africa) did far better.

The Reasons Why

The basic explanation for these persistent gaps between aspiration and business reality is simple: the propaganda about Asean portrays the grouping as a potential or embryonic regional marketplace – something which the region's politicians and their business cronies have no intention of allowing to happen. Free trade within this tropical Asian archipelago would upset far too many comfortable monopolies and cornered import agencies.

Truly free, or even minimally constrained entry for regionally produced manufactures would also hurt each country's lavishly nurtured but often poorly performing 'infant industries'. The falsely named 'Malaysian Car Project' is a perfect example of a coddled business destined for quick insolvency if a genuine common market ever tears down protective tariff and tax barriers.

Quite apart from this, however, economic nationalists in each Asean country have other reasons for fearing a dismantling of intra-Asean trade barriers. They see the victor in a truly free market tussle as invariably the enterprise most adroitly backed by foreign capital (read: Japanese) in league with non-indigenous retailing networks (read: overseas Chinese) and benefiting from generous licensing agreements (read: native politicians in cahoots with both of these demons).

It is thus no paradox, the nationalists say, that Japan strongly supports a wider Asean marketplace while nationalist-minded businessmen spurn even the vague promise of a bigger Asean market as a device to help Japanese corporations to consolidate their position. Yet this may happen anyway, in view of the colossal direct investment flows out of Japan after 1985.

Because no independent authority resides in Asean, unlike the European Community, its machinery for making decisions is painfully slow. The real power remains tightly held by each member country; diplomats tend to be distant from matters of commerce at the best of times, and Asean's performance lends credence to this time-tested rule. In a review of the 1987 Asean summit, Donald Crone said that as 'the agenda proposals ascended the political ladder from theorists and business managers to government ministers, the more integrative measures were simply culled out.'

In truth the grouping's utility is primarily as a diplomatic device, while increasing regional trade comes far down the list of priorities, despite the communiqués. Every trifling protocol to recognise one another's driving licences dodges the real issue: will a wider market emerge, or is the opposite happening?

Asean Be Damned: When Necessary

Much evidence points the other way. Decisions since 1980 by most Asean countries to impose exit visa restrictions, and to tax foreign travel without regard to final destination, severely hampered intra-Asean movement of people. Another example: unilateral moves in the mid-1980s to slap huge tariff increases on cement imports said more about Malaysia's commitment to regional trade than a hundred communiqués.

All the 'integrative' exercises thus cannot disguise a stubbornly national bias in Asean. Praise from outsiders bestows what the grouping does not deserve and may never attain, despite grand talk, like that from Malaysian prime minister Mahathir Mohamad, who envisages united Asean markets as a step towards a 'new Pacific economic locomotive'. The truth is that no common institutions have emerged in Southeast Asia that have a scrap of independent life.

Industrialists from Europe, America and Japan none the less have flocked to pay court. Various Asean Business Councils did service to the idea, if not the reality. Asean promised much that was new. While European business writers predict a new common market, Japanese commentators more accurately discern a fancy new dress for (temporary) regional stability. Meanwhile, the American business press is pursuing the notion that Asean contains another raft of ever-more-efficient Asian market economies, now conveniently grouped in one acronym. Asean's biggest growth industry seems to be enthusiastic foreign reportage.

Preparations for the 1987 Summit

By the late 1980s therefore, the facile game of Asean make-believe had taken on a shopworn look. Before the heads of government consented to meet each other for 65 minutes in Manila in December 1987, eighteen months had gone into preparing another batch of economic initiatives. This time, the economic ministers and their myriad working parties assured themselves, some real, forward motion would be achieved. The summit had been delayed for ten years because of Malaysia's refusal to go to Manila, the prearranged site of the summit, until and unless the Philippines renounced its claim to Sabah.

The committees generated enormous paperwork. The arguments for free-trade areas, customs unions and even a full economic union were gone over again. Only Singapore and, perhaps, Brunei have a commitment to genuine free trade. The others reinforce the truism that Asean comprises countries with competitive, not complementary economies. Indonesia, Malaysia, Philippines and Thailand grow the same tea, coffee, coconuts, palm oil, tobacco, sugar, spices, timber, rubber and cocoa.

That is only the start of the competitive problem. All of them, plus Singapore too, manufacture or process cement, urea, nitrogenous fertilisers, steel, crude oil and textiles. Most have heavily protected light and medium industries, mostly working under licence. And even Singapore's devotion to the free market falters on the principle of free movement of labour. This is unacceptable to the racially conscious island republic, which has mandated expulsion of *all* foreign workers (which comprise domestic helpers from the Philippines and industrial workers from neighbouring Indonesia and Malaysia) by the early 1990s.

While much progress has occurred in developing intra-Asean trade (see Table 8), the figures are often misleading. In the continuing debate about regional commerce, lies, damned lies and Asean trade statistics predominate. Most of all, approximately one-sixth of all trade flow noted as occurring within the region results from commodity flows; Thai rice goes to Indonesia, Indonesian and Malaysian oil goes to Singaporean refineries prior to onward shipment to Japan or California.

Commodity processing or even transhipment helps keep Singapore rich. Special, one-off sales of oil to Thailand in times of scarcity as a brotherly gesture have

Table 8   Intra-Asean trade (% of national totals)

Country	Exports to other Aseans	Imports from other Aseans
Indonesia	11.4	14.0
Malaysia	26.0	19.5
Philippines	9.7	11.6
Singapore	21.9	17.9
Thailand	14.1	13.7

SOURCE: International Monetary Fund, 1985

occurred. But the data reflecting these and other flows must not deceive us into believing that variegated, balanced intra-regional trade is blossoming. Far from it.

Some Straight Talk

Ten months before before the Manila summit, specialists on these issues met in Singapore. The Institute of Southeast Asian Studies, or ISEAS, published the results of their colloquium (1987), perhaps the clearest-headed meeting about Asean's regional business prospects for many years.

'Asean countries owe their prosperity to trade and investment links with the outside world,' the assembled economists and businessmen said flatly. Thus 'the ideal of Asean economic cooperation is to create an outward-looking economic area with compatible economic policies, constituting a powerful production unit and permitting continuous expansion.' This is the right emphasis.

But given the 'wide diversity of trade regimes among Asean countries', the only realisable goal is an 'Asean Trade Area', the group said, achievable over ten years. They argued that this was realistic timing. But even this move, timid by comparison with market creation in other regions such as Europe, North America or Australasia, requires elaborate 'tariff restructuring formulae' to make it work. And even these, the gathered businessmen and economists said, would allow 'each [Asean] country to establish levels of protection appropriate to their development needs.'

Asean's most tangible achievement in trade has been the creation of 'preferential trading arrangements' or PTAs, covering an impressively long list of traded items attracting reduced tariff charges if they were 'non-sensitive'. But the 18,000 PTA items have earned that appellation precisely because they are minor and, usually, non-traded. Sixty-five per cent of Thailand's traded items, for example, are exempt from the PTA system; nothing that might remotely threaten each country's domestic industries has been allowed to reach the tariff-cutting lists.

The Manila Summit: So What?

The summit took place in Manila in December 1987, under bizarre circumstances. Fearing efforts by President Corazon Aquino's opponents to disrupt the occasion,

Asean governments sent their own security teams. Indonesia even dispatched frigates to anchor in Manila Bay.

The summit itself resulted, inevitably, in the unveiling of more promises of economic integration. The heads of government said they had decided to streamline the Asean Industrial Joint Ventures, in which new projects with at least 40 per cent equity held in the region will get tariff breaks. They raised the equity level to 60 per cent.

At Manila the proclaimed aim became an Asean 'trade community' by 1992, with PTAs giving 50 per cent tariff margins while lowering the Asean local content requirements needed to win this favoured treatment to just 35 per cent. Brunei, which has no industrial base, chose to stay uninvolved. Indonesia is already acting, since Manila, as a drag on rapid progress while Singapore, which has almost no tariffs any more, will keep its free port status. This left only three of the Asean Six with any real interest in the reforms: the Philippines, Malaysia and Thailand.

The 1987 summit predictably endorsed these long-discussed steps to take the region towards substantive economic collaboration. Predictably also, the measures carefully avoided dramatic moves towards such exotica as a hybrid customs union or a free trading zone. The four agreements, signed under intense security arrangements in a cordoned-off convention centre, aimed to harmonise investment guarantees, to put half of Asean's intra-regional trade into the PTA scheme, to expand existing margins-of-preference tariff schemes for industrial joint ventures and finally, to freeze and gradually to reduce non-tariff barriers to intra-Asean trade.

Of all of these long-negotiated, timid steps, the move to bring 50 per cent of intra-Asean trade within the PTA system seemed the most ambitious step. The others broke little new ground. The margin of preference in Asean's PTA system had given an insignificant 5 per cent. The 1987 pact, if implemented (a big 'if'), will cut back by 1992 the exemptions to the PTA list to 'not more than 50 per cent of the value' of intra-Asean trade while chopping back the exclusion lists (which now have 9,000 important exceptions) to just 10 per cent of the total *number* of traded items.

New 'rules of origin', which determine realistically how much a product can claim a 'made-in-Asean' label, will supposedly bring more categories of industrial products into the PTA system. Finally, a minimum margin of preference of 25 per cent should speed up the changeover.

Another Charade?

But will it? Every key industrial and investment decision made by these governments over two decades flies in the face of their regional rhetoric. Autarchy, not regionalism, claims their attention. *Dirigiste* thinking still dominates. Their commodity-based economies did not complement each other; in industrial investment they intensified this competitiveness.

As a confidential, Asean-commissioned study in 1984 reported, the 'emergency [rice and oil sharing] schemes are possible because Thailand is a rice surplus country . . . and because Indonesia and Malaysia are petroleum producers. On the other hand, the industrial structures of each [member] country are similar; at present they produce similar goods or plan to do so in the future.' Nothing has changed since 1987. Even the petroleum sharing scheme was really, to quote from one report, 'a nice political idea' because of Indonesia's membership of OPEC.

Other moves did little to change this basic business landscape of complementarity. Eliminating ambiguity in intra-Asean investment rules, both for any type of investor in a neighbouring country, to specific changes to the Asean Industrial Joint Venture (AIJV) concept, has gone nowhere apart from investments in some fertiliser plants that have chronically lost money.

Singapore soon saw the futility of the exercise, and showed its level of interest by cutting planned equity (in an AIJV methanol plant in Bintulu, in Sarawak) from 20 to 1 per cent. Another agreement just dressed up earlier trading commitments in a new guise. Dismantling non-tariff barriers to intra-Asean trade looked good – until analysts realised that the immediate undertaking by the Six in their 'standstill' agreement at Manila (which has them promising not to 'introduce new or additional non-tariff measures which would impede intra-Asean trade') did not commit the region to doing one iota more than the countries separately had promised to do at the 'Montevideo Round' of the Multilateral Tariff Negotiations in Uruguay the same year.

The 1987 agreements supposedly creating an Asean Trade Community show plenty of loopholes. The memorandum enables any of the Six to withdraw from keeping its standstill or 'rollback' promises; one clause allows suspension of promises 'if imports . . . are increasing in such a manner as to cause or threaten to cause serious injury to sectors producing like or similar products.' The word 'injury' for this purpose meant 'actual or potential decline in output, sales, market share, profits, productivity, return on investments or utilisation of capacity.' A more widely drafted escape clause would be hard to find. And the accord, inevitably perhaps, also allows 'protection of deserving infant industries.'

Promises to 'phase out or eliminate non-tariff measures', (the so-called 'rollback' option), also came in Manila without any timetable for reductions. Even a much publicised agreement to give Asean national investors 'no less favourable' treatment 'than that granted to investors' with the normal most-favoured-nation status added little or nothing that was not already there for outsiders. Not content with this, the Six specifically put 'taxation matters' outside the reciprocal investor treatment agreement. It would be hard to identify an aspect of investment more crucial to decision-making than a new firm's tax position.

For a grouping that runs strictly by consensus, the test for these cautious steps now lies in whether continuing political will would carry them on to completion by 1995. Halfway across the world, the European Community, already light-years down the integrative road by comparison, has set itself a fully common market as a goal to achieve by 1992. The Closer Economic Relations pact between Australia and New Zealand is ahead of its original, free market creating timetable. The North American free trade arrangement has survived electoral challenge in Canada and may, before the end of the century, embrace Mexico.

Whether Asean will manage its much more modest proposal remains unclear, but the immediate signs are not promising. Against these broad undertakings the petty but pressing alarms of vulnerable infant industries, special-pleaders and monopolists have already surfaced. The key indicator of how serious the region is lies in whether the Asean Six will keep to their strict, five-year timetable for increasing the margin of preference in the PTA traded items to 50 per cent.

Invest Now, If . . .

If they do, then outside businessmen should start cementing licensing and joint venture arrangements for the longer term. The litmus test comes in measuring rhetoric against achievement in bringing their competitive markets into closer alignment. 'Are they ready to accept some kind of regulatory mechanism like the Brussels Commission?' a Singaporean minister asked me rhetorically at the 1987 summit. He doubted it.

Although a few of the 1987 summit decisions had designated the mainly paper-shuffling Asean Secretariat as a 'surveillance body' to monitor the agreements, the intent seemed to make the Jakarta-based bureaucrats more of a registry and less of a regulator in their own right. This continued disdain (or suspicion) of their own creation contrasted with the call of the economists from the Institute of Southeast Asian Studies (1987) for a 'special Asean body to monitor non-tariff barriers', and to 'adjudicate and arbitrate in conflicts arising from the liberalisation policies.'

At Manila there was not a hint of other measures promoted by a private business group, the 'Group of Fourteen', which urged relaxing intra-Asean travel formalities, greater mobility of labour, 'standardising educational accreditation' and introducing other Asean languages into business schools. Just getting the Asean Six to their third summit required more than one-and-a-half years of negotiation.

A cumbersome, public/private jumble of committees and working groups is one problem; another is that tough issues cannot be fudged any longer. One of these is the hoary old problem of assessing, for tariff calculation purposes, the local content of manufactured imports from other Asean countries. It is not enough to want to liberalise this trade; differential tariffs must either be imposed or not.

The Japanese Dimension

Yet the dithering continues. The knowledgeable Southeast Asians realise who will become the real beneficiaries of these preferential arrangements. It is no accident that Japanese-licensed or Japanese joint venture manufacturing businesses are promoting the expansion of PTAs. Matsushita subsidiaries or Nissan's local plants will lobby long and hard for local content rules agreeable enough to give their wares preferential access.

Thus, at the end of the day, even Asean's timid steps forward may do little more than advance work for yet another wave of Japanese industrial penetration of regional markets. The orchestration of calls for 'market-widening' in Asean have already begun. For example, Reiichi Shimamoto, the deputy president of Japan's Export-Import Bank, told a Manila audience in 1988 that Japan wants Asean to 'create a broader market for area producers [which will] promote direct investment taking advantage of intra-regional integration'. The ultimate beneficiaries, as the region's economic nationalists suspect, are not that hard to discern.

When it finally convened, the December 1987 Manila summit welcomed just one foreign visitor, a sharp contrast to the normal inclusion at the foreign ministers' gatherings of all Asean's dialogue partners. The sole invitee? Japan's prime minister, Noboru Takeshita.

The reasons for this special honour were clear. Asian economic realities had now reached a point where all the region's leaders had no doubt about which country stood 'first among equals'. After 1985 the yen held increasingly triumphant sway over the region. Takeshita's presence signalled more about the shape of the future Asean marketplace than all the summit's trumpeted accords aimed at creating an internal trade community.

Despite the fireworks however, Japan's US$2 billion birthday present to Asean's twentieth anniversary summit in Manila simply reaffirmed Tokyo's propensity to reach into its pocket; the maverick economist and Malaysian government adviser Kenichi Ohmae in March 1989 even criticised this propensity 'to throw money at Southeast Asia without thinking first'. Prime Minister Takeshita's Asean-Japan Development Fund like its many predecessors had the look of a package rather too rapidly cobbled together.

As time went on, the fund's purposes became more evident. A 3 per cent concessionary inducement went way beyond the more modest proposals received in Tokyo from Singapore's prime minister Lee Kuan Yew during 1987. Embroiled in their balance-of-payments diplomacy with the US, the Japanese found Lee's plan as one more way to recycle money. Singapore's diplomats hoped that the fund would be disbursed 'equally', codetalk for allowing Singapore to dip into the funds if necessary. But Tokyo would only agree to an 'equitable' use for the money, codetalk for a strong bias towards the failing Philippines.

Could the right projects be found? Japanese public opinion had seethed after Marcos's fall from a barrage of stories about Japanese multinational corporations paying the dictator or his cronies to do business, and keep business. It soon became apparent that the latest Asean fund from Tokyo had become, with Asean consensus, a thinly disguised booster programme to lubricate the slowly awakening Philippine economy. Yet Manila could not digest the money; by mid-1989 the amount of already committed aid – outright grants or concessionary money offers – stood at a staggering US$ 4.3 billion dollars just from Manila's 'Big Four' donors: Japan, the US, the Asian Development Bank and the World Bank.

The Regional Vacuum

For a region with two-thirds of the world's population, Asia lags behind the rest of the world in the creation of vibrant, regional institutions. The Asian Development Bank remains stuck in the groove of the role it narrowly defines for itself: building capital infrastructure. Still, the ADB does have a type of near-universality and a common institutional 'presence' in Asia. (See Chapter 10.)

In Southeast Asia, Asean goes through the motions of putative importance, substituting a complex committee structure for substantive economic achievement. What else is there of regional importance for outsiders doing business in the region or for the Southeast Asians themselves? The list of regional economic groupings is embarrassingly short, even for specialised industries or interest groups.

The professional associations bearing an 'Asean' tag have mostly degenerated into rarely convened social clubs having little clout and even less intention to apply it to dealings with national governments. An International Tropical Timber Organisation, centred in Yokohama, concerns itself with prices for tropical timber yet it also includes countries from outside Asia. What else reveals regionalism? A Southeast Asian Ministers of Education Organisation, known by the awkward acronym SEAMEO, runs a sleepy regional language centre in Singapore.

Not very impressive, is it? After completing a survey of Southeast Asian institutions, a sneaking suspicion begins to appear. Could this striking dearth of regional organisations suggest that there is little about which to be 'regional'? In an analysis (1986) of Asean's 'Four Farms', an Australian National University economist, Helen Hughes, made the point in another way: 'Although those four countries are often considered as the second most rapidly growing group after the NICs [that is, the newly industrialising countries comprising Hong Kong, Singapore, South Korea and Taiwan], and frequently regarded as "near-NICs", their economies are in fact very diverse.'

As the substance behind Southeast Asian regionalism becomes clearer, Gertrude Stein's description of Oakland, California seems ever more appropriate; 'the problem about being there', she is supposed once to have written, 'is there is no there, there.' But an even more germane question is waiting to be asked: why should Asean become a broader economic unit? John Wong, an economist at the National University of Singapore, snipes at the very idea of regional business in Asean.

'Economic cooperation in the Third World sometimes assumes value overtones that dwarf' such basics as 'inefficiency of use and pooling of resources,' he has written (quoted in Kintaner and Tan, 1986). 'Regional economic cooperation is commonly viewed . . . as a "good thing",' he says, but finds good financial and economic reasons why this may be misconceived. Looking at the seemingly endless list of unsuccessful Asean economic plans, Wong notes that

in Asean, as in many other Third World regional groupings, not many industries could be competitive at world market prices *even if* all the national markets in the region were fully integrated [emphasis added].

Taken as a whole, the [Asean] package deal approach was conceptually sound and theoretically appealing; in practice . . . it [was] difficult to identify economically viable projects that also passed the test of political acceptability.

At root lies one unchanging fact of life, a political unwillingness to take the economic integrative process any distance down the road.

Game Playing

In a 1988 issue of the *Asean Economic Bulletin*, a visiting foreign academic described the negotiation of Asean trade preferences as a 'game'. He said 'the game of Asean is a so-called "non-cooperative" game . . . the result is that, unless *all* players agree to do something, it is not done.'

Perhaps the effort would be futile, whatever the amount of political will. 'The reality is that external forces can only be counteracted at great cost,' note Mohamad Ariff and Hal Hill in their *Export-oriented Industrialisation: the Asean Experience*, published in 1985. H. Edward English, another authority on Asean-area economics, describes (1988) the inescapable 'basics' of Southeast Asian business life, including 'the resource intensity of all the national economies except Singapore', plus the lucky windfall of oil price rises in the 1970s and the 'arrival of the electronic age with technical characteristics leading to vertical segregation of production of low-weight-per-value components' made by Asean's cheap labour.

English also tilts at the pretensions of a region-wide, Southeast Asian economic community. Despite the incessant talk of a future Asean free trade area, 'the most remarkable feature of [the various published] tables of nominal and effective [tariff] protection rates . . . is how little change occurs overall in the levels of Asean protection.'

It is beginning to be understood just how vulnerable these Asean economies are. A secret memo prepared for Ronald Reagan's visit to Bali in May 1986 predicted that, 'unless economic growth can be nurtured and developed, Asean support for democratic ideals and institutions may be undermined and can cause [it] to be vulnerable to external and internal threats.' In other words, regionalism may depend entirely on continuing founts of wealth flowing in from outside donors and outside markets.

Others Play Games Too

Asean's economic side-stepping mirrors the experience of just about every Third World economic grouping. Who remembers the Latin American Free Trade Association, the Central American Common Market, the Andean Pact or the Caribbean Community? Others, of this genre included the Central African Customs Union, the East African Community and the Economic Community of the West African States.

Like most of them, Asean is more a creature of intent than substance. Antonio Periquet of the Philippines, one of the businessmen pleading in vain for real market liberalisation, has described Asean's sterile superstructure as 'leaving the uninformed observer with the impression that the organisation is bustling with cooperative undertakings . . . A broad survey of the files however will quickly unmask the unfortunate reality: beneath the impressive bureaucratic paraphernalia', he said, 'there has been scant progress.'

The Future as an Extension of the Past

It is difficult to disagree with Donald Crone, a specialist in Asean economics, who wrote in 1988 that 'the future of Asean is essentially an extension of its past. Extreme caution and the careful maintenance of governmental control will continue in regional economic affairs.'

The 1988 *Asia Yearbook*, published by the *Far Eastern Economic Review* in Hong Kong, put it another way: 'relations with the [Western industrial countries] remained steady but had more form than substance,' it said. 'Part of the problem centred on Asean's structure, with a plethora of committees, but little in the way of a single corporate authority.' The yearbook continued by noting that

[the] one fundamental factor which hampers the Six in seeking their elusive goal of economic integration is a lack of political will. While there is plenty

of that in forming a joint diplomatic front over such issues as Cambodia, it appears to evaporate when members are confronted with a challenge to subvert their selfish national economic interests for the common regional good.

Five levels of commercial cooperation can be attained in an ideal world of evolving regional trading blocs, either in lock step, one after the other, or by moving immediately to higher levels of free marketeering.

These stages range from simple preferential trading arrangements through a limited free trade area and on to a full free trade area. Thereafter a grouping can opt to go on to a customs union and, finally, to establish a real common market such as that targeted for 1992 by the European Community. Despite twenty years of incessant talk, Asean has moved only partially, with many reservations, into the first category.

Leifer has concentrated on the diplomatic history of Asean, the area of its most important usefulness. He reminds us (1989) that

Asean's record is one of mixed achievement. It has displayed a facility to sustain quasi-friendships [but] . . . there is an absence of interest in transforming [it] into a different kind of corporate entity . . . [It] has the natural defects of its inherent qualities, which cannot be overcome by any indulgence in symbolic forms of achievement.

Most of all, Leifer emphasises that Asean began its corporate life as a '*diplomatic device for subregional reconciliation* [my italics].' Nothing has fundamentally changed since then, except the largely unsuccessful attempt to make the running on the diplomacy surrounding the Cambodian problem, a diplomacy which, perhaps inevitably, would also be directed by the outsiders to whom the region's markets must also respond so often. Remembering these basic circumstances, and looking ahead to the turbulent leadership changes now beginning in the Asean countries, those hoping for a regional market millenium in tropical Asia must prepare themselves for a long wait.

References

Ariff, M. and Hill, H. (1985) *Export-oriented Industrialisation: the ASEAN Experience.* Sydney: Allen & Unwin

Crone, D. (1988) 'The ASEAN summit of 1987: searching for new dynamism', in *Southeast Asian Affairs 1988*, the annual yearbook of the Institute of Southeast Asian Studies. Singapore: ISEAS

English, H. E. (1988) 'Dynamic comparative advantage and the search for a coherent industrial policy in ASEAN', *Asean Economic Bulletin*, vol. 5, No. 1

Hughes, H. (1986) 'Asian and Pacific developing countries: performance and issues', *Asian Development Review*, vol. 4, No. 1

Institute of Southeast Asian Studies (1987) *The Way Forward: the Report of the Group of Fourteen on ASEAN Economic Cooperation and Integration.* Singapore: ISEAS

Kintanar, A. and Tan, L. E. (1986) *ASEAN–US Economic Relations: an Overview.* Singapore: ISEAS

Langhammer, R. J. (1988) 'EEC trade policies towards Asian developing countries', *Asian Development Review*, vol. 6, No. 1

Leifer, M. (1989) *ASEAN and the Security of Southeast Asia*. London and New York: Routledge

McCloud, D. G. (1986) *System and Process in Southeast Asia*. Boulder, Colorado: Westview Press

Palmer, R. D. and Reckford, T. J. (1987) *Building ASEAN: Twenty Years of Southeast Asian Cooperation*. New York: Praeger

Schulze, D. L. (1988) 'The ASEAN Finance Corporation', *Asean Economic Bulletin*, vol. 5, No. 1

12

THE CLOUDED FUTURE

Steady as She Goes?

An afterburn of success still surrounds Southeast Asia's market economies as the twenty-first century approaches. Yet a mood of stubborn wariness also persists among the region's business communities. Why?

At first glance this uneasiness seems oddly at variance with data showing how well the Asean countries have weathered the sharp recessions during the 1980s. Indeed, their regained growth rates as the 1990s begin almost mirror the first, headlong expansion of their economies during the 1970s.

Certainly, in the eyes of most foreign investors at least, commercial success continues to bestow a halo-like aura on these archipelagic Asian countries. Even at the nadir of business confidence, at mid-decade point in the 1980s, outside specialists still pronounced that all was well. Southeast Asia specialist Gareth Porter said in 1985 that, except for the Philippines, the Asean countries were 'self-confident, economically dynamic and internally stable.'

This reputation has a strong hold. For example, an assessment at the end of 1988 for the US Agency for International Development ranked 'investment climate' in ninety-five countries. Asian countries took four of the top nine slots; two of the top-rankers, Singapore and Thailand (first and fifth place respectively), are Asean states. Although less trumpeted, Indonesia's position in that survey (forty-fifth), or the Philippines (nineteenth), still stood up well against most African or Latin American economies.

The World in Flux

Memories are short. Few in the early 1980s would have forseen Thailand's meteoric rise to this favoured pre-eminence or, two decades earlier, would have presumed as much for Singapore, then an abandoned starveling after an unhappy period in federation with Malaysia. No matter which regional country is favoured by current investor fashion, Southeast Asia's business success in the long term will ride or fall on three factors: stable politics, a vibrant world economy and, most of all, pass-it-around patrimonial habits.

Only the last factor seems well assured of indefinite currency; large question marks now hang over the other two. One by one, there are various challenges appearing to confront the easy expectations of continuing boom. The remainder of this chapter deals with the trends and transitions, both locally and globally, that cloud the region's future.

These include the prospect of renewed recession in major foreign markets, the accumulated effect of stockmarket crashes in December 1985 and in October 1987, and higher interest rates. Political uncertainties hang over the regimes in Indonesia, Malaysia and, in a much more contained sense, in Singapore as well. In an institutional sense, questions must surround the survival, in their present form, of the Brunei and Thai monarchies, and of the irresponsible élite now governing the Philippines.

Yet, for all their importance, these are merely short-term worries. Farther down the road lie structural changes now remaking the nature of industrial society around the world. Traditional commodity demand patterns are also changing, for reasons that include changes in diet, in production costs and in the substitution of new materials.

Yet these, also, form only part of the darkening picture. In addition the region must contend with ever more volatile exchange rates that have already altered the region's debt burden, usually with negative effect. Declining oil prices are derailing the fast-growth dreams of the Indonesians and other petroleum producers in Southeast Asia. True, Singapore and Thailand are awash in foreign investor funds, but slackening investment applications trouble their laggard Asean neighbours. Many local businessmen live in the shadow of persistent uncertainty: currency devaluation risks or portended political upheaval are just two of these.

Looking back, it is clear that twenty years of free-riding on the world economy paid large dividends to these trade minded economies. Yet this era, now in flux, also created a mounting agenda of problems for the region's easy-going, commercial culture. Free-riding, or 'rent-seeking' by another name, remains the favoured commercial norm, a tried and tested road to wealth – so long as financial and commodity markets outside the region continue to pour enough wealth through the cornucopia.

The impending third millennium presages basic, and unwelcome changes for this style of business culture. Before the end of the 1990s, the political leadership in nearly every Asean country is destined to pass from the scene. Just one year after Porter's steadying words in 1985, economist Hans Christoph Rieger took a decidedly more sombre view of the future. 'The optimism and confidence encountered in the "fastest growing region of the world" has given way', he said (1986), 'to pessimism and gloom over the prospects for further growth.'

If this view is correct, then the business turnaround of the late 1980s amounts to little more than a reprieve from underlying, and essentially negative trends. That Southeast Asia's commercial prospects should still be a matter of debate is, in itself, somewhat surprising; with as much land as India and many more people than in North America, this free marketeering region should already have taken a commanding place in the Asia Pacific.

Less flattering but more specific data than trade figures bolster a dissenting assessment of the region's prospects. In particular, doubt must surround claims that Asean is well on the road to achieving self-generating industrial growth, fuelled by indigenous technology and serviced by indigenous skills. Earlier chapters have offered much of this contrary view and it remains only to sketch some of the less encouraging trends now apparent throughout the region.

Inexorable Growth of Another Kind

All of Southeast Asia, except perhaps Malaysia, faces severe risk of human over-crowding. Even Malaysia seems eager, under its present leadership and within the context of its enervating ethnic calculations, to fill in its blank and forested spaces by a pro-procreation policy aimed at breeding 70 millions during the next century. In Singapore 2.7 million people crowd a territory, only a fraction of the size of neighbouring Indonesia. In Thailand the population has grown threefold in the last half-century; even its birth control successes during the 1980s cannot halt the demographic momentum spawning a 3 per cent growth in the labour market each year for the rest of the century. On Java and Bali, the old Malthusian nightmares recurringly haunt the export-led orthodoxy of Indonesia's technocrats.

In the checklist of any investor, the region's human numbers game must take first place. More people mean bigger local markets, to be sure, and the Japanese above all others have never forgotten how useful a large demand base can be when setting up their export-oriented factories. Inexorably rising numbers also presage slipping standards, inundated educational systems, declining health standards and dreadfully overcrowded cities, however. The imbalance between rural and urban opportunity is vivid in Bangkok, Manila and other regional cities, as is their overload on road and rail in the region's cities.

The implications of this growth are simple enough to comprehend, and abating rural population pressures and land hunger obviously requires work opportunities to be created elsewhere. This can only come through an industrial base that has self-sustaining possibilities. Yet the trends in industrial investment by outsiders in Asia point the other way, toward dependence, especially on the Japanese. So do trends in global production, technology and marketing.

Specifically, these trends point to labour displacement, not absorption. Even within the region's established and highly protected manufacturing base the future leads towards redundancy, towards continuing foreign control and towards a growing number of unemployed, volatile and educated youth flocking to cities.

Indonesia's labour force grows by 1.6 million annually. The Philippines and Thailand must find 800,000 new jobs each year, at a time when investors want higher value-added from each worker, an effect belying the usefulness of foreign investment to mop up unemployment. World manufacturing trends, despite the agility of light, 'footloose' industries to set up in Southeast Asia, are towards factories sited ever closer to end users and towards factories making ever lighter products, with less raw material and with the aid of robotic hands.

Who's in Charge Here?

Foreign investors entranced by Southeast Asia also tend to overlook a second trend. The region's politics will become increasingly fluid and unpredictable in coming decades. With the exception of Singapore (where a forward-looking if somewhat authoritarian party leads a tenaciously honest administration) changes in top personnel will result in a costly and confusing period in which multiple claimants for patronage will emerge during political transitions.

A foretaste of this confusion was evident in the Philippines after 1986. The disarray following Marcos's departure resulted, to a great extent, from an ambiguity in which outsiders, not to mention local Chinese and the old moneyed families, had no idea who in the new administration they needed to cultivate, and whom they could safely ignore. In a very real sense, the Aquino government's 'consolidation' after 1987 simply means that investors now know the 'ropes', that the patrimonial lines of authority are now relatively clear. Given a long-established business culture of this type, political transitions now bearing down on the region throughout the 1990s also guarantee an unsteady time of contending claims to the national purse. Very few foreign investors, apart from the Japanese, have anticipated this flux; the Japanese have prepared for it by sedulous homework and by cultivating all major factions.

Neglected Agriculture, Neglected Land

The impending demographic footfall of 600 million Asean citizens within the next thirty years also signals acute pressure on Southeast Asia's resource base. Population pressure, single-crop agriculture and the impending loss of the last of the region's tropical forests are already savaging land quality. In the surrounding seas, other signs mirror the pressure on land; fishermen use dynamite and cyanide to increase their catch in the increasingly depleted waters. Purse-seine fishing techniques and trawling also chase dwindling survivors of the two thousand edible fish species once thriving in the archipelago's warm waters.

In the Philippines alone, enormous quantities of topsoil wash into the adjoining seas every year. Java is ringed by a seeping red ring of lost soil, choking its estuaries and fouling its coasts. These facts are normally recited to squeeze out an ecologist's tear but Southeast Asia's businessmen should think again about the destruction; these trends suggest greater scarcity for the commodities that still enrich Southeast Asia and an approaching need for expensive prospecting or refurbishment of old plantation investment. Even global weather, by the late 1980s, was conspiring to make the monsoon less predictable, and agricultural failure correspondingly more likely.

All this will have, and has had, a profound effect on the daily lives of the region's people, the majority of whom must make their living from the land. Yujiro Hayami of Aoyama-Gakuin University, one of Japan's more sensitive economists, noted in 1988 that 'the real wages of [Asean's] agricultural labourers have declined, or at best, stayed stagnant for the previous two decades.' Instead, he said, 'the propertied income rose at the expense of labour income.' Hayami cites the relentless problem of population pressure in Southeast Asia:

> The increase in industrial employment has been grossly insufficient to absorb the increased labour force. Meanwhile the possibility of opening new land for cultivation has been exhausted . . . as population growth presses on land resources under constant technology, cultivation frontiers expand to ever-more marginal land, and greater amounts of labour are applied per unit of cultivated area: the marginal return to labour input declines and the cost of food production rises . . . in the end, the labourers' income becomes *the minimum sufficient to maintain a stationary population*. [Hayami's emphasis]

By 1989 some governments, notably Indonesia and Thailand, were moving to save the last of the endangered forests while senators in the Philippines debated a measure to achieve the same goal but the ability of consumer nations to shift their sources of supply quickly made modification of extractive forestry methods a tricky economic question.

In these circumstances, the financial press for the most part is ignoring a looming investment need of another kind in Southeast Asia. In coming years much money must go towards simply maintaining what has already been built or preserving what is in danger of being lost. Much of the base of roads, bridges, irrigation schemes and the like must, as noted, be rebuilt from scratch. This re-investment extends far beyond public sector responsibilities. New plantation cropping, new crop replanting or new petroleum prospecting by private businesses must also occur, and soon, if past momentum is to be maintained.

More Giveaways

In a region bankrupt of ideas, the solution for this investment shortfall will be sought via more generous investment incentives. Devising more enticing lures could prove difficult, however. Economic nationalism, no matter how misconceived and abused by patronage and monopoly, is already in full retreat throughout the region, hastened by disappointment at the waste of public enterprise. The earlier foreign equity restrictions and local content rules have fallen away, one by one, as Asean countries step up their competition for foreign investment.

The Thai authorities, as noted, have already opted for generosity in order to retain a competitive edge over their Asean neighbours, now striving to lure investors away from Bangkok. The abandonment by the Malaysians of formerly strict foreign ownership rules is another sign. There is, of course, a certain logic to hacking away bureaucratic clutter, but it must be recognised that the resulting investment gained has little to do with indigenously generated development.

From a position of spurning suitors at the height of the boom, the Asean economies have become mendicants hungry for the investment capital they cannot, or will not, generate themselves. The lengthening list of tax-free holidays, duty exemptions, preferential tax breaks and other bribes have, however, only had an intermittently positive effect. In a 1988 Asian Development Bank seminar on foreign investment in the region, the International Finance Corporation pointed to 'considerable evidence that fiscal incentives have little effect on investment decisions . . . incentives are little more than a drain on the treasury of the country giving them.'

The long-term trend is running in the direction of declining flows of foreign investment to most Asian countries,' an IFC senior official, Richard Richardson, told the gathering. Investment levels for all the Asean economies plummeted after 1982. As it happened, all of Asia received declining foreign investment after the mid-1980s, except for China. And much of the investment going into China, such as that for textile manufacturing or light engineering, had the effect of diminishing Southeast Asia's competitive edge.

'The declining trend in direct investment in Asia during the 1980s was particularly noticeable in two countries, Singapore and Malaysia,' said Richardson. He added that, 'in the case of direct investment in Asia, the popular media have overplayed a forecast of problem-free growth. Asia as a whole certainly has been a relatively bright . . . but this has been largely due to flows to one country – China.'

These then are a few of the more sombre, underlying trends which the oscillation of commodity markets often disguise or blur. Yet, in characteristic paradox, the spectre of quasi-permanent surplus also haunts commodity markets, even as the environmental foundations for sustained production are eroding before one's eyes.

In some places the point of absurdity has already been reached: Indonesia will soon have to import more oil, admittedly of a poorer quality, than the quantum of 'sweet' (i.e., non-sulphurous) oil it now exports. In the Philippines, sugar began to be imported in 1987, another anomaly among many distortions plaguing what once was Asia's pre-eminent sugar producer. Sugar, oil? Enough in plenty elsewhere. Timber? Not much left to sell. Burgeoning populations are biting into the surplus left for export, surpluses produced at ever increasing cost by comparison with other competitors in South and East Asia.

Debt Valley

To the introverted casino markets of Southeast Asia, these issues seem far away, irrelevant fretting when measured against immediate commercial opportunism. But another issue of more immediate impact has also emerged. Limits to land quality and resources are one thing; limits to credit are quite another. In hindsight, the region's breathless run of good luck looks increasingly like a precipitate gallop into colossal debt. Reinforced by debt finance, profligate public spending and policies hostile to the free market are now deeply entrenched in these economies.

The investment economist, Mari Pangestu, measures 'investment intensity' in this part of free marketeering Asia. Her studies show strong correlations between Asean's manufacturing 'successes' and outsiders' direct investment.

For example, the foreign investment share of Singapore's total financial resources, including domestic investment, stood at a huge 73.6 per cent in 1986. By comparison, Indonesia's share stood at 9.2 per cent. Pangestu's work, and others', suggests that industrialisation remains the creation of foreigners, not only in its reliance on external demand, but also in its dependence on foreign investors' decisions to site, or not to site, their plants in any particular Southeast Asian country.

Yet another economist points to American investment in Singapore's refinery business during the 1970s which, she says, meshed with marketing decisions by US oil companies in neighbouring Malaysia and Indonesia. These decisions were 'instrumental in linking Singapore to the region and have in turn linked Asean to the US and world markets,' writes Marjorie Suriyamongkol from Thailand (1988).

Recent research also shows a slowing down of indigenous investment growth in areas where the brightest hopes still linger. Capital formation, a key yardstick of indigenously powered economic growth, began to fall back in Thailand, the Philippines and Indonesia after an improvement in the early 1980s. Efforts to increase government revenues, rather than rely on foreign loans, have fared poorly. 'Widespread tax evasion' occurs in areas like Asean, says Kohli of the Asian Development Bank, 'because of high marginal tax rates and lax enforcement.'

Economists in the region play down the role of foreign capital investment in building a truly indigenous industrial society. 'There is no escaping the implication that reliance on foreign capital does not offer the solution for high and rapid growth,' the ADB said in 1986. 'Instead of taking measures to increase revenues or limit expenditures the countries [have] resorted to heavy domestic and external borrowing to meet growing expenditures,' the bank said.

Indonesia, for example, finances its deficits almost entirely from foreign loans. 'The gap between saving and investment has widened considerably since 1975,' the ADB noted. Much of domestic borrowing was in the form of captive government paper. Much of it put harsh credit squeezes on the private sector. Southeast Asia's debt has now become a structural feature of the region's economies. And although the Philippines seized most attention during its rescheduling talks with 486 private creditor banks during 1986–88, the foreign bankers' knuckles have also gone white over other debt prospects.

Overshadowed in global reporting by concern about Latin American exposure, external debt in Southeast Asia also became worrisome during the 1980s, to creditors and debtors alike. Even rich Malaysia became a source of anxiety; by 1986 its per capita debt was nearly four times higher than that in the Philippines.

A study by ADB economist Jungsoo Lee (1987) notes that 'in 1980 there was no [Asean] country whose ratio of debt to GNP exceeded 50%, but in 1985 the ratio of the Philippines rose to 80.6%' and even to 62.5 per cent in Malaysia. It went above 45 per cent during that year for Indonesia and Thailand, and went over the 50 per cent barrier for both countries during the following year.

Juggling the debt has showed a wizard streak in many central bankers. They have become skilled at beating the so-called 'bunching' phenomenon, the occurrence of too much repayment obligation in too short a period of time. Bunching distorts the 'maturity structure' of their foreign loan portfolios. Some central banks, as in Thailand and Malaysia, have prepaid some of the debt. More juggling will be needed in the coming years: in the two decades after the late 1960s, public debt alone (private indebtedness is an astronomical extra) swelled by a factor of five or six in most Asean countries.

The figures really do 'tell all'. In the Philippines, public debt as a percentage of GDP in 1975 stood at 6.9 per cent but, ten years later, this had climbed to 33.5 per cent. In Thailand the equivalent figures were 4 per cent, which rocketed to 20 per cent a decade later. The Indonesians' external debt in the mid-1970s was already high, thanks to the profligacy of the national oil company, Pertamina. Afterwards however, Jakarta allowed its public debt to climb from one-quarter of GDP in 1975 to 40 per cent ten years later.

Debt service burdens reached critical levels, exacerbated by unwise borrowing in Japanese yen loans, which appreciated by 100 per cent after 1985. This happened while 'real', or constant, commodity prices, invariably denominated in dollars, fell during the 1980s; the unkindest cut came from the ever higher cost of converting those dollars to pay back Japanese loans. No wonder that one of the few common Asean economic initiatives to succeed is a currency swap scheme for central banks short of hard exchange.

Loans Unwisely Spent

How wisely was the debt-financed money spent? Not very, suggest many studies. The International Monetary Fund's fiscal affairs director, Vito Tanzi, has studied (1987) benefits in Asia from the huge boosts in public spending. 'My basic and admittedly impressionistic conclusions about the market economies of developing Asia are the following,' he says.

'By and large, economic policy has been better than in other regions . . . however, the good results were achieved at higher costs than necessary.' According to Tanzi, these governments often spent unwisely: from 20 to 40 per cent of GDP in Asean still comes from government spending, but 'public sector investment has often not followed efficiency criteria,' as he notes diplomatically. 'The net result,' he says, is that the 'rates of growth [are] lower than they should have been, considering the high level of total [public] investment.'

Publicly-owned businesses lose money by the bucketful in the Asean region. In the Philippines, for example, the rate of return on equity of the top fifteen public enterprises was a laughable 2.8 per cent during the first half of the 1980s. In Indonesia, except for the oil giant Pertamina, all 142 non-financial public enterprises returned an even more embarrassing 1 per cent on their assets in 1985.

By the mid-1980s, bad commodity prices meant dismal returns for just about every publicly owned company, many of them milked by business associates of those in power. With crimped commodity earnings becoming the norm by the mid-1980s, revenues dropped while income from grandiose, debt-financed investments dwindled or, in many cases, vanished altogether. Yet the recurrent spending needs, let alone operational costs, of fancy projects put many happy-go-spending regimes in a double bind.

Inexorable consequences began to catch up with the region by the mid-decade. Interest payments on foreign debt climbed from trivial amounts in the mid-1970s to US$8 *billion* a year in 1987. The exponential rise in debt payment outgoings, measured in constant dollar values, was 600 per cent for Indonesia, 1,800 per cent for both Malaysia and the Philippines and a huge 1,380 per cent for Thailand.

Another way to look at the debt load was through the ratio between the GDP and external debt. In Indonesia in 1981 for example, foreign debt amounted to 21.2 per cent of its GDP. That is to say, its debt was US$20.4 billion and its GDP stood at about US$100 billion. Examine the picture five years later. The ratio had rocketed to over 46 per cent. In Malaysia the GDP/debt ratio rose from 34 per cent to 85.3 per cent, while in the Philippines it climbed from 54.4 per cent to 85 per cent. In Thailand, it rose from 30.6 per cent to 45 per cent. Tanzi unsurprisingly calls these figures 'disturbingly high'. And more disturbing still was the yen-denominated proportion of this debt in all countries except the Philippines. (See Table 9.)

Not only do debt and declining public investment weigh down on Asean. Private domestic investment during the 1980s has also plummeted: in Indonesia it dropped from 21.3 to 12.2 per cent. In Malaysia, the Philippines and Thailand, the figures in 1980 and 1985 were respectively as follows: from 20.5 per cent to 16.5 per cent; from 16.2 per cent to 13 per cent, and from 16 per cent to 12.7 per cent of GDP. Coming out of the recession in the late 1980s these figures improved somewhat but still lagged far behind foreign investment. Is this then the region where private enterprise was triumphantly on the rise?

Who Needs Maintenance?

Not only was much of the money wasted, but the investments themselves have been badly looked after. 'These countries have been more successful at building infrastructure than at its maintenance or use,' Tanzi says. He describes a 'serious

Table 9   Another 'miracle?: mushrooming foreign debt (US$ billion)

Country	1975	1981	1987
Indonesia	10.3	20.4	42.6
Malaysia	1.9	8.2	22.2
Philippines	3.4	21.1	29.0
Thailand	1.7	10.3	17.0

SOURCE: World Bank and IMF statistics

deterioration' in 'public sector capital stock', meaning roads, railways, communications equipment and all the other things that make economies work better by
making it easier to produce and get to market.

In the Philippines operating and maintenance spending dropped to half of what
it had been in 1977, ten years earlier. 'In Indonesia much . . . built over the past
two decades is reported to be deteriorating and in need of costly rehabilitation,'
wrote another economist in 1986.

'For example, only 40 per cent of national and provincial roads are considered in
a stable condition and such a situation is also reported for irrigation canals.' This
is known in development jargon as a 'recurrent cost problem'; the Philippines and
Thailand figure prominently in a study by the London-based Overseas Development Institute (quoted in Tanzi, 1987) showing the most affected countries. This
added up to a self-inflicted weakness becoming apparent just as the mid-1980s
downturn hit Southeast Asia's economies.

Asean Economies: How Resilient?

This might matter less if Southeast Asia's macroeconomic management was more
agile. But various studies suggest otherwise. In 1983, for example, ADB economists
led by the bank's former chief economist Seiji Naya measured the impact of external
economic 'shocks' on different Asian countries.

This involved measuring policy responses through measures to increase export
volumes (to compensate for deteriorating terms of trade); to boost savings rates
and increase investment; and to slow external debt growth and to reduce the
debt-serving burden. Naya's group concluded that the Northeast Asian industrial
countries had 'withstood the impacts of external shocks much more successfully
than the countries of Southeast Asia.'

Worsening terms of trade and abrupt rises in the cost of external borrowing
meant that the Asean economies became entangled in current account deficits in the
mid-1980s. Their record at containing inflationary pressures was also unimpressive.
Finally, the ADB group said, 'many [Asean] industries have survived only because
of protection, which hindered exports because of higher costs and prices.'

Who Gains?

It hardly bears comment that the Asean grouping has achieved an incomparably
better result than the 'planned economies' imposed on much of Indochina. Anyone

visiting Vietnam after 1975 cannot escape noticing the poverty, corruption, government apathy and an almost desperate wish to get out by many Vietnamese. The socialist dream has led to Vietnam's ranking by the International Monetary Fund as one of the world's twenty poorest countries, with per capita income just over US$160 a year in 1985. That was a static figure: Vietnam's second five-year plan, 'implemented' during 1976–80, achieved *zero* growth.

Free-marketeering Southeast Asia's achievement stands in gleaming contrast although not in every respect. Social surveys, beginning back in the 1970s, show that the highest 10 per cent of the social strata in the Philippines and Thailand still receive over 40 per cent of the national income. Few researchers in Southeast Asia believe that these differentials are altering in the direction of a more generous portion for the poor. East Asian scholars make the point themselves; Ryokichi Hirono, for example, an economics professor at Japan's Seikei University, points out that while the Asean countries have 'experienced sustained growth, the rates of open unemployment and underemployment have not necessarily declined.'

Education: Quantity, Not Quality

Even the best achievement, of education levels gained throughout Asean, has a hollow ring. The Philippines have the highest percentage of 20- to 24-year-olds enrolled in higher education in all the region: 26 of every 100 young men or women spend their time in 'college', far more than in Singapore (12 per thousand) and equivalent to the percentage achieved in France, where per capita income is fifteen times more than in the Philippines.

Even Switzerland has fewer young people at tertiary levels than the Philippines, although its per capita income exceeds that of the Philippines twenty-five times. Once the second richest country in Asia during the 1950s, the Philippines now slides inexorably towards Indonesia's chronically low per capita income (US$450 a year), thanks in part to a myopic preference to do nothing to slow Asia's fastest population growth rate.

The point needs no labouring. There is no obvious correlation between sheer numbers in tertiary education and material welfare. And even within the bloated figures, Filipinos choose status rather than skills. Fewer than 20 per cent of Filipino students in university-level education choose engineering or technical subjects. By comparison, 65 per cent of Japanese students do.

More telling still, most of the Philippines' far fewer technical graduates can only find work outside their country, notably in the Middle East. They work there for a fraction of the wages paid to South Korean, British, West German or Japanese supervisors who have equivalent degrees. In 1988, only 5,000 Filipinos, in a population of 60 millions, worked in true research. This is less than 0.001 per cent of the population; by comparison, the figure in Japan is well above 2 per cent in the same year, a differential of 1:2000!

In Asean's much publicised success story, these are the percentages and the figures that really matter. The details of education enrolment from Thailand (see Chapter 5) and other Asean countries tell the same tale. In short, the engine of Asean's industrial 'take-off' remains fitful, stalled or barely idling on the runway despite figures showing big surges of production from export zones riding high on tax giveaways, or from companies importing almost all their components duty free before sending the product on to world markets.

Lacking: A Culture of Innovation

This is the next troubling trend, a rock-hard truth smashing through transparent claims of a Southeast Asian manufacturing 'miracle'. In his book, *The Rise of Ersatz Capitalism in South-East Asia* (1988), Yoshihara Kunio says 'the political leaders of these [Asean] countries have not faced up to the gross distortion of efficiency created by heavy government involvement in industry . . . the trouble is that national leaders do not realise that true industrialisation is based on an economic system that encourages people to strive for innovation and creativity.' He also emphasises that

> Today's large technological gap frustrates in many ways Southeast Asian efforts to catch up with the technology of developed countries. This problem should not be overemphasised however, for against similar odds [South] Korea has been catching up rapidly. But none of the Southeast Asian countries is making comparable technological progress. The gap may even be widening.

Protected industry has become the norm for Asean's internal markets while loose-footed foreign firms produce a quickly shifting range of electronic and other light products for the global market only. Some analysts see good news in the growth of the services in these economies, but they should look again. Far from being the type of computer-at-home service industries so beloved of the American financial press, services in Asean increasingly reflect what economists call a 'pathological' service industry, comprising millions of underemployed, mostly unskilled people.

For all the vaunted industrialisation in the Asean countries, Indonesia, the Philippines and Malaysia have achieved only marginal increases, of 7 per cent or less, in the numbers of people employed in industrial work. Brave talk about a 'fundamental shift' away from agriculture and towards manufacturing remains a myth, a dynamic fuelled by outsiders' investment decisions and outsiders' markets. Nearly all Asean's service sector, with the exception of Singapore, comprise non-tradable items in the informal sector of the economy. They do not bring in foreign exchange. On the contrary, services of the quantifiable kind, such as insurance and other trade 'invisibles', make for a constant net drain on Asean trade accounts except, as always, for Singapore.

Industrialisation Without Technology

The skills issue is crucial for Southeast Asia's industrial hopes. Where are the hands-on technicians, the laboratory hot shots whose achievements in applied research must quickly pass into flexible heads and hands of production line engineers? Information from Dr Uwe Parpart, a US physicist living in Bangkok, shows how even Thailand's rocketing growth has not yet pushed the country over the threshold into self-sustained scientific research. The country has yet to produce a PhD in physics – a symptomatic sign, says Parpart. In Asean, as the economist Rieger points out, 'it is now being realised that "high-tech" can be a very misleading word.'

Charles Lindsey, an economist from Trinity College in Connecticut, distinguishes (1986) between 'transported' and 'transferred' technology to the Asean economies.

Foreign-owned manufacturing, 'with a few conspicuous exceptions, remains last-stage assembling and highly import-dependent.' And when it comes to technological skills, foreign firms understandably aim only at raising the minimal competence of their workforce.

With exceptions, notably in Singapore, Lindsey disparages local R & D spending in Asean. 'The local economic élite appears to be willing to play a secondary role in the economy,' he claims, a damning judgement when contrasted to most accounts of industrial take-off elsewhere in Asia, the US and Europe, where a deep personal and intellectual involvement of the élite made the transition possible.

Singapore economist Chia Siow Yue (quoted in Chew, 1988) notes that 'major manufactured exports in this country [Singapore] are in the non-resource based product groups . . . in other words, the major exports are the products of the electronics industry established in the late 1960s and the 1970s.'

He continues, 'it is debatable whether much of the exports of electronic products can really be classified as "technology intensive", as many of the processes performed in Asean countries are highly labour-intensive and much of the technology is imported.' The same assessment applies to textiles, Asean's second largest export. Despite the blossoming growth, much of that trade is to some extent 'passive': regional trade figures usually conceal intra-firm trade between globally-controlled subsidiaries.

Mingsaarn Kaosa-ard, a Thai economist, has also analysed technology agreements between Asean countries and outside investor countries. Over 1970–80, for example, Malaysia negotiated twice as many such agreements with Japan as with the US, and those with the latter concentrated on only a few industries.

'Thailand usually had to pay higher technology acquisition fees to American suppliers than they did to Japanese suppliers,' Kaosa-ard says (1986). Even in industries where Southeast Asian firms should have an edge through processing indigenous raw materials, little happened during the richest two decades to increase their share of down-market manufacturing or distribution. Malaysia, for example produces over 40 per cent of the world's natural rubber. It makes less than 1 per cent of the world's total rubber products, however.

The issue goes beyond narrow definitions. From a recipient's point of view, foreign direct investment should provide five desired elements: financing; salesmanship (market for final product); plant and equipment at current technological levels; technology of the productive process itself; and management plus quality control. Yet virtually every study of foreign firms doing business in Asean describes foreign managers as loathe to surrender either knowledge or management control to the locals. As Penang's experience, noted in Chapter 3, illustrates, very little passes through the ostensibly permeable walls dividing the local economy from the transplanted visitor.

Market Moves of Another Kind

How then are skills being inculcated? Sadly, most of the region's educational establishments pitch their teaching programmes at what Asean students would *like to be*, rather than at what the job market needs. Stratospheric hopes are indulged, partly for marketing reasons (the vast majority of tertiary establishments are private businesses or poorly funded provincial establishments). Rather than meshing study with business and commercial reality, students train for work appropriate to industries that most Asean economies cannot independently sustain.

Where do these trained people go upon completion of their studies (the quality of which suffers from poor resource allocation and overcrowding)? Migrant labour from Indonesia, the Philippines and Thailand sends back money from the Middle East, Japan, the US and even Europe. Teachers work as maids. 'College graduates' take jobs as the ever euphemistic 'hostesses' or 'entertainers' in Tokyo. Engineers drive trucks in Saudi Arabia.

A useful safety valve for chronic unemployment, migrant labour prospects have darkened however with the oil price stagnation of the 1980s. 'Today', says an International Labour Organisation researcher in Bangkok, 'stiff competition among labour suppliers in a very weak market has led to a situation where workers practically have to bid for the few jobs available [overseas].'

These migratory trends, another less comforting side of Southeast Asia's economic future, cut in varying ways. Even Singapore's Lee Kuan Yew, had cause, by the late 1980s, to bemoan the exodus of some of his island's best trained and most cosmopolitan citizens. They have chosen to get out even as Singapore's economy had turned the corner after 1985 to clock up, once again, double-digit growth rates. Yet high growth regained availed nothing against the tyranny of geography which places the city-state forever within a differently motivated archipelago.

Some Singaporeans cannot lose the sense that their island republic must remain forever an entrepôt bubble, no matter how successfully it is organised and run. It is not just Singapore that loses its most professionally qualified people: the same applies, with varying shades of Chinese ethnic tint, to the steady out-migration of Malaysians, Indonesians and Filipinos.

Many of the Southeast Asians seeking their livelihood elsewhere have made impressive strides. The 'refugee exodus' from Indochina perfectly illustrates the point: the mainly ethnic Chinese leaving Vietnam by the millions after 1975 have sought and gained new business locales anywhere but in the Southeast Asian countries which unwillingly received them.

These footloose Chinese have moved to the US, Canada, Australia and Western Europe bringing problems, but also a dynamism suppressed or discouraged in Southeast Asia. The Chinese and Filipino middle classes are most conspicuous in this permanent migration although many 'native' Malaysians, Thais and Indonesians also go abroad in search of work.

After 1985 the US press began to devote attention to what *Fortune* magazine called 'America's super minority'. It referred to America's fastest growing minority, the Asians. This and other articles mentioned Robert Nakasone, a Japanese-American now president of a major US toy retailing company.

Gerald Tsai, a Chinese who became chairman of American Can Corporation, also received attention as the first Asian American to head a Fortune 500 company that he had not established himself. And most readers of even the popular press learned that the Chinese migrant An Wang is responsible for Wang computer laboratories, worth US$2.4 billion in 1988.

Although just 2 per cent of America's population, Asians have comprised over 12 per cent of Harvard's freshman classes since 1985. Their share has reached 20 per cent at Berkeley. Twice as many Asian Americans graduate from university level studies as white Americans. The median Asian family's income topped US$23,600 per year in 1980, three thousand dollars ahead of white Americans. The next census, in 1990, will almost certainly show a bigger differential.

Asians consistently edge ahead of other ethnic Americans in scholastic testing. Scores of studies fret over the much greater time spent studying mathematics by Asian children, than by other Americans. 'America's future is likely to be increasingly Asian,' said the Population Reference Bureau, a Washington group. So is Australia's and Canada's.

Where does this flood of talent and energy come from? In the Philippines alone, 150,000 visa applications to the US were pending in 1988; the backlog in processing them went back to applications lodged in 1971. And racial unease in Malaysia has prompted new surges out by ethnic Chinese in that country – Australia, Canada and the US remain favoured destinations. Even Singapore's gilded professionals, who live in an efficient city-state peopled largely by Chinese, feel the need for greater security or scope, and target the same destinations. The author of *The Australasian Who's Who?* lists 500 Asians now prominent in Australian life.

Writing in the *Asian Wall Street Journal* in 1985, Ronald Nairn, a Bangkok-based American businessman put it this way: 'Asians in America embody virtually all those old-fashioned virtues characteristic of the old US prescription for economic success: family cohesion, pursuit of education, loyalty, respect for law and tradition, self-discipline and hard work.' He claims that 'freedom' in the US allows these virtues to cohere, to flower and to meld into a great dynamic. Nairn's description, though overblown, hints at reasons why some in Asean, no matter how big the recent returns, seem to want out.

To be sure, there are risk-takers, Chinese or non-Chinese, in plenty in Southeast Asia. Duppy behaviour does not reign supreme. We are not dealing with ideal types here; it is rather instead a matter of predisposition, of the tug between two contrasting commercial impulses.

Ivan Zimonyi, an ADB specialist on venture capitalisation, notes that a pay-off time of 7–10 years for many product-financing agreements seems beyond most quick-in, quick-out risk-taking. One thing is clear: regional investment by local entrepreneurs remains minuscule in computer development, telecommunications, semiconductors, biotechnology, computer software, robotic engineering and other cutting edge technologies for the next century.

Let The Market In, Get the Governments Out?

One premise of a free market is this: as business becomes broader and more sophisticated, government intervention should decrease. In Southeast Asia, at least, it is difficult to deny that the cost of doing business rises in these top-heavy economies, crowded with free-riders. Economies like these spawn underground markets, as in the region's 'Chinatowns', for credit and services.

Regional economists are now coming to believe that mass capitalism in Southeast Asia must wait, as the recent Latin American vogue for an 'invisible revolution' asserts, for the retreat of the state. A low quality of government intervention drives up costs by rampant cronyism and, more benevolently, with tariffs, artificially high exchange rates and the like. Hernando de Soto and other Latin American writers say that government paternalism merely frustrates the innate business abilities possessed by ordinary people throughout the Third World. In a truly free market, 'the basic idea', says Asean specialist Bruce Clapham, 'should be a minimum of regulation with a maximum of freedom.'

Yet the crony instinct proves terribly resilient. It has endured into the Aquino-ruled Philippines with scarcely a break in pace or a change of clothes. In Malaysia, a government policy to bring the politically dominant group into the market mainstream becomes, in part, a vehicle for enriching the so-called 'bumi billionaires' among the top Malay leadership. In Indonesia, monopolies and licensing networks linked to the highest families defeat the operation of even a qualified market. Perhaps my few years as a correspondent have immersed me in too much commercial cynicism. Yet, from my experience in the region, public spending in Asean in its essence still means distributing unearned largesse to one's business friends.

For All That, an Achievement

Dare one disparage the Southeast Asian achievement, especially when contrasted with the continuing fiasco in Africa or the drift of debt-ridden Latin America? Even Europe sometimes seems a less than robust rival to Asean dynamism. After all, the region's growth rates during 1980–87 were 4.8 per cent per annum, for Indonesia and Malaysia; 6.1 per cent per annum for Singapore; and 5.2 per cent for Thailand. Only the Philippines dipped into that econometric absurdity, 'negative growth'. As Lucian Pye, a doyen of Asian studies in the United States, puts it (1985), 'during the twenty years of the sixties and seventies, the peoples of East and Southeast Asia were living through the longest period of rapidly rising economic growth ever experienced in human history.'

At a business conference in 1987, Sanjoy Chowdhury, Merrill Lynch's chief economist for Asia, noted the factors that point to continuing buoyancy. 'Demographic factors can provide a boost to domestic demand [and] the virtually untapped potential of expanding intra-regional trade, the high saving/investment ratios of most Asian countries and the very important changes in policy direction' all add up, in his view, to a sustained achievement. Maybe he is right.

Chowdhury also sketched a picture of poor times ahead for East Asia's industrial 'Four Dragons' (Singapore, Hong Kong, South Korea and Taiwan). He also described how what he called the 'Four Farms', the four largest Asean countries, will also face continuing stagnation in commodity prices 'or even dip slightly as deflationary trends develop in the major industrial economies.'

The Second Time Around: Japan in Southeast Asia

Dwarfing all calculations about Southeast Asia's future is the emerging financial, trade and investment power of Japan. Spurred by the yen's rapid appreciation since September 1985, Tokyo's major and minor companies pumped more direct investment into Southeast Asia in the following three years than the total of Japanese direct foreign investment, or DFI, to that region in all the preceding postwar years. In February 1985 the markets had given 260 yen to the dollar; by the beginning of 1988 it took only 125 yen to buy the same dollar, an appreciation of more than 100 per cent in less than three years.

This trend alone signals the end of Southeast Asia's old road to wealth. During the 1960s and 1970s the spread of foreign investors was wider than it has become since 1985. US-controlled equity or loan finance remains concentrated in oil production and exploration, and in some electronics and food-processing lines. Investment from Japan, by way of contrast, has spread out more widely, 'with a tendency', as Reiichi Shiamoto, deputy president of Japan's Export-Import Bank told a conference in 1988, to 'concentrate on the low wages and low production costs.'

During 1986 the outward flow reached the equivalent of US$2.3 billion, at December 1985 exchange rates. This amounted to 40 per cent of all Japanese DFI. The depreciation of all Southeast Asian currencies against the yen also lifted the profile of Japanese creditors. Other consequences appeared. 'Figures for 1987 for some Asian countries suggest exports by Hongkong, South Korea, Taiwan and Thailand to Japan have vastly outstripped those to the traditionally important US market,' said a Merrill Lynch report in 1988.

In constant terms the flow of DFI into Asia keeps on increasing, exceeding US$3 billion during just the first half of 1987. By mid-1988 Japanese DFI to Asia was probably at a higher level than to the US itself. The momentum has not slackened as Japan continues its 'ambitious programme of capital recycling', as Shiamoto describes it. The aim is to move at least US$20 billion into Asia, including Southeast Asia, over the three years ending in 1990.

By 1988 the influential Pacific Rim Consulting Group (PRCG) warned of an 'imminent competitive leap [by Japan] in Asia.' Japanese companies are 'rapidly shifting huge portions of industrial capacity offshore, with Asia a prime target.' This means, the PRCG said, that the sheer size of Japanese investment will allow that country's multinationals to hold on to their market share, taking short-term losses because of yen appreciation.

'By 1993, the industrial production capacity that Japan adds to the region will equal the *entire industrial output of Asean today*,' the report concluded. This means the equivalent of US$55–65 billion in industrial investment is flowing into Southeast Asia in just six years. The consultants' group had this piece of advice for US and European firms: 'get serious, or get out.'

Is Japan Irresistible?

These trends accompanied a strong preference by Japanese companies for 100 per cent equity ownership, an attitude that capital-starved Asean economies have little choice but to accept. Their earlier strictures against complete foreign ownership have become irrelevant. Anyway, Japanese business ascendancy operates at many levels, of which equity ownership is just one.

The methods include technology licensing deals, management contracts, leasing (both financing and operations), franchising and turnkey contracts that keep Japanese construction firms on site from ground-breaking to plant commission. Other devices include 'risk-service' and production-sharing contracts, especially (though not exclusively) in the petroleum business, and on into murkier 'international sub-contracting' reminiscent of the old 'piece-work' system of nineteenth-century English textile mills.

It is no coincidence that Tokyo is no longer so insistent upon restricting imports from Southeast Asia to raw materials; greater value-added is slipping in to Japan-bound exports from Asean. Miyohei Shinohara, who chairs the prestigious

Institute of Developing Economies in Tokyo, told a business conference in 1988 the Asean countries face a dilemma in reacting to Japan's financial power. If Southeast Asians 'distance themselves from Japan economically, he said, their growth will eventually decline; on the other hand, attempts to increase their growth rates may well result in increased dependence.'

Many Southeast Asians see a new Japanese Greater East Asia Co-prosperity Sphere in the making; the creation of such a sphere of influence had been Tokyo's ostensible aim during the 1941–45 war. The world trading system, unable to cope with the gross distortions in US-Japanese trade and with violent exchange fluctuations in the late 1980s, now seems to vindicate views that the international trade environment will become ever more dominated by bilateral trade relations. In a game of these stakes, the United States is seen in Southeast Asia as having entered a status which is the modern financial and sovereign equivalent of indentured servitude, its naval forces a gendarmerie increasingly reliant on contributions from Japan.

Southeast Asia's missed opportunities for self-sustained growth will become increasingly painful in coming years as Japanese fiscal supremacy meshes more closely with Tokyo's role as the region's pre-eminent foreign investor. 'The 1990s will see Japan playing a role *vis-à-vis* the rest of Asia similar to that played by the USA in Latin America in the 1950s,' says Chowdhury of Merrill Lynch. Some straws are already flying in the prevailing wind: Indonesia's approved foreign investment in 1987 reached the equivalent of US$1 billion. Forty-five per cent of this came from Japan. A Chemical Bank official tells a Manila conference that, 'at the macro level, statistics show that Asean has become a Japanese lake.'

Practising What They Don't Preach

Meanwhile, Asean's older markets are looking harder at restrictive trade practices about which Southeast Asian countries have complained to the European Community but which they themselves impose in their home markets. 'The frequency of tariffs [in Southeast Asia] is very high,' writes Asian Development Bank economist Dean DeRosa (1986). He says the average frequency of tariff barriers in the region reaches 80 per cent in all the Asean economies except (as one might expect in a free trade port) in Singapore. Data for the mid-1980s show average rates of tariff protection approaching 92 per cent in Indonesia; 100 per cent in the Philippines; 56 per cent in Thailand and 64 per cent in Malaysia. The protection spreads across a spectrum touching over a third of all Asean imports.

Protectionism of this less frequently discussed type falls into varying categories. Beside normal tariffs, these shrill advocates of free trade impose such impediments as quantitative restrictions and advance sales taxes. Not least, various government trading monopolies, such as Malaysia's Pernas or the bevy of family-linked import companies in Indonesia, distort trade. Malaysia imposes import taxes on food, beverages and tobacco. Similar tariffs operate in the Philippines. The Thais discriminate against natural oils, machinery and food.

No one cared much about these during Asean's first twenty years. Now, protectionist sentiment in North America and Europe, plus the evolution of regional trading blocs in both these markets, have put a different complexion on Asean trade barriers. 'The "free-rider" aspect of [Asean's] non-participation [in tariff cutting] . . . has been conspicuous,' DeRosa says. Despite promises of

Asean economic integration, US business groups began, by the mid-1980s, to complain loudly about a 'lack of freedom across [Asean] borders for trade-related investments.'

He also claims that, as the Southeast Asians gained most-favoured nation preferences from trade liberalisation during the 1960s, they should 'no longer expect to remain passive beneficiaries of efforts to liberalise world trade.' DeRosa also says that 'export controls and subsidies are more serious and pervasive in the Asean countries than in the US.'

Trade Disputes

In trade friction, Asean increasingly feels the sort of pressure normally applied against the sharper side of the 'East Asian Edge', that is, the rapidly growing, autonomous industrial economies of Northeast Asia. Both the European Community and the United States have become less patient with special textile advantages for Asean. A restrictive, 'Multi-Fibre Agreement' has resulted from protectionist pressures. Retaliatory moves have been threatened by Washington against Asean firms producing fake or pirated goods, an infringement of intellectual property rules. The European Commission has demanded the same standard of protection.

Even Asean's ties to America no longer promise the same, gilt-edged ride that propelled these economies into prosperity when demand from the US market fuelled the expansion. From 1967 to 1986, US-Asean trade grew twenty-fivefold, to US$23.5 billion a year. This amounted to an average annual rate of 10 per cent, twice as fast as that of world trade.

A Generalised System of Preferences, or GSP, had applied to about 10 per cent of Asean's exports to the US by the mid-1980s. Singapore especially did well, with the GSP applying to one-fifth of America-bound exports. The turning point came in 1984, with a new US Trade and Tariff Act that revised the GSP. Pressure grew to withdraw the privileges from Singapore, which clung to 'developing country' status despite a per capita GDP higher than New Zealand's.

As we have seen, the trading climate deteriorated further after sales from US surplus stocks of rice, tin, sugar and rubber caused bickering. The Thais complained that rice subsidies and foreign sales of that foodgrain at the end of the Reagan administration 'threatened the livelihood of 30 million poor Thai farmers.' By mid-decade point, American congressmen and women had introduced 2,300 bills proposing measures to restrict imports in one way or another. The 1988 trade act required the President to identify countries, sure to include some in Asean, 'unfairly' trading with the US.

China is Eyeing the Same Markets

If Japan looms increasingly as paymaster, then China may eclipse the infant Asean industries in another fashion. China has grown by an average of 6–7 per cent since 1985. Even its balance of payments and budget deficits at the end of the decade cannot long inhibit the languid move of the giant's arm, sweeping away the comparative advantage enjoyed by the comparatively pygmy-sized textile industries or finished consumer product industries in Southeast Asia. Little by little, another set of characters is on the wall, staring Asean in the face.

If – a big 'if' still – the Chinese keep to their liberalising road and are not side-tracked by party bureaucrats or inflation jitters, the industrial conceit of the Asean countries will become the purest of delusions. As the evidence of formal Asean economic cooperation shows (see the Chapter 11), no regional economic counterweight is emerging. Indeed, 'even the Aseans' export plans have created new competition among them in certain types of manufactured exports,' writes Marjorie Suriyamongkol of the Bangkok-based UN Economic Commission for Asia and the Pacific (1988). 'This has stimulated an international division of labour for Asean that produces differences and inequalities among its members.'

Already Peking's trade with the rest of Asia amounts to 57 per cent of its world trade (Japan takes 15 per cent of China's exports only). When those massive economies of scale finally mesh with the rest of the world economy, very few of the carefully nurtured, little gardens in the southern archipelago will survive the competition.

So Are Other Eyes

The same applies to another giant, India, now stirring in the west. Although fitful and uneven, free marketeering moves in that country could also portend another competitor (if only in the supply of cheap labour in the same bonded warehouse zones pioneered in Asean). Until its collapse into communal violence, Sri Lanka was also moving purposefully to win some of the footloose investment now flowing into Asean. Even Vietnam may close the gap. John Elliott, writing in the London *Independent* in March 1989, tells the tale:

Take a country with one of the world's lowest per capita incomes but one of Asia's highest levels of literacy, located on international air and sea routes in a booming economic region where businessmen are urgently looking for factory locations with cheap but intelligent labour . . . [Vietnam's] leaders hope foreign aid and investment will enable Vietnam to become one of Southeast Asia's 1990 generation of 'tiger' economies.

Some signs were apparent in 1989, when Vietnam signed its first foreign joint venture in banking, with the Summa Handelsbank AG of Düsseldorf. And in the same year, Hanoi approved four petroleum joint venture agreements with foreign companies.

Politics, Politics

Finally, the omnipresent political uncertainties in Asean dog its economic and business future. The impending departure of many leaders, in the saddle for up to two decades or more, will tax the region's shallow institutional forms to the limit. The complexities involved would fill another book; suffice it to say that expectations of an easy transition are likely to be disappointed, largely because the gap between the fading leaders and the future leadership generation is already very wide.

Nor are these the only political caveats. One hundred and fifty thousand Indochinese refugees sit in camps among four Asean countries, almost a decade

and a half since the first rush of boatpeople floated out of Vietnam and into the
South China Sea. Another 150,000 'displaced people of Filipino origin', as the
UN High Commissioner for Refugees describes the Muslim Filipinos, now find
the Borneo state of Sabah more congenial to them than the southern Philippines.
There they live, in legal limbo, complicating politics and becoming an insoluble
problem as new generations grow up within their community. Border problems
bedevil Indonesia's relations with Papua New Guinea. A simmering insurgency
also afflicts East Timor. China's navy grows. Muslim fundamentalists plot. The
communists may find fertile ground in slipping living standards amid overcrowded
conditions.

'To sustain the economic achievements of the last ten years, Asian countries must
have stable political structures,' said former US assistant secretary of state for East
Asia and the Pacific Richard Holbrooke in 1986. 'If they lose that, the past ten or
twenty years will be remembered as a brief golden age for the region.' The point
remains valid today.

A Crippled Culture?

Ultimately it all comes down to that old dodge, culture. The Malay critic
Shaharuddin Maaruf, in his *Concept of a Hero in Malay Society* (1983), has
scathing words for the type of ideal man exemplified in his country's past and
still honoured today. A role model more inimical to market-mindedness would
be hard to imagine.

'The central problem faced by Malay society is . . . having an underdeveloped
élite. The qualities necessary for development which the Malay élite lacks are
ethical integrity and standards, intellectual capacity and stamina for productive and
creative endeavours,' Shaharuddin writes. This élite 'is Westernised superficially,
beneath which it bears deeply ingrained characteristics of the culture of the feudal
past.' He adds that 'among the negative ideals of the dominant Malay élite is the
love of gain, the desire to get rich at all costs, a craving for material comfort and
easy living, regardless of ethics.'

Harsh words indeed, but similar work in Indonesia points to a cultural mix
that hinders, not helps, market capitalism. One authority on leadership values
in Indonesia, Ahmad Kamar, of the University of Malaya, dismisses the 'so-called
technocrats, who . . . are only in a position to function as effective leaders as long
as the actual power holding group, the military, put their trust in the capacities of
these technocrats . . . as soon as [they] fail to meet these expectations, they will
cease to function.'

At the fiftieth anniversary in Jakarta of the so-called 'Cultural Polemic' of
1937, in which advocates of Western rationalism clashed with proponents of the
'Eastern' methods, one observer said the battle had seemed won by the rationalisers.
'Indonesians today are far more rationalistic, more individualistic, more pragmatic
and worship the West more. Schools of [a non-Western model] are giving way to
graduate schools in business administration, which are mushrooming.'

But is this so? Another participant asked pointedly, 'have we been able to build a
dynamic and prosperous society?' 'I am afraid the answer is no,' said Arief Budiman;
'Indonesia depends on the West for financing, export marketing and investments.'
Indonesian students 'use their money to buy what is popularly called "aspal"
diplomas,' says novelist Mochtar Lubis. 'Aspal' means *asli tapi palsu*, 'original,

but fake.' The issuing college gives a real diploma, but it is fakely won and fakely earned. Although 'Indonesia is going through a change of generation on a national scale,' according to Mochtar Lubis, 'the problem is that during the past 20 years the formation of new cadres for leadership has been grossly neglected.'

Donald McCloud's comments (1986) are appropriate here. He describes the old élites of pre-colonial Southeast Asia as

> a collection of revenue producing regions which the rulers allocated to individual members of the élite, who were linked together by personal ties and derived their status from royal recognition.

> Other elements of traditional state practices have re-emerged in the contemporary period . . . the states of Southeast Asia are in many respects traditional in both domestic and international outlooks. The capital city is still the locus [and] the new states are primarily resource extractive . . . at [their postwar] independence the typical extractive pattern of state organisation was evident in Indonesia, Thailand, Malaysia and the Philippines [where the] economic systems tended to be controlled by resident Chinese often with close links to the political élite. Concomitantly, there was little participation by the general population in the system.

Little seems to have changed, despite the glossy appearances.

Underlying Potential

At root the original thesis stands. The Asean economies are rich. Their peoples are as creative and innovative as any other. Their governments eschew socialist cant, and are alert to market dynamics. There is much potential.

But the peoples there themselves have now come to believe that there must be a thorough spring-cleaning. The countries must find more of their own investment capital and they must move beyond feudal dispensation of favours. Contrast the English aristocracy of the eighteenth century with the Southeast Asian élites today. Where is the latter's delight in innovation, in experimentation, in the application and encouragement of new technologies? The public words, and even the public spending, embrace such forward movement yet behaviour lags behind.

To be sure, Asean will remain an attractive region for investment although increasingly perhaps on a more selective basis. The region's frequent business seminars abroad correctly point out that the Asean investments, overall, have yielded an average rate of 26 per cent return during 1975–85. That is one-and-a-half times better than elsewhere in the developing world.

Yet that is not the point. What matters is how much of this was self-sustained. A US$211 billion combined GDP in 1987, or trade volumes reaching US$111 billion that year count for little against the basic questions.

To counter that dimming of opportunity in the future the Asean Six must start to lift the efficiency of corporations set up with earlier, debt-funded largesse and staffed with cronies and second-raters. All those hidden costs must be cut away. There must be more earnings from non-commodity exports – which means making products that can stand up in the world's markets and not, as the farce of Malaysia's national car' illustrates, to rely on a thicket of subsidies, subventions and tariffs to break even.

The region's governments moreover, staffed by feudal-minded free-loaders, have to retract from their meddling role in the economy. It is not enough, as in the Philippines after Marcos left in 1986, to replace one band of free-riders with another, or to displace one lot of monopoly-minded bureaucrats with another set. And privatisation must come to mean just that, not a hand-out for would-be cronies all too happy to take over a public asset with loan finance readily provided by government mentors. That comes far closer to racketeering, not marketeering, and impresses no one. Nor does the charade of 'new listings' on the casino-like stock exchanges where the game is stacked in favour of the existing players.

Finally, and not least, the empty moves towards a regional marketplace, outlined in the Chapter 11, must become real. There will always be risks, not least to monopoly interests created in the 1970s and 1980s. Even with the bigger market-place, it will be touch and go how much independent dynamism can be generated in a regional economy so effectively dominated by Japan and overshadowed by China and, perhaps one day, by India as well.

Bigger Stakes

There are wider stakes than just the challenge to create a real marketplace instead of passive economies. The consequences for the rest of the world of a failure to retain Asean's currently impressive stability stare one straight in the face. The impact of a declining regional ability to influence commodity demand, of ageing leadership, of restless minorities, of supply problems (either overproduction or, as in timber, petroleum or some minerals, elimination of the resource) will be profound.

To take just one issue, the Philippine insurgency seems set, in the absence of any fundamental change, to grow slowly, year by year, its organisational roots setting deeper into areas of marginality – marginal land, marginal subsistence, marginal influence of even the most basic government services. Yet in this context Manila's best business research centre, an institute funded by the conservative papal prelature Opus Dei, sets its face and formidable propaganda against acknowledging the monstrous problems created by galloping population growth. It is no accident that a direct correlation exists between a government of looters and a communist-led rural revolution that promises only socialist poverty. One extreme evokes the other, in dialectic duet.

This insurgency, a well-prepared and patient one, also augurs poorly for essential security interests in the Philippines, a complex of US naval, air and communications bases 'unmatched in scope and sophistication anywhere else in the world,' as Gareth Porter (1985) puts it. And the Philippines' neighbours are not exempt from these pressures: between Malaysia and Indonesia lie all the major passages between the western Pacific and the Indian oceans. The Malacca, Lombok and Sumba straits figure in all naval strategies of denial or access. So does the South China Sea, with horrendously complex and overlapping territorial and resource claims centred on the Spratlys and Paracel islands in that sea. In March 1988, China's navy opened fire on Vietnamese gunboats there; the area remains a trouble spot.

The point is that business confidence in the Asean economies depends, ultimate-ly, on a settled balance of power. As the Malaysian *New Straits Times* noted in the

1980s, 'it was the balance of power that has enabled free market economies to thrive in Asean.'

During this same period of time a process began, one of the mightiest changes in world trade since the European Age of Discovery. By this I mean the shifting of trade and economic dynamism increasingly towards the Asia Pacific. By the early 1980s, America's trade westwards had already surpassed its commerce across the Atlantic. More than half the world's goods and services and much more than half the world's population now come from the nearly four dozen nations lining the Pacific Basin. Intra-regional trade has grown significantly although not, as we have seen, within Southeast Asia itself.

Trade reflects many things, only some of which have anything to do with a deeper, harder question: how much of Southeast Asia's economic miracle resulted from its own work? And how much is the achievement reflected in a self-sustained, technical and genuinely market-minded business culture? The answers to those questions must, I am sure, be 'not much'. As Kunio remarks, 'the capitalism that has emerged in Southeast Asia has some intractable problems . . . because of these problems the region has been dependent on the market economy and the government for its growth rather than being the vanguard of economic change.'

Sadly, other answers were possible. They still are: the reserve of talent is there, as are the skills and energy. Behind the 'miracle' of twenty, mostly free-riding years waits the chance to give marketplace economics a real chance. As facts and figures – debt, population, ageing leaderships, lost opportunity costs, Japanese stewardship – are compounded daily, there is still a chance to win for this wealthy arc of the world's largest archipelago the marketplace reputation it has won but does not yet deserve.

References

Budiman, A. (1988) 'The emergence of the bureaucratic capitalist state in Indonesia', in Lim, T. G. (ed.) *Reflections on Development in Southeast Asia*. Singapore: ISEAS

Chew, S. B. (1988) *Small Firms in Singapore*. Singapore: Oxford University Press

DeRosa, D. (1986) 'Trade and protection in the Asian developing region', *Asian Development Review*, vol. 4, No. 1

Hayami, Y. (1988) 'Asian development: a view from the paddy fields', *Asian Development Review*, vol. 6, No. 1

Kaosa-ard, M. (1986) 'Technology transfer in Thailand', in Kintanar, A. and Tan, L. E. *ASEAN–US Economic Relations: an Overview*. Singapore: ISEAS

Kunio, Y. (1988) *The Rise of Ersatz Capitalism in South-East Asia* Singapore: Oxford University Press

Lee, Jungsoo and David, I. P. (1987) *A Survey of the External Debt Situation in Asian Developing Countries*. Manila: Asian Development Bank

Lindsay, C. (1986) 'Technology transfer – how real?' in Kintanar, A. and Tan, L. E. *ASEAN–US Economic Relations: an Overview*. Singapore: ISEAS

McCloud, D. (1986) *System and Process in Southeast Asia*. Boulder, Colorado: Westview Press

Naya, S. *et al.* (1983) 'Asian and Pacific developing economies: performance and issues', *Asian Development Review*, vol. 1, No. 1

Porter, G. (1985) 'The region: an overview', in the January 1985 issue of *Current History* (devoted exclusively to Southeast Asia)

Pye, L. W. (1985) *Asian Power and Politics: the Cultural Dimensions of Authority*. Cambridge, Massachusetts: Belknap Press

Rieger, H. C. (1986) 'Southeast Asian economic performance: growing doubts', *Asian Development Review*, vol. 3, No. 1

Shaharuddin, M. (1983) *The Concept of a Hero in Malay Society*. Singapore: Eastern Universities Press

Shiamoto, R. (1988) 'The future of foreign direct investment in the Asian-Pacific region', paper presented at an Asian Development Bank/International Finance Corporation symposium on foreign direct investment, 27 January, Manila. Unpublished.

Suriyamongkol, M. L. (1988) *The Politics of Asean Economic Cooperation: the Case of Asean Industrial Projects*. Singapore: Oxford University Press

Tanzi, V. (1987) 'The public sector in the market economies of developing Asia', *Asian Development Review*, vol. 5, No. 2

GLOSSARY

Abri: Angkatan Bersenjata Republik Indonesia, the Armed Forces of the Republic of Indonesia.

ADB: Asian Development Bank. Created in 1966.

Asean: Association of Southeast Asian Nations. Founded in 1967.

Barisan Nasional: National Front, Malaysia's coalition of political parties that has formed the government since 1971. The Barisan Nasional is dominated by UMNO (see below).

Berhad: In Malaysia the word meaning 'limited' in the sense of a limited liability company.

Bumiputra: 'son of the soil', an indigenous or 'native' Malaysian as opposed to members of the immigrant Chinese or Indian communities.

Cukong: (pronounced 'choo-cong'). In Indonesia the word denoting a Chinese financier who backs a 'native' Indonesian politician or military man.

Dwi fungsi: Dual Function. The principal doctrine relied upon by the Indonesian military to justify their extensive involvement in civilian affairs, including business and commerce.

Duppy: a word coined from the expression 'derived unearned profit', or 'DUP'. Hence a 'duppy' is a person, often a self-styled entrepreneur, who usually acts as a dummy partner in businesses centred in the import monopoly business or other privileged licensed trade, in which the running is left, invariably, to the active partner, usually a local Chinese businessman.

'Free-riding': Passive business participation or derived gain in which the person receiving income or benefit 'free-rides' on the energies of another business partner or on demand for a product which the free-rider has done nothing to create.

Futures: Commodities trading in contracts promising the delivery of the specified commodity at some future date.

Golkar: An Indonesian acronym for Golongan Karya, the 'group of functionaries' or coalition of different social sectors. Golkar is the government's 'political party' in Indonesia's elections held every five years but is otherwise largely dormant. It has won each of the elections since its formation in 1971.

Hua chiao: The commonly used Chinese expression for 'overseas Chinese'.

Mamak: In Malaysia the word is used to describe Malays who have South Asian ancestry, usually Pakistani or Gujarati.

Nanyang: Chinese for 'South Sea' but referring to the region known in present times as Southeast Asia.

NEP: New Economic Policy. Launched by the Malaysian government in 1970 to correct racial imbalances in the distribution of wealth and corporate ownership in Malaysia, especially as between Malays and Chinese.

PAP: People's Action Party. The ruling political party in Singapore which has won every general election since Singapore became independent.

Pribumi: 'son of the soil', meaning a 'native' Indonesian, as opposed to Indonesians belonging to immigrant groups, such as the Arabs or, especially, the Chinese. (See *bumiputra*).

PT: Perusahaan Terbatas, or 'limited liability company' in Indonesia.

Shophouse: Usually found in Chinese quarter of Southeast Asian cities, the word means a ground floor shop with the upper floors inhabited by a family.

Sogo Shosha: The multifaceted Japanese trading houses that dominate Japanese investment and trade in Southeast Asia.

Taipan: A word used in Hong Kong to describe a major merchant family.

Towkay: A word used in Malaysia to describe a well-off Chinese businessman.

UMNO: United Malays National Organisation. After 1987 the legal existence of UMNO became disputed as rival factions contested the legality of leadership elections. As of 1989, UMNO takes the name UMNO Baru, or 'new' UMNO, and has evicted most of the opponents of Malaysian prime minister Mahathir Mohamad.

FURTHER READING

1: The End of an Era

Adam Smith's Money World radio programme, transcript of 17 March 1986 programme entitled 'What to Do with Your Money if You Have to Leave the Country Fast: a Dictator's Guide to Secret Money'. New York: National Broadcasting Corporation

Carino, L. (ed.) (1986) *Bureaucratic Corruption in Asia.* Manila: University of the Philippines' College of Public Administration

Clad, J. (1986) 'The neighbour watch', *Far Eastern Economic Review*, 20 March

Hofheinz, R. and Calder, K. E. (1982) *The East Asia Edge.* New York: Basic Books

Kunio, Y. (1988) *The Rise of Ersatz Capitalism in South-East Asia.* Singapore: Oxford University Press

Robison, R., Hewison, K. and Higgott, R. (1987) *Southeast Asia in the 1980s.* Sydney: Allen and Unwin

2: Full Circle in the Philippines

Adriano, F. D. and Adriano, L. S. (1983) 'The development of capitalism in Philippine agriculture', *Philippine Social Sciences and Humanities Review*, vol. 47, No. 1

Clad, J. (1986) 'The struggle to decentralize the Philippines', *International Herald Tribune*, 15 August

Clad, J. (1987) 'Claims of cronyism dog Aquino's government', *Far Eastern Economic Review*, 26 March

Clad, J. (1987) 'In Asia, insecure regimes are cracking down hard', *International Herald Tribune*, 1 April

Clad, J. (1987) 'Philippine housecleaning: tarnished crusade', *Far Eastern Economic Review*, 17 September

Clad, J. (1988) 'Philippine privatisation: sale of the century', *Far Eastern Economic Review*, 7 July

Clad, J. (1988) 'Philippines population: genesis of despair', *Far Eastern Economic Review*, 20 October

Clad, J. (1988) 'The politics of plunder', *Far Eastern Economic Review*, 24 November

Fenner, B. (1985) *Cebu Under the Spanish Flag.* Cebu City, Philippines: University of San Carlos Press

Hawes, G. (1987) *The Philippine State and the Marcos Regime: the Politics of Export.* Ithaca: Cornell University Press

Ileto, R. (1979) *Pasyon and Revolution: Popular Movements in the Philippines.* Quezon City: Ateneo de Manila University Press

de Jesus, E. (1980) *The Tobacco Monopoly in the Philippines.* Quezon City: Ateneo de Manila University Press

Joaquin, N. (1983) *The Aquinos of Tarlac.* Manila: Cacho Hermanos

Karnow, S. (1989) *In Our Image: America's Empire in the Philippines.* New York: Random House

Mijares, P. (1976) *The Conjugal Dictatorship of Ferdinand and Imelda Marcos*. San Francisco: Union Square Publications

Miller, M. (1987) 'Journalist caught in Manila muddle over expulsion', *Asian Wall Street Journal*, 3 December

Ofreneo, R. E. (1980) *Capitalism in Philippine Agriculture*. Quezon City: Foundation for Nationalist Studies

Rosett, C. (1988) 'A revolution starts to die', *Asian Wall Street Journal*, 29 February and 1 March

Tiglas, R. D. *et al.* (1982) *Feudalism and Capitalism in the Philippines: Trends and Implications*. Quezon City: Foundation for Nationalist Studies

Turner, M. M. (1984) *National Level Élites in the Philippines 1945-1984*. Hull: Centre for South-East Asian Studies

3: Malaise in Brunei and Malaysia

Bartholomew, J. (1989) *The World's Richest Man: the Sultan of Brunei*. New York and London: Viking

Chee, P. L. (1985) 'No reverse gear: the economic burden of Malaysia's Car Project' in Jomo, K. S. (ed.) *The Sun Also Sets: Lessons in 'Looking East'*. Petaling Jaya, Malaysia: Institute for Social Analysis

Clad, J. (1984) 'The profit of the East', *Far Eastern Economic Review*, 14 June

Clad, J. (1985) 'Mahathir leads Malaysia towards heavy industrialisation', *Far Eastern Economic Review*, 14 February

Fisk, E. K. and Osman-Rani, H. (eds) (1982) *The Political Economy of Malaysia*. Kuala Lumpur: Oxford University Press

Gale, B. (1981) *Politics and Public Enterprise in Malaysia*. Singapore: Eastern Universities Press

Gill, R. (1985) *The Making of Malaysia Inc*. Petaling Jaya, Malaysia: Pelanduk Publications

Gill, R. (1985) *George Tan: the Carrian Saga*. Petaling Jaya, Malaysia: Pelanduk Publications

Gullick, J. M. (1983) *The Story of Kuala Lumpur (1857-1939)*. Singapore: Eastern Universities Press

Haflah Piei, M. (1987) *Malaysia: Isu-isu Pembangunan*. Bangi, Malaysia: Penerbit Universiti Kebangsaan

Jenkins, D. (1983) 'Sultans as symbols', *Far Eastern Economic Review*, 30 June

Jomo K. S. (ed.) (1985) *The Sun Also Sets: Lessons in 'Looking East'*. Petaling Jaya, Malaysia: Institute for Social Analysis

Kenichi Ohmae (1985) 'Rethinking global corporate strategy', *Asian Wall Street Journal*, 1 May

Khor, K. P. (1987) *Malaysia's Economy in Decline*. Penang: Consumers' Association of Penang

Kwan, N. and Peyman, H. (1988) *Malaysia*. Singapore: Merrill Lynch

Lim, K. S. (1986) *BMF: Scandal of Scandals*. Petaling Jaya, Malaysia: Democratic Action Party publication.

Lim, M. H. (1981) *Ownership and Control of the One Hundred Largest Corporations in Malaysia*. Kuala Lumpur: Oxford University Press

Mahathir bin Mohamad (1970) *The Malay Dilemma*. Kuala Lumpur: Federal Publications

Rowley, A. (1984) 'The politics of business', *Far Eastern Economic Review*, 10 May

Seaward, N. (1987) 'Fleet Group sails into heavy weather', *Far Eastern Economic Review*, 3 September

Seaward, N. (1988) 'The Daim enigma', *Far Eastern Economic Review*, 1 September

Seaward, N. (1989) 'Bank on the run', *Far Eastern Economic Review*, 19 January

Stern, J. J. (1984) 'Malaysia: growth and structural change', background paper for a conference on the Malaysian economy. Fletcher School of Law and Diplomacy, Tufts University, Medford, Massachusetts. Unpublished

4:   ABRI-culture: Dual Functioneering in Indonesia

Anderson, B. (1972) 'The idea of power in Javanese culture', in Holt, C. (ed.) *Culture and Politics in Indonesia*. Ithaca, New York: Cornell University Press

Barlow, C. and Thee, K. W. (1988) *The North Sumatran Regional Economy: Growth with Unbalanced Development*. Singapore: ISEAS

Budiman, A. (1988) 'The emergence of the bureaucratic capitalist state in Indonesia', in Lim, T. G. (ed.) *Reflections on Development in Southeast Asia*. Singapore: ISEAS

Crouch, H. (1978) *The Army and Politics in Indonesia*. Ithaca, New York: Cornell University Press

Dick, H. W. (1987) *The Indonesian Interisland Shipping Industry: an Analysis of Competition and Regulation*. Singapore: ISEAS

Dickie, R. B. and Layman, T. A. (1988) *Foreign Investment and Government Policy in the Third World*. New York: St Martin's Press (Heavy emphasis on Indonesia.)

Erquiaga, P. (1987) 'Improving domestic resource mobilisation through financial development – Indonesia', Asian Development Bank Economic Staff Working Paper No. 40, November

Garnaut, R. and McCawley P. (eds) (1980) *Indonesia: Dualism, Growth and Poverty*. Canberra: Australian National University

Gelb, A. (1985) 'The impact of oil windfalls: comparative statistics with an Indonesia-like model', World Bank Discussion Paper No. DRD133, October

Hill, H. (1988) *Foreign Investment and Industrialization in Indonesia*. Singapore: Oxford University Press

Hobohm, S. (1987) *Indonesia to 1991: Can Momentum be Regained?* London: Economist Intelligence Unit

Jenkins, D. (1984) *Suharto and His Generals: Indonesian Military Politics 1975–1983*. Cornell Modern Indonesian Project Monograph No. 64. Ithaca, New York: Cornell University Press

Jones, S. (1986) 'Power and privilege in Indonesia', *Asian Wall Street Journal*, 25 November

Jones, S. (1987) 'Swiss firm revamps Indonesia imports', *Asian Wall Street Journal*, 29 September

Lubis, M. (1979) *Manusia Indonesia*. Jakarta: Sinar Jaya

McCawley, P. (1978) 'Some consequences of the Pertamina crisis in Indonesia', *Journal of Southeast Asian Studies*, vol. 9, No. 1

McDonald, H. (1980) *Suharto's Indonesia*. Honolulu: University Press of Hawaii

Makarim, N. (1978) *Companies and Business in Indonesia*, doctoral dissertation, Harvard Law School. Unpublished

Nasution, A. (1983) *Financial Institutions and Policies in Indonesia*. Singapore: ISEAS

Palmer, I. (1978) *The Indonesian Economy Since 1965*. London: Frank Cass

Panglaykim, J. (1983) *Japanese Direct Investment in Asean: the Indonesian Experience*. Singapore: Maruzen Asia

Pawitra, T. (1988) 'Marketing in the automotive industry of Indonesia', *Asean Economic Bulletin*, vol. 5, No. 1

Robison, R. (1986) *Indonesia: the Rise of Capital*. Sydney: Allen & Unwin

Shahrir (1988) *Basic Needs in Indonesia: Economics, Politics and Public Policy*. Singapore: ISEAS

Spehoed, A. R. (1981) 'Japan and the development of the Indonesian manufacturing sector', *The Indonesian Quarterly*, October

de Soto, H. (1989) *The Other Path: the Invisible Revolution in the Third World*. New York: Harper & Row

Vatikiotis, M. (1988) 'Major donors increase aid pledge despite Indonesia's huge debts', *Far Eastern Economic Review*, 30 June

5: Boomtime in Bangkok

Brown, I. (1988) *The Élite and the Economy in Siam, 1890–1920*. Oxford: Oxford University
   Press
ten Brumanelhuis, H. and Kemp, J. H. (eds) (1984) *Strategies and Structures in Thai
   Society*. Amsterdam: University of Amsterdam Press
Bunbongkarn, S. (1987) *The Military in Thai Politics 1981–1986*. Singapore: ISEAS
Handley, P. and Friedland, J. (1989) 'Bangkok Bank: can it perform?', *Far Eastern
   Economic Review*, 13 April
Hewison, K. (1981) 'The financial bourgeoisie in Thailand', *Journal of Contemporary Asia*,
   vol. 11, No. 4
Hewison, K. (1985) 'The state and capitalist development in Thailand', in Higgott, R. and
   Robison, R. (eds) *Southeast Asia: Essays in the Political Economy of Structural Change*.
   London: Routledge & Kegan Paul
Ingram, J. C. (1971) *Economic Change in Thailand, 1850–1970*. Stanford: Stanford Uni-
   versity Press
Khanthachai, N. and Tanmavad, K. (1987) *Technology and Skills in Thailand*. Singapore:
   ISEAS
Kirsch, T. and Skinner, G. W. (eds) (1975) *Change and Persistence in Thai Society*. Ithaca,
   New York: Cornell University Press
Kraisak Choonhavan (1984) 'The growth of domestic capital and Thai industrialisation',
   Journal of Contemporary Asia, vol. 14, No. 2
Krikkiat, P. and Kunio, Y. (1983) *Business Groups in Thailand*, Research Notes and
   Discussion Paper No. 41. Singapore: ISEAS
Pasuk Phongpaichit (1980) *Economic and Social Transformation of Thailand*. Bangkok:
   Chulalongkorn University Social Research Institute
Shaplen, R. (1979) *A Turning Wheel*. London: André Deutsch
Sricharatchanya, P. (1988) 'Thailand's Crown Property Bureau: the King's conglomerate',
   Far Eastern Economic Review, 30 June
Wilson, D. (1962) *Politics in Thailand*. Ithaca, New York: Cornell University Press
Wongtrangan, K. (1988) 'Thai bureaucratic behaviour: the impact of dual values on public
   policies', in Lim, T. G. *Reflections on Development in Southeast Asia*. Singapore: ISEAS

6: Singapore: The Exception that rules the Proof

Balakrishnan, N. and Pann, L. (1989) 'Confucius and confusion', *Far Eastern Economic
   Review*, 9 February
Ch'ng, H. K. and Kau, A. K. (1988) 'Marketing factors and small and medium enterprise
   improvement in Singapore', in James, K. and Narongchai, A. *Small and Medium Business
   Improvement in the ASEAN Region: Marketing Factors*. Singapore: ISEAS
Chen, P. S. J. (1983) *Singapore: Development Policies and Trends*. Singapore: Oxford
   University Press
Chew, S. B. (1988) *Small Firms in Singapore*. Singapore: Oxford University Press
Chong, L. C. (1983) *Multinational Business and National Development: Transfer of Managerial
   Knowhow to Singapore*. Singapore: Maruzen Asia
George, T. J. S. (1973) *Lee Kuan Yew's Singapore*. London: André Deutsch
Ooi, J. B. and Chiang H. D. (1969) *Modern Singapore*. Singapore: Singapore University
   Press

Quah, J. S. T. (ed.) (1985) *Government and Politics of Singapore*. Singapore: Oxford University Press

Soon, T. W. (1988) *Singapore's New Education System: Education Reform for National Development*. Singapore: ISEAS

7: Chinatown

Coppel, C. (1983) *Indonesian Chinese in Crisis*. Kuala Lumpur: Oxford University Press

Goldberg, M. (1985) *The Chinese Connection*. Vancouver: University of British Columbia Press

Lim, Y. C. and Gosling, P. (eds) (1983) *The Chinese in Southeast Asia*. Singapore: Maruzen Asia

Limlingan, V. (1987) *The Overseas Chinese in ASEAN: Business Strategies and Management Practices*. Manila: Vita Development Corporation

MacKie, J. A. C. (ed.) (1976) *The Chinese in Indonesia*. Honolulu: University Press of Hawaii

Purcell, V. (1980) *The Chinese in Southeast Asia*. Kuala Lumpur: Oxford University Press (reprint)

Song, O. S. (1984) *One Hundred Years History of the Chinese in Singapore*. Singapore: Oxford University Press (reprint)

Sricharatchanya, P. (1988) 'Chinese in Thailand – a good mix', *Far Eastern Economic Review*, 18 February

Suryadinata, L. (1979) *The Chinese in Indonesia*. Singapore: Singapore University Press

Wu, Y. L. and Wu, C. H. (1980) *Economic Development in Southeast Asia: the Chinese Dimension*. Stanford: Hoover Institution Press

Yeap, J. K. (1984) *The Patriarch*. Singapore: Federal Publications

Yong, C. F. (1980) *Tan Kah-kee; the Making of an Overseas Chinese Legend*. Singapore: Oxford University Press

8: Wellsprings of Wealth: Southeast Asia's Commercial Crucibles

Akrasanee, N. and James, K. (1988) *Small and Medium Business Improvement in the Asean Region*. Singapore: ISEAS

Ariff, M. (1988) *Islamic Banking: Islam and Economic Development in Southeast Asia*. Singapore: ISEAS

Brooks, M. R. (1985) *Fleet Development and the Control of Shipping in Southeast Asia*. Singapore: ISEAS

Clapham, R. (1985) *Small and Medium Entrepreneurs in Southeast Asia*, Research Notes and Discussion Paper No. 49. Singapore: ISEAS

Findlay, C. and Garnaut, R. (eds) (1986) *The Political Economy of Manufacturing Protection: Experiences of Asean and Australia*. Sydney: Allen & Unwin

Hiron, R., Ng, C. Y. and Siy, R. Y. (1988) *Technology and Skills in ASEAN: an Overview*. Singapore: ISEAS

Rowley, A. (1987) *Asian Stockmarkets: the Inside Story*. Hong Kong: Review Publications

9: Commodities: Gluttered Cornucopias

Bartholomew, J. (1988) 'Commodities bounce back', *Far Eastern Economic Review*, 9 June

Clad, J. (1985) 'Primary commodities fall across the board', *Far Eastern Economic Review*, 14 November

Drabble, J. H. (1973) *Rubber in Malaya*. Kuala Lumpur: Oxford University Press

Duncan, R. C. (ed.) (1984) *The Outlook for Primary Commodities, 1984 to 1995*, World Bank Staff Commodity Working Papers No. 11. Washington, DC: World Bank

Gelb, A. (ed.) (1988) *Oil Windfalls: Blessing or Curse?* Oxford University Press and World Bank

de Jesus, E. (ed.) (1980) *The Tobacco Monopoly in the Philippines*. Quezon City: Ateneo de Manila University Press

Ooi, J. B. (1982) *The Petroleum Resources of Indonesia*. Kuala Lumpur: Oxford University Press

US Embassy, Kuala Lumpur (1985) 'Malaysia: Sabah forest products report', unclassified report of 10 September

10: Development Bunk

Cassen, R. *et.al.* (1986) *Does Aid Work? Report to an Intergovernmental Task Force*. Oxford: Clarendon Press

Clad, J. (1986) 'Unhappy returns', *Far Eastern Economic Review*, 28 November

Clad, J. (1988) 'The ADB reviews its role and its critics', *Far Eastern Economic Review*, 24 March

Clad, J. (1988) 'Vote buying in Manila: Japan, the US and Sweden to boost ADB shares', *Far Eastern Economic Review*, 14 July

Huang, P. W. (1975) *The Asian Development Bank: Diplomacy and Development in Asia*. New York: Vantage Press

Krasner, S. D. (1981) 'Power structures and regional development banks', *International Organization*, vol. 35 (spring)

Rix, A. (1980) *Japan's Economic Aid: Policy-making and Politics*. London: Croom Helm

Wihtol, R. (1988) *The Asian Development Bank and Rural Development: Policy and Practice*. London: Macmillan

Yasutomo, D. T. (1983) *Japan and the Asian Development Bank*. New York: Praeger

11: Reluctant Regionalism

Akrasanee, N., Hirono, R. and Ng, C. Y. (1988) *Industrial Restructuring in Asean and Japan*. Singapore: ISEAS

Ariff, M., and Hill, H. (1985) *Export-Oriented Industrialisation: the ASEAN Experience*. Sydney: Allen & Unwin

Arnfinn, J. D. (1982) *Regional Organization and Order in South-East Asia*. London: Macmillan

Awanohara, S. *et al.* (1987) 'Asean cooperation: who cares?' *Far Eastern Economic Review*, 3 December

Broinowski, A. (ed.) (1982) *Understanding ASEAN*. London: Macmillan

Chanda, N. (1986) *Brother Enemy: the War After the War*. San Diego, California: Harcourt Brace Jovanovich

Cheng, B. and Chia, S. (1980) *Asean Economic Co-operation*. Singapore: ISEAS

Clad, J. (1987) 'Full of good intentions', *Far Eastern Economic Review*, 24 December

Evans, P., Rueschemeyer, D. and Skocpol, T. (eds) (1985) *Bringing the State Back In*. Cambridge: Cambridge University Press

Far Eastern Economic Review (1984) 'Asean exit taxes stunt intra-regional tourism', 29 March

Garnaut, R. (ed.) (1980) *Asean in a Changing Pacific and World Economy*. Canberra: Australian National University Press

Harris, J. (1979) 'Financial deepening as a prerequisite to investment growth: empirical evidence from five East Asian economies', *Journal of Developing Economies*, September

Indorf, H. H. (1984) *Impediments to Regionalism in Southeast Asia: Bilateral Constraints among ASEAN Member States*. Singapore: ISEAS

Institute of Southeast Asian Studies (1984) *Asean: a Bibliography*. Singapore: ISEAS

Institute of Southeast Asian Studies (July 1984–) *Asean Economic Bulletin*, quarterly, various issues. Singapore: ISEAS

Institute of Strategic and International Studies (1987) *The Way Forward: the Report of the Group of Fourteen on ASEAN Economic Co-operation and Integration*. Kuala Lumpur

James, K. and Akrasanee, N. (1988) *Small and Medium Business Improvement in the Asean Region*. Singapore: ISEAS

Kintanar, A. and Tan, L. H. (1986) *ASEAN–US Economic Relations: an Overview*. Singapore: ISEAS

Leifer, M. (1989) *ASEAN and the Security of South-East Asia*, London and New York: Routledge

Palmer, R. D. and Reckford, T. J. (1987) *Building ASEAN: 20 Years of Southeast Asian Cooperation*. New York: Praeger

Solidum, E. D. (1982) *Bilateral Summitry in Asean*. Manila: Foreign Service Institute

Sopiee, N., Chew, L. S. and Lim, S. J. (1987) *Asean at the Crossroads: Obstacles, Options and Opportunities in Economic Cooperation*. Kuala Lumpur: Institute of Strategic and International Studies

Suriyamongkol, M. L. (1988) *The Politics of Asean Economic Cooperation: the Case of Asean Industrial Projects*. Singapore: Oxford University Press

Talisyon, S. (1988) 'Designing the future of ASEAN electricity trade', *Asean Economic Bulletin*, vol. 5, No. 1

Tan, G. (1982) *Trade Liberalisation in Asean: an Empirical Study of the Preferential Trading Arrangements*. Singapore: ISEAS

Waelbroek, J. (ed.) (1985) *Asean–EEC Trade in Services*. Singapore: ISEAS

12:   The Clouded Future

Bank of Japan (1988) *Greater Role of Asian Economies in the World*. Tokyo: Bank of Japan Research and Statistics Department

Bradford, C. I. and Branson, W. H. (1987) *Trade and Structural Change in Pacific Asia*. Chicago: University of Chicago Press

Billerbeck, K. and Yasugi, Y. (1985) *Private Direct Foreign Investment in Developing Countries*. Washington, DC: World Bank

Buszynski, L. (1986) *Soviet Foreign Policy and Southeast Asia*. London: Croom Helm.

Chichilnisky, G. and Heal, G. (1986) *The Evolving International Economy*. Cambridge: Cambridge University Press

Evans, P., Rueschemeyer, D. and Skocpol, T. (eds) (1985) *Bringing the State Back In*. Cambridge: Cambridge University Press

Evers, H. (1980) *Sociology of Southeast Asia: Readings on Social Change and Development*. Kuala Lumpur: Oxford University Press

Faber, M. (1988) *The Great Money Illusion: the Confusion of the Confusions*. Hong Kong: Longman

George, S. (1988) *A Fate Worse than Debt*. London: Penguin Books

Girling, J. (1981) *The Bureaucratic Polity in Modernizing Societies: Similarities, Differences and Prospects in the Asean Region*. Singapore: ISEAS

Hall, K. (1985) *Maritime Trade and State Development in Early Southeast Asia*. Honolulu: University Press of Hawaii

Higgott, R. and Robison, R. (eds) (1985) *Southeast Asia: Essays in the Political Economy of Structural Change*. London: Routledge & Kegan Paul

Institute of Southeast Asian Studies. (1975–) *Southeast Asian Affairs* (annual yearbooks). Singapore: ISEAS

Johnstone, B. (1988) 'Fading of the miracle: scientists strive to develop new rice varieties to feed Asia', *Far Eastern Economic Review*, 1 December

Lee, J. and David, I. P. (1987) *A Survey of the External Debt Situation in Asian Developing Countries*. Manila: Asian Development Bank

Lee, Y. L.(1980) *The Razor's Edge: Boundaries and Boundary Disputes in Southeast Asia*. Singapore: ISEAS

Lim, T. G. (ed.) (1988) *Reflections on Development in Southeast Asia*. Singapore: ISEAS

McCloud, D. G. (1986) *System and Process in Southeast Asia: the Evolution of a Region*. Boulder, Colorado: Westview Press

McCoy, A. W. (1972) *The Politics of Heroin in Southeast Asia*. New York: Doubleday

McNeely, J. A, and Wachtel, P. S. (1988) *Soul of the Tiger: Searching for Nature's Answers in Exotic Southeast Asia*. New York: Doubleday

Naylor, R. T. (1987) *Hot Money and the Politics of Debt*. London: Unwin Hyman

Preston, P. W. (1987) *Rethinking Development: Essays on Development and Southeast Asia*. London and New York: Routledge & Kegan Paul

Pye, L. W. (1985) *Asian Power and Politics: the Cultural Dimensions of Authority*. Cambridge, Massachusetts: Belknap Press

Redwood, J. (1988) *Popular Capitalism*. London: Routledge

Scalapino, R. A., Sato, S. and Wanandi, J. (1986) *Internal and External Security Issues in Asia*. Berkeley: University of California, Institute of East Asian Studies

Steinberg, D. J. (ed.) (1971) *In Search of Southeast Asia*. New York: Holt, Rinehart and Winston

Syed Hussein Alatas (1977) *The Myth of the Lazy Native*. London: Frank Cass

Tate, D. J. M. (1979) *The Making of Modern South-East Asia*. Kuala Lumpur: Oxford University Press

Tilman, R. O. (1987) *Southeast Asia and the Enemy Beyond: Asean Perceptions of External Threats*. Boulder, Colorado: Westview Press

US Department of Commerce (1988) *International Direct Investment*. Washington, DC: US Government Printing Office

INDEX

Oriental names are given according to custom, i.e. Chinese and Malayan names are entered under the first part of the name, Indonesian and Filipino are under the surname.